INTIMACY AND EXCLUSION

E D I T O R S

Sherry B. Ortner, Nicholas B. Dirks, Geoff Eley

A LIST OF TITLES

IN THIS SERIES APPEARS

AT THE BACK OF

THE BOOK

PRINCETON STUDIES IN
CULTURE / POWER / HISTORY

INTIMACY AND EXCLUSION

RELIGIOUS POLITICS IN
PRE-REVOLUTIONARY BADEN

Dagmar Herzog

PRINCETON UNIVERSITY PRESS
PRINCETON, NEW JERSEY

LIBRARY OF CONGRESS CATALOGING-IN-PUBLICATION DATA

HERZOG, DAGMAR, 1961–
INTIMACY AND EXCLUSION : RELIGIOUS POLITICS IN
PRE-REVOLUTIONARY BADEN /DAGMAR HERZOG
P.   CM.—(PRINCETON STUDIES IN CULTURE/POWER/HISTORY)
INCLUDES BIBLIOGRAPHICAL REFERENCES AND INDEX
ISBN 0-691-04493-7 (ALK. PAPER).—ISBN 0-691-04492-9 (PBK. : ALK. PAPER)
1. BADEN (GERMANY)—POLITICS AND GOVERNMENT.   2. LIBERALISM—
GERMANY—BADEN—HISTORY—19TH CENTURY.   3. JEWS—EMANCIPATION—
GERMANY—BADEN.   4. FEMINISM—GERMANY—BADEN—HISTORY.   5. BADEN
(GERMANY)—ETHNIC RELATIONS.   I. TITLE.   II. SERIES.
DD801.B18H47 1996   320.943′46′09034—DC20   95-19577   CIP

THIS BOOK HAS BEEN COMPOSED IN GALLIARD TYPEFACE

PRINCETON UNIVERSITY PRESS BOOKS ARE PRINTED ON ACID-FREE PAPER,
AND MEET THE GUIDELINES FOR PERMANENCE AND DURABILITY OF THE
COMMITTEE ON PRODUCTION GUIDELINES FOR BOOK LONGEVITY OF
THE COUNCIL ON LIBRARY RESOURCES

PRINTED IN THE UNITED STATES OF AMERICA BY
PRINCETON ACADEMIC PRESS

1   3   5   7   9   10   8   6   4   2

1   3   5   7   9   10   8   6   4   2
(PBK.)

IN MEMORIAM

Frederick Herzog

NOVEMBER 29, 1925–OCTOBER 9, 1995

CONTENTS

ACKNOWLEDGMENTS

I HAVE incurred a considerable number of debts in the course of writing this book, having depended throughout on the kindness of strangers and friends. My first thanks go to my professors, Joan Scott, Volker Berghahn, Mary Gluck, and Dietrich Rueschemeyer. Inspirational models as teachers and scholars, they combined the most rigorous standards with generous warmth and support. I am indebted as well to a number of other scholars. Vicki Caron, Geoff Eley, Daniel Goldhagen, James Harris, Isabel Hull, Mary Jo Maynes, Lewis Siegelbaum, and Jonathan Sperber graciously subjected themselves to earlier versions of the manuscript, and their incisive critical commentary immeasurably clarified my focus and strengthened the book's arguments. In addition, crucial insights on earlier versions of individual chapters were offered by Jane Caplan, Deborah Hertz, Larry Eugene Jones, Doris Kaufmann, Claudia Koonz, Carola Lipp, Kathy Peiss, and David Sabean. I thank them all. Further thanks go to my students at Brown, Harvard, and Michigan State, sources of constant joy and challenge.

A dissertation research fellowship from the Deutscher Akademischer Austausch Dienst enabled me to live in Germany in 1987–88, and to travel widely in search of source materials. An Andrew W. Mellon Faculty Fellowship in the Humanities at Harvard University in 1993–94 gave me the precious time and space not only to reread all the primary documents on which the dissertation had been based—as well as to collect many additional sources in the treasure trove that is Widener Library—but also to rethink and rewrite the book in its entirety. I am deeply grateful for the support of both organizations. Portions of chapters 2 and 4 first appeared in the *Leo Baeck Institute Year Book* XL (1995) and *Jewish History* 9/2 (1995), respectively. The material is reproduced here by kind permission of the editors of both publications, and I would like to thank them as well for their advice and support.

I am also profoundly appreciative of the many archivists and librarians who assisted me in the course of my initial research. Free Religious preachers Dr. Eckhart Pilick and Mr. Heinrich Keipp generously opened their congregations' archives to me; this study would not have been possible without them. The staff at the Leo Baeck Institute in New York assisted me in finding a broad array of German-Jewish newspapers from the 1840s. Mr. Bernhard Müller-Herkert and Mr. Heinrich Raab of the Generallandesarchiv Karlsruhe, Dr. Hans Schenk of the Bundesarchiv

(Aussenstelle) Frankfurt, Dr. Franz Hundsnurscher of the Erzbischöf-liches Archiv Freiburg, and Mr. Hans-Günther Bäurer of the Stadt-archiv Stockach all made indispensable interventions. The many hours my friends Francisca Loetz, Roland Jakob, and Benedikt Achten spent in dealing with overseas document requests, copying, and shipping, and their perceptive comments on the work-in-progress, put me consider-ably in their debt as well. On this side of the Atlantic, I have been lucky to have had two outstanding research assistants, Maureen Stewart and Amy Lagler, whose sharp intelligence and unflappable cheerful compe-tence saved me endless hours of aggravation.

I also owe a great deal to my parents, Kristin and Frederick Herzog, not only for nurturing me with their love, but also for never—in all those intense debates at the dinner table over the Bible or the day's newspaper—letting me get away with easy answers. I owe a similar debt to my aunt Ruth Karwehl, whose personal support and interest in my work were unstinting and unflagging, and who supplied me with a steady stream of news from Germany.

In addition, I would like to thank those many wonderful colleagues at Michigan State who from the start made the state of Michigan feel like a warm place, even in the deepest winter. I also want particularly to thank Scott Aversano, Kathie and Sam Dunbar, Victor Jew, and Joanne Wellman for turning both East Lansing and Ann Arbor into "home."

Finally, my most profound thanks go to those whose abiding friend-ship, love, and wisdom have sustained me throughout the many stages of this project, most particularly Jennifer Fleischner, Ellen Furlough, Flora Keshgegian, Irina Livezeanu, Paul Podolsky, Dianne Sadoff, and Tracey Wilson. Above all, I thank my very best friend, Michael Staub, who has read and edited more versions of this book than either he or I can count, has debated every idea in it with passion and patience, and whose presence in my life has blessed it in every imaginable way. This book is dedicated to our daughter, Lucy Milena Staub, and to the mem-ory of my father.

INTIMACY AND EXCLUSION

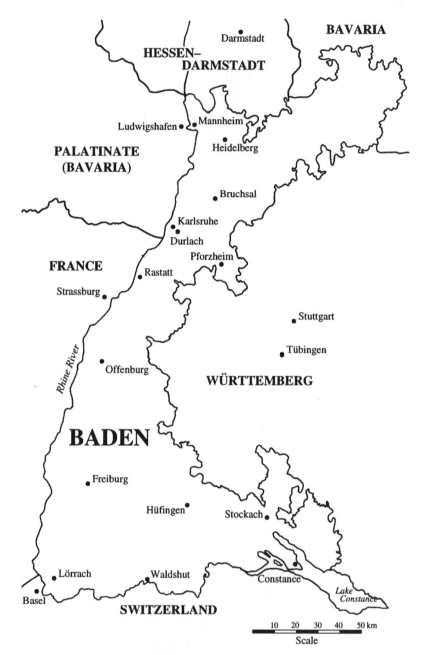

Baden in the 1840s

Drawing by Dirk J. Arnold

INTRODUCTION

W HICH is more expressive of true Christianity," the preeminent German liberal Friedrich Hecker asked in 1845, "to leave people's consciences in liberty or to subject them to spiritual coercion?"[1] Hecker raised this question in a tract demanding that a just-then emerging movement of Christian dissenters be granted freedom of worship and political rights equal to those held by members of the two traditional Christian confessions. He embedded his appeal in a broader call for the full separation of church and state, and Hecker's own answer to the question was implicitly obvious as he went on to assert that Christianity was a religion of love, equality, and free self-development, rather than exclusivism, hierarchy, or authoritarianism.

Strikingly, Hecker couched his patently secularizing gesture in religious language. Moreover, while in this instance Hecker criticized state intervention in matters of individual conscience, at other moments in the 1840s he openly defended state intervention into the purview of the Christian churches, especially the Catholic church. Finally, despite his paeans to equality and inclusiveness, Hecker did not support either Jewish rights or women's rights. Although the dynamics of exclusion operated differently for the two groups, Hecker held that both Jews and women should be denied political equality on the basis of their supposed "differences" from the Christian male norm.[2] In all these respects, Hecker was a classic mainstream liberal of his generation. To account for these various conjunctions and contradictions within mid-nineteenth-century German liberalism will be one of this book's tasks.

Another of the book's objectives will be to illuminate the broader intellectual and political terrain within which liberals' efforts were situated. It thus reconstructs and analyzes, on the one hand, a phenomenon which disoriented and alarmed liberals at just the moment a modern participatory political culture was beginning to emerge: the rise to prominence of an increasingly politically active religious right led by conservative Catholics, a movement which, not coincidentally, aggressively employed anti-Jewish rhetoric and sexual innuendo in its bid for political power. And, on the other hand, it describes and evaluates the contributions made, and dilemmas encountered, by both moderate movements for Jewish and women's rights and more radical forms of philosemitism and feminism, all of which, significantly, were born in the context and on the ground of religious dissent and criticism.

Intimacy and Exclusion documents the persistence of religious conflicts in a supposedly secularizing age.[3] Reconnecting to each other the heretofore separately examined histories of religious and political developments in the pre-revolutionary era, it shows how inextricable these developments were for contemporaries. Once this reconnection has been effected, it becomes apparent that far from being an era of steadily increasing secularization, the first half of the nineteenth century actually saw a major battle over the place and content of Christianity in a post-Enlightenment, post-French Revolution world, a battle that involved all the key political players and reached up to the highest levels of state. To conceive of this conflict as a simple contest between those seeking to advance secularization and those advocating a religious renewal, however, would be to miss the complexity of the interaction between the two sides. Each side thought *it* was advancing "true Christianity" and, from the point of view of contemporaries, no one could guess which version would emerge triumphant.

Reintegrating the religious and political histories of the age in this way also suggests the need to rethink the relationship between progressivism and conservatism at the beginning of the modern political era in Germany. Most scholars, for example, think the 1830s and 1840s were a time of ever-increasing liberalization culminating logically in the revolutions that erupted across Germany in 1848 and 1849. But the pre-1848 period is better understood as a time of ever-increasing ideological polarization. By identifying how distressed progressives were by the rise—already in the first half of the nineteenth century—of a politically sophisticated Catholic conservatism, a phenomenon most historians place much later in the nineteenth century, I demonstrate how defensive and reactive political liberals and radicals were already in this, their formative phase.

Furthermore, *Intimacy and Exclusion* shows that it was above all in contests over interethnic and sexual relations that the competing visions of the proper content and meaning of Christianity were most urgently put forward and reformulated—even as the political conflicts over religion led to new understandings of both ethnic and gendered identities. Examining the views of religious conservatives, political liberals, religious dissenters, and Jewish rights and women's rights activists, this study is thus situated at the intersection of religious history, intellectual history, Jewish studies, and women's studies. Using insights drawn from both Jewish studies and women's studies, but turning the lens around onto Christian men, brings into focus issues too frequently marginalized in mainstream accounts of German political and religious history. It reveals not only that religious conflict was the arena in which activists of the 1830s and 1840s were most fully confronted with what we would now call the problem of ideology—that is, with the limits of rationalism, with the thorny issues of prejudice and desire, and with the irresolvable puzzle over whether the self had autonomy or was socially constructed. It suggests as well that intra-Christian conflicts cannot be fully understood without close attention to two matters which have proved to be stumbling blocks for Christianity since its inception: its relationship to Judaism and its attitudes toward sexuality. As this study will show, the contests over both Christian-Jewish and male-female relations which evolved in the 1830s and 1840s ultimately had a profound impact not only on the relationship between church and state, but also on the particular formations of conservative, liberal, and radical thought.

The *Musterländle*

Fascinated by ideological conflict but not wanting to forfeit an understanding of the concrete context in which people were engaged, and the concrete interconnections between various debates, I chose to write a regional study. For a reconsideration of German liberalism and its conservative and radical critics, the Grand Duchy of Baden was a logical choice. The Grand Duchy of Baden was, by general consensus, the most liberal of all the nineteenth-century German states. As Lothar Gall, Loyd Lee, Norbert Deuchert, and Paul Nolte in particular have described, Baden was home to many of nineteenth-century Germany's most illustrious liberals, both the moderate liberals in the government and the diet, and the radical liberals who most boldly challenged Restoration Germany's restrictions on press and associational life, and spearheaded the revolutionary upheavals of 1848 and 1849. It was in Baden that liberalism first became an influential political movement. And given the strength of Badenese liberalism in the pre-revolutionary period, it was no coincidence that Baden became the site of nineteenth-century Germany's only revolutionary upheaval in which the revolutionaries were successful in taking over the entire apparatus of state: From May 13 to July 23, 1849, when the revolutionaries were defeated by Prussian and Hessian troops, Baden was a democratic republic. Yet 1840s Baden was also, although this is less frequently acknowledged, the birthplace of conservative political Catholicism in Germany, and it was conservative Catholic activists that Badenese liberals and radicals identified as their most formidable ideological opponents. Finally, 1840s Baden was home to a small experimental group of religious dissenters who, calling themselves the Mannheim Monday Club, were dedicated to bringing together socially Jews and Christians, women and men. It was this group's existence that first inspired me to sort out the interconnections between religion, politics, Jewish rights, and women's rights, and to place questions of ethnicity and gender at the center of an analysis of the religious politics of the pre-revolutionary era.

Historians have long recognized that the Grand Duchy of Baden had a political relevance that extended far beyond its borders. They invariably label Baden's bureaucratic elite, its constitution and franchise, its Lower Chamber, and the law on local government passed in 1831 as the "most liberal," "most progressive," "most modern," "most freethinking," or "most enlightened" in all of nineteenth-century Germany, and these accolades are usually applied to the grand duchy itself as well. Baden has been seen, in Gall's words, as "the great field of experimentation for all new ideas that pushed their way into Germany in the wake of, or in reaction to, the great upheaval [of 1789] in France," and the development of Badenese liberalism is considered "paradigmatic" for all of German liberalism.[4] Baden is often called the "*Musterländle*," an untranslatable bit of dialect which means, roughly, "little exemplary land." To take on Baden's liberals—in both their moderate and radical variants— is, then, in many ways, also to take on German liberalism as a whole.[5]

Religion and Economics in Baden

The Grand Duchy of Baden, a long, narrow, c-shaped strip of land encompassing approximately 15,000 square kilometers, was nestled in the southwest corner of Germany between France and Switzerland.[6] Formed between 1803 and 1806 out of many small principalities as part of the larger Napoleonic reorganization of Europe, it was the most artificial of all the nineteenth-century German states. During those three years, due largely to the protection of Napoleon and the diplomatic prowess of his minister Sigismund von Reitzenstein, Margrave Karl Friedrich of Baden acquired the parts of the Palatinate lying east of the Rhine, portions of the bishoprics of Constance, Basel, Strassburg, and Speyer, as well as the formerly Austrian territories of Breisgau and Ortenau and the city of Constance. By joining the Federation of the Rhine, Karl Friedrich (now Grand Duke) also acquired sovereignty over the principalities of Fürstenberg and Leiningen.

The close to one million inhabitants of this new political entity were heterogeneous not only in custom and political loyalties, but also in religious affiliation, and those religious divisions were compounded by geographic and socioeconomic disparities. Although the Grand Duke was Protestant, fully 66 percent of his subjects were Catholic. The Protestants were also divided amongst themselves, for 27 percent of Baden's population was Lutheran and 7 percent Evangelical-Reformed. (Although the Grand Duke quickly united the two Protestant churches administratively, it was not until 1821 that the two groups formally merged to form the Evangelical Protestant church.) In addition, 0.3 percent of the population were Mennonites, and 1.5 percent were Jews. While fully half of Baden's Protestants lived in the more urbanized and prosperous northern half of the grand duchy, only one out of five Badenese Catholics lived there, and far more Catholics than Protestants lived outside of the actual urban centers. The other 50 percent of Protestants and the other 80 percent of Catholics lived in the largely rural and poorer southern half of the country, with the less fruitful land typically farmed by Catholics.

In the first half of the nineteenth century, Baden was still a primarily agricultural society. Farmers and artisans predominated, while the tiny middle class consisted largely of civil servants and professionals. As late as the eve of the revolution of 1848, three-quarters of the population still lived on the land. Only twelve towns had more than 5,000 inhabitants, and the two largest (Mannheim, the major commercial center, and Karlsruhe, the seat of government) had only 24,000 people each. Heidelberg in the north and Freiburg in the south were university towns and hence prominent cultural centers. Pforzheim was a major center of jewelry production, and a number of towns were centers of textile manufacture. But, as contemporaries complained, there was no economic bourgeoisie to speak of, and industry was yet in its infancy. Although Baden joined the Prussian-German Customs Union in 1835 (and this encouraged more factories to set up shop within its borders), the Mannheim-Basel railroad was built, and steamboats plied the Rhine River and Lake Constance, by the time of the revolution there were but 130 factories in Baden, employing a total of only 12,500 workers.

But the socioeconomic situation was far from tranquil. There were recurrent agricultural crises (especially in 1817, 1829, and 1846/47) which shook other sectors of the economy as well. The population grew dramatically, reaching nearly 1.4 million in 1848. Inheritance patterns caused farms to be divided into ever-smaller units. And meanwhile, fully one-third of Badeners still lived in partial feudal servitude, for the nobility mediatized in 1806 tried to compensate for its subordination to the new grand duke by reactivating long-forgotten privileges. Not only did the nobles control the local police, and play a major role in choosing village mayors, teachers, and clergymen, they also denied the rural population their traditional rights to use forest land to hunt game, gather firewood, and graze livestock. As a consequence of the ensuing rising expenses and loss of supplemental sources of income, coupled with the nobles' transformation of the traditional requirement of payment in kind (recognized as being dependent on the success of a given harvest) to an inflexible demand for payment in cash, many Badenese farmers were led into debt and eventually the foreclosure of their farms and utter immiseration. These developments caused profound hostility not only toward the nobles themselves, but also to the farmers' creditors—who were often (though by no means always) Jews. This animosity toward Jews was shared as well by that majority of farmers who, although not beholden to a nobleman, had nonetheless become indebted due to crop failures or other setbacks. Increasingly, furthermore, conservative Catholic activists in particular—far more attentive to the economic suffering of the rural population than the liberals—also worked to revive and legitimate centuries-old traditions of religious distrust against Jews.

The Jews of Baden (numbering 12,000 in 1806, 23,000 in 1845) were in some ways much better off than Jews in many other German states. Already in the seventeenth century, Elector Karl Ludwig of the Palatinate had actively sought to bring wealthy Portuguese and German Jewish families to Mannheim (the site of his court) to help rebuild the city into a commercial center after its destruction during the Thirty Years War. As incentive, he offered them a degree of freedom extremely unusual for that time, and eliminated many of the restrictions and burdens to which Jews were traditionally subjected. Numerous Jewish families took up the offer, and Jews came to play an important role in the economic and cultural life of the city. But it was not until the late eighteenth century that Badenese Margrave Karl Friedrich, impressed by the writings of Moses Mendelssohn and C. W. Dohm and Joseph II's Edict of Toleration, began to improve the lot of the Jews under his rule— always with the classic Enlightenment goal also of "improving" the Jews themselves. Karl Friedrich extended this project much more generously once he had become Grand Duke. In some of the first edicts promulgated by his new government, Jews across the new land were finally granted permanent rights of residency, and no longer had to fear either potential expulsion or limits on the number of Jews in each generation who would be allowed to marry. They were granted the rights to purchase land and to enter the trades. In legal matters, they were considered Christians' equals. Jews were conscripted into military service, and Christian elementary schools were required to take in all Jewish children. Jews were also granted complete freedom of worship, and their rabbis (like Catholic and Protestant clergymen) doubled as civil servants at marriages and other occasions. When a franchise was instituted in conjunction with the constitution developed in 1818, Jews were given voting rights equal to those the Christians had (although the right to be elected to office was denied them until 1849, except at the very lowest level, the town's citizen advisory board). By the 1840s, only Jews in Electoral Hesse, Luxemburg, and some of the formerly French-owned

Rhenish territories had a better situation, while policies were comparable in Württemberg and in some of the Prussian provinces; conditions were far more oppressive in Bavaria, Saxony, the Free Cities, and in vast stretches of Prussia, especially the province of Posen.[7]

While many Jews in Mannheim and Karlsruhe were prosperous and at least partially integrated into the local educated elite (though those cities too had long had their share of poor Jews), the majority of Baden's Jews lived in rural poverty and eked out only a meager subsistence through trade in livestock, produce, and retail goods, and/or through moneylending. Jews were still denied the right to move from one community into another without permission from the new community (a right not granted until 1862). With most occupational niches in a given community already filled, it was not particularly desirable to take advantage of the just-granted right to enter an artisanal trade or take up agriculture, and those Jews who did so, especially those who did so successfully, often met with hostility, jealousy, and violence from their Christian competitors. In 1816, fully 89 percent of Badenese Jews lived by trade of some form, and by 1833 it was still 67.5 percent, slightly more than a third of which was in irregular trading. As vulnerable to downturns in the rural economy as their Christian neighbors, those Jews who engaged in moneylending often had no choice but to raise their interest rates or call in loans when times were hard. As competitors and as creditors in both town and countryside, and as those responsible for transporting goods into and out of the rural economy, Jews were easy targets for the violent animosity of their neighbors. For although there were Christian moneylenders as well, phantasmagoric anxieties and time-honored rituals of violent "sociability" (especially among young apprentices) fixed on Jews in particular. But many members of the urban intellectual elite did nothing to discourage and frequently encouraged popular anti-Jewish sentiment, and only became alarmed when the waves of anti-Jewish violence which recurred regularly in the first half of the nineteenth century (especially in 1819, 1830, 1846, and 1848) threatened to disturb the social order more generally.[8]

Badenese Politics

Because of the exceptional heterogeneity of the area he had come to govern by 1806, Grand Duke Karl Friedrich and his ministers soon set about finding ways to integrate the various regions of the new grand duchy into a unified whole, and to encourage among his new subjects a sense of identification with him and with each other. This need for inner unity was made even more pressing because of Baden's awkward geopolitical location between the warring powers of Austria and France, and the strong possibility, in Baden's early years, that either Austria or Bavaria might want to recover some of the territory now under Badenese rule. The first step Karl Friedrich thus took was to institute, in the classic tradition of enlightened absolutism for which he was already well known, a strongly centralized administrative bureaucracy which would govern and regularize all local affairs.

Fully aware, however, that unification from above could not induce a sense of unity at the grass roots, his successor Karl (who ruled from 1811 to 1818), and Karl's minister Karl Friedrich Nebenius, supplemented the centralized bureaucracy with another integrative strategy: the granting of a constitution (1818) and the development of a two-chamber diet (which first met in 1819). They conceived the diet's function as providing a forum in which diverse estates and interest groups could debate and process their conflicting goals, developing loyalty to the sovereign and a sense of mutual political responsibility. The Upper Chamber (whose size fluctuated) was composed of members of the monarchical family, representatives of the nobility, one representative each from the two Christian churches and the two universities, and a handful of prominent men appointed by the grand duke without regard to rank.

The Lower Chamber (composed of sixty-three delegates) was designed to represent "the people," but it really represented the educated middle strata. The granting of indirect voting rights to all men over the age of twenty-five for elections of the chamber's delegates—it was the broadest franchise in all Germany (only apprentices, servants, and those not economically self-supporting were excluded)—was designed to encourage the formation of a more unified sense of political belonging also in the general populace. Popular politicization around elections initially only developed slowly, however, and as a result, the delegates were generally drawn from the middle-class elite in town and country. They were either the very same bureaucrats the government had sent to administer a given area, or they were village mayors, tavernkeepers, members of the narrow strata of businessmen, or professionals like academics, clergymen, doctors, or, increasingly, lawyers. At times, fully half of the delegates were civil servants. Overrepresentation of the urban elites was also encouraged by the peculiarities of electoral districting which deliberately privileged the cities over the countryside (this was justified by pointing to the cities' larger tax base), a phenomenon which also typically caused the confessional composition of the chamber to be half-Protestant and half-Catholic, despite the one-third/two-thirds proportions in the populace at large. (This is not to imply, however, that confessional differences mattered to the delegates; as the delegates themselves frequently remarked, they did not. There was in almost all cases no correlation between a delegate's political views and his religious affiliation. Protestants and Catholics alike could be found on both the left and the right.)

The Lower Chamber was technically only a debating chamber. The delegates could not initiate or develop legislation themselves, they could only make recommendations in the form of "motions"; and although the chamber had the right to approve or veto budgets, it could not develop them. Furthermore, if the delegates raised issues the monarch would rather have left unaddressed, or if it stalled for too long in approving a budget, the grand duke could simply dissolve the chamber and set new elections. Grand Duke Karl's successor Ludwig (who ruled from 1818 to 1830), for instance, much more autocratic than his predecessors, both made use of his right to dissolve the chamber (in 1823) and employed extraordinary intervention in subsequent elections in order to guarantee a preponderance of government loyalists among the delegates. In short, the introduction of a diet had in no way been intended as a move toward genuine democratization of Badenese government, but rather as a way to defuse potential conflicts and build consensus. Indeed, the two-chamber system generally worked quite well for the government, for the Upper Chamber usually provided the grand duke and his ministers with a reliable conservative counterbalance to any impetuous demands the Lower Chamber might make, while the Lower Chamber's self-defined role as advocate of the citizenry-at-large occasionally offered a useful wedge against any overweening political aspirations of the nobility still recurrently evident in the Upper Chamber.

What had not been anticipated, however, was the way in which the Lower Chamber would become an important political force in its own right. This became particularly apparent when Grand Duke Ludwig died in 1830, and the far more enlightened Leopold acceded to the Badenese throne. For the first time in years, elections were held without government interference and, as a result, a majority of the delegates elected (though, as always, a high proportion were civil servants) were men who understood themselves as liberals. Throughout the 1830s and 1840s, to the profound alarm of other German monarchs, who constantly pressured Leopold to become more repressive, Baden's Lower Chamber functioned as Germany's major forum for the airing of all manner of progressive and enlightened views. The educated public across Germany followed the chamber's debates with rapt interest. Although a variety of other German states had diets, no other one had as much freedom to address a broad range of political issues, and in no other one were so many liberal luminaries gathered under one roof. There were government loyalists and conservatives in the Badenese chamber as well (typically constituting slightly less than one-half of the delegates), but the liberals unquestionably set the tone. Karl von Rotteck and Carl Theodor Welcker, for instance, editors of the encyclopedic *Staats-Lexikon*, the "bible" of southwest German liberalism, were influential delegates for many years, as were other prominent liberals like Adam von Itzstein, Adolf Sander, Johann Baptist Bekk, and Friedrich Bassermann; in the 1840s they were joined by Lorenz Brentano and the aforementioned Friedrich Hecker, both future 1848 revolutionaries. Furthermore, until the mid-1840s, political identities in the chamber were remarkably fluid; many of the delegates styling themselves as government loyalists also considered themselves liberals, and voted in unison with the more clearly oppositional liberals on a variety of issues.

At the center of the liberals' political vision lay the ideal of the freely self-developing, mature citizen, thinking and acting for himself, yet always alert to his responsibility for the good of the whole. This starting-point determined their views on politics and the law, economics, and religion. Government was to be made as rational and responsive to the governed as possible, and informed civic participation in government was to be encouraged. It was in this spirit, for example, that liberals demanded increased communal self-government and the reform of civil and criminal law, and insisted that government ministers be accountable for their policies to the chamber and not just to the monarch, all goals that, at various points in the 1830s and 1840s, were crowned with significant success. It was also in this spirit that they continually called for an end to press censorship, achieving the passage of Germany's most liberal press law in 1832, only to have other German governments force its retraction a few years later.

In economic views, Baden's liberals were not the stereotypical advocates of unfettered freedom of trade many historians imagine, and indeed, freedom of trade was not written into Badenese law until 1862. Rather, most of the delegates shared with the grand duke's government the fantasy of an idyllic and harmonious society of independent small producers—mostly composed of farmers and artisans, interspersed with a few thrifty and hardworking capitalists who took excellent care of their workers—and thus haphazardly advocated state subvention of industry in some instances, the removal of trade barriers in others, as the individual occasion seemed to demand, while being consistent in their insistence that feudal privileges be eliminated. The liberals' reluctance to envision the economic realm as an arena of conflict made them peculiarly unprepared for both conservative Catholics' and political radicals' eventual success in mobilizing the economic disaffection of the rural populace for their own (albeit conflicting) ends. Liberals' preoccupation with responsible autonomy and free self-development of the individual also explains their choices in the realm of religious politics. Their hatred of the religious authoritarianism (the mostly extraparliamentary) conservatives were advancing with renewed vigor in the 1830s and 1840s caused Protestant and Catholic liberals alike to advocate separation of church and state when defending religious dissenters, while vociferously supporting the government's autocratic supervision of the churches whenever the subject turned to the Catholic church's ambitions to control the hearts, minds, and personal lives of its members.

Although the Lower Chamber was the primary cause for Baden's status as the main locus of Germany's pre-1848 liberal movement, the role of the radical liberal press cannot be underestimated. It was precisely the interplay between chamber debates and activist newspaper reportage and analysis (constantly pushing against and exposing the limits set by government censors) that encouraged the formation of an active, politically informed, even radically inclined, citizenry. The *Seeblätter* (Constance), the *Oberrheinische Zeitung* (Freiburg), the *Mannheimer Abendzeitung*, and the later revolutionary Gustav von Struve's *Mannheimer Journal* and *Deutscher Zuschauer* in particular played important roles in articulating and shaping progressive public opinion in the 1840s. Although these papers typically had only 1,000–3,000 subscribers each, they were passed from hand to hand and debated in homes and on the streets. Their influence was far greater than that of the conservative papers like the *Karlsruher Zeitung* or the *Mannheimer Morgenblatt*, or even than the moderately liberal *Deutsche Zeitung* (Heidelberg).

The 1840s also saw the explosive growth of associational life, as radical liberals in particular gathered in athletic and singing clubs, in reading and social clubs, in clubs "for the benefit of the laboring classes" and, eventually, from 1845 on, in the religious dissenting congregations of (what in Baden was called) the *deutschkatholische* movement. The *Deutschkatholiken* (German-Catholics, as opposed to Roman Catholics) had both Protestant and Catholic members, but they were united in their anger at the authoritarianism gaining ground within the Catholic church in particular, and they were devoted to individual freedom of belief and cross-confessional cooperation. Although the movement only attracted 700 official members in Baden (even though across Central Europe the various strands of dissent gained somewhere between 100,000 and 150,000 adherents), the Badenese *Deutschkatholiken* acquired an extraordinary symbolic significance. Their emergence would fundamentally reconfigure the relationship between liberalism and conservatism in Baden and, for a series of complicated reasons, it was also their emergence that would cause progressives to rethink their stances toward both Jewish and women's emancipation. The aforementioned Mannheim Monday Club, for example, which brought together Jews and Christians, women and men, was born in 1847 out of a schism within Mannheim's dissenting congregation. Furthermore, although expressly political organizations were formally banned in Baden, by 1847 radicals were testing the limits of the law with routine impunity, forming into clubs whose political purpose was only thinly veiled and, when the police shut down their meetings, simply launching others. Large athletic and singing festivals, bringing together more than 1,000 activists at a time, made supraregional organization possible; celebratory banquets provided the occasion for developing and publicizing political programs. The most famous of these took place in Offenburg in September of 1847, under the leadership of Friedrich Hecker, Gustav von Struve, and the liberal Jewish lawyer Elias Eller; it was considered by many to be the first rumbling of the impending revolution. In sum, then, clubs, dissenting congregations, and demonstrations offered progressive activists concrete forums for articulating their views to a broader populace, and for challenging the more hesitant leaders in the Lower Chamber to make good on liberalism's radical potential.

The War of Words

Concerned as this study is with ideological conflicts, the sources on which I have primarily relied are the sorts of sources often inherently concerned with persuasion: parliamentary debates, religious and political newspapers, polemical tracts, correspondence between religious and political leaders, and sermons. I have, in short, been particularly interested in *how* nineteenth-century people made their arguments, how they tried to persuade others of their point of view, what rhetorical strategies and narrative devices they used, and what metaphors they employed to lend weight to their claims. I thus particularly explore the strategies by which social inequalities were legitimated or protested, as well as the rhetorical tactics by which speakers or writers sought to evoke a sense of pleasure or danger, hope or anxiety, for their audiences. This reevaluation of the *content* of liberal, conservative, and radical ideas (too often presumed to be self-evident) provides a crucial—indeed often corrective—supplement to social historical investigations.

At the same time, my approach diverges from traditional intellectual history in a number of ways. For instance, rather than focusing on (what is called) "high" intellectual history—the subjects of which are usually the canonized philosophers of Western civilization—I have instead concentrated on the middle range of thinkers, those political and religious activists who saw themselves as mediating between the philosophers and popular culture, the state and its subjects, and the churches and their members. These activists saw themselves (however partially or inaccurately) as speaking to and for "the people." I have tried to take the ideas of these middle-range people as seriously (and to analyze them as fully and as critically) as other intellectual historians have taken the ideas of G.W.F. Hegel or John Stuart Mill, while seeking explanations for the contradictions, presumptions, preoccupations, and silences evident in their arguments in the social, political, and cultural context.

Furthermore, influenced by new developments in literary criticism, I have also started from the assumption that texts can be at war with themselves, and produce meanings in excess of their own intent. I have thus particularly looked for textual repetitions and fixations, as well as gaps in logic, moments of inconsistency, or striking suppressions. I have, in short, tried to analyze the multiple layers of meaning in a variety of texts, attending both to a given text's programmatic intent *and* its inadvertent gestures and rhetorical flourishes (and the implicit assumptions those reveal). I have also been interested in the mutual entanglement of discourses and counter-discourses, as well as the unintended side effects of efforts at resistance to seemingly hegemonic ideologies.[9] I have thus tried to show the ways opposing sides in a given controversy borrowed from each other's argumentative arsenal, even as they pushed each other into ever more extreme positions. I have tried to analyze as well how seemingly discrete conflicts were intertwined with one another, and how images or phrases from one controversy showed up in the midst of another one. For finally, then, rather than identifying one ideological conflict as primary, *Intimacy and Exclusion* is above all an experiment in writing a (more historically accurate) de-centered intellectual history, one which shows how various religious and political debates, because they were interwoven in their time, also need to be read by us with and against each other in order for the full meaning of each to emerge.

The book's organization reflects this conviction. The first chapter, "Bodies and Souls," analyzes conflicts between various progressives and the rising religious right over sexuality and marriage from the late 1820s to the 1840s, documenting in particular the profound but generally underacknowledged investment liberals and other progressives had in celebrating the intimate realm of the private sphere and protecting it from outside intervention. The chapter focuses on how disputes over priestly celibacy and mixed Protestant-Catholic marriages raised complex questions about the relationship between individual subjectivity and religious authority, and about the proper boundaries and proper relationships between social groups, and explains why these conflicts led to a reconfiguration of the religious and political landscape in Baden.

The next two chapters explore the consequences of this reconfiguration for Jews and women, respectively. The second chapter, "Jewish

Emancipation and Jewish Difference," begins by challenging most historians' assumptions that liberals were natural advocates of Jewish emancipation by documenting Badenese liberals' long-standing hostility to emancipation. It then shows how it was liberals' efforts to reconceive their views of Christianity in light of both their alarm at the rise of religious conservatism around the issues of sexuality and marriage and their delight at the emergence of *deutschkatholische* dissent that ultimately caused liberals to make Jewish emancipation a central plank in their political platform. But the chapter also shows how these intra-Christian disputes created a space in which Jewish "difference" from Christian Germans could be conceived in racial terms. The third chapter, "(Wo)Men's Emancipation and Women's Difference" calls into question the historiographical consensus that the dissenting movement of the 1840s is best understood as the seedbed for the first organized German women's rights movement. The chapter shows that when the movement's leaders' ambiguous rhetoric about women is taken seriously, and is interpreted in light of the long history of intra-Christian conflict over sexuality and marriage which was a central cause of the movement's emergence, the dissenting movement can just as helpfully be understood as a men's rights movement whose overarching goal was to resist Roman Catholicism's renewed denigration of human sexuality and free choice in love. The movement thus emerges as primarily concerned with an intra-male conflict between dissenters and priests over whether or not women might be considered worthy love objects.

The final two chapters provide close readings of the work of a few key individuals who—in the context of radical religious criticism—put forward more innovative and utopian visions of Jewish-Christian relations (chapter 4) and gender relations (chapter 5) than most of their contemporaries; their writings shed light on what kinds of social transformations were imaginable in that millenial moment immediately preceding and coinciding with the outbreak of revolution in 1848. "Problematics of Philosemitism" looks at two of the most radical religious dissenters, the Mannheim dissenting preacher Carl Scholl and the radical liberal lawyer and journalist Gustav von Struve. Scholl and Struve were the main leaders of the Mannheim Monday Club, and an examination of their philosemitic activism—as well as the Reform Jewish response to their efforts—paradigmatically reveals the strengths and weaknesses of Christian humanism. Their efforts show that rethinking the meaning of Christianity, and generating Jewish-Christian social intimacy, were essential supplements to Jewish political equality; but the homogeneity implicit in their humanism, and their simplistic assumptions about historical progressivism (from Judaism to Christianity to humanism) made them condescending toward Jews and incapable of hearing Jewish activists' insistence on the equal moral value of Judaism as a religion. "The Feminist Conundrum" examines the writings of Louise Dittmar, an autodidact philosopher and women's rights activist, and the Monday Club's most significant product. Dittmar's work is interesting because of the difficulty she had inserting women into the two main intellectual paradigms available to her: liberalism and radical religious criticism. Trying to extend liberty and equality to women was difficult because the liberal story of the social contract was not written with women in mind; from the start, the sexual contract a man concluded with a woman was conceived of as an indispensable but always subsidiary supplement to the social contract men concluded among themselves. Including women in the liberal agenda was also hard because of the tenacity with which contemporaries held to the notion that women were naturally different from men, and hence not deserving of full equality; Dittmar's efforts to question the notion of natural differences were pathbreaking for the mid-nineteenth century, and ultimately unsuccessful for precisely that reason. Finally, including women in the project of radical religious criticism was difficult because the whole history of this project's evolution had to do with male subjectivity and desire. Providing a reprise of many of the themes raised in "Bodies and Souls," this chapter shows how near-impossible it was to speak of women as subjects and as sexual beings within the conceptual frameworks available at the time; all Dittmar's work could do was to expose the exclusionary foundations of her contemporaries' ideological systems.

In the broadest sense, then, this book is an exploration of the locating and relocating of *boundaries*—the identification and contestation of where the relevant differences between people lie, and about the ordering and reordering of *relationships*—between individuals, between individuals and various forms of authority, and between social groups. My purpose is to track the effects of the intensification of religious conflicts in the pre-revolutionary era, and to analyze how contemporaries sought to advance their conflicting notions about interethnic and sexual relations in the context of their larger battles over the meaning both of Christianity and of the Enlightenment's legacy. In this context, I am particularly interested in how anti-Judaism and assaults on progressives' investment in amatory happiness became central strategies in conservatives' efforts to advance their own political agenda. I am especially concerned as well with self-styled progressives' guilty conscience—around two issues: brotherly love and heterosexual desire, the social contract and the sexual contract. Jews provided the test case, the outer limit, of who would be included in the circle of brothers. Women, meanwhile, were revered and defended as worthy love objects against conservatives' tendencies to denigrate them (and love itself); but most progressives were not quite willing to see women as subjects in their own right. And finally, I am interested in radical critiques of mainstream liberals' attitudes about both interethnic and sexual relations, and in analyzing the difficulties radicals encountered in reconceptualizing both classical liberalism and Christianity in order to make room for the claims of Jews and women.

1

BODIES AND SOULS

THE GRAND DUCHY of Baden was well known to be nine-teenth-century Germany's most liberal state. Ruled (from 1831 on) by an enlightened monarch and his like-minded bureaucrats, Baden was also home to many of Germany's most illustrious liberal and radical-democratic publicists and activists. The decades preceding the Badenese revolutions of 1848 and 1849 are often described as an era of ever-increasing liberalization culminating logically in the revolutionary years. What most historians have failed to note, however, is that in the 1830s and 1840s Baden was also the seedbed for a politically sophisti-cated religious conservatism, led by neoorthodox Catholics, and that the very intensity of liberal activism in Baden was in no small part due precisely to liberal alarm at the growth of this religious right. When reli-gious history is reintegrated into the history of political developments, then, it becomes clear that the pre-revolutionary decades are better un-derstood as a time of ever-increasing ideological polarization.

The major conflicts around which neoorthodox Catholicism orga-nized itself in Baden had to do with priestly celibacy and mixed mar-riages between Protestants and Catholics. These phenomena were only seemingly marginal. As the fervor with which all sides addressed the top-ics attests, the controversies raised profound questions about the rela-tionship between individual subjectivity and religious authority, and about the proper boundaries, and proper relationships, between social groups in an era of ever-greater mobility and mixing. Each side ad-vanced its own understandings of the values, or dangers, of sex, love, and the pursuit of earthly happiness; at stake were individuals' attitudes toward their own bodies and the bodies of others, as well as the most intimate reaches of individuals' souls.

The conflicts over sex and love also led to a major rearrangement of the religious and political landscape in Baden. In the first decades of the nineteenth century, for example, Baden's Catholic leadership included many men deeply influenced by Enlightenment thought. The struggle over priestly celibacy in the late 1820s and early 1830s provided conservatives with the occasion to rid the Catholic church in Baden of these reformist elements. The controversy over mixed marriages, in turn, allowed conservatives successfully to challenge the Badenese state government, and to undermine the state's efforts to keep the church subordinate to itself. It was, moreover, through these two disputes over sex and love that political liberals and radicals came to identify neoorthodox Catholics as their most formidable ideological opponents. This development was to have important and unexpected consequences. As subsequent chapters will show, due to a complex conjunction of circumstances it was on the ground of this militant anticlericalism that movements for both Jewish rights and women's rights, as well as more radical forms of philosemitism and feminism, were born in Germany.

Unearthing the roots of liberal irritation at conservative Catholicism, then, is important for a number of reasons.[1] One is that reconstructing religious conflicts between liberals and conservative Catholics sheds light on the serious philosophical dilemmas confronting liberals just as they were coming to self-consciousness and self-confidence as a coherent political movement. For example, as conservatives increasingly used calls for liberty, equality, and tolerance to advance their own cause, liberals were pressed to come to terms with the malleability of those cherished ideals, a phenomenon that intensified liberal insecurity just at the moment that a modern mass political culture was beginning to emerge.

Another reason is that the ongoing battle with religious conservatives decisively shaped the character of German liberalism in its formative phase, and analyzing the substance of the controversy reveals elements of liberal thought obscured in most traditional studies. These elements include: liberals' preoccupation with male sexual rights, the fervor of liberals' efforts to circumscribe a private sphere free from the control of religious authorities in particular, and the special investment liberals had in the institution of marriage—not only as the foundation of a stable and beneficent social order, but also as a site of untrammeled bliss and individual self-development and perfectibility. In short, it becomes apparent that such seemingly private matters as sex and marriage were important elements of public debate in general, and were central to the liberal political agenda in particular.

Furthermore, historians have often wondered why political liberals, typically associated with religious tolerance and support for the separation of church and state, were so profoundly hostile to institutional Catholicism in particular. Liberals' anxiety about church encroachment on the domestic realm goes far toward explaining the roots of this hostility. As the Catholic church in the first half of the nineteenth century recaptured much of the political and spiritual power it had had before the Enlightenment and the French Revolution, it took on a phantasmagoric status in the liberal imagination. Although the Protestant church also underwent a conservative revival in the first half of the nineteenth century, liberal apprehension fixed upon the Catholic phenomenon as the far more potent threat.[2] Not only did the Catholic church provide a convenient and acceptable target for anti-conservative hostilities in a land ruled by a Protestant monarch. Much more important was the fact that the revival of Roman Catholicism called into question liberals' expectation that historical progress was inevitable. In addition, the psychological power the church openly sought to exercise over the hearts and minds of its members raised doubts about the viability of the rational and autonomous individual subject that was the starting point of liberal thought. Most significantly, because it insisted on its own right constantly to scrutinize its members' personal lives, no institution more forcefully contested liberals' efforts to circumscribe a private sphere than the Catholic church, and no other institution so strongly contested human beings' rights to sexual pleasure and to free choice in love.

Finally, an investigation into the religious politics of the pre-revolutionary era forces a reconsideration of conventional conceptions of the relationship between religious revival and efforts at secularization. For what evolved in the 1830s and 1840s was no simple opposition between these two forces, but rather an elaborate, inter-reactive dialectic, in which religious conservatives increasingly intervened in the ostensibly secular realm of politics (publicizing their views in newspapers and polemical tracts and organizing petition drives and election campaigns), while liberals and radical democrats persisted in making their claims in religious language, and insisting on the viability of their more humanized, but nonetheless sincerely spiritual, interpretation of Christianity. In short, the various combatants were not only wrestling over the place or role of Christianity in a post-Enlightenment world, but also over its very content.

Church and State after the French Revolution

To make sense of how the conflicts over celibacy and mixed marriages developed in Baden in the 1830s and 1840s, it is necessary to turn back briefly to the French Revolution of 1789, and to the first decades of the grand duchy's existence. The French Revolution (and its Napoleonic aftermath) must be seen as the touchstone of crisis for the first half of the nineteenth century in Germany. Its effect was both material and symbolic. On the one hand, it was the event which permanently stripped the Roman Catholic church of its formal political and economic power and catalyzed the political reorganization of Europe. On the other hand, it was the trauma which was repeatedly to supply debaters at different points on the political spectrum with a rich reservoir of threatening metaphors.

Paradoxically, the same events which robbed the Catholic church of its territorial powers and made it so desperately eager to reestablish itself, also created the conditions which made the striving for a new sort of power possible. For, freed from the concerns of ruling separate territories, the church could centralize its organization and universalize its focus. Faced with this phenomenon, many state governments attempted both to deemphasize confessional differences, and to assert and secure the primacy of their own power over that of the Catholic church.

At this juncture, however, another paradox emerged. The experience of the French Revolution had also forced governments to recognize their dependence on religious authorities, and the usefulness of the churches in maintaining social order and obedience. As historian Franz Schnabel observed in discussing the 1830s,

> The modern state was formally sovereign, and yet it was practically and politically dependent upon the Christian churches due to the incredible influence which these exercised on the sensibilities of their members. . . . That the state could reach and mobilize the attitudes of its subjects on its own, this Hobbes and basically also Hegel had taught. But the French Revolution had shown where this path led; the time seemed too serious to . . . undertake experiments.[3]

Catholic activists mocked the state's functionalist understanding of religion—"the old idea, that religion is just a political bridle for the people."[4] But they also missed few opportunities to advertise their religion as the antidote to revolution. At the Congress of Vienna in 1815, for example, German Catholic leaders pointed out the crucial role of the Catholic church in "elevating the denatured era back to religion, and leading it back to awe before its monarchs and obedience to the laws." For "once a human being has been disturbed in his internal peace, in his religion . . . there can no longer be any doubt that this will have a dangerous effect on the external order."[5]

In sum, then, the governments' contradictory needs in their own attempts to come to terms with the post-revolutionary world, and their vulnerability to the Catholic church's persuasive efforts, necessarily created an ambiguous situation. At first, efforts made by papal representatives at the Congress of Vienna to regain church lands and funds from the nations assembled there were unsuccessful. The states confirmed their refusal to return land and money to the church, and confirmed their commitment to parity and peace between Catholics and Protestants. But soon thereafter, Rome turned its attention to the goal of establishing a new network of dioceses to be distributed among the various states that had emerged in the wake of the Napoleonic era, and here the ambivalence of the state governments toward the Catholic church became strikingly apparent.

In the 1820s, Baden, together with a group of other small central and southern German states anxious to establish a permanent but controlled relationship with Rome, came to a secret agreement with the papal curia and accepted the establishment of a new archdiocese to be based in Freiburg. In addition to the Catholics in the tiny territory of Hohenzollern, the jurisdiction of the Freiburg archdiocese was to include all the Catholics in Baden; the political territory of the Grand Duchy and the religious territory of the archdiocese were thus basically coextensive. The state governments also agreed to the establishment of subsidiary dioceses in each of the other states. Lengthy maneuverings between the governments and Rome ensued over the details of the agreements. The states made some concessions to Rome, but after permitting the dioceses to be established (the Freiburg archdiocese was founded in 1827), and allowing Rome to determine the manner in which bishops would be chosen, the states proceeded unilaterally to publish decrees reiterating each monarch's ultimate supremacy over the church. Referring to the principle of *Staatskirchentum* primarily developed by Joseph II of Austria, the states insisted that churches should be subordinate to the state. Their decrees to this effect, which were (understandably) never formally recognized by Rome, asserted that governments had the right to review and potentially to veto any church policy before it was publicized within a state's boundaries, that the states would maintain legal control over the clergy, and that priests must receive education at public (state-controlled) universities. In practice, then, the states had allowed Rome to gain a foothold inside each of their countries, but in principle, they wanted to retain the ability to hold the church in check.

The situation in Baden had its own special complexities. The grand duchy had been formed between 1803 and 1806 as part of the Napoleonic reorganization of Europe. Created out of many tiny principalities, it was the most artificial of all the newly forged German states, a circumstance which led the government to be particularly preoccupied with securing peace and parity between its subjects of different confessions. A Protestant monarch ruled over a population that was two-thirds Catholic and only one-third Protestant. Nonetheless, initially there were few conflicts between the state and the Catholic leadership, for in the early decades of the nineteenth century, much of Baden's Catholic hierarchy and clergy was Enlightenment-inspired and sought out reconciliation with Protestants and distance from Rome.

The most powerful Catholic leader in the first decades of Baden's existence was Ignaz von Wessenberg. Wessenberg, the leading administrator of the old diocese of Constance from 1802 until 1827 when it was supplanted by the new archdiocese in Freiburg, was a loyal Catholic dedicated to defending the church's rights against the state.[6] But he was also one of the leaders of the movement to develop a national German church with only loose ties to Rome, a decentralized church in which bishops provided a counterbalance to the papacy and adapted church life to the peculiar needs of the region under their jurisdiction. To the priests under his tutelage and care, he stressed the value of a scholarly education, of reform of the worship service in keeping with the times—such as saying Mass in German instead of Latin, and of dialogue with Protestants. Like many of his contemporaries, he identified complete lack of faith, not the blurring of differences between Catholics and Protestants, as the gravest threat to society.[7] These attitudes contributed to Rome's decision to reject him as a potential archbishop for the new archdiocese, and from the 1820s on his influence would decline.

Furthermore, the University of Freiburg, where most young men in training for the priesthood in Baden studied, had been a center of reform Catholicism already in the eighteenth century, when Freiburg had belonged to the Austrian territories. Joseph II of Austria had seen to it that the professoriate at Freiburg, while Catholic, was theologically progressive, and the Badenese government followed in his footsteps. Professors at Freiburg routinely excoriated corruption in Rome and called for structural church reform. Some of the more radical professors, like Karl Alexander von Reichlin-Meldegg, Heinrich Schreiber, and Heinrich Amann, were also said to question the doctrine of the Trinity and even the divinity of Christ, teaching their students to think of biblical events historically, and to understand that there was no uniform truth emanating from Rome but rather that the church had taken a great diversity of positions over the centuries. The result of all this encouragement in rebellious thinking, as one of the few less liberal professors complained, was a strong sense of individual autonomy among many of Baden's Catholic priests, for "every lowly clergyman dares to tinker with the worship service, with the handling of the sacraments, to celebrate the Holy Mass in German language, to present his very own catechism."[8]

The Anti-Celibacy Campaign

The great drama of the 1830s and 1840s was the eventual displacement of all the reformist Catholic leaders by conservatives loyal to Rome; by a peculiar twist of fate it was the reformists' efforts to abolish priestly celibacy which catalyzed the revival of Catholic conservatism. For the same professors at Freiburg who challenged Rome and questioned its teachings also aggressively promoted the ideal of priestly marriage and discussed that which was, in Professor Schreiber's oft-quoted phrase, "immoral, unlawful and unnatural" about the celibacy rule.[9] No sooner had the new archdiocese been established, and an archbishop, Bernhard Boll, installed, when already in the spring of 1828 twenty-three prominent Catholic laypeople from Freiburg, a number of them professors, sent a petition authored by Professors Heinrich Amann and Karl Zell to the Lower Chamber of the Badenese diet, soliciting the Lower Chamber's assistance in convincing the grand duke to induce the archbishop to abolish priestly celibacy within Baden's borders. They also delivered addresses directly to the grand duke and the archbishop.

The petitioners made four main arguments. One was that the celibacy rule, which they considered "dangerous" and "violent," encouraged sexual immorality. "Who does not know," they asked, "what secret crimes and public scandals this coercive law has caused and still causes? There are so many loud complaints and so much evidence before us in this matter that we assume we can spare ourselves the unpleasant business of elaborating in more detail the disadvantages of priestly celibacy from this angle." A related line of argument both insisted on the naturalness of sex and drew on Enlightenment rhetoric to announce that the "unnecessary coercion" of the celibacy rule robbed the individual of his "personal freedom" and of the "enjoyment" of "one of the most essential natural rights." The third argument was that the church needed to recall itself to the purity of its origins: "That which we demand is no innovation, but rather a return to the old way," for "history shows that in the first three centuries of the Catholic church there was most definitely no commandment against priestly marriage," and it was only in the eleventh century, with the "destructive measures" taken by Pope Gregory VII, that priestly celibacy had become generally required. This call for a return to the "very oldest arrangements of the Catholic church" was absolutely compatible with the petitioners' assumptions about historical progress: "We cannot conceive of the idea that our request for improvement, which was already in the sixteenth century solemnly and formally demanded by German Catholic monarchs, could be ignored by a German diet of the nineteenth century."[10]

As this last remark suggests, and as indeed the entire effort to get the Lower Chamber and the grand duke involved demonstrates, the petitioners were deliberately politicizing what was generally considered to be an internal church matter. Thus the petitioners' fourth main rhetorical strategy was to flatter the state government in its attachment to the principle of church subordination to the state by speaking of "our Catholic state church" and by reiterating the state's prerogative to control church policy. The petitioners particularly sought to cast the institution of compulsory celibacy as a danger to the state, arguing that since its inception in the eleventh century, its main goal had been to ensure Rome's authoritarian control over its clergy, and thus that celibacy was the linchpin in the church's efforts to remain autonomous from state control. Marriage, they proposed, was a "mighty bond . . . which ties the individual state citizen more intimately to the monarch, to the fatherland and to his fellow citizens"; an unmarried clergy, by contrast, was "all the more given up to foreign influences." The petitioners insisted that the government had the legal right to abolish priestly celibacy within Baden's borders even if the archbishop could not be persuaded to do so himself, for this would be "a measure imperative for the well-being of the state."[11]

There was nothing particularly novel about any of these strategies. Complaints about compulsory priestly celibacy were as old as the institution itself, and had been particularly common during the Reformation and the age of Enlightenment, with another flurry inspired in Germany after the French revolutionary Assemblée nationale had demonstrated in 1790 (although Napoleon subsequently allowed this to be reversed in his concordat with Rome) that a political body could abolish compulsory celibacy by fiat. As one commentator pointed out, "It is impossible to say something new about celibacy, for there are whole libraries of books about it."[12] Across the German lands, also in the first decades of the nineteenth century, Catholic reformers documented in extraordinary detail the purported sexual proclivities of only ostensibly celibate priests.[13] Some mocked the church, turning the Apostle Paul's dictum that "it is better to marry than to be aflame with passion" on its head by arguing that the church acted as though "it is better to be aflame with passion than to marry."[14] One tract focused on defending the "blameless sexual drive," criticized the "unnatural, painful condition" of priests, and sought to document the celibacy rule's "unbiblical origin, its fanatical extension, its illegal introduction . . . its physical, economic, political and moral perniciousness."[15] Another called the celibacy rule "something evil," "not of divine origin," but rather something "which the *Roman curia* used to secure and extend the worldly might of the popes"; because of this, the author argued, it was "more than ever necessary . . . to separate the Catholic church from the Roman curia."[16] Still another stressed both that celibacy, like castration, "demolishes inalienable rights," and that celibacy was "detrimental to the welfare of the state."[17]

What was new after 1828 was the support the Badenese petitioners received from a political phenomenon that was just evolving into a recognizable entity: liberalism. Although Baden's diet had been established in 1819, it was only after the accession to the throne in 1831 of Grand Duke Leopold, more open-minded than his predecessor, that the Lower Chamber of the diet acquired the freedom to discuss any and all political matters that made it the envy of all the rest of Germany, and *the* leading forum for the airing of liberal views in the pre-1848 era. Predictably, the still quite intimidated chamber of 1828 had not felt competent to take a stand on what it perceived to be a purely religious matter. Indeed, in 1828, efforts by a minority of five delegates to get the petition formally discussed had caused an enormous commotion, with many delegates threatening to walk out. But in 1831, for the first time in years, elections to the Lower Chamber were held without evidence of corruption and vote-rigging, and these elections brought into the chamber many more self-identified liberals than ever before. The new delegates were optimistic and full of a sense of their own importance as a progressive political force. Inspired by the transformed conditions, Professor Amann, one of the authors of the 1828 petition, circulated a memorandum to all of the 1,149 priests in Baden, asking them to support a renewal of the petition to the Lower Chamber and assuring them of confidentiality. One hundred and fifty-six priests responded with signatures in sealed envelopes supporting the proposed petition; eleven Catholic university professors and twelve other laypeople joined them.[18]

ʹ This time Amann succeeded in getting the political support he wanted. In a rush of supreme self-confidence, the predominantly liberal chamber of 1831, fully half of which was Catholic, ridiculed the delegates of 1828 and enthusiastically supported the reformers' demands.[19] Discreetly veiling references to sex with paeans to the joys of domesticity, the delegates celebrated the awakening of a "permissible human wish in a man's breast," argued that "without family life our existence has little charm; only domestic bliss gives value to life," and decried how "inhumane it is, to exclude a whole class from the greatest of life's pleasures." Justifying their own right to adjudicate this topic, the delegates also explicitly emphasized its political import, stressing that the celibacy rule "intervenes so deeply in the civic order of the state." The prominent liberal Karl von Rotteck contended that it was the "*double* nature of the issue, on the one side *religious* and on the other side *civic*" that made it entirely appropriate for the Lower Chamber to get involved, for, as he put it, the "matter of celibacy has so profound an influence on the *welfare of the state*" and "its abolition is a measure demanded by politics, humanity and law." Rotteck's colleague Carl Theodor Welcker also insisted that the topic of celibacy "is one of the most important ones that can be discussed anywhere, especially in a diet. . . . All enlightened friends of humanity consider the abolition of this institution unendingly important from a moral and a civic point of view." In a classic example of how liberals tended to freight marriage with great expectations, Welcker anticipated that the state government's intervention in the matter would "plant new seeds which must lead to the most beautiful and most glorious development for the morality, freedom, civilization and culture of our land."[20]

Furthermore, the delegates of 1831 were strikingly convinced that the celibacy rule's demise was inevitable. "Its abolition must sooner or later necessarily occur," one declared, while another intoned that "the case is closed on the offensiveness, the unnaturalness of celibacy and on its irreconcilability with the progress of the human spirit and of true morality." A third delegate said that "I don't believe a single enlightened Catholic would defend the notion that celibacy belongs to the [church's] fundamental religious principles, and no sensible Catholic exists who does not express the wish that in this matter things might become different." And, as with the petitioners themselves, this assumption about the inescapability of progress was inextricable from the presumption that such progress involved a return to "the pure *conditions of original times.*"[21]

Only one of the sixty-three delegates spoke in favor of retaining the institution of celibacy, and only one other delegate silently concurred with him, for at the end of the discussion the chamber voted all against two in favor of urging the grand duke to plan for a Catholic synod at which the matter of priestly celibacy could be discussed and appropriately resolved. The call for a synod was an attempt to apply the principle of democratic representation and participation, which was just gaining ground in political life, also to the realm of religion. The delegates found the idea of mixed lay-clerical synods, in which laity could help determine church policy, particularly appealing. Rotteck had been pushing the idea of such a synod for more than a decade already. The delegates' demand for a synod was both strategic—since they were fully aware that they could not themselves in one stroke achieve the abolition of compulsory celibacy—and it was also an end in itself, for the introduction of a more democratic decision-making process within the Catholic church would inevitably undermine many aspects of the church's hierarchical structure.

Although this may seem almost unimaginable in hindsight, it is crucial to understand that the anti-celibacy petitioners' and the delegates' hope of success was in many ways quite reasonable. In the wake of the French Revolution, Rome's power indeed appeared to be at a nadir; many Germans assumed that national or even regional German Catholic churches only loosely affiliated with Rome would in fact be created, and that these would be fully capable of instituting priestly marriage without ceasing to be Catholic. Also well known was the Badenese state government's commitment to keeping the Catholic church in check; liberals could not see why the government, which in previous decades had promoted legitimate marriage wherever it could in the interests of both social order and population production, could have any objections to a married clergy.[22] In general, German liberals were tremendously self-congratulatory about German states' abilities to implement progressive social reform without a revolution, and they were above all convinced that such reform would most definitely occur in almost all realms of social life. Finally, the individualistic tendencies of Baden's Catholic clergymen in the early nineteenth century were legendary. It was an independence that apparently extended to sexual matters, for many Catholic priests in Baden in the 1820s and 1830s were said to live openly with their housekeepers; no resistance to changing the rule was thus anticipated from these quarters.[23] The younger generation seemed amenable as well. Fifty-one of the sixty-one young candidates in training for the priesthood at the Catholic seminary publicly declared their opposition to celibacy.[24]

But the reformers had fundamentally miscalculated when they tried to play church and state authorities off against each other. For despite its resistance to Catholic autonomy, the state felt itself far too dependent on the Catholic church as a guardian of order and morality even to consider intervening in the church's handling of celibacy and therefore rejected the reformers' request out of hand. As one delegate had pointed out already in 1828, to change the celibacy law would be to "shake profoundly" the "hierarchical system" of the Catholic church, to "undermine . . . its very foundations."[25] This was a destabilization in which the state was not interested. (Indeed, even such a devotee of church subordination to the state as Joseph II of Austria had not seen fit to abolish celibacy.) The Lower Chamber, which had made the issue its own, reminded the government to take action in 1833 and again in 1835, but Minister of State Ludwig Winter clearly expressed the state's position when he declared in 1833 that "the government will not be so foolish as to make a single move to abolish celibacy."[26]

Even more significant, the reformers had inadvertently catalyzed the revival and mobilization of Catholic neoorthodoxy. The movement against celibacy in Baden had, as one historian put it, "made waves throughout all of Germany." In Hessen, Württemberg, Bavaria, Silesia, and elsewhere, anti-celibacy activists lobbied diets, wrote tracts and/or started clubs with the abolition of celibacy as a central goal, and "the daily political press took on the issue and gave the topic of celibacy a great deal of space in its pages."[27] In response, conservative observers warned of the Badenese campaigners' revolutionary purposes, and lamented how "theological professors [in Freiburg] are mobilizing . . . against the mother-church Rome," recommending that "the bishops of Germany might tie themselves more tightly to Rome . . . and seek advice and help from there."[28] Conservatives also rejected the idea of holding synods, both because synods were identified as incompatible with the felt need for a hierarchical church organization, and because they perceived demands for synods to be simply covers for the anti-celibacy movement.[29]

The most influential critic of the Badenese petitioners, Johann Adam Möhler, a Catholic theologian from the neighboring state of Württemberg, argued that the assault on celibacy was an assault on the church as a whole, an assault on its very existence and essence. He insisted that "whoever denies the infallibility of the church [by, for example, questioning its doctrines] . . . thereby denies its origin in Christ, as well as its eternal permanence." As a result, critics were excluded from the community of the faithful, were indeed, "un-Christian": Möhler not only declared that the "fleshly minded person . . . stands outside the Gospel," but also associated criticism of celibacy with "the most vulgar Jewish and pagan . . . weakness." To these assertions, Möhler added an element of sarcasm, noting his surprise at the idea "that in order to revive the frozen members of the moral body of Christ, or in order to win thorough and spirited theologians and inspired preachers . . . one must above all provide *women*."[30] Möhler's tract found wide distribution, and was credited with sparking the profound reconsideration of celibacy's virtues that subsequently ensued particularly among the younger clergy.

As Möhler's remarks suggest, conservative Catholics held to a worldview that was utterly divergent from that of reformist Catholics or political liberals. Not only were diversity of opinion within the church and an attitude of skepticism toward authority considered a sacrilege, but conservatives also had especially well-defined and hostile conceptions of the body. As one conservative Catholic put it, "Christianity demands the suppression of every passion, the mortification of every purely earthly stirring."[31] The goal was to be "dead to the world and glowing with enthusiasm for the Savior and his Holy Church."[32] Priests were solicitously advised to avoid "secular concerns, idleness, pleasure-seeking" and instead devote themselves to "prayer, imploring of God's grace, serious study," for then "the battle is not hard, one can achieve moral manliness."[33] One pro-celibacy polemicist called on his readers to have "courage in the battle with the flesh" and celebrated those who demonstrated "virile strength and brave resistance against lust." He repeatedly ridiculed the physiological arguments of those opponents who claimed priests suffered from being unable to express the "creative force" God had put into their "generative organs" by accusing them of "weakness" and calling them "softies" and "woman-craving whimperers."[34] Similarly, the young Badenese seminarians' "rage for women" was taken by the seminary director as a clear sign that they were "not fit to be clergymen," and under pressure from the archbishop, they retracted their previous views and promised in their "own lives to uphold this doctrine [of celibacy] in a manly way."[35]

Quite apparently, then, closely associated with conservatives' animus against the body was a mistrustful attitude toward women. Even the venerable old reform-minded diocesan leader Wessenberg, who had encouraged critical discussion of celibacy among his students and was convinced celibacy was a dying institution, criticized those who attacked compulsory celibacy simply because they wanted to get married themselves. "How," he asked a liberal friend in a revealing formulation, "can one avoid the suspicion that the friends of reform in the clergy are only interested in women?"[36] In an era in which the Enlightenment and Romanticism both had brought a new rhetoric of reverence for women's special moral qualities (though this rhetoric too was not without its darker undertones of suspicion vis-à-vis women) conservative Catholics held fast to and refurbished an age-old Christian view of women as more susceptible to sin than men.[37] Thus, for example, conservative Catholics accused the women of their day of having "made themselves into real daughters of Eve instead of children of Mary" and announced that "the Prophet Isaiah's description of the degeneracy of the Jewish women, a major cause of the general deterioration of morals and the divine punishment which followed, is unfortunately only too faithful a mirror image of the degeneracy of Christian women."[38] Conservatives believed that women tended toward craftiness and vanity and too great a loquacity. They further complained (as one prominent Catholic theologian put it in a textbook on Christian morals) of

the *weaker*, more *negative* nature of this sex in general: it is stimulated by *jealousy*, by *lustfulness* etc. and succumbs. . . . Namely, *fleshly* missteps are with this sex of a profoundly destructive nature. They cause the foundations of its virtue—fear of God, shame and morals—to crumble abruptly. . . . And once the female sex has lost its morality, then the *savage*, the *hideous and unnatural* lies closer to it than to the male. . . . And because she is in general more passionate, and (when once fallen) more given over to drives, therefore she is also more given over to the demonic.

As definitive evidence for this analysis, the author cited the biblical figures Salomé and Jezebel, and—in a rhetorical but nonetheless indicative flourish—"so many scenes from the French Revolution."[39] Such distrust or dislike of the female sex was closely intertwined with the felt need to defend celibacy. Alban Stolz, who was to become one of the leading conservative Catholic activists in Baden, made this unabashedly explicit. While granting that some women retained an inner beauty throughout their lives (though only if their spirits were ennobled by a deep Christian piety), Stolz warned his readers that the vast majority of women quickly lost their youthful charms and became so "boring, miserable, bizarre, cantankerous . . . that every Catholic clergyman from the bottom of his heart thanks the church that through celibacy it has saved him from such a supplement and life-sweetener."[40]

Related concerns motivated the Catholic hierarchy in Baden. Particularly because of the reformers' success in making celibacy a major public, political issue, the archdiocesan office could not allow the petitioners to go unchallenged. Although himself initially a pragmatist without strong opinions on the value of celibacy, Archbishop Boll, under increasing pressure from more conservative Catholics in the neighboring states of Württemberg and Bavaria, rapidly went on the offense against the anti-celibacy campaigners.[41] His report to Pope Gregory XVI in October of 1832 revealed his new forcefulness:

> At the university [of Freiburg] there are professors who present pernicious teachings, tickle the ears, lure the spirits of the young people with a propensity to licentiousness, flatter the fleshly lusts. [They are] people who deny divine revelation . . . , who ridicule the external forms of worship, who seek to make the people turn away from the submissiveness they owe to their worldly and spiritual superiors, who sow the seeds of revolt against both powers [state and church]. . . . Furthermore, there are among us those, who take up matters that belong before the forum of the Church, and give them to laypeople to decide, . . . [whose goal it is] to rip apart the sacred bond of oneness that ties us to Rome.[42]

Archbishop Boll, as well as his immediate successor Ignaz Demeter, have been variously described by historians as either too weak to challenge the Badenese state, or as themselves believers in *Staatskirchentum*, the state's right to determine church policy.[43] But when it came to the issue of protests from within the church itself, neither description of the two archbishops is applicable. Boll, for example, took his concerns directly to the grand duke, announcing that the Catholic church "does not honor private opinions. . . . Every teacher who challenges a single dogma of the church . . . has separated himself from her."[44] Consequently, Boll demanded that the government remove the more liberal Freiburg professors. He threatened to revoke the priestly ordination of those professors who were known to lecture against celibacy and to forbid theology students to hear their lectures or risk never being ordained as priests themselves. Boll also informed his clergy of the importance of giving no credence to the anti-celibacy activists; priests, he argued, must "belong undivided to the church" for, as he put it in an illuminating comment, "the office of Christian teacher and shepherd requires the total powers of those who take it on."[45]

Pope Gregory XVI and his staff, in turn, continually encouraged Boll to keep up the pressure on the government to remove liberal members of the Freiburg faculty, and also communicated their distress directly to the government. For example, in his encyclical of August 1832, *Mirari vos*, Gregory XVI criticized the "abominable conspiracy against clerical celibacy," castigated those clergy who forgetting the duty of their office "have been carried away by the enticements of pleasure," and expressed particular indignation that opponents of celibacy had turned to their monarchs for assistance, thereby overstepping the proper bounds between church and world.[46] Papal secretary of state Tommaso Bernetti criticized the way "the young clergy is forced to study theological scholarship at public universities, being instructed in books that have a corrupting influence and under the leadership of professors who do everything to teach their students the poison of vice and the most vile doctrines."[47] In a reference both to the anti-celibacy campaigns and the call for synods, Gregory XVI pushed a number of the German bishops, including Boll, to be even more active in resisting the "impudent" and "godless machinations" of those who would, "as they call it, reform" the church—those who had attacked its "divine authority." He declared that

> We are constantly determined that We will leave nothing that is within our power untried, until the Catholic church is reconstructed in its former liberty . . . and the mouth of each and every one who speaks falsely is silenced. Also you, honorable brothers . . . are responsible for guarding the holiest treasure of faith and sacred doctrine, [and] for warding off every innovation which emerges from a secular way of thinking.[48]

These were the themes that would recur in all conservative Catholic rhetoric from this point forward: the intimate interrelationship between the dangers of sexuality, secularity and insubordination, the unacceptability of democratization and dissent and the need for absolute conformity of belief within the church, and the necessity for strict boundaries between church and world. Particularly evident in Boll's remarks was also the effort to threaten the state by portraying sexual desires as political dangers, as signs of immanent revolution. The warm support political liberals repeatedly gave to the campaign against celibacy made it even easier to portray the campaign as a political threat.

Grand Duke Leopold made his own motivations apparent when he eagerly reassured Boll that he recognized, "how through reckless teachings the peace and quiet of souls can be disturbed" and contended that he would "never approve of efforts which only develop reason and do not . . . have as their goal the establishment of a devout faith."[49] Thus, although initially the state government had been reluctant to accede to Rome's wishes, eventually all the progressive Catholic professors at Freiburg were replaced by men who had, as one historian phrased it, "overcome . . . the Enlightenment."[50] For example, after repeated complaints to the government from Boll about Professor Reichlin-Meldegg, an ordained priest, the professor himself asked to be moved from the theological to the philosophical faculty in 1831, and in 1832 he converted to Protestantism and was moved to the faculty at Heidelberg; there, as a conservative chronicler sarcastically observed, "he 'brought home' his bride."[51] Due to complaints from both Boll and Rome, Professor Schreiber was also moved to the philosophical faculty in 1836, only to lose this job as well (and never have another one) after he too got married and left the Catholic church in 1845. The anti-celibacy petition author Amann, due to complaints from both Boll and Archbishop Demeter, had his right to teach church law rescinded in 1840 and was completely removed from his professorial position in 1842, allowed only the position of senior librarian. Shaken by the success of neoorthodox attacks against him and worn down by continuing battles with the church hierarchy, he succumbed to mental illness in 1843, and died in a sanitorium in 1849.[52]

More conservative men were hired in 1836 and 1837, such as Franz Josef Buss, Johann Baptist Hirscher, and Franz Anton Staudenmaier. Hirscher and especially Buss were to become enormously influential, with both men's own liberal pasts a great boon to them as they worked to dismantle whatever remnants of reform Catholicism persisted in Baden. As one conservative Catholic historian put it, "religious liberalism ruled" in 1831 among the Freiburg faculty, and there was not a single strictly conservative professor on staff. But only "one decade later the power relations had already shifted in fundamental ways. The tendency was now primarily church-oriented."[53] Young men studying for the priesthood would now be exposed primarily to teachers loyal to Rome, and this tremendously alarmed political liberals. Two important results of the anti-celibacy campaign, then, were that the reformers themselves lost their jobs, and therewith their influence over the education of Baden's Catholic clergy, and that conservatives were, from this point on, ascendant.

A third outcome was that political liberals became obsessed with defending men's rights to sexual expression (within the setting of legitimate marriage). Whether in the Lower Chamber, or in the *Staats-Lexikon*, in newspapers, or in tracts, liberals missed few opportunities to denigrate the institution of priestly celibacy, and extol the virtues of marital relations. While ostensibly discussing the enforced celibacy of military officers in the Lower Chamber, for example, a number of delegates made asides about priestly celibacy and "its sad consequences for morals."[54] In 1843, Carl Theodor Welcker also used the *Staats-Lexikon* to continue promoting the anti-celibacy petitioners' cause, asking whether there could possibly still be those "who were so ignorant of real life, such dreamers or hypocrites, that they could seriously claim that a coerced exclusion from *legitimate* marital relations would keep *even a significant* portion of priests, to say nothing of *the majority*, free" from "extramarital, illegitimate, even unnatural . . . satisfaction of the sexual drive." As usual lumping together physiological arguments about bodies with a pseudo-spiritual ode to marital companionship and family life, Welcker asserted that marital and familial relations "have a beneficial purifying and developing power. . . . In this way marital and familial relations belong to the most supreme and noblest life joys. Exclusion from these relations as a rule causes one-sidedness, immorality, mental and physical agonies." And strikingly, Welcker still believed that his side would triumph. For, he concluded, "the current new hierarchical and jesuitical efforts which do indeed already have a broad, mostly still secret effectiveness and breadth, and which until now have opposed all reform efforts in relation to celibacy, are surely only a transitory phenomenon. They are a solitary setback and relapse in the general forward-striving movement."[55] A few years later, this liberal confidence would be severely shaken.

The Controversy over Mixed Marriages

While the dispute over priestly celibacy in Baden had been initiated by liberal reformers within the Catholic church, and the church leadership had been forced to respond defensively, the controversy over mixed marriages, by contrast, was clearly initiated by conservatives in the Catholic hierarchy, and was part of Catholic conservatives' larger counterassault on the ways the Enlightenment, and the French Revolution and its aftermath, had shaped church practices and church-state relations. Having succeeded in pushing progressive elements out of leadership roles in Baden's erstwhile reformist church, Catholic conservatives now turned their attention to a new opponent: the state government itself, which believed mixed marriages to be *the* major site at which the Catholic and Protestant populations of the grand duchy could be harmoniously unified.

The explosiveness of the mixed marriage conflict was due in part to the multifaceted nature of marriage itself as a simultaneously private and public, religious and civic institution. As one government spokesperson put it, "This much is certain: the question is serious and has many consequences for public and private life in Germany, as few others do, and particularly for states in which there is parity [between Protestants and Catholics] it is becoming a truly existential question." "So fertile is the debate of our time over mixed marriages," he further elaborated, that "it easily brings danger to the whole legal relationship between state and church."[56] Another reason for the heat of the conflict was that utterly clashing conceptions of Christianity were mobilized within it. Defenders of mixed marriages saw no significant differences between Protestants and Catholics. As the former anti-celibacy activist Heinrich Amann, for example, put it in his anxious, tortured syntax,

> Whoever has managed to rescue his spirit over into the realm of Christian freedom, proceeding from the conviction that Catholicism, which is after all supposed to be Christianity, can in fact as its final foundation recognize only the genuine teaching of Jesus, . . . he cannot help but . . . struggle [to the conclusion that] that which is truly lastingly valid of the difference between the two major Christian confessions can only still be found in the forms, which do not hinder the holding of the same views in all the important questions of the shared Christianity.[57]

Conservative activists, by contrast, increasingly contended that a vast gulf separated Protestants and Catholics.

Despite their many differences, however, and this was a further factor contributing to the escalation of conflict around mixed marriages in particular, the combatants shared fundamental assumptions about how marriage and family life provided the building blocks for the social order. As one conservative Catholic phrased it, "Marriage, as the foundation of family life, is the educator of humanity . . . whoever controls marriage, controls the future human race—reason enough for church and state, firmly to make their claims on this institution."[58] Similarly, in the liberal *Staats-Lexikon*, Karl von Rotteck announced that "*marriage is the first foundation of the family*" and (despite the evolution of other social relations) "the family *remains* the foundation of all nobler human and civic life, all human and civic happiness."[59] Also in the *Staats-Lexikon*, in an essay on "Relations between the Sexes," Rotteck's fellow diet delegate Welcker explained how the life of the state, and civilization itself, rested on "happy family life . . . this Christian and German family life—the greatest and most hopeful progress in the whole history of humanity—the most noble bloom and fruit of our more recent culture."[60]

As especially Welcker's effusiveness already suggests, and as liberal involvement in the anti-celibacy campaign had also shown, yet another reason for the controversy's intensity lay in the extraordinary expectations liberals placed on marriage as a site for personal fulfillment and perfection. Happiness within marriage was becoming a central element in the self-understanding and self-definition of the liberal-leaning members of the German middle strata.[61] Although for many middle-class people, just as for many in the lower strata, material interests continued to outweigh romantic considerations in choosing a mate, the ascendancy of the new norm made them feel compelled to describe their choices in romantic terms as well.[62] But this programmatic insistence on glorifying the power of love (whether defined as sentiment or eroticism or a vague muddle of both) was also strongly and openly contested by the Catholic church, which profoundly distrusted love and sexual attraction as the bases for a marriage.[63] The church was of course not concerned about a couple's material compatibility, but about the demands of faith. This questioning of the value of interpersonal love was, as we will see, deeply threatening to liberals. In short, despite the divergence of their views, the seriousness of both liberals' and conservatives' preoccupation with sexual and marital relations in the early nineteenth century cannot be underestimated. For these reasons, and because of the growing polarization between liberals and conservatives, the debate about mixed marriages became the vehicle for a larger conflict between competing visions of the relationship between the individual's conscience and religious authority, and the relationship of social groups to each other.

The climax of the conflicts over mixed marriages in Baden would commence in early 1845 when the new and very conservative archbishop, Hermann von Vicari, secretly circulated a directive to his clergy without—as he was legally bound to do—soliciting the state's prior consent. In this directive, he called on his priests to report every instance of a planned marriage between a Protestant and a Catholic to him, and await directions from him, before proceeding to participate in the marriage service. His ultimate goal was to get priests to refuse to give the church's blessing to a couple that had not agreed to raise their children as Catholics, and in general, to encourage them to dissuade mixed couples from marrying at all.

This secret move set in motion a fierce dispute within Baden, where at that time many hundreds of couples lived in mixed marriages—more, in proportion to the size of the population, than in any other German state—and where mixed marriages had long been blessed by both the Catholic and the Protestant clergyman.[64] According to one government source, such dual blessings had been given, without any preconditions being attached, already for "more than a century," and indeed such a practice had been evolving since the Peace of Westphalia in 1648.[65] Another government commentator suggested that some territories which later became part of Baden had officially instituted the relaxed practice already in 1705.[66] The archdiocesan office would only acknowledge that the relaxed practice had existed for half a century, and, characteristically, it blamed the emergence of such a practice on "the time of religious indifference, of political disorders, of chaotic conditions."[67] But indisputably the practice had been established in the region well before it was formalized into law as Baden was being formed in 1803.

The contradictions embedded in Badenese law explain why the government would eventually find itself on a collision course with Vicari. While each of the successive proclamations the fledgling government made on religious matters technically referred to both the Catholic and the Protestant churches, they primarily addressed the state's relationship to the Catholic church. Because Baden's ruling family was Protestant, because the Protestant churches tended toward subservience to state authority, and because Protestantism neither claimed to be the only true church nor considered marriage a sacrament, conflicts between the state and the Protestant churches were far less likely.

Each of the laws promulgated on religious matters touched on the issue of mixed marriages, and the significance of all this legislation lay precisely in its ambiguity. First, in 1803, the state proclaimed its interest in defending the rights and needs of individuals. It defended the couple's freedom to choose a clergyman, and it defended the individual's right, if he or she so desired, to have "his [or her] conscience put to rest" with an additional blessing from the clergyman of the other confession.[68] But then in 1807, in a new edict, the state assured the churches that they too had rights, granting to each church the right to rule on all purely religious matters, including, by implication, the right to refuse to bless a marriage it opposed. Already a contradiction had been established between the individual's right and the church's right. Finally, also in 1807, in trying to address this impasse, the state established itself as the ultimate arbiter of church practices. It gave itself the right to decide if a new church ruling was acceptable, to decide who could marry, to force priests to perform the civil aspects of a marriage even if they refused to perform the religious aspects, and then to recognize such a marriage as legitimate. Implicitly, here, the state acknowledged that it would accept purely civil marriages as legitimate. But simultaneously, it revealed its desire to maintain the religious aspects of marriage, and—by implication—to uphold the religious dimension of social life as a whole.[69] The state was eager to preserve the dual character of marriage as both a civil and a religious institution, and it sought to do so in part by insisting on the clergyman's dual role as servant of the church and of the state. But that dual role remained tenable only so long as church authorities did not challenge the primary authority of the state.

As we have seen, in the years immediately following the establishment of the archdiocese at Freiburg in 1827, Rome was most concerned with combating the reform movement within Badenese Catholicism itself. Thus Rome's efforts with respect to Baden in the late 1820s and early 1830s were primarily directed toward removing liberal members of the Freiburg faculty, trying to regain control of the education of the clergy, and resisting all calls for synods and the changes in church doctrine and worship practice they were meant to bring. But related to these concerns was also Rome's effort to resist the state's insistence on its own supremacy. The battle against the state was intertwined with the battle against reformers, for the state and its laws tied the archbishop's hands, and the state's initial protection of Freiburg faculty and its insistence on a public education for the clergy made Rome fear Badenese Catholics would forever be under liberal influence. Until these issues were resolved more to Rome's satisfaction, Rome would not bother to tangle with the Badenese state over mixed marriages. In Prussia, Pope Pius VIII already intervened in the state's handling of mixed marriages in 1830, calling on the Catholic clergy there to tell Catholic brides that "no one can find salvation outside of the true Catholic faith," and that any woman planning to enter a mixed marriage was already "proceeding most cruelly against the children she is expecting from God."[70] But as Pius well knew, in Prussia he had much of the Catholic clergy on his side.

The only bright spot in Baden, as far as Rome was concerned, was that since 1826, each couple there was allowed to determine, completely at its own discretion, in what religion it would raise its children, and to settle this before the marriage with a contract. Previously, the law required that children be raised in the father's faith; exceptions were made only under very specific circumstances.[71] The state intended for this shift to enhance individual freedom of choice. But the church saw in it an opportunity to pressure Catholic brides into insisting on Catholic childraising.

This last point was to become the central bone of contention. Already the first Archbishop of Freiburg, Bernhard Boll, had sought to convince the state government that it was the priest's right, indeed his "sacred duty," "to speak to [the bride's] conscience" so that she would conclude such a premarital contract.[72] Rome's position was that if a mixed couple did not promise to raise all children as Catholics, then the Catholic priest must refuse to bless the marriage, and must refuse the Catholic spouse both absolution and the communion typically taken in preparation for marriage. But under Badenese law, the church could issue no directives to its clergy without prior government approval, and any publication of those particular principles would have been rejected out of hand. The government's view was that any untoward "mental influencing of the betrothed" constituted a "proselytizing" of unborn children and impinged on the "equal rights" of the other confession, and that the actual clerical practice the archdiocesan office was encouraging—in the case of a Catholic bride dragging out official permission for the wedding until such time as the couple had signed a pro-Catholic contract, in the case of a Catholic husband actively discouraging a contract so that by default the children would follow in the father's faith—was "unquestionably incompatible with peace between those of different, but related, confessions."[73] In view of the state's hostility, Boll relented.

A pivotal moment came in 1837, when a dramatic conflict over mixed marriages erupted in Prussia, the so-called Cologne Upheavals (*Kölner Wirren*), which reached their climax when the Archbishop of Cologne was arrested by the Prussian government. Due to the incorporation of large Catholic territories under a Protestant monarch, a situation arose in which Protestant bureaucrats in the Catholic regions typically married women they met there. Since the most likely combination for a mixed marriage was therefore a Protestant man and a Catholic woman, Prussian law required that all children of mixed marriages be raised in the religion of the father (a rule which had the combined appeal of benefiting Protestantism and upholding the principle of paternal authority). Although previously, the Catholic hierarchy in Prussia had acquiesced to the rule, the new archbishop, Clemens August von Droste-Vischering, refused to continue this practice and announced (in spite of a government ultimatum) that he would start handling such marriages in strict accordance with Rome's wishes. In response, the Prussian government arrested him.

The effect of the arrest was monumental, enraging not only the Roman curia, but also stirring discussion all over Germany. Pamphleteers immediately took the opportunity to make larger claims about the oppression of the Catholic church by German governments. The Prussian state had inadvertently set in motion a rapprochement between Catholics of all classes and political persuasions throughout Germany, and stimulated the renewal of Catholic solidarity and religiosity. Within a few months of the Cologne archbishop's arrest, the Prussian government was forced to modify its stand on mixed marriages, and Rome was soon determining the way they were handled throughout the Prussian territories. It was a battle the Prussian state had clearly lost.[74]

The most famous of the pamphleteers who attacked the Prussian government was Joseph Görres. He argued that

> under no circumstances can the church be forced to bear mongrel bastards for another confession which has become powerful in the secular world, and whoever wants to force her to do this is intending to rape her. The right to resist this with all her might, using the same self-defense that an individual may use against a murderer, cannot be denied her.

Görres also revived the reference point of revolution, arguing that it was "the revolution, in reciprocal interaction with absolutism, which brought us this as well as so many other ruinous phenomena." This argument led directly into Görres's proposed solution: "The pacification of the world can only be achieved through a sincere and thorough return to the laws of eternal order, which can never become obsolete." Görres had already explained the content of that "eternal order": Just as Christ was both "true God and true human, one and the same Christ," so "the Christian society, as antiquity understood it, should also be: true godly and true human order, church and state, one and the same Christianity."[75] Görres's distinctive combination of vulgarity and piety would provide a great inspiration for Baden's conservative Catholic activists as well.

The huge debate unleashed by the Cologne Upheavals placed the Catholic church everywhere under much closer scrutiny. Baden's Archbishop Boll had died in 1836, a few days after Rome had written to him and directly pressured him to confront the Badenese government more forcefully on the issue of mixed marriages.[76] The new archbishop, Ignaz Demeter, although initially just as reluctant to confront the state as his predecessor, knew that after the events in Cologne he had no other choice, for, as he told representatives of the state, "we would fall outside of the church unity, if we allowed the more recent praxis [i.e., the more relaxed practice] to develop further in our archdiocese." Taking Görres's cue, and echoing arguments Boll had made in criticizing the anti-celibacy campaign, Demeter suggested that if the practice in Baden's Catholic church stayed different from the Roman Catholic church, there could be a schism which would have "repercussions for civic relations" and "would also endanger the political peace."[77] Such a threat carried intensified weight in light of the renewed outbreak of revolution in France in 1830. Surely, Demeter argued, the state also wished to avoid political disturbances, therefore it would understand his need to instruct his clergy in the stricter praxis by formally publicizing the papal curia's guidelines for mixed marriages.

Predictably, however, the Badenese government rejected Demeter's request, stressing that there was no Catholic consensus across the centuries that mixed marriages were unacceptable, and that Catholicism also varied by region and nation; the Catholic church in Baden should thus be allowed to maintain the character appropriate to Baden's peculiarities as a mixed state, and retain conciliatory practices that were much older than Demeter claimed they were. Once again, then, the state sought firmly to defend individual rights and hold in check the church's power over the hearts and minds of its members—and yet at the same time also tried urgently to keep the church's role in social life alive. And once again, in view of the state's resistance (even Grand Duke Leopold had intervened personally, pleading for the church to desist from damaging the harmony and love between his subjects), the church hierarchy backed down. In private meetings with his staff, Demeter declared that he found mixed marriages without Catholic childraising to be "godless" and "unbelievably abominable." Thus (in a practice already begun by Boll) he allowed his staff to urge individual priests who consulted with him to warn Catholics wishing to enter a mixed marriage about the dangers this posed for the salvation of their souls, and, if this did not work, to warn of the ease with which Protestants could obtain divorce, while the Catholic partner would have to remain alone forever (a threat which inevitably would be felt as more distressing in an era increasingly verbose about the importance of matrimonial happiness).[78] But Demeter was unwilling to challenge the state more openly, and thus Baden remained one of the last German states to resist Rome's wishes, a situation that became even more precarious in 1841, when the Austrian government conceded to the institutionalization of the stricter practice in its German-language territories.[79]

The Success of Neoorthodoxy and the State's Ambivalence

Throughout these negotiations, it had been clear that Demeter, a moderate, was under pressure to be more militant toward the government primarily from two sources: from Rome, and from one of his own assistants, Hermann von Vicari. Thus it came as no surprise that when Demeter died and Vicari was elected archbishop, Vicari—aware of the fruitlessness of engaging the state directly—chose the path of secrecy. But Vicari's directive to his clergy did not remain secret for long, and the Ministry of the Interior soon issued a sharp rebuke, demanding that the directive be retracted. The archbishop, however, ignored the government and told his priests that the directive would remain in effect. Indeed, on August 9, 1845, he sent out a further circular which amplified the first and openly detailed how mixed marriages should be handled more strictly. Vicari told his priests that the Catholic spouse, who withdraws his children from the Catholic church, has the blessing of the church withdrawn from him, because he does not deserve it. Receiving such a blessing may in any event be a matter of indifference to him, since after all educating children in the true religion is a matter of indifference to him. . . . The love for our Protestant brothers is not damaged by this decisiveness and firmness of faith: we love them, as ourselves, and would give our lives for them. But out of a poorly understood love we may not weigh down our conscience.[80]

Subsequently, in explaining his move to the government, Vicari deemphasized his views on Catholic superiority and instead stressed the dangers that could ensue for the state if the church were not assuaged: "The demand to my clergy that they break their religious oath has established the principle of rebelliousness and revolution; may God protect our fatherland from it."[81]

On November 21, 1845, the state went on the offensive and released its own decree to the Catholic clergy of Baden, informing them that they would be punished by the state if they intervened in a mixed couple's decision-making process through "inappropriate meddling or importunate exhortation." As the Ministry of the Interior analyzed it, Vicari's "planned innovation" was not simply incompatible with a couple's legal freedom, but would also constitute a form of "moral coercion" which would "threaten the harmonious coexistence of members of the two Christian churches, the peace of countless families and the [social] peace."[82]

As they observed this mounting conflict between state and Catholic church, liberals had been deeply anxious about how the government would respond to Vicari. Liberal diet delegate Friedrich Hecker warned in November 1845 that "everywhere there is an attempt to rob marriage of its secular character, and make it once again into a *res ecclesiastica*; Protestant states . . . are forgetting, that nobody lusts for power like the priest. If marriage is turned over again to the realm of religion, then he will rule over education, family and the state."[83] The liberal Protestant newspaper *Der Morgenbote* asked anxiously in October 1845 whether "the state will preserve its citizens' right, in free choice to found a family? [or] will it tolerate that in the conflict between church and love the latter is devoured?"[84] The paper argued that "despite the love Mr. Archbishop claims he has for the Protestants, his refusal to bless allows us to doubt his sincerity; and because he bestows the blessing only at a price— the price of the incipient progeny, he is actually unabashedly exercising a coercion of faith." *Der Morgenbote* could not avoid sarcasm: "The Archbishop of Freiburg allows his priests to bless only those persons, who, before they enter a mixed marriage, sign over the anticipated children to the Catholic church ahead of time. What a very special kind of blessing, an asset that only becomes liquid when you pawn that which has been lent to you! That is like saying: I will pray to heaven for a blessing for your fields, but only if you give me the harvest."[85] In view of these concerns, it was no surprise that political liberals were delighted by the Badenese government's resolve to challenge Vicari, and delegates in the Lower Chamber praised the decree of November 21, 1845.[86]

Vicari, however, was not impressed with the flurry of liberal consternation, and would not be cowed by the government's aggressive posturing; two strategies helped him force the state to back down, and to begin the process of dismantling *Staatskirchentum* in Baden. One tactic was to turn to the pope; the other was to take his case to the public. Vicari warned the government's High Church Council that after the government's November 21 decree further negotiations between him and the government "are . . . out of the question. I am turning this matter over to the Holy See to decide."[87] Pope Gregory XVI responded in a brief on May 23, 1846, praising Vicari's defense of "the right and the freedom of the church," and expressing his "sorrow" over the "great number of marriages between Catholics and non-Catholics in your diocese." He warned that he would actually prefer to forbid such marriages entirely. The only conditions under which he would allow mixed marriages, "very reluctantly," would be if there was some expectation that the non-Catholic spouse could be converted to Catholicism and, most importantly, if it could be guaranteed that the anticipated children would be raised as Catholics; at stake, he emphasized, was "the sanctity of marriage and the salvation of individuals' souls."[88]

Vicari further embarrassed the state by allowing Adolf Strehle, a high-ranking member of his staff, to publish (albeit anonymously) *Die gemischten Ehen in der Erzdiöcese Freiburg* (Mixed Marriages in the Archdiocese of Freiburg) in 1846. This was a collection of items drawn from the correspondence between state and church about mixed marriages over the preceding decades, all interpreted from the neoorthodox point of view. Its publication marked the first time the majority of these documents had been made publicly available, and was an explicit attempt to affect the course of the conflict, a move which clearly revealed the self-assurance of the conservatives.[89] Strehle was unambiguous that what was at stake was the Catholic church's "freedom" from state control: he was confident that the pope "does not allow the spotless bride of the Lord to languish in chains." Contrasting the Catholic church, "God's church," with the merely "*human* church" of Protestantism, Strehle, like all neoorthodox Catholics, stressed that the Catholic church was "the *only true* church, the *only* church *through which one can attain salvation*," "the holy church, that knows its worth, and knows itself to be in possession of the Christian truth and grace." Strehle warned that the ways Catholics and Protestants in Baden lived "so mixed among each other" made the "danger" of "indifferentism, this plague of our age, this death of all religiosity and morality" particularly pressing.[90]

Overwhelmed by an intransigence and counterattack it had not anticipated, distressed at the prospect of potentially massive civil disobedience on the part of a sector of its employees, and after much inconclusive wrangling, the government finally sought to escape the deadlock with the archbishop by promulgating a new law on November 6, 1846, a law which provided for the possibility of secular civil marriage in the event of the noncooperation of religious authorities.[91] On the surface, it seemed as though the liberal premise of equality between the confessions and every individual's right to marry whomever he or she chose, had once more emerged victorious. In fact, however, the outcome of the dispute was far more ambiguous. Not until 1862 did the first couple in Baden get married in a purely civil ceremony.[92] So the promulgation of the new law had nothing to do with actually opening up new freedoms for mixed couples. Rather, the real and immediate effect of the November 1846 law was that the state had implicitly given up its legal right to intervene in the Catholic church's handling of marriage. As one conservative Catholic put it: "From 1846 on the clergymen were not ever bothered again."[93] With very few exceptions, priests immediately began to follow Vicari's directives.[94] There was now no longer any legal basis upon which the state could hold in check the intimidating pressure some priests placed on those parishioners desiring to enter a mixed marriage.

Neoorthodox observers at the time, while critical of the trend toward secularization of marriage the November 1846 law seemed to imply, could not quite contain their sense of satisfaction at this outcome of the mixed marriages controversy. In discussing the effect of the law, for example, conservatives noted that "the state appeared to defend its rights, but actually, it yielded to the church," and asked, "So what do we have left here? Exactly the same state of affairs as before, . . . one of those unclear, unsteady situations . . . in which the state forfeits far more than the church."[95]

The effect of this development was doubly intense because it came at precisely that moment when a conservative renewal was taking place within Badenese Catholicism. Not only had the reformist professors in Freiburg been replaced by conservative ones. In 1841, the conservative lay activist Franz Josef Mone had also anonymously published a programmatic tract, *Die katholischen Zustände in Baden* (Conditions for Catholics in Baden), which laid out all the ways the Catholic church felt itself to be disenfranchised in Baden, and which spurred many prominent Catholic laypeople to rally to the church's defense. At the same time, a group of leading laypeople had founded a new Catholic newspaper (the *Süddeutsche Katholische Kirchenzeitung*, later transformed into the more openly political *Süddeutsche Zeitung für Kirche und Staat*) which tried to spread ultramontane and other conservative ideas among the clergy and the educated bourgeoisie, and soon superseded the *Mannheimer Morgenblatt* as the most conservative newspaper in Baden.[96] Even though it never had more than eight hundred or nine hundred subscribers, due to its high price and, at times, its scholarly tone, it succeeded dramatically in expanding the terms of debate on a wide range of issues, and papers of all other persuasions continually engaged with its perspectives. Furthermore, in 1842, the prominent priest Alban Stolz had begun annually to produce a wildly successful almanac with explicit ultramontane tendencies, the *Kalender für Zeit und Ewigkeit* (Almanac for Time and Eternity).[97] Written in an accessible, earthy, populist style, this almanac became one of the very few texts typically read in the impoverished rural Catholic areas, and one contemporary remarked that "the first two volumes [of Stolz's almanac] were read and passed around here with great eagerness . . . In this area no other one is bought as long as [his] is available."[98] (In 1848, Stolz would join the other new conservatives on the Freiburg faculty; for decades thereafter he was one of the university's most beloved and influential teachers.) The new archbishop Vicari also contributed to the conservative revival through his many travels throughout Baden, which brought him into consistently close contact with the lower clergy and with local parish life, and which worked to spread his popularity.[99] He was also successful in establishing a new seminary for priests and a new theological college in 1842, as well as a small seminary for boys (to lead them to the priesthood) in 1845.[100] These men, along with Heinrich von Andlaw in the Upper Chamber and Professor Franz Josef Buss in the Lower Chamber, were the ones who were to shape and promote theological and political conservatism among Baden's Catholics for years to come.

Secondly, the conflict between state and church did not remain confined to correspondence between these two authorities, but rather spiraled into a much larger public debate with far-reaching consequences. In affecting priests' attitudes and behavior, the conflict necessarily affected the lives of countless citizens. From the pulpit, in the daily press, in polemical tracts, and in scholarly reference works, mixed marriages became the subject of the most heated outpourings.

In one final burst of energy, the state sought to vindicate its own previous intervention in church matters. It produced its own anonymously edited document collection, *Der Streit über Gemischte Ehen und das Kirchenhoheitsrecht im Grossherzogthum Baden* (The Struggle over

Mixed Marriages and the State's Sovereignty over the Church in the Grand Duchy of Baden). The editor was either Karl Friedrich Nebenius, the liberal Minister of the Interior and the man who had been most passionately involved in trying to change Archbishop Vicari's mind, or Nebenius's close associate, the liberal Catholic priest and civil servant Joseph Beck.[101] *Der Streit* included almost all the same documents Strehle's collection had, but framed them with a more liberal interpretation. The author focused particularly on how the 1826 law allowing premarital contracts was being misused for "a strange sort of *competitive soul-snatching game*," and—in a clear indication of just how potent the matter of mixed marriages was—questioned "whether the Grand Duke's government would ever have consented to subject this region, by letting it be included in the new archdiocese, to the rule of the Catholic church, if in the matter of mixed marriages the demands had been made that a few years later were made."[102]

The state's position, as always, was internally contradictory. It wanted to assert its own sovereignty over all other institutions, and yet, as already in the grand duchy's very earliest years, the government also wanted the church's support. These warring needs could of course only be met if the Catholic church in Baden was more cooperative. Struggling over the impasse between the priest's conscience and the couple's conscience, for example, the editor of *Der Streit* clearly sided with the couple, and worried over the "*disquieting of the couple's conscience by the clergyman*," the "attempt at influencing the couple's determination of will," "the harshness against the peace of mind of a person of faith," when, after all, decisions about childraising "in the majority of cases depend less on the will of betrothed and far more on a complex of circumstances in face of which the individual is powerless." In contrast to conservatives' assertions that those who entered mixed marriages were religiously indifferent, the editor stressed that the reason the church's stricter stance was so painful for an individual was precisely because he or she was still a "believer," a "person of faith."[103]

The state's perspective on religious coexistence was also closely entwined with liberal faith in the "reconciling power of marriage." Marriage was "a connection to which [the individual] is drawn by the noblest feelings." The editor especially celebrated the way mixed marriages had helped to "overcome the damaging mutual prejudices, antipathies and hesitations, interwoven the physical and spiritual interests of families of different confessions in the most intimate way, and therefore in all these ways like almost no other thing worked toward the inner unity and strengthening of the life of the state and the life of the *Volk*." It was this beautiful development the church was trying to destroy: "To insist upon the doctrine that for a Catholic to enter into such an intimate relationship as marriage with a Protestant is a *sin*, which can only be atoned for by promising to raise all anticipated children in the Catholic religion, is clearly incompatible with the peaceful coexistence of both confessions." Such a doctrine would naturally lead, the author argued, to "far more serious consequences," among which were "mutual antipathies" and "sharp separation and mutual exclusion between the religious groups."[104]

Yet despite its liberal investment in the power of love to transcend differences of faith, the state still felt itself to be dependent on both Christian churches, precisely in the matter of marriage. This was reconfirmed by the editor of *Der Streit*, who wanted marriage to be not just a civil act, but rather wanted "its higher nature also to be brought to light through the consecration of the church." On the one hand, the state wanted to protect "the higher spiritual nature [of marriage] against every hurtful use of psychological or legal pressure." But on the other hand, it wanted to "resist indifference to the religious aspects of such an important act as marriage is."[105] These remarks made clear that, even in light of the rise of Catholic conservatism and ultramontanism over the preceding ten years, the state's basic attachment to institutional religion had not changed.

Sex and Sin

It was precisely in this situation that neoorthodox and ultramontane activists could promote their own views on proper social boundaries, on insubordination to authority, and on the dangers of sexuality, ever more forcefully. As had already been evident in the church hierarchy's correspondence with the state government, the Catholic church was now explicitly starting from the position that Catholicism was superior to all other confessions and religions, and that boundaries between Catholics and all others needed to be drawn far more strictly—that "Catholics and Protestants are substantially different from each other," and that "between the confessions there can be no mixing, no union; what there can be is recognition, tolerance and justice."[106] Conservatives were especially distressed at the ways the merging of different principalities to create the Grand Duchy of Baden, and the government's encouragement of mixed marriages, had made it "impossible to preserve the purity of the communities" that had existed previously; the goal was to reverse this trend.[107]

Related to this need for clear boundaries was the necessity of absolute obedience to authority. The church began from the premise that the individual had no rights—that the individual's task, indeed the individual's only guarantee of salvation—was to be obedient to the church's position as it was expressed by Rome. The archdiocesan office announced that "according to Catholic principles the private perspective and the private conscience are not the norm for the church's actions, rather the individual must, *out of conscience*, be governed by the teaching, doctrine and ritual of the church."[108] Furthermore, as Franz Rosshirt, author of a tract criticizing the state's position, summarized it, "The Catholic church itself, which recognizes *only one* way of thinking, . . . must defend its way of thinking to the utmost, . . . [and must] earnestly warn against every *ambiguity* and *inobedience*." For "a Catholic can not diverge from the unity. That unity is in the pope."[109] Even the slightest compromise was unacceptable, because as one member of the archdiocesan staff had put it, "Whoever denies even one single dogma, is declared by the Catholic church as no longer belonging to her, but rather as having stepped out of her. As Christ . . . is only *One*, so . . . the true church of Christ is only *One*."[110] Almanac-writer Stolz put it most succinctly: "Whoever does not listen to the church, has no part in the Savior."[111]

Conservative Catholics' most powerful rhetorical strategy was to denigrate mixed marriages by portraying them as purely motivated by lust. For example, in response to the government's repeated defense of individual freedom of choice, the archdiocesan office castigated those whose "marriage was dearer to [them] than [their] religion," and heatedly asked: "What? The conscience of the couple . . . bribed by the most powerful sensual attraction, should *decide*,—decide in . . . their own case?! What? The defendant should also be the judge?"[112] Such bodily motivations, of course, put the soul in grave peril. Stolz was blunt on this point: Unless "your repentance is genuine," he warned, "your prospects beyond the grave look dismal, and I would not recommend to anyone to hang themselves from your feet trying to rise to heaven."[113] Over and over again, conservatives established imaginative links between individual subjectivity, sexuality, and sin.

One way the newly self-confident ultramontanists tried to spread their views was through newspapers. Ultramontane professor and diet delegate Franz Josef Buss, in *Capistran*, a journal he launched in December 1846 for the express purpose of combating mixed marriages, announced that mixed marriages were "carriers of indifference to faith, of an its-all-the-same religion. . . . The quantity of these mixed marriages has poisoned the society and made it . . . indecent." Buss was unabashed about delineating the differences he saw between Protestantism and Catholicism: "Protestantism robbed our nation of its empire . . . and erased it from the circle of world-determining peoples," whereas "the Catholic church has already spiritually solved all the problems with which the German nation is presently confronted." The proliferation of mixed marriages in Baden, Buss told his readers, was the strongest sign of "the rising pleasure-seeking and the daily growing incapacity to control and moderate oneself, the uncontained reign of private caprice." Unimpressed with the government's pleas for harmony ("we will be criticized as disturbers of the peace, but only by those who are stupid or evil"), Buss argued that the state was forgetting who its best ally was: In this "licentious present," it was "the Catholic church, as the religion of *authority*" that "brings order. Whoever liberates her, liberates the throne."[114]

Conservatives also made use of the power of the pulpit. An example is provided by a sermon delivered in the spring of 1847, *Die Musterehe* (The Model Marriage). Lumping together the "marriages without religion, the mixed marriages, the marital conflicts, the divorces, the shamelessness" as signs of the "new barbarism breaking in," the priest expressed particular alarm that "faith—and that means sameness of faith" was "the very last thing which is considered these days when people contract marriages," for although "the powers of this world have bestowed such particular favor on *mixed marriages*," such marriages actually ran counter to "the fundamental law of God." The priest warned his listeners that

> the foundation of human society—the family—is tottering; the ground under us is threatening to give way, and it must necessarily collapse entirely, if we do not reach for the sole means of salvation, if marriage is not once again prepared in a Christian way, contracted in a Christian way, and preserved in a Christian way.

What he meant by "Christianity" he had already made clear: "Therefore only Christianity as it is carried by the holy Catholic church, is the ground on which a holy marriage can grow, a happy family life in which love, fidelity and respect rule, and which guarantees a better future."[115]

Similar assumptions and concerns characterized the stance of the *Süddeutsche Zeitung für Kirche und Staat*, the ultramontanists' premier mouthpiece. It asserted that "in marriage a brutal, powerful sensuality must be combatted. If marriage becomes debased, then the spouses, the children, the family, and the state—which is built on an ordered family life—are all endangered." Marriage "needs the cooperation of all authorities, in order to prevent degeneracy within it, and in order to sanctify this crucially important institution." The paper warned the state not to meddle with the church's handling of marriage, for without the church's assistance in marriage, "overpowering sensuality and licentiousness would seek to break out."[116]

On the one hand, the purpose of marriage, according to conservative Catholics, was procreation and childraising.[117] On the other hand, sexuality—even within marriage—was a problem, a potential evil, which required constant vigilance and self-examination. Stolz, for example, told the readers of his almanac that sex within marriage could also fall under the rubric of "fornication": that "old vice number six which is for the soul, what cholera is to the body." This was a very worrisome thing, for "even in hell a damned person may feel lighter and better, if he was at least free of licentiousness." Meditating on the Apostle Paul's words to the Corinthians—"do you not know that you are God's temple?"—Stolz asked his readers: "How do things look on this matter on your insides? . . . Search yourself and your life, whether such brandmarks and stains of disgrace can be found. . . . Have you never treated your body, or the body of another disgracefully? . . . . Truly wretched are in this matter some married people; they abuse marriage grotesquely and live and die carelessly in deep sins, as if being married were a license for lust."[118]

Only a shared faith saved sexual relations within marriage from being purely "animalistic"—as Johann Baptist Hirscher, one of the newly installed conservative professors at Freiburg, put it—only "the friendship of souls . . . the most intimate union of hearts," served to "sanctify the fleshly communion" and make it into an "image of the union between Christ and His church."[119] It was this "union of hearts" that mixed couples could not achieve. According to Hirscher, "Marriages between spouses of different confessions (mixed marriages) have an element in them which never ever lets them arrive at a proper life union, and only a very superficial conception of marriage can advocate such connections. Already there is missing the most profound aspect of oneness in living and striving: the oneness of religious conviction; and so from the start no genuine bond *in and before God* is created." Hirscher asked how anyone could allow his children to be raised in a "foreign confession" without

> revealing himself as an indifferentist? or without sacrificing his sincere attachment to his confession to a sexual attraction or to material advantages for his children? But will the sexual stupefaction last? The material advantage continue to glitter? No. When this stupefaction and self-delusion have disappeared, what a long silent grief will grow on account of the children, who . . . have been raised in falsehood!

Hirscher was convinced that "there is perhaps not one single mixed marriage in which (although they have otherwise peacefully coexisted) the spouses have not after years expressed the conviction that it would have been better if they had never met. At least I do not know of any counterexample. There remains in their relationship a diseased sore, *which can never be healed.*"[120]

Not only was a mixed marriage sinful and sick, and destined for inevitable unhappiness, but the introduction of secular civil marriage was even worse. The *Süddeutsche* reinforced this point by linking civil marriage with the fearsome political event which had first introduced it: "It really took the French Revolution, which shattered all positive foundations in church and state, to carry through such a revolution in marriage law."[121] A further effect was to imply that support for mixed marriages would lead to a new revolution. As the author of *Die Musterehe* put it, in mixed marriages, there was "only love of the flesh, of sensual, perishable beauty, and of personal advantage." Such disregard destroyed one's children's children, for "out of the relations of the flesh a purely fleshly race grows, that with every further generation goes farther astray from the Christian doctrine and life, and through the sins of the parents transmits the poison over and over." And such disregard was politically dangerous: "But where self-interest creates the marital union," there "civic strife, insubordination and rebellion against every authority have their source. We fear for the future, when we contemplate the great mass of un-Christian marriages and families." The fact that revolution did break out in 1848 only confirmed the conservatives' predictions.[122]

In sum, in the two decades of conflict between Catholic conservatives and their various reformist, liberal, and etatist opponents, years in which the conservatives undeniably gained strength and confidence, they were also increasingly able to elaborate on a larger vision of what ailed their society and how it could be cured. Not only were the conservatives ever more effective in silencing diversity of opinion about sex, love, and marriage within Catholicism's own ranks, enforcing conformity where once there had been a rich internal debate, they were also increasingly successful in raising the specter of revolution to their own advantage. And they were ever more bold in asserting the superiority of their "true" faith over all other faiths and in insisting on strict separation between Catholics and all other people, thus sending the message that divisions between social groups should be upheld as a matter of sacred conviction— a development which, as the next chapter will show, held ominous implications for Baden's Jews. Meanwhile, although the moderately liberal state government had given in to the Catholic hierarchy, liberals in the diet and elsewhere were alarmed and incensed by the rise of theological neoorthodoxy and politically active ultramontanism. This radicalized many liberals, but also made them more reactive. The battle against the new religious right became a central preoccupation for them, determining (for better or worse) their programmatic choices and the very character of liberalism itself.

2

JEWISH EMANCIPATION AND

JEWISH DIFFERENCE

THE ASSUMPTION that German Jews owed their emancipation to the rise of German liberalism saturates German history and Jewish studies scholarship. Although occasionally one or another scholar documents some liberals' ambivalence or hostility toward Jews, the general consensus that liberals were Jews' most reliable friends, and that liberal dedication to the Jewish cause was a logical outgrowth of liberals' commitment to equality and human rights, seems to remain untouched by this evidence.[1] In the introduction to a recent collection of essays on the relationship between German liberalism and Jewish emancipation, for example, Werner E. Mosse commented that in the nineteenth century, "liberals were the staunchest, indeed the only allies of Jews in their struggle for emancipation and civil rights" and that "liberals regarded Jewish emancipation as an integral part of their political program."[2] This can be taken as a fair summary of the prevailing view.

Because Baden was renowned as nineteenth-century Germany's most liberal state, an examination of debates over Jewish rights there is especially helpful in demonstrating how imperative it is that the reigning consensus be substantially modified. Many Badenese liberals resisted emancipation with all the rhetorical strength they could muster; most pro-emancipationist liberals revealed themselves to be quite ambivalent about Jews, even as they styled themselves as defenders of Jewish rights. Most strikingly, the debates in Baden reveal that even though many reluctant, initially anti-emancipationist liberals eventually came to support emancipation as a central plank in the liberal platform, this shift had little to do with any logical unfolding of liberal principles, expanding to include ever more social groups in the circle of those who deserved equality. Rather, what emerges is that it was a complex conjunction of intra-Christian conflicts which ultimately made it advantageous for liberals to take a pro-emancipation stand.

The debates over Jewish rights can be more fully understood when we grasp how these debates were interwoven in complex ways with the various intra-Christian conflicts over sex, love, and marriage that were analyzed in the previous chapter. In the course of Catholic reformers' anti-celibacy campaign, men's rights to sexual expression and freedom from church coercion had become a major plank in the liberal platform. The controversy over mixed marriages, and especially the ways in which conservative Catholics sought to portray married love as base and sinful unless both spouses were obedient Catholics, only unnerved liberals further—the more so since conservatives were appropriating liberal ideals such as liberty, equality, and religious tolerance as they sought to advance their own extraordinarily rigid views. The aggressively dismissive attitude conservatives expressed toward individual subjectivity and personal happiness, the ways they excluded from the ranks of the properly faithful many people who felt themselves to be deeply religious, and their ever more unabashed defense of their own intervention in individuals' most intimate choices, caused liberals to develop a profound and abiding hatred of neoorthodoxy. For a series of reasons which will be discussed below, it was actually this long-standing fight over men's sexual and romantic rights that ultimately led the most admired and respected of German liberals finally to become the defenders of Jewish rights many historians assumed they were all along. This was so because the intensification of conflict over the content and meaning of Christianity caused a fundamental recasting of the terms in which the "Jewish question" was understood and debated.

Liberal Ambivalence about Jews

As mentioned in the previous chapter, the year 1831 was a turning point for liberalism in Baden, and thus by extension for the rest of Germany. The year 1831 marked the moment that liberalism came into its own as a political—and philosophical—force to be reckoned with. In the Lower Chamber of the Badenese diet, it was a year of triumph for liberal agendas such as free elections and a freer press, for the principle of the diet's right to be involved in the legislative process, and for the development of an ordinance on local government (*Gemeindeordnung*) hailed as the most advanced and liberal in all of Europe.[3] This new law established increased self-government in each community and made full community citizenship more easily acquirable. The year 1831 was also the year the chamber delegates had so vigorously supported reformist Catholics' anti-celibacy campaign.

When discussion turned to the issue of Jewish emancipation, however, liberals joined conservatives in rejecting the Jewish community's petitions for full equality. Thus, as of 1831, the 18,000 Jews in a population of more than one million Badeners (by 1845 there would be approximately 23,000 Jews in a population of more than 1.3 million Badeners) continued to lack four fundamental rights: the right to be a delegate to the Lower Chamber, the right to all military and state offices, the right to be a mayor or town councilman, and the right to move from one community into another where no Jews had as yet lived without permission from that community (a right that was particularly contested because it would potentially involve sharing in the use of a community's commons).[4] Over and over again, in the years that followed, in response to petitions submitted by Baden's Jewish leadership, liberals tried to justify their resistance to Jewish rights.

On the issue of Jewish emancipation, the self-identified liberals in Baden's Lower Chamber tended to divide into two general camps. A majority of liberals (and herein they concurred with the majority of those who saw themselves as government loyalists) insisted that emancipation could not be granted until Jews had proven themselves worthy by becoming more assimilated into Christian society. Nonetheless, except for a dogged few who expressed doubt that Jews were capable of or interested in such moral self-improvement, this group continually averred that it favored emancipation as an ultimate goal. A minority of liberals, by contrast, pressed for immediate emancipation, arguing that only the granting of emancipation would cause Jews to assimilate in the desired ways.

The majority resistant to emancipation included some of the most illustrious liberals in Baden, men roundly esteemed for their consistent commitments to securing all manner of free institutions and expansions of civic rights, men like Karl von Rotteck, Adam von Itzstein, Adolf Sander, Ignaz Rindeschwender, and Friedrich Hecker. These men were vehemently opposed to Jewish emancipation as long as Jews did not "give up their Jewishness."[5] They perceived Jews to be the ones who were peculiarly illiberal, resistant to modernity, and uncompromising toward Christians. Rotteck, for example, asked how any liberal could defend Jews, the "most stubborn devotees" of the "system of stagnation," and Sander complained that "everything in the world has changed, only the Jew has remained a Jew."[6] Sander even went so far as to declare that "if we were to change positions, and to trade places with them, if we 18,000 Christians placed ourselves vis-à-vis one million Jews, I ask you, would they emancipate us? No, they would devour us, as the hated children of [M]oab, with fire and the sword. Don't think that these are empty words."[7]

The majority of liberals these men represented found three dimensions of Jewish distinctiveness objectionable—they referred to them as religious, national, and social peculiarities—and they tended to see these three dimensions as inextricably fused with one another. Thus, for example, in response to those leaders of the Jewish community who stressed that it was unconscionable for the delegates to demand that Jews change any of their religious practices, that no human being should be asked to trade his faith for political advantage (as one Jewish leader put it, "They call us a bartering people, but with our religion we will not trade"),[8] these delegates vehemently denied that they harbored any religious hatred toward Jews, even as they continually referred to Baden as a Christian state. But because they saw the three dimensions of Jewish difference as interconnected, they then typically proceeded either to argue that the problem with the Jewish religion was that it was "theocratic"—that Jews' longing for their Messiah made them incapable of genuine obedience to the laws of a non-Jewish state, and/or that rabbinical teachings caused Jews to behave in socially obnoxious ways, and thus that it was the national or social difference of Jews that was the "real" problem.

Within this tautological framework, the national dimension of Jewish difference was also emphasized by constant reference to the notion that Jews constituted a separate nation, that they were foreigners, not Germans, not Badeners—a homeless, displaced people that refused to mingle with any other peoples and, above all, clung rigidly to the faith of its fathers. Arguments about the social dimension also circled back to religious matters. Here the two main complaints had to do with Jewish self-segregation, believed to be expressed in such elements of Jewish religious practice as dietary laws or the observation of the Sabbath on Saturdays, and with the perception that Jews were dishonest in their economic dealings with non-Jews—that the petty trading and money-lending on which the majority of Baden's Jewish community subsisted was necessarily usurious and exploitative, and that this "unproductive" behavior took its justification from the Talmud. Friedrich Hecker, for example, declared that while Christianity called on its followers to "love thy neighbor as thyself," "Mosaism," by contrast, "in its totality creates an insurmountable barrier of nationality between Christians and Jews."[9] Similarly, Ignaz Rindeschwender, elaborating on the beauties of the "Christian state," announced that Judaism's religious principle "is different from our Christianity in its innermost essence," because it "offers none of those great ideas that raise a human being above himself."[10]

In short, despite the disclaimers about religious prejudice, these liberal delegates tended to portray Judaism as a religion vastly inferior to Christianity, and to stress a causal connection between this religion and Jews' much-maligned economic roles. As self-understood representatives of "the people," the majority of liberals used popular hostility toward Jews as the justification for their own hesitancy to extend emancipation. They did so without bothering to analyze how the transition from a feudal to a market economy had forced rural Christians into a dependent relationship with that group responsible for exporting and importing goods out of and into the rural economy, and the group most willing to offer small credit. They also failed to consider how the ongoing restrictions on Jews' residence rights limited the feasibility for Jews of taking up their only recently acquired right to enter the trades or agriculture, for in most villages all occupational niches were filled.[11]

The more progressive minority of liberals sought to counter all these arguments in a variety of ways. They tended to emphasize that the major difference between Jews and Christians was a religious one, and that religious difference should be no excuse for political inequality. But they also stressed the ways Baden's Jews were modernizing their religion—how they were replacing the Hebrew language with German in their worship services, or how the new books for religious education of their children contained only the purest moral principles. They insisted that Baden's Jews were indeed Germans and Badeners, that they had lived in the land for centuries, that they were loyal to the monarch, that they had fought impressively in the recent Wars of Liberation. They reeled off statistics about the number of Jews who were taking up respectable trades and entering the professions. They reminded their colleagues that there were Christian usurers as well as Jewish ones, that by no means all Jewish moneylenders were usurious, that the operative moral distinction should be between usurers and non-usurers, not Jews and Christians. Finally, they stressed that they too were faith-filled Christians, and many, though not all, also said they valued the notion of a Christian state, but they pointed out that Christianity was a religion based on love and equality, not hatred and hierarchy.

Yet these counterarguments were almost invariably embedded in a more problematic line of reasoning as well, which turned on the notion that the granting of equality would lead to the dilution of difference, and that such dilution was eminently desirable and urgently necessary. In short, they posited that a "character change" must take place, and that the Jewish "personality must disappear with equalization."[12] Pro-emancipationists conceded a great deal to their opposition when they argued that Jews' unappealing traits of "cunning and cleverness" and "unrestrained craving for profit" were products of centuries of oppression and persecution, even as they used such assertions to press their claims that "liberty is especially the right means to improvement of character."[13] The prominent pro-emancipationist Friedrich Daniel Bassermann, for instance, contended that the great advantage of a rapid emancipation lay in the way "equalization with the Christians is the greatest enemy of the old rabbinicalism": "If one had equalized the Jews with the Christians one hundred years ago, I maintain, they would long since no longer be the Jews we have today."[14] Pro-emancipationists wanted to "help Jews come closer to Christians and make them as bearable and useful as possible."[15] One fervent pro-emancipationist, Karl Mez, put it quite bluntly:

> I want to give them freedom . . . because I want to better them, and because I am convinced, that only in freedom . . . can one truly thrive. . . . We should seek justice, and *then* all else will be given unto us. *Then* also the Jews will be given unto us, that means they will no longer hesitate . . . to accommodate themselves more fully to our conditions.[16]

Liberalism, in short, had a double aspect: It could be used to empower disadvantaged groups through its discourse of liberty, equality, and rights, but simultaneously, largely because it imagined the supposedly universal rights-bearing individual as a (white, male) Christian, those who were in some way "different" from this norm could not easily be accepted as equals.[17] Precisely liberalism's intrinsic preoccupation with progress hampered liberals' ability to embrace Jewish equality without trying to remake Jews, for pro-emancipationists shared anti-emancipationists' assumptions about Jews as uniquely backward, trapped in an earlier stage of history. No matter how militant their defense of the principle, as one pro-emancipationist put it, that "by nature every human being has equal rights," then, this insight was routinely coupled with the notion that "emancipation should not be . . . the *reward* for enlightenment, but rather the means by which that enlightenment will be achieved."[18] Similarly, one who contended that the Jews' political equalization was required by "humanity and justice" also argued that the "moral improvement of the Jews" should not be demanded as a precondition for emancipation, but rather that "emancipation is the means to this improvement."[19] Yet another avid pro-emancipationist, Josef Merk, insistent that "precisely now is the time to banish all legal difference because of religious difference," also argued, in a classic formulation, "it is my conviction that nothing remains but to throw the Israelites, with equal rights, into the mass of the Christian population, so that, ripped along by the torrent, they will, like the pebbles rolling along in a riverbed, round themselves off and fit themselves in."[20] Although unable to pin down precisely where Jewish "difference" from Christian Germans lay (since they believed that religious differences had no relevance from the state's point of view, and since they found the notion of Jews as a separate nation ridiculous), pro-emancipationists nonetheless assumed that there was a difference that was in some way disturbing, and they shared with anti-emancipationist liberals and conservatives the firm conviction that difference and equality were irreconcilable. In sum, also the self-declared pro-emancipationists contributed to a discourse about the dangers of Jewish difference from Christian Germans which was to have damaging consequences even after emancipation was, eventually, granted.

Contemporary observers were well aware that most liberals in the diet shared conservatives' hesitancy about Jewish rights. One anonymous contributor to the *Mannheimer Journal* expressed despair over how "the fate of a people can depend on the moods of a liberal."[21] And another commentator (from as far away as Hamburg) remarked that "since the year 1830 the Lower Chamber of the Grand Duchy of Baden shines as a model for all German parliaments. All the starker is the contrast, all the more glaring is the shadow, when we see how that chamber has until now cared so little about the most well-founded requests and laments of the Jews."[22]

In response to Jewish petitions, Baden's Lower Chamber debated Jewish emancipation in 1833, 1835, 1837, 1840, 1842, and 1845, but nothing much changed either in the terms of debate or in the proportion of delegates supporting equality. From a high of nineteen (out of a total of sixty-three) in 1835, the number of pro-emancipationists in the chamber slipped to fifteen in February 1845, even as the number of self-identified liberals in the chamber climbed in the 1840s to more than half the delegates. However, only a brief eighteen months later, in August of 1846, a dramatic reversal of opinion occurred: fully two-thirds of the delegates, in a triumphant landslide, voted in favor of full Jewish emancipation. Yet this sudden shift was due not so much to a change in attitudes toward Jews, but rather to liberal alarm about rapidly intensifying conflicts over the content and meaning of Christianity. The abrupt transformation in the liberal position cannot be understood unless we recall how in the 1830s and 1840s the liberal majority in the Lower Chamber had become increasingly distressed about the growth of a religious right outside the chamber—a level of distress that was to make liberals extraordinarily receptive to a new phenomenon: Christian dissent.

The Emergence of Christian Dissent

Right in the midst of the battle over mixed marriages, in the summer of 1845, the religious landscape of Baden changed. Just as elsewhere in Germany, so also in Baden a protest movement emerged specifically in reaction to the rise of Catholic neoorthodoxy and ultramontanism. The

Catholic dissenters were joined by Protestants disaffected by conservative trends in their own church; together, they split from the established churches and founded democratically run congregations dedicated to individual freedom of belief, cross-confessional cooperation, and the separation of church and state. Across the German lands, the movement reached a peak of between 100,000 and 150,000 members by 1848, making it the largest protest movement of any sort in pre-revolutionary Germany. In Baden, there were ten dissenting congregations, encompassing 700 official members, although there were many more sympathizers. The first congregations to be established in Baden were in Mannheim and Heidelberg in August 1845, and other, smaller congregations sprang up in Pforzheim, Durlach, Constance, Stockach, Waldshut, Hüfingen, Bonndorf, and Neukirch in the following months.[23] Like many of the dissenters elsewhere in Germany, the Badenese dissenters—despite the substantial number of Protestants among them—called themselves *Deutschkatholiken*, or German-Catholics, as opposed to Roman Catholics. Those hostile to the movement tended to call it "Rongeanism," after Johannes Ronge, a former Catholic chaplain from Silesia who was one of the movement's main founders and its most charismatic leader.

There were multiple reasons for the emergence of organized dissent. The largest reason lay in the widely felt need to create an organized humanist form of Christianity. The dissenters sought to provide individuals with a tolerant, supportive community in which they could combine reason and spirituality, and express a faith that was no less fervent despite its disgust at hierarchical control and rigidly exclusivist doctrines. Joining or supporting the new congregations was also a way to express a more general discontent with both the persistence of political authoritarianism in Germany, and with Rome's growing intervention in Germany's religious and political affairs. Indicatively, the most immediate catalyst for the creation of the dissenting movement had been a stunningly popular pilgrimage organized by conservative German Catholic leaders in 1844 to the Holy Robe of Trier, purportedly worn by Jesus at his death.[24] Critics were shocked at neoorthodoxy's apparent ability to attract massive public support by blatantly lying about the robe's authenticity in the midst of the supposedly so "enlightened" nineteenth century, and it galvanized them to create a concrete alternative; Ronge's open letter to the Archbishop of Trier protesting the pilgrimage became the movement's founding document. But over and over again, the dissenters also stressed that it was Rome's new authoritarianism in marital matters in particular which was causing them to mobilize.

Not only did the dissenters express their opposition to Rome's authoritarian agenda by promoting equality between clergy and laity and instituting equal voting rights for all members of a congregation; they also particularly welcomed priests who wanted to marry as their spiritual leaders, and especially encouraged mixed Protestant-Catholic couples to join their fold, thus directly snubbing the Catholic hierarchy in its stances on sex and marriage. Not only did the *Deutschkatholiken* bring all the contentious issues together, but they also gave them practical form. The Catholic reformers of the 1820s and 1830s had simply requested that church structures be democratized, and that celibacy be abolished. The state government had primarily tried to ease restrictions on mixed marriages, and (as it turned out, unsuccessfully) to protect mixed couples from undue psychological pressure. But in one fell swoop, the dissenters created not just a concrete democratic experiment. They also gave priests desiring to marry both complete respect and a new forum for pastoral activity. And they offered mixed families a community in which they could worship together, and be supported rather than maligned, while in general providing the space in which Protestants and Catholics could identify their commonalities.

The nascent dissenting movement met with immediate official resistance in Baden, as elsewhere in Germany. Predictably livid about how brazenly the dissenters were taking on the Catholic hierarchy, Catholic conservatives vied with each other to defame them in the most lurid terms. But many Protestant leaders and municipal and state administrators were equally alarmed. Frequently prohibited by the censors from advertising their worship services in the newspapers and by town governments and local clergy of both confessions from using school or religious buildings, the dissenters struggled to attract members and to find a meeting space. Even when they resorted to gathering in taverns, police repeatedly broke up the meetings. Dissenting preachers from other states were banned from preaching in Baden. In order to discourage proselytizing, the dissenters were often only allowed to hold private home prayer meetings, and they were denied the right to give their children a dissenting religious education.[25]

Although a number of historians have analyzed the nationalist, anti-Rome impulses reflected in the dissenting movement's chosen name, and others have studied its important role in launching the first organized German women's movement, the movement's central preoccupation with men's sexual rights has received no attention.[26] Yet because of the evolving tension between liberals and ultramontanists over men's sexual and romantic rights, it was precisely this element of the movement's vision that was to have important consequences for how liberals came to reconceptualize the "Jewish question." Because of their own indignation at conservative Catholic views on individual freedom and on sex and marriage, political liberals were thrilled with the emergence of dissent and rushed vociferously to the dissenters' defense when these dissenters, by stepping out of the traditional Christian churches, lost the political rights they had previously held—and thereby became similar in status to Jews.

Liberals waxed rapturous over the significance of the dissenters' emergence, extolling the movement as "the Reformation of the Nineteenth Century," and the movement's leader, Ronge, as the "New Luther." Some spoke of "Germany's Second Easter, or the Resurrection of the Church," while others compared the *Deutschkatholiken* with Christ's early disciples. In Baden, liberal politicians, journalists, and academics echoed sentiments elsewhere when they argued that the *Deutschkatholiken* would inaugurate a new era of national rebirth, an end to hypocrisy in public life, and an end to both religious indifference and to the new religious tyranny emanating from Rome. The *Deutschkatholiken* would unite Germany because they would overcome the divide between Protestants and Catholics that had for so long weakened the German people.[27]

Liberal delegate Bassermann, for example, called the dissenting movement the "beginning point of a reformation of the life of the German people," and rhetorically asked, in a clear reference to the rise of Catholic conformism, "What is the main principle of the *deutschkatholische* teachings? It says that we do not want uniformity of belief. . . . Uniformity of belief . . . leads to hypocrisy, whereas only uniformity in morals and in Christian teaching leads to unity." Georg Gottfried Gervinus, a liberal Protestant historian at the University of Heidelberg, praised the movement's "impulse toward unification of the confessions" as a "blessing" and the potential "beginning of a general reform of the whole life of the nation." Likewise, liberal diet delegate Carl Theodor Welcker proclaimed that the dissenters' concrete implementation of the "principle of brotherly love" would demonstrate "how far humanity can come in the nineteenth century in Germany," and that through "the new Reformation . . . the spirit of God will be capable of . . . making the German nation a chosen people of God in sensibility, feeling and education."[28]

Supporters particularly hailed the triumph of individual subjectivity and human reason demonstrated by the movement's emergence, as well as the concrete resistance to Rome it represented. Liberal delegate Hecker was especially insistent that "religious conviction in and of itself is something inner" and that therefore "every coercion in relation to religious conviction is an attack on the human spirit, which is capable of and necessarily strives for perfection." Hecker railed against the exclusion of the *Deutschkatholiken* from "even the smallest political right," arguing that thereby the state "cast itself as lord of the conscience and of reason"—while also warning the government of the dangers of a "priests' state" and the need to resist "power-hungry" priests' encroachments into education and family life. Bassermann announced that "whoever knows German history knows that the greatest disaster that ever hit Germany came from Rome," adding snide remarks on Catholic priests' inability to stay celibate. Similarly, the reformist Catholic professor Heinrich Schreiber (having already lost his position on Freiburg's theological faculty and about to be excommunicated and permanently unemployed), also weighed in on the topic of dissent, decrying "prostitution with the foreigner" and suggesting that "when the heart lies in Italian Rome, then it is not in the German *fatherland*."[29]

Zittel's Motion

It was in this context of liberal delight in dissent and concern about rising ultramontanism that liberal delegate Karl Zittel, on December 15, 1845, advanced before his colleagues in the Lower Chamber the principle that every citizen in Baden ought to be able to profess his faith without thereby forfeiting any rights of citizenship. He introduced a motion that would implement this principle, yet he also included a clause that would limit its implementation to avowed Christians. Although the realization of complete religious freedom was his genuine goal (Zittel, a recent convert to Jewish emancipation, had already expressed strong support for it in the last debate on that topic ten months earlier), he added this limiting clause because his most immediate goal was to secure the right of the *Deutschkatholiken* to organize themselves as a church. He was well aware that his motion could face severe objections even with this clause, but given the continuing hostility to Jewish emancipation among the majority of his colleagues, the motion had almost no chance of passing without it.

Therefore, in the speech introducing his motion for universal religious freedom, Zittel went to great lengths not to mention Jews by name, in an obvious attempt to strengthen the motion's chances. He did, however, albeit in a convoluted fashion, refer to the implications the motion inevitably held for Baden's Jews:

> I would be unfaithful to my own principles if I would limit my motion from the outset through the exclusion of any one religious party. But—I cannot say this without a certain shame—I cannot insist on this, for I can have no hope that my motion, phrased so generally, will receive the approval of the

house. The majority of you feels itself more accountable to the general antipathy against a religious party which lives among us, an antipathy which
it has of course primarily incurred through the way of life of its lower
classes, than to justice. . . . In order therefore not to cause the motion for
religious freedom itself to fail, [a freedom] which has recently become so
very important because of the movement in the *Christian* population, I at
this point of course see myself forced *possibly* to limit the motion in the
second instance to those who profess the Christian religion.[30]

Recognizing that this willingness potentially to limit the motion only
to Christians necessarily called attention to the question of whether the
dissenters were in fact Christians, Zittel knew he had to counter the new
strict definitions of Christianity that had been advanced ever more insistently by conservative Catholics in the contentious debates surrounding
priestly celibacy and mixed marriages. In particular, Zittel needed to undermine the neoorthodox Catholics' assertions that the Catholic
church, under the guidance of Rome, was the only true expression of
Christianity, and the notion that without obedience to the church hierarchy and uniformity of belief within the church, disintegration of the
social fabric and the spread of immorality were inevitable.

Against such conservative conceptions, Zittel stressed the sacred invi-
olability of an individual's own understanding of spiritual matters. He
also argued that the drive for community was fundamental to human
nature, that each individual should be free to join with like-minded others to satisfy his or her spiritual needs, and that society as a whole bene-
fited from such freedom of spiritual expression. In sum, Zittel wished to
"let truth everywhere cut its own path, and give the spirit freedom; true
religiosity is rooted only in this freedom. Even if this may seem problematic for the church, religion is more important than the church; better
no church than no religion."[31]

It was clear that it was the growth of ultramontanism that was moti-
vating Zittel to attempt to ensconce religious freedom in the law of the
land, for he offered his colleagues an extended summary of the whole
rise of the religious right over the preceding years, replete with references to the battles over mixed marriages in Prussia and Baden, and to
the Trier pilgrimage that had catalyzed the dissenting movement.
"Worse things yet are being silently planned," he warned, "the dark
spirit of fanaticism has almost everywhere moved in to the educational
institutions for future religious teachers. . . . A dark mysterious force
has arisen from the grave and has spread itself over our fatherland. . . .
Jesuitism is marching forwards with giant steps, trampling under its feet
our century's budding seeds of freedom and enlightenment."[32]

Acutely aware that the *Deutschkatholiken* were not considered Christians by conservative Catholics, Zittel addressed this point directly. "Are the *Deutschkatholiken* Christians?" he asked:

> Who will answer? Who should decide? . . . Look around, gentlemen, in the whole realm of the state you find no tribunal of faith; the nineteenth century no longer tolerates one. For the state, it must be enough that a religious corporation declares, *that it wants* to be *Christian*. The *deutschkatholische* community has done this; it has declared that it wants to develop a community in the sense and the spirit of Jesus the Christ, and that it seeks nourishment in His gospel for its religious meaning and life. The state must see to it that the spirit of immorality does not gain ground within it and that it does not nurture principles dangerous to the state; but as long as that is not the case, the state cannot deny it the label and recognition as a *Christian* community.[33]

In his concluding remarks as well, Zittel reiterated the Christian identity of the dissenters when he stressed that the movement for religious freedom they represented would lead to the reconciliation of all Christian Germans that had for so painfully long eluded the German people.

Similar tendencies appeared in the remarks made by other liberal delegates in the brief discussion following Zittel's statement. Liberals who favored Jewish emancipation extolled the virtues of dissent, continually reinforced the idea that dissenters were Christians, and made only indirect gestures in favor of Jewish equality by applauding the inclusion of "all religions" in Zittel's motion.[34] The fervently pro-dissent but anti-emancipationist Hecker, however, made the distinction he saw between dissenters and Jews explicit. Hecker, whose hatred of conservative Catholicism was profound, took the opportunity to describe in glowing terms the "great moment in our history" signaled by the emergence of dissent, and declared that it would be "blasphemy," "slander of that which is most sacred, if one were to try to prevent a human being from worshipping the Eternal in his own way." Yet he failed to connect such sentiments with his attitudes toward Jews; the allusion was indirect, but Hecker's meaning was unmistakable: "In the interest of freedom, I do not support the motion for one part of the population of this land. I do not want the priests' state, and I also do not want the theocratic state."[35]

Less liberal delegates lamented their colleagues' assaults on Catholicism and/or indicated that they were not in agreement with Zittel on all points, but they acknowledged that the motion was "maybe the most important matter that will be discussed in this session of the diet," and they were willing to let the motion be debated further at a later date.[36] In fact, the discussion that day was only supposed to decide one thing:

whether Zittel's motion should be printed and sent to committee, so that a report could be prepared and then the matter could be discussed substantively at a future point by the full house. At the end of the discussion, the sixty delegates present unanimously decided that this would indeed happen.

The Religious Right's Response

The relaxed attitude of conservatives in the Lower Chamber incensed conservatives elsewhere in Baden. While the *Süddeutsche Zeitung für Kirche und Staat* had been fiercely criticizing the *Deutschkatholiken* since their emergence, the unanimous vote to send Zittel's motion to committee turned its single-handed effort into a broad-based protest.[37] A rash of tracts criticizing the *Deutschkatholiken* appeared, stirring up public opinion, alerting Grand Duke Leopold's government to the dangers of religious freedom, and castigating the conservative delegates for their inattention.[38]

In stark contrast to the vague allusions to Jews made by Zittel and his liberal supporters in their endorsements of the dissenters, critics of the motion for religious freedom constantly worked to link dissenters and Jews. The pamphleteer Ludwig Castorph, for instance, articulated clearly what he saw as the logical implication of granting full equality to the dissenters: "The requested religious freedom, in the way *they* mean it, is unacceptable, because then, to be fair, the *other sects* and *the Jews* would also have to be granted equal rights and privileges."[39] The prominent conservative Catholic professor Johann Baptist Hirscher similarly warned that "immorality . . . is decisively encouraged when good and bad are treated equally in social life. Thereby the worth of morality sinks in the eyes of the public. Likewise, the worth of religion must sink in the eyes of the people, when the law . . . treats Christians, Jews and pagans as equals."[40] Franz Josef Buss, in his *Das Rongethum in der badischen Abgeordnetenkammer* (Rongeanism in Baden's Lower Chamber), exposed the implications of Zittel's reasoning most pointedly: "But you, Mr. Friend of Light, believe that as long as the spirit of morality finds its place in your protégé congregation, and as long as no principles are nurtured there that threaten the state, then the state could not refuse it recognition as a *Christian* community. But according to this logic, a Jew, a pagan, and a Turk would also be a Christian."[41]

Aside from Buss, the other most influential anti-dissent activist was Alban Stolz, who wrote three tracts against the dissenters. His *Landwehr gegen den badischen Landstand* (Civil Defense against the Badenese Diet) was sent into every Catholic community in Baden and was read aloud to the townspeople by priests and mayors.[42] It explicitly urged the readers and listeners both to pray daily that God might rescue Baden from the dissenting movement and the faithlessness, sin, and sexual corruption it represented, and to send petitions to the grand duke requesting that the Lower Chamber be dissolved for having let Zittel's motion go to committee. This dissolution of the chamber had been Buss's express goal as well.

Furthermore, in a striking parallel with the way religious and economic arguments had long been intertwined in attacks on Jews, Stolz used a similar combination of arguments against dissenters. He accused the diet delegates of using the dissenting movement to destroy Catholicism, and he claimed that if Zittel's motion passed, the townspeople would be forced to pay heavily for dissenters' churches, pastors, and schoolteachers. As other pamphleteers had, so Stolz too stressed that the dissenters were just as un-Christian as Jews or Turks.[43]

Stolz's two other anti-*Deutschkatholiken* tracts, also self-consciously designed to be read to an only partially literate rural audience, were even more graphic in the way they both sexualized and "judaized" the dissenters. In *Amulett gegen die jungkatholische Sucht* (Amulet against the Young-Catholic Mania) Stolz repeatedly associated dissent with lust and adultery, and slyly suggested that dissenters were offering Catholic priests a trade: the "priests of the flesh" could have women, if the parishioners no longer had to go to confession. Furthermore, after having established that "God destroyed the Jews' temple and rejects their worship," he declared that "now the *Rongeaner* want to become like the Jews, they want . . . only rabbis who will sing for them and make pretty speeches." In criticizing dissenters' rationalist rejection of the notion that Christ was literally present in the communion wafer, he declared that "if Christ were not in the Host, then we Catholics would be idol-worshippers, we would thus be more wicked than Jews and Turks."[44]

Merging these two rhetorical maneuvers in *Der neue Kometstern mit seinem Schweif, oder Johannes Ronge und seine Briefträger* (The New Shooting Star with its Tail, or Johannes Ronge and his Letter-Carriers), Stolz described those Catholics who would be attracted to dissent as those who "grew up lasciviously in arrogance and licentiousness, whose synagogue is the tavern, whose gospel is newspapers with rotten principles." Among the dangerous newspapers he named was also "that Jew-paper, the *Frankfurter Journal*." Equating Christianity with Catholicism, he also argued that "the most precious thing the human being can possess is the Christian religion, the secure, solid Catholic faith, the holy sacraments. But now there are peddling Jews [*Schacherjuden*] at the door, traders in souls . . . who want to swindle you, Catholic folk, out of your precious faith. . . . Whoever has good sense and love of religion will be filled with nausea at . . . this carnal lust and haughtiness."[45]

Both the sexualizing and the "judaizing" served to undermine dissenters' claims to be Christians. The sexualizing was a logical rhetorical tactic because of the genuine significance of sexual matters for the movement and its supporters, but it also served as a more general signifier of the all-too-human and thus not properly spiritual concerns of the dissenters. The "judaizing" of dissenters was obviously a way to undercut their self-understanding as Christians and to constrict and consolidate the meaning of "true Christianity." Throwing in references to Turks for good measure was not only a time-honored rhetorical attack on the medieval enemies of Christendom (with particular ongoing relevance in the south of Germany where popular memories of the sixteenth- and seventeenth-century Turkish sieges of Vienna were still strong). In the nineteenth-century context, these references also served to exoticize both Jews and dissenters even more, reinforcing the implication that these were foreign elements.

Buss made similar connections between sex, dissent, and Jews. For example, this is how Buss described the entry of the *Deutschkatholiken* into the Lower Chamber's agenda: "A few dissolute chaplains begin the business. A debauched press, usually led by Jews, seizes upon the inflammatory subject-matter. Political radicalism, having exhausted its formal constitutional questions, throws the material onto its dying embers." Buss mocked the concessions to anti-Judaism evident in Zittel's willingness to limit his motion solely to regularizing the dissenters' situation—"because you fear the consequences of Jew-hatred in the chamber and among the people for your little miserable bit of popular appeal"—but also contributed to anti-Jewish sentiments with his own remarks, taking swipes at "Young Israel's" role in the "crusade against Catholicism" and telling Zittel that his comments in his speech about the archbishop's handling of mixed marriages showed the speech could just as well have been delivered by "a Jew, a Turk." Buss also called dissenting groups "these untested suddenly-surfacing sects, germinated in the lasciviousness of radical rabblerousing," and declared that "they have done all frivolous and sensuous people a favor by offering them a religion of convenience, because it is still somewhat part of good manners to be religious."[46]

Buss again linked *Deutschkatholiken* and Jews in his imaginative final sequence:

See—now the Lord is crucified a second time. Or do we perhaps lack a *Judas Iscariot* who kissed Christ and betrayed Him for 30 silver coins? . . . Do we lack Christ's sleeping disciples, to whom the Lord could say '*Sleep for the remaining time and rest. See, the hour is near and the Son of Man will be delivered into the hands of sinners.'* . . . Do we lack *Pontius Pilate*, the representative of the pagan state, the governor who barely dares to ask as [Pilate] did: Which one do you want me to release, Barrabas the state subverter—or Jesus who is called the Christ? And do we lack the *people* who call: [We want] Barrabas. Christ should be crucified!. . . And do they not in our days lead Him to the place of the skull [Golgotha] to be crucified? You ask, where is the place of the skull? Do you not recognize it? There you see the three crosses on the dismal plain: in the middle the Lord in His church, one criminal to His left, one criminal to His right. That is your Golgotha.[47]

In this dramatic conclusion, Buss likened the response to *Deutschkatholizismus* in Baden to a second crucifixion of Christ. The parallels were fairly transparent. Judas, the unfaithful disciple, was like the priests and pastors who left their churches to join the dissenting movement for—as Buss had repeatedly asserted earlier in the text—their immediate gratification, symbolized here by the silver coins. The sleeping disciples were the delegates of the Lower Chamber, particularly the self-defined conservatives, "sleeping" while Zittel's motion was sent to committee. Already early in his book, Buss had asked the conservatives what was wrong with them, and declared that "the unanimity with which Zittel's motion was sent to committee without any intervention is—say what you will—a loud testimony for the religious indifference of the administration and the chamber."[48] Karl Friedrich Nebenius and Franz Anton Regenauer, the Grand Duke's ministers who sat in on Lower Chamber proceedings, together were Pontius Pilate, the representatives of the *pagan*—no longer Christian—state, and Golgotha, the place of crucifixion, was the Lower Chamber itself. The crucifying crowd consisted of the laypeople rushing to join dissenting congregations, or perhaps even all those who were no longer active members of the traditional congregations. But underneath these immediate parallels, Buss also maneuvered more subtly to evoke another set of associations for his readers, deliberately invoking and thereby reinforcing the commonly held misconception that it was Jews who were responsible for Christ's "first" crucifixion. Finally, in his image of the three crosses, Buss conjured up a metaphor for the way religion was in the process of becoming the central object of contention between left and right in Baden. For nothing so polarized political sentiment in the pre-revolutionary years as the cluster of religious conflicts that had emerged from the conjunction of the controversy over mixed marriages with the advent of religious dissent and with the recurrent demand for Jewish emancipation.

Banking on popular animosity toward Jews (but obviously also digni-fying it as an article of faith), casting aspersions on dissenters' character and motivations, playing on the economic fears of a predominantly agri-cultural population whose financial security was frequently shaky, the anti-dissent activists successfully convinced thousands of Badenese Catholics that dissent was a mortal danger. Archbishop Hermann von Vicari too had thrown his weight behind the anti-dissent campaign, re-leasing an "emergency call" to his flock that "they are trying to steal your faith!"[49] Already in January of 1846, petitions against Zittel's mo-tion started arriving in the Lower Chamber, and, in keeping with Stolz's suggestions, the petitions stressed the religious and economic dangers dissent presented.[50] Defenders of the motion tried to organize petitions as well, but the opponents were in the overwhelming majority.

The right was not only more in touch with grassroots sentiment on religious and economic matters than the left, but also in a better posi-tion to organize petitions. Priests across the Catholic areas of Baden an-nounced from the pulpit that their parishioners should sign petitions against the motion, and the petitions were laid out for signing immedi-ately after church. Liberals had no forum like the church in which to display petitions or solicit signatures, with the exception of newspapers, and (according to liberal delegates) censors saw to it that every an-nouncement about petitions in the newspapers was excised.

Already by the middle of January 1846, liberal delegates were becom-ing upset by the preponderance of anti-*Deutschkatholiken* petitions. This was so not least because the petitions often demanded that the Lower Chamber be dissolved by the grand duke for having allowed Zittel's mo-tion to go to committee in the first place. But it was also because the liberals saw whatever hopes they had had for religious liberalization in Baden slipping away under the impact of an unforeseen radicalization and organization of the right.

Bassermann tried to forestall this trend by reevoking the vision of love and harmony that had motivated liberals to support Zittel's motion in December 1845. He described a typical *deutschkatholischer* worship ser-vice in Mannheim in an emotional speech on February 3, 1846. He urged his listeners to attend a service:

> Only a schoolroom serves as the church . . . but the grandest cathedral can-not move you to reverence like this. . . . Packed tightly together . . . all the way into the halls outside the doors, in solemn silence all listen to the en-thusiastic words of joy in faith and of comfort and encouragement, in these days of oppression and persecution. . . . And while perhaps at the same hour from many pulpits in the land abuse is heaped on the meager little congregation, the worship service ends with the prayer: "God bless our

enemies." Go there, see up close that which you seem ready to damn from afar, and if any one can still then in well-meaning zeal pick up a stone against these his human brothers, may God forgive him.[51]

But despite efforts like Bassermann's, also within the chamber, conservatives now started to mobilize. Countering demands for religious freedom became a matter of principle for conservative delegates, who had been silent only a few weeks earlier, and had voted with the liberals to send Zittel's motion to committee. The same tracts detailing the dangers of *Deutschkatholizismus* that had convinced local priests to organize petition drives, had also persuaded them. Now the conservative delegates began to argue, as Johann Baptist Karl Junghanns did, that passage of the motion would lead to "the disintegration of Christianity in the Grand Duchy of Baden."[52]

Conservatives also now took the pamphleteers' cue to expose how liberals' humanist redefinition of Christianity, taken to its logical conclusion, made religious differences uncomfortably difficult to pinpoint. Gideon Weizel expressed the conservative view clearly when he said,

> How can you hold it against a Catholic if he resists with all his strength this motion, which in its first sentence requests that *every* religious association, no matter of what name, whether it is a *Christian* one *or not*, should be granted already through the *fact* of its emergence alone *full* and *equal rights* with both of the existing Christian churches in our land, whereby the delegate who made the motion sets up no other precondition except that the members of that society should only fulfill the *state-citizen* duties, for the rest it could be Christian or Mohammedan. Gentlemen, against such a motion I would vote as a *Christian*, not as a Catholic or Protestant. . . . After all, they are not only requesting religious freedom for Christian associations, but also for *un-Christian* ones.[53]

Ultimately, the "petition storm" organized by conservatives brought 347 petitions with close to 50,000 signatures against the *Deutschkatholiken* into the Lower Chamber. Only 31 petitions had been sent in support of Zittel's motion.[54] It was the first mass petitioning campaign in German history, and the birthdate of political Catholicism in Germany.[55] The general state of uproar in the land convinced Grand Duke Leopold's ministerial advisors that the Lower Chamber should indeed be dissolved, and the grand duke did so on February 9, 1846.

Thinking that the petition storm also reflected a politically conservative trend in the population, the grand duke and his advisors assumed that in the new elections set for April 3, 1846, a majority of conservative candidates would win. But there were confessional tensions within the conservative camp which hampered campaigning. Traditional Protestant government loyalists, for example, were quite uncomfortable making common cause with upstart ultramontane Catholics. Meanwhile, the emerging tension between radical and moderate liberals was temporarily put aside in the interests of combating the religious right. Furthermore, as liberals later analyzed it, it is also likely that although rural Catholics would mobilize to defend their faith and economic interests in a petition campaign, many still saw their political interests best guaranteed by liberals, who were not tainted as conservatives were by association with the local government administrators they often detested. Conservative observers, by contrast, called attention to the peculiarities of Baden's indirect voting system, which favored the persistence of a "politics of notables" in which well-known individuals routinely got voted into public office regardless of their ideological affiliation. For all these reasons, an even larger liberal majority was returned to the Lower Chamber than before.[56] Thirty-six liberals faced twenty-seven conservatives when the Lower Chamber reopened on May 1. In fact, the only new conservative to win a seat was Franz Josef Buss himself.

Dissenters' Rights

On June 26, 1846, the liberal delegate Ignaz Rindeschwender delivered the report of the petition committee on the *Deutschkatholiken*'s request for revocation of the grand duke's decree (promulgated on April 20) which had officially deprived them of political rights and formalized the already-existing restrictions on their ability to worship and organize. The committee was very favorably disposed to the petitioners. The major thrust of Rindeschwender's argument was that

> it would offend healthy common sense and moral feeling alike, if a citizen who previously enjoyed *all* state-citizen rights, should now find himself . . . robbed of . . . the most important of these, because on a few points he is changing his religious opinion—to be more exact, because he is honest enough to speak openly, that which thousands and thousands think of as he does, but do not profess loudly.[57]

Thus Rindeschwender not only placed the *Deutschkatholiken* firmly among the Christians from whom they had emerged, but also portrayed them as even better Christians than those who remained in the traditional churches.

Rindeschwender, who as a long-standing fierce opponent of Jewish emancipation had once been a pioneering articulator of the "Christian state" concept, now made arguments which fundamentally undermined that ideal. He noted that many feared "an atomistic disintegration of the existing great churches," but he said that this was not the concern of the state, whose only purpose was to guarantee justice (which included full freedom of conscience) and whose justification only derived from its capacity for *"satisfaction of the general needs of human nature."* He further redefined both Christianity and the purpose of the state when he argued:

> If it lies in the course of the development of humanity that from time to time the Christian religion creates other forms for itself . . . if periodically there emerges . . . a dissatisfaction with the old structure, *the state should let it be*; the movement will either, in league with the *truth*, safely break ground for itself and bear good fruit, or it will—if its foundation is *frivolous*—silently seep into the sand like undammed water, without leaving a trace. . . . A government . . . does not comprehend its position, its well-being, if it with intensified heartpounding tightens the reins of domination ever more, instead of letting go freely that which has outgrown its minority and can control itself in a manly prudent manner. Let religious life take care of itself.[58]

It was a fact not lost on any of the men in the liberal majority that it was the issue of religious freedom that had caused the chamber to be dissolved in the first place, and that religious conservatism was their most immediate enemy. As one newly elected liberal put it, "Let's admit it, the chamber was dissolved . . . as a result of a *monstrous priestly lie*, the petition storm, or if you prefer, as a result of the religious upheaval in the land."[59] Buss and Stolz and their cohorts had made opposition to the *Deutschkatholiken* a matter of principle for the right; in response, the *Deutschkatholiken* became even more of a *cause célèbre* for the left. No longer was it only the promise of national unity and an end to the religious divisions which rent Germany, no longer was it only the appeal of a democratic experiment in brotherly love that inspired the *Deutschkatholiken*'s defenders. Despite their electoral triumph, they had also had to confront the political effectuality of conservative Catholicism, its ability to expose liberals' distance from "the people" in whose name they pronounced their views on matters great and small, its ability, indeed, to rob them, however temporarily, of their exalted status and identity as members of a diet which had the eyes of all Germany on it. Religious freedom, once a matter of ambivalence for liberals, became their rallying cry. And—especially given the comparisons between dissenters and Jews their opponents were pressing—this could not help but affect their stand on the "Jewish question" as well.

The liberal delegates' overriding concern, however, was with resisting the ways the religious right was trying to define the content of Christianity. In the two days of debates about Rindeschwender's report, on

August 12 and 13, 1846, one liberal after another certainly called for religious freedom, but the bulk of liberals' statements was given over to an elaborate defense of the *Deutschkatholiken*'s identity as Christians. Some delegates went so far as to compare the dissenters with the early disciples of Christ, taunting those who opposed dissent that if they had lived 1,800 years earlier, they would have, "in the name of peace, order, unity," opposed Christ himself.[60] Because the grand duke's decree limiting dissenters' rights had implicitly acknowledged that the dissenters were Christians, giving liberals a wedge with which to argue that the decree itself was unconstitutional, the focus on dissenters' Christian identity was a logical strategy to pursue.[61]

Yet the insistence on dissenters' Christianity was not purely strategic, but also the result of a deeply felt revulsion at those who would arrogate to themselves the right to determine the value of another person's faith. As Friedrich Hecker put it to those of his colleagues who denigrated dissent: "How can you be so presumptuous as to present yourself, as it were, as identical with God and say: these alone are the true paths that lead to temporal and eternal happiness?"[62] Others criticized Buss and everything he stood for directly, either declaring that "not one Badener out of a thousand wants a Catholicism like *Buss*'s," or trying to point out that "we all stand on the ground of subjectivity, Representative *Buss* just as much as we."[63] The general message of most of the liberals' statements was that Baden was in grave danger because of "jesuitical" and "ultramontane" machinations, and that supporting dissenters' rights was an excellent way to resist such trends.[64] Thus, given the preponderance of liberals in the chamber, it was no great surprise that, when the vote was held on whether the *deutschkatholische* petitions should be forwarded to the Grand Duke's government with the "*urgent recommendation*" that the petitioners' requests be satisfied, this recommendation passed by a vote of thirty-six to twenty-six.[65]

Significantly, in this debate on the dissenters it had been left to the Lower Chamber's conservatives to point out that liberals caught themselves in a contradiction when they demanded freedom of religion for those who left the Christian churches, even though they had not been particularly eager to work for the equality of non-Christians. Christoph Trefurt, one of the very few pro-emancipationists who was also a government loyalist, specifically asked Hecker how he could reconcile his previous opposition to equalization of Jewish rights with his indignant demands for equalization of the *Deutschkatholiken*. It was this challenge which prompted Hecker to declare a change of heart with respect to Jewish emancipation, though not quite without ambivalence. For Hecker first turned the accusation around and criticized Trefurt for supporting the rights of Jews "whom one has always reproached for having a separate nationality," while trying to deny rights to the *Deutschkatho-liken*, "our Christian brothers and brothers in name—German and Christian." Yet he also acknowledged that his own position needed to change:

> I must admit that this religious persecution, this repression for the sake of faith, makes quite clear to me what sort of oppression has weighed on the Jews, and from that moment on that I saw the oppression of our *Deutsch-katholiken*, I vowed to vote for the emancipation of the Jews. (Many voices cry bravo.). . . . I was caught in the prejudice of youth, of custom, and now I have returned to freedom. . . . I would not be able to justify it before God and the people to put someone in a worse or lower position, because he cannot worship God as I do, but rather wants to serve Him in his own way.[66]

Both the liberal and the conservative press recognized the significance of Hecker's public change of heart, because of the important leadership role he played among his fellow liberals. The progressive *Mannheimer Abendzeitung* notified its readers that "many previous opponents of emancipation among our delegates have changed their opinion on this matter, and particularly the delegate Hecker has publicly declared in the midst of the debates on the *Deutschkatholiken*, that with respect to Jewish emancipation he has changed his previous views; and so it cannot be doubted that an imposing majority will be for emancipation." The conservative *Mannheimer Morgenblatt*, however mockingly, conveyed the same message: "Now various of the most bitter opponents of emancipation have converted; Mr. Hecker has transformed himself from a Christian Paul into a Jewish Saul; without fail, the great man will carry away the little ones with him."[67]

Jewish Rights

And indeed, so it was. One week after the debate on the dissenters, on August 21, 1846, when debates were reopened on Jewish emancipation, it quickly became evident that the terms in which the debates had for so long been cast had been fundamentally transformed. Previously, the debate had centered on whether equality would cause the dilution of difference or whether it should be the reward for such dilution. In the most recent debate on the subject, in February 1845, for example, one anti-emancipationist had summarized the delegates' choices this way:

> The giving-up of nationality is either the prerequisite or the result of so-called emancipation. . . . We and all diet decisions since 1831 demand certain concessions, the clearing-away of the obstacles inhibiting equalization,

we attach to emancipation *conditions that must be fulfilled beforehand*, but the petitioners and their Christian friends say: emancipate us *first*, and then the fulfillment of your demands will come of its own accord; for this is the necessary effect of emancipation.[68]

In August 1846, the operative question had changed entirely. Now, what was at stake was deciding between the realization of the principle of religious freedom, on the one hand, or the maintenance of a Christian state, on the other. As the pro-emancipationist Anton Christ put it,

> Choose one or the other of the two opposing possibilities, either take a stand for emancipation or against it. In both cases, what is at stake is the principle of religious freedom, and here everyone is consistent if he says, I demand sameness [*Gleichheit*] of religion in a state, or if he says, in relation to the state it is not necessary for all members to have the same religion. . . . If one starts from the principle [that the religion of the individual should be irrelevant to the state], then one can with respect to the Jews no longer be in doubt even for a moment, that one must also declare them to have equal rights in relation to the state.[69]

In short, Christ urged consistency from those who a week earlier had propounded the notion that there was more than one acceptable way to be a person of faith. Newly fervent for the cause of emancipation, Hecker similarly called attention to the way the emergence of dissent and the conservative attack on it had changed the ways Jewish emancipation needed to be conceptualized. He too, as his colleagues well knew, had once been ambivalent about Jewish rights. "But in the meantime," he said, "an event has intervened, that challenged everyone to think more closely about persecution for the sake of faith."[70]

Other liberal pro-emancipationists sought to provoke still-reluctant liberals in similar ways, particularly by focusing on the concept of the "Christian state" which had in previous years so successfully been used to justify the maintenance of Jews' political inequality. Some pro-emancipationist liberals had already in earlier debates argued that a truly Christian state was one in which everyone was treated in accordance with the Christian values of love and justice, not one in which everyone had to be Christian, and this kind of argument recurred in 1846 as well. But now that religious conservatives had given the idea of the Christian state a new, and for most liberals, quite frightening meaning, there was a greater pugnaciousness in liberals' comments on the term. One expressed gratitude that his opponents' concept of a Christian state did not exist, for, he charged, "it would necessarily lead to an inquisition or to hypocrisy."[71] Another delegate compared the idea of the Christian state to the Ottoman Islamic state—where Christians were being persecuted.[72] Others provocatively equated the Christian state with the notion of the "theocratic state" more typically evoked in standard criticisms of Jews, pleading instead for a "state of law" (*Rechtsstaat*) in which the state "has no right to demand of its citizens . . . that they belong to a particular faith."[73]

A newly elected radical liberal delegate, Johann Georg Christian Kapp, played out the comparison between the new conservative Roman Catholicism and the old stereotypes against Judaism with particular wit and rage. Reminding his listeners that German Jews had modernized their faith over the centuries just as most German Christians had, Kapp responded to the venomously anti-emancipationist liberal Ludwig Weller—who had just warmed over all the hoary clichés about Jews' rigidity, self-segregation, and arrogance vis-à-vis Christians—by contending that the Roman Catholic church was just as separatist as Weller claimed the Jews were, and that conservative Catholics also thought themselves to be the chosen people of God. "According to this theory of exclusivism the state government would, to be *consistent*, finally also have to take away the rights of all who belong to the Roman church, insofar as it wants to be exclusive." But Kapp went on to note that "the humorous side of such consistency harbors a tragic seriousness."[74]

Another effect of the reconfiguration of Baden's religious landscape was that liberals came to feel differently about "public opinion." The petition storm had driven home for liberals their distance from "the people," and this had clearly created an awkwardness in many liberals around the old tactic of wrapping themselves in the cloak of "public opinion" when they sought to justify their resistance to Jewish emancipation. Furthermore, the entire conservative mobilization against dissent had revealed that the strategic deployment of anti-Jewish rhetoric in general was a gambit that was now being used more effectively by the right—not just against dissent, but also against liberalism itself, and the issues dear to its heart. (Typical devices designed to rile up public opinion against liberalism and its values, for example, were to call liberal newspapers "Jew-papers," and to portray mixed Catholic-Protestant marriages as just as "unacceptable" as a Christian-Jewish marriage.)[75]

As a result, liberals were suddenly theorizing the gaps in their relationship to the populace as never before, and commenting on the phenomenon of mass politics and its vulnerability to demagogic manipulation. Alexander von Soiron, for example, suggested that "there is also a sort of public opinion that one shouldn't really recognize."[76] Lorenz Brentano called on his colleagues to "have the courage to resist public opinion when it wants something unjust . . . especially when public opinion has been led astray. For who represents public opinion? Surely not those who consider themselves justified when they persecute another because of his faith."[77] And Kapp announced that Jews "are almost only hated in those places where one *fanaticizes the people against them*," and reported that conservatives were already plotting how to use the pro-emancipationist stand the chamber was to take that day to embitter public opinion against liberals.[78]

But not all liberals were convinced. The diehard anti-emancipationist Weller, although he had favored religious freedom for dissenters, was not to be converted in his feelings about Jews. He thus reiterated the old argument that Judaism was not simply a religion like any other, but that, because of the peculiar fusion of the religious and the political in Judaism, Jews were also a separate nation:

> The Jew is completely incapable of amalgamating himself with the peoples among whom he lives, so that a homogeneous whole can emerge, he remains a Jew in all situations. . . . The history of this tribe shows that his religion teaches him that he is of nobler blood than all the other children of the earth. . . . The Jew always marries only among his own kind, and therefore any blending is impossible. . . . If we allowed Jews to take part in the government, we would not equalize them, we would be founding a new aristocracy of birth. We have enough aristocrats of birth in our state, I . . . therefore vote against emancipation.[79]

This line of argument, however, met with immediate resistance from Kapp:

> What is at stake here are primarily two points, one is the question of *freedom of conscience*, and in this my honored friend will agree with me, *this* can no longer be a concern, the matter is finished, and only a *hypocrite* could base himself on imperative dogmas and attack Jews on the basis of their faith. The second point is that the Israelites form a *different race* [*andere Race*] that keeps itself separate.

Pushing on Weller's inconsistencies, Kapp pointed out that

> when the Israelite becomes a Christian, one allows him [political] rights without further ado. So if the source of the evil . . . lay in the tribe, then also the converted Israelite could not receive the rights that had been denied him. . . . Conversion does not change the tribe. Therefore the denial of rights cannot only lie in the *nature of the tribe*.

Kapp then went on to expose the complaint of anti-emancipationists that Jews were unwilling to amalgamate as the sham that it was, for no one actually feared amalgamation more than opponents of emancipation: "The difficulty of *amalgamation* lies primarily in the obstacles, with which the so-called *Christian state* opposes those who believe differently. This state seems to fear the visible *interbreeding of races* almost as much as the *intersection of faiths.*"[80]

Kapp's defense of Jewish rights was paradoxically generating new problems, for in putting pressure on his opponents to reject the realm of religion as the site of difference, Kapp suggested a new site: that of race. Related images were evoked in Hecker's speech. While calling for fellow liberals to join him in his admittedly belated conversion to a pro-emancipationist position, Hecker sympathized with those who had difficulty accepting fully the new principle of religious freedom for everyone, for, as he put it, "I know well, that it makes a peculiar impression upon one with Christian Germanic sensibilities, when he sees the sharply etched Oriental face suddenly invading."[81] For the time being, however, these novel subtexts did not affect the fundamental issue at hand: the debate over religious freedom.

In the end, it was the way in which the "Jewish question" had been recast that caused the answer to that question to be a new and different one as well. Characteristically, it was again the conservative Catholic Buss who articulated more clearly than any other the new division between defenders and opponents of emancipation: The choice no longer revolved around whether "*Gleichheit*" (sameness, equality) would be the precondition or the reward for overcoming difference. Now the choice was: support for complete religious freedom *or* support for the hierarchical Christian state. Thus the anti-emancipationist Buss echoed the pro-emancipationist Christ's remarks, but from the opposite perspective. Both sides were aware how much the terms of debate had shifted. Buss said:

> The question of emancipation, which is a source of embarrassment for many a political character, is not so for me. Someone who starts from the principle that our states are Christian states, and that also Baden is still a Christian state, who strives to restore the quality of a Christian state, which has in recent times become completely weakened under the impact of legal religious indifference, cannot be for emancipation. But all who are for this religious indifference, all who advocated the civic recognition of Rongeanism, must, if they are to be consistent, vote for the emancipation of the Jews.[82]

Though they disagreed with Buss, many delegates agreed with his summary of the choices facing them. A number of previous opponents of equal rights for Baden's Jewish community indicated clearly that—although they retained deep ambivalence about Jews and about some aspects of emancipation—the changed context was leading them to support emancipation for the first time; other long-standing anti-emancipationists simply voted quietly for emancipation, without making any speech at all. Thus, for the first time in its history, on August 21, 1846, the Lower Chamber voted for Jewish emancipation by a margin of thirty-six to eighteen.[83]

Jewish observers across the German lands were absolutely delighted, and expected that Jewish emancipation would soon become law in Baden. For example, the *Allgemeine Zeitung des Judenthums* in Leipzig argued that "it is true that the vote has as yet no immediate practical result; . . . [and] that until its realization it must still pass through three authorities. . . . But let us not forget, that in Baden it is *usually* a matter of *principle* rights, less of material [rights]. . . . Restrictions, reservations, clauses may therefore become popular, but the principle has been decided, it has conquered, and after a short time it will also conquer them."[84] But as it turned out, these observers were wrong, for precisely at this moment when Baden's famed liberals were being most visionary, their hands were tied. The grand duke, his ministers, and the Upper Chamber stalled and failed to entertain the Lower Chamber's recommendation.[85] Although emancipation was partially implemented in the revolutionary year of 1849 (indicatively, it was understood as part of a larger move to make political rights independent of religious affiliation and to assure that churches should have no influence on the state), there were many post-revolutionary setbacks and it was not until 1862 that Jews were given complete equality with Christians in Baden.

Indeed, the most immediate effect of the vote was to inspire outbreaks of anti-Jewish violence in a number of Badenese communities.[86] And as Kapp had predicted, conservative Catholics tried to turn this popular hostility to their own advantage. The *Süddeutsche Zeitung für Kirche und Staat* reported smugly that "the vote on the issue of Jewish emancipation has generated a great deal of hostility among the people, something that can be excused by anyone who is familiar with the situation in places where Christians and Jews live beside each other and therefore knows how much the domestic welfare of the latter is ever increasing at the expense of the former."[87] The paper noted with glee how in the wake of the vote, "the popular halo of certain people has been severely tarnished" and how "every now and then one of our parliamentary men-of-the-people trembles in fear of losing his popular glory."[88] Increasingly, liberals returned the favor—comments about how conservative or "jesuitical" forces were fanaticizing the masses against Jews became standard elements in liberals' arguments.[89]

It was not then, at bottom, the emergence of the *Deutschkatholiken* themselves that made religious freedom a matter of principle for liberals, and led them to change their minds about Jewish rights. Rather, it was the conservative counterattack on liberalizing tendencies within Christianity, the conservative assault on free choice in matters of faith and love, culminating in the stricter handling of mixed marriages and in the petition storm and the rhetoric in and around the dissolution of the chamber, that had confronted liberals with the reality of conservative Catholicism's increasing political effectiveness. It was this that provoked Baden's leading liberals into taking an emancipatory stand. In short, it was above all liberals' hatred of conservative Catholicism, and not a commitment to universal equality, that led them to reframe how they understood the "Jewish question," and to revise their previous stance on it.

Jewish Difference

Since the Lower Chamber's newly embraced advocacy of emancipation had no immediate effect, what was the long-term relevance of the Lower Chamber's debates? As Joan Scott has pointed out in a different context (in explaining the relevance of deconstructionist methods for gender history), meaning is created through the establishment of oppositions, and the "positive definition" of a particular term always rests "on the negation or repression of something represented as antithetical to it." She therefore argues that "contests about meaning involve the introduction of new oppositions, the reversal of hierarchies, the attempt . . . to challenge the natural status of seemingly dichotomous pairs, and to expose their interdependence and their internal instability."[90] Such dynamics were also at work in the Badenese debates about Christians and Jews. Only as long as Christianity was perceived of as internally coherent, and "Jewish nationality" could be presented as absolutely antithetical to the "Christian state," could liberals consent to the exclusion of Jews from rights granted to Christians.

When the rise of Catholic neoorthodoxy and the emergence of the *Deutschkatholiken* exposed the internal instability of Christianity, the dichotomous opposition between Christians and Jews was necessarily destabilized. Nevertheless, as Scott indicated, contests about meaning also tend to introduce new oppositions. As the debates in Baden showed, the very same dislodging of entrenched oppositions both caused liberals to advocate emancipation *and* caused a subtle new nuance to creep into the discussion. It was not exactly racism, in the sense that racial arguments against Jews would be more fully developed in the second half of the nineteenth century.[91] But there was indisputably a new tone that no delegate in the chamber had bothered to bring up in any of the earlier discussions. In pressing their opponents to downplay the significance of Jews' religious difference from Christian Germans, two of the most radical delegates volunteered an alternative site for difference in their references to the "Oriental face" and the "nature of the tribe."

As the work of Sander Gilman, Yosef Hayim Yerushalmi, and others has shown, a focus on physiognomy and on blood, on visible and/or biological markers of Jewish "difference" had been available for centuries.[92] But such language was quite infrequent in the first half of the nineteenth century, at least within the dignified forum of a diet, and this makes it valuable to attend to the specific context in which it surfaced.[93] The debates in 1840s Baden show that it was the competing (and yet mutually entangled) pressures for secularization and religious renewal, and especially the widespread conflict over what it meant to be Christian and what exactly justified Christian superiority over Jews, that caused the combatants to push on each other's logic and to attempt to sort out where exactly Jewish "difference" lay. Significantly, it was precisely liberals' (also self-identified *pro*-emancipationists') long-standing collaboration in elaborating that there was some discomfiting Jewish difference which they could not quite name that caused the move away from theological explanations for difference to leave intact a potent residue of assumptions that Jewish difference from Christian Germans might lie elsewhere . . . a conceptual vacuum in which old notions of Jewish national difference would be refurbished with new scientific-sounding racial overtones.

For all the reasons suggested here, the widely shared model of an increasingly pro-Jewish trajectory of Germany-wide liberalization running from 1780 to 1870, followed by an antiliberal, antisemitic countermovement from 1870 on, requires fundamental revision. Too many historians have taken liberal commitment to universal emancipation for granted, assuming—as one put it—that the eventual inclusion of Jews in the circle of those who had equal rights was simply a matter of "erosion."[94] But in practice, the boundaries of that circle were not extended without heated contest, and, as the Badenese situation suggests, often such contest emerged out of an unexpected conjunction of circumstances. Furthermore, even when—through such a conjunction of circumstances—many liberals did come to see Jewish equality as a matter of fundamental human rights, liberals' participation in confirming that equality and difference were irreconcilable had already done lasting damage. The very terms in which liberals advocated emancipation contributed to the persistence of anti-Jewish sentiment throughout the supposedly liberalizing period. Liberalism itself was part of the problem.

Lest this documentation of liberal complicity in sustaining negative attitudes toward Jews be misunderstood as further evidence for the supposedly peculiar illiberalism of German liberals, however, it is important to position the Badenese debates within a larger historiographical context.[95] An enormous body of literature assumes that the tragedy of German history resides in large measure in an insufficient absorption of Enlightenment ideals, and/or in the conceptual inadequacy of the German Enlightenment in comparison with its presumably healthier western counterparts, an inadequacy that was carried forth into nineteenth-century German liberalism. Yet a smaller, though growing, body of scholarship has been interrogating those supposedly normative western Enlightenments, documenting the disturbing authoritarianism and intolerance of religious differences—not to mention racism—intrinsic to them.[96] Thus, for example, in analyzing the French Enlightenment, Arthur Hertzberg has argued that "there was a price on the Jew's ticket of admission into society":

> Having accepted, and even having helped to create, the new premise that the Jews ought to be admitted into society, theologians and economists had agreed without any doubt that they were accepting not of the concretely existing one, but of some new Jew that they would remake, or who would remake himself, in the image of what they thought he ought to be.[97]

Similarly, Shmuel Trigano has analyzed "the philosophico-political impasses of the Enlightenment conception" and criticized "the violent and radical negation of the Jew in the man which one does oneself the pleasure of emancipating."[98]

If historians of German liberalism and of Jewish emancipation in Germany take these findings of western-focused scholars seriously, it appears that anti-Jewish sentiment in Germany was not so much due to the failure of a "western-style" Enlightenment to take proper hold there, but rather to a contradiction at the heart of the western ideal itself. It was not, then, the impotence of liberalism in Germany that caused difficulties for those who were disenfranchised, but rather liberalism's own fundamental duality: its simultaneous tolerance and intolerance—the elastic, always potentially inclusive aspects, and the continually contested and renegotiated exclusions which characterized it as well. Another key lesson emerging from a close examination of the Badenese debates is that while the 1840s seem like an era of growing liberalization, the reason they seem that way is actually in large part because of the growing effectiveness of conservative forces—especially conservative Catholic forces—who provoked the liberals. As the next chapter will explore, the conjunction of these two phenomena—liberalism's intrinsic inconsistency, and liberals' growing hostility to a resurgent religious neoorthodoxy—had entirely different, but nonetheless similarly profound, complex, and contradictory consequences for yet another disenfranchised group: women.

3

(WO)MEN'S EMANCIPATION AND
WOMEN'S DIFFERENCE

IN THE LAST few years it has become an established consensus among German women's history scholars that the first organized German women's movement had its origins in the religious dissenting movement of the 1840s.[1] The strong support for women's equality voiced by the dissenting movement's male leaders, the voting rights granted women by many dissenting congregations, and especially the proliferation of activist and social-service women's clubs within and alongside these congregations, make this a compelling claim. In Baden, women constituted approximately 30 percent of the membership of the dissenting congregations; elsewhere in Germany women often made up 40 percent of the members.[2] This high level of female participation was undoubtedly a response to male leaders' active concern to address and include women. Women's organization of fundraising and charitable activities were essential both to the survival of the movement, and to its practical people-serving vision, and these activities, in turn, gave women's rights activists an institutional base and a great deal of leadership experience. As one contemporary noted, among the important achievements for which *deutschkatholische* congregations could take credit was also the "*lifting-up of the female sex*, through expanded participation of the same in childraising and service to the poor, through women's clubs, [and] through the ... free speech they have been granted."[3] Similarly, the most famous women's rights activist in nineteenth-century Germany, Louise Otto, remarked in 1847 that "it is above all the religious movement [of the dissenting congregations] to which we are indebted for the rapid advance of female participation in the issues of the times."[4]

A close examination of dissenters' sermons, tracts, and newspaper essays, however, both in Baden and elsewhere in Germany, reveals a far more ambiguous and confusing phenomenon. The dissenting movement's male leaders were certainly intensely preoccupied with analyzing and debating gender relations. But as they did so, they mobilized many different, indeed contradictory, images of womanhood, thereby complicating and undermining their own feminist demands in subtle, but unmistakable, ways. Male dissenters routinely called for greater equality for women within marriage and for a broadening of women's spheres of activity. But their calls for women's emancipation were always coupled with a celebration of marital companionship and with a reaffirmation of women's difference from men.

The belief in gender difference was and is, in and of itself, not *necessarily* oppressive to women. Almost everyone in 1840s Germany—though, crucially, as chapter 5 will show, not entirely everyone—thought women and men were, by nature, different, and that that was as it should be. (Significantly, however, since nature was hard to read, they disagreed on what the difference consisted of.) Especially in light of centuries of denigration of "woman's nature," the new validation of women's (purportedly) distinctive moral qualities ushered in by Enlightenment and Romantic thinkers and put forward with particular fervor by the religious dissenters, was welcomed also by many women. Countless activist women sought to develop and extend the ideas about women's special qualities many male thinkers had come to ascribe to women in order to buttress their own demands for more egalitarian marriages and/or a greater range of acceptable activities. For these women, the prevailing insistence on gender differences seemed an appealing ground from which they could press their political claims, as well as develop a greater sense of self-worth.

But too often, the description of the difference between the sexes slid over into a constricting prescription. Any woman overstepping the bounds of "proper" female behavior was castigated as unnatural and immoral, as were men who acted "inadequately" masculine. And as we shall see, the dissenters did indeed envision gender difference in these ultimately quite limiting ways. Most important, while dissenters generally rhapsodized about women's unique capacities and characteristics, with striking frequency there was another undercurrent as well. For in dissenting texts, women appear as both a source of salvation and a source of danger, as both loyal and seducible, vulnerable and unreliable.

These contradictory valences can best be explained when texts by male dissenters are read against the background of the context in which dissent emerged.[5] It was, after all, the two-decade-long history of fierce battles over sex and marriage pitting first Catholic reformers, and then political liberals, against a reviving Catholic neoorthodoxy, that caused the *deutschkatholische* movement to be born in the first place. Not only did the emergence of *deutschkatholische* congregations inspire the related protest movement of Protestant Friends of Light to launch their own "free congregations"; the problem of Catholic neoorthodoxy, especially in light of neoorthodox views on mixed marriages, also formed a frequent theme among Protestant dissenters, and was certainly a major factor in each group's ability to attract adherents from the other confession, and ultimately, for the two movements formally to merge. Whether originally Protestant or Catholic, dissenters were united in their hatred of the new authoritarianism gaining ground within the Catholic church. As one formerly Protestant Badenese dissenter put it in 1846, "The action of the Jesuits has resulted in the reaction of the *Deutschkatholiken*."[6] Dissenters were only the most recent, and most radical, incarnation of the phenomenon of Christian anticlericalism in Germany.

The complicated ways gender figured in dissenting rhetoric makes most sense when this context is kept in mind. My goal here, then, is not to make a hindsight-inspired fuss about mid-nineteenth-century dissenters' misogyny, and to measure them by present-day standards. Rather, the point is to show, by reconstructing the imaginative world dissenters inhabited, how religious polarization around sexual matters could both produce a feminist vision, *and* complicate that vision. However paradoxically, what becomes clear from a close reading of male dissenters's writings on gender relations is that the battle against the religious right's views on sex and marriage both spurred dissenters to seek to emancipate women—*and* to be exceedingly anxious about whether women were worthy of that effort.

There were various reasons for dissenters' interest in greater equality between the sexes. One important cause was the feminization of religion already being remarked upon in the first half of the nineteenth century.[7] Women were understood to be the backbone of the traditional Christian churches, and no upstart religious movement could afford to ignore this constituency. Another significant reason lay in the dissenters' democratic and anti-authoritarian tendencies, and their rejection of distinctions between clergy and laity. As the interest in advancing women's equality shown by the contemporaneous movement of Reform Judaism reveals as well, there seemed to be an almost necessary relationship between calls for women's emancipation and challenges to traditional religions. This was both because of the perceived links between women and religiosity, and because the questioning of traditional authority arrangements implicit in a critique of traditional religions invariably called all forms of authority and inequality into question. This phenomenon took on even greater significance because of the dissenters' belief (widely held at the time, also by those elsewhere on the ideological spectrum) that the family was a microcosm of society and that social transformation could only be grounded in self-transformation: Democracy had to be practiced in the private realm if it was to have any hope of conquering the public realm. But in order to understand why the dissenters' calls for women's emancipation were also consistently embedded in glorifications of marital partnership and of women's special difference from men, and why that delight in women's difference at times slid over into more negative representations of female nature, it is necessary to examine what dissenters did with the legacy of liberal hostility to Catholic neoorthodoxy they had inherited—beginning with their frequently articulated disgust at the institution of priestly celibacy.

Rights of Men

Outrage about priestly celibacy was a major motif in dissenting rhetoric. Enforced celibacy was thought to emasculate men in two ways: It was a sign of their lack of independence, their pathetic subservience to other men within a hierarchical system, and, quite concretely, it meant that they were deprived of any (legitimate) sexual expression. In 1845, in his earliest efforts to mobilize interest in dissent, Johannes Ronge, the founder of *Deutschkatholizismus*, challenged German fathers whether they really wanted to let their sons be "humiliated" into becoming "Romish choirboys."[8] Similarly, in an open letter he circulated to his fellow Catholic clergymen, urging them to convert to his movement, Ronge asked whether they really would "choose supinely to remain in circumstances of blind surrender to your judgment?" He called on them to resist "the pain of blinded, passive slavery to Rome," to stop behaving like "automata," and to "become men, filled with a sense of your great dignity as such." He accused them of being "hirelings of the pope" rather than "men full of ardour to exhibit your convictions in your actions—to turn your words to truth and actual realization." Finally, describing love and marriage as "the holiest concerns," Ronge reminded them of how they had been deprived of "the stamp of open manliness" by being robbed of their right "to the possession of a virtuous wife."[9]

In light of these preoccupations, it was no surprise that dissenters and their liberal supporters rushed to congratulate those Catholic priests who joined the movement so they could get married. They exulted in the courage these men displayed in freeing themselves from the church's "coercion of conscience, slavery of conscience" by making such a "manly, truly Christian decision: to choose a wife."[10] The only priest to take this step in Baden was the former anti-celibacy activist and professor Heinrich Schreiber; his case, however, encapsulates all the elements of the broader phenomenon.

After having been excommunicated for publicly joining the *Deutsch-*

katholiken in March 1845, Schreiber proceeded a year later to marry the woman who had been his housekeeper, Maria Anna Fuchs. At least three liberal, pro-dissent newspapers greeted this move with admiration and exhilaration. In doing so, they confirmed the ongoing centrality of male sexual rights in the liberal agenda. The *Seeblätter* in Constance, for example, edited by the *Deutschkatholik* and radical liberal Joseph Fickler, proclaimed in its lead story on May 21, 1846, that

> we are delighted that the courageous man, who gained the agreement and respect of the great majority of thinking people by taking the first step— speaking his conviction openly, without hesitation and fear—has also transcended the second hesitation which usually keeps weakminded people stuck at the half-way point.—If I have the courage to speak the truth, then I must also have the courage to act accordingly.[11]

With this introductory announcement, the *Seeblätter* located Schreiber's action in the context of a prevalent left-liberal concern with turning words into deeds, and with becoming a wholly committed person—one of the "wholes," in the terminology of the day, rather than one of the cowardly "halves."[12] Well known throughout Baden for having spoken out against priestly celibacy in his lectures and books, Schreiber was now welcomed into the fold of those men of courage who put their bodies on the line as well. The *Oberrheinische Zeitung* in Freiburg similarly stressed how Schreiber's marriage demonstrated the way the dissenting movement offered concrete solutions to long-standing anti-Catholic complaints:

> Whoever . . . does not have the courage to reject celibacy *also through the deed*, him we consider a weak man, unsuited to advance the great cause of *Deutsch katholizismus*. . . . What a desolate enlightenment that is, that is not man enough to bring life into harmony with the refined concepts. Therefore honour to that man, who does not stop at the half-way point, who . . . listens more to the voice of God than to the old wives' prattle of fear, prejudice and anxious hesitation.[13]

Such remarks show clearly how male liberals' and dissenters' self-understanding was intimately bound up not only with a certain history of anti-Catholic preoccupations, but also with certain attitudes toward masculinity and that, indeed, these two matters were intricately interrelated. Dissenters, whether initially Protestant or Catholic, established, confirmed, and defined their own masculinity by attacking Catholicism. At the same time, their male listeners and readers were continually provoked to display their manliness by embracing their right to sexual expression, by (quite literally) embracing women, and they were constantly enjoined that this end could best be achieved if they embraced dissent.

Spiritualizing Sex

Another key element evident in Ronge's rhetoric and in the applause for Schreiber's marriage was dissenters' felt need to present marriage, and by extension marital sexuality, as something holy. The overheated language used by religious reformers and political liberals in the earlier battles with religious conservatives was taken up again, and indeed developed further, by the liberals' dissenting heirs. Dissenters were livid that—as the Mannheim congregation told Archbishop Hermann von Vicari—"through the *commandment of priestly celibacy, marriage in and of itself* is, strictly speaking, branded as an *immoral* relationship."[14] In response to this perception of the Catholic stance, one dissenting newspaper referred to sexual love as a "sacred yearning," a "so mighty drive, permeating living organisms by the laws of Nature's Founder."[15] Ronge announced that "true love," that is, "the union of two in one," "leads to God and sanctifies and redeems in him."[16] Others argued that marriages were "the holiest natural relationships," "the holiest ties," or that a loving marriage was a "God-ordained happiness" and a "heaven on earth."[17] A collection of dissenting songs celebrated matrimonial love as "heavenly balsam" and "heavenly pleasure," and countless dissenters described marriage as "paradise."[18]

A particularly good example of this general phenomenon emerges in the writings of Friedrich Albrecht, who ministered to the *deutschkatholische* congregation in the town of Stockach, in the deeply Catholic south of Baden.[19] For example, in his *"Ave Maria"* (Hail Mary) sermon, Albrecht proclaimed: "I have already said this before, that I do not share the belief in Jesus' divinity and in his supernatural birth, and therefore I also do not recognize the consequences of this belief."[20] Significantly, humanizing God and affirming the sanctity of human sexuality were, for Albrecht, integrally related. Other Albrecht sermons make this connection even more clear. In a sermon on *"Erbsünde"* (Original Sin), Albrecht elaborated:

> The manner in which a human child is created is considered so immoral, so sinful, so unworthy, that [the churches consider Jesus] to be insulted if one does not make an exception in how [he] became human. Except for Jesus . . . every human being thus owes his existence to sin. That I live, that you live, is proof of the sin of our parents. Against no other church doctrine has my heart so revolted as against this one.

Commenting on how conservative Catholics associated sensuality not only with sin but also with secularity, Albrecht further exclaimed: "Everything that provides sensual pleasure, must therefore be a sinful worldly lust from the devil. . . . What a slandering of marriage!" And more clearly than any other dissenter, Albrecht articulated the standard *deutschkatholische* spiritualization of nature: "For is not the law of Nature the law of God? Whoever then wants to find something unholy, unclean in the eternal law and its governing order, does he not blaspheme God, who gave the law as it is, who designed the order in such a way?"[21]

Similarly, in his "statement of faith" expressed as a series of sonnets, *Glaube, Hoffnung, Liebe* (Faith, Hope, Love), Albrecht asserted that "Love remains the highest good of all." The (marital) sexual subtext was unmistakable, as was the effort to spiritualize that sexual love. Albrecht announced that "Fidelity consecrates the hot desire of the senses/ The rush of bliss becomes love's revelation/ As fruit of love the child becomes conceived," and concluded that "Love sanctifies all struggle of the spirit/ The universe itself—'thout love it would be lost/ For Love is God and only loving is living."[22] In a sermon delivered at a dissenting marriage service, Albrecht was even more explicit, for, as he put it with inimitable circular logic, "if love blesses the bond, . . . then this love will . . . ennoble all those pleasures, through which pure lust unfortunately lets so many people sink into animalistic rawness, into the sweet revelations of *a love made holy.*"[23]

Previously, church reformers and political liberals in Baden had simply insisted that sexual relations were *natural*; dissenters' insistence that sex was *divine* raised the debate to a new level. The new rhetoric was a logical response to the routine denigration of human sexuality among conservative Catholics as well as Protestants;[24] it was a logical response especially to the increasingly central place of sexual matters in Catholic conservatives' assaults on humanist forms of Christianity. Catholic conservatives, for example, portrayed sexuality even within marriage as profoundly problematic; couples were urged to model themselves on the sexual restraint shown in the marriage of Mary and Joseph.[25] Spouses were warned from the pulpit that "matrimony is no place to be beasts" and that "also between married people . . . lustful licentiousness" was physically and spiritually dangerous: "On the one hand it debilitates primarily young spouses and makes them sickly weaklings, and on the other hand it produces a series of children who carry the sin of the parents within them."[26]

Conservatives used sexual rhetoric to denigrate dissent the moment it emerged.[27] The influential Badenese ultramontanist Franz Josef Buss, for example, responded to the celebration of dissenters by the liberals he so fervently detested by declaring that "it is not rationalism which confronts us here, it is a disgraceful sensualism, whose wretchedness is glued together with a few rags of humanitarianism of the sort which all lewd people appeal to."[28] Archbishop Vicari, in April 1846, while threatening the Badenese dissenters with excommunication if they failed to return to the fold within four weeks, also challenged the dissenters to ask themselves "whether the lust [to leave the church] had come from God, or rather from world and flesh?"[29] The new conservative Catholic professor Franz Anton Staudenmaier asserted that the dissenters' attitude toward marriage made it into something "exceedingly vulgar" and removed it from "divine grace."[30] Dissenting preachers were called "priests of the flesh" and dissent itself labeled a "religion of the flesh."[31] Dissenters in Heidelberg were accused of being "debauched."[32] The dissenting community in Stockach was accused by its fellow townspeople of all manner of sexual deviance (a campaign that was so successful that the authorities shut down the congregation in 1852).[33] And one disenchanted Mannheim dissenter who returned to the Roman Catholic church announced that dissenters "know no other God than the God of passion and sin."[34]

This was the context in which Ronge declared that his movement's mission was to tell people they need not live in fear of God, that they were not ruined by original sin, but that "we can recognize ourselves as free in God, in purity and sinlessness born of God's love."[35] Because conservatives vociferously denigrated human sexual relations, because conservatives were using sexual rhetoric to denigrate dissent and deny its spiritual validity, dissenters appropriated religious language to defend sexual relations. Their very legitimacy as a spiritual movement turned on their ability to present sexuality in spiritual terms. They worked, in short, to spiritualize sex.

The Religion of Love

For dissenters, marital love was divine. It was also, they argued, the best means to advance the spiritual perfection of the individual, and the best means to transform the whole world into "heaven on earth."[36] The preacher at the Schreiber-Fuchs wedding in Freiburg, for example, declared that the "*marital connection*" was the "*most beneficial,*" "*most noble,*" "most effective means" for the development of "our spiritual and moral perfection, and therewith the means to achieving the highest end-purpose of our existence!"[37] Another dissenting preacher, ridiculing "the poor pious idiots who think an unmarried life is more sacred than marriage!" told his readers that "precisely the combination of man and woman produces the perfect human being; without this connection perfection is much harder to achieve than with it." Marriage was also represented by the *Deutschkatholiken* as a prime vehicle for the transformation of the whole society, for marital love prepared for and enabled brotherly love. One dissenter argued that "a good marriage is simultaneously the fruitful ground on which the highest ideal of humanity grows into beautiful reality, on which all of humankind should grow together into one family joined in justice and love."[38] As Ronge put it, with "the emancipation of love . . . the principle of love, emanating out from marriage and family, will shape all conditions *newly, truly and sacredly*."[39] In short, dissenters sought to preach "the eternal gospel of divine love" and to redefine God as the "Father of Love."[40] They developed, quite self-consciously, a "religion of love."[41]

Without question, dissenters—fully in the liberal tradition—understood marriage as the main site at which social and religious boundaries could be transcended, and the divisive effects of Catholic exclusivism most effectively resisted.[42] In light of their conviction that conservatives' insistence on the irreconcilability of faith differences was a major evil, dissenters, like liberals before them, threw themselves into a strenuous defense of interfaith marriages, while constantly citing Rome's renewed assault on mixed marriages. Carl Scholl, for instance, the main preacher to Mannheim's dissenting congregation, told his listeners that "our era wants love": "Not that love of which Rome speaks in its pastoral letter, while it forbids the love-tie between two hearts if both do not believe as Rome believes! Our era wants a different, true, full, unconditional love! Love that reaches further than faith, love that unites what faith divided! . . . love that creates heaven on earth."[43] Never prone to understatement, Ronge preached that his movement had "restored peace in thousands of families, [the peace] that had been wantonly destroyed through the prohibition of mixed marriages; [the movement] has transformed thousands, who had become alienated from religion and church through Roman hypocrisy, into the most eager members and defenders of the new congregations."[44]

There must have been some truth to Ronge's claims, however, for the relationship between the emergence of the *Deutschkatholiken* in Baden, and the intensity of the mixed marriages conflict there, is striking. The founding of the dissenting congregation in Pforzheim, for example, was said to have been sparked by Rome's "arrogant" opposition to the Badenese state government with respect to mixed marriages.[45] The dissenting congregation in Mannheim repeatedly complained of "the assault on mixed marriages begun and pursued with such stubbornness by the Archbishop of Freiburg," and particularly decried the way "the bond between two hearts is disrupted through violent insistence on educating children in the Roman religion."[46] Mixed Catholic-Protestant couples, moreover, did seem particularly attracted to the *Deutschkatholiken*. Already among the twenty-six founding members of the *deutschkatholische* congregation in Heidelberg were ten who lived in mixed marriages.[47] By the spring of 1846, the Heidelberg congregation had grown to 136 members. Out of a total of sixty-three marriages represented in the congregation, at least twenty-three were mixed.[48] Similarly, of the fourteen couples who joined the Mannheim *deutschkatholische* congregation as couples, nine were mixed; in all likelihood, many more who had officially joined alone also lived in mixed marriages.[49]

Dissenters further argued that the love between a man and a woman was so powerful that it could reconcile not only Protestants and Catholics, but also Christians and Jews. They were especially riveted by one particular case in Prussia. In the city of Königsberg, the authorities persistently resisted the marriage of a Jewish man and a Christian woman, Ferdinand Falkson and Friederike Möller, who ultimately had to get married in England, although this did not stop the Prussian authorities from refusing to recognize their marriage and calling it an "offensive concubinage."[50] The drama of their efforts to marry captured the imaginations of liberals and dissenters across the German lands.[51] One newspaper declared that the Falkson-Möller case was *the* reason people across Germany took such a great interest in the issue of mixed marriages, and the *Mannheimer Abendzeitung* reported that "no event has received more attention in all newspapers."[52]

One explanation for this "unusual amount of interest aroused in the German public" was provided by Falkson himself. He believed the explanation lay in the way dissenters' rights, Jewish rights, the effort to separate church and state, and "the great culture-historical successes which must result from marriages between Jews and Christians" were all closely interconnected.[53] The *Mannheimer Abendzeitung* concurred: "When these marriages become more frequent in Germany and are allowed *by all the states*, then also *all barriers* will *fall*, that . . . have been erected between Christians and Jews."[54] The dissenting newspaper *Kirchliche Reform* offered a supplementary explanation, and one that illuminated more clearly why dissenters in particular were so attracted to the Falkson-Möller case. The author, a Königsberger like Falkson, writing under the pen name J. Kinorhc, took as his theme the urgent need for an "emancipation of love": "We live in a time of emancipations, or at least the efforts to achieve them. One wants the emancipation of faith; an emancipation of thinking; an emancipation of human rights. But yet one other emancipation impatiently awaits the time, it is: that of love." Moreover, he announced, "in the emancipation of love . . . we see a new guarantee arising for another emancipation that . . . no less impatiently and unavoidably awaits its realization, it is this: the civic emancipation of the Jews." And more explicitly than most dissenters, Kinorhc hastened to explain, "I am not speaking here of love for your neighbor, I am speaking of sexual love, of that divine and deifying love between man and woman."[55] In short, dissenters believed wholeheartedly in the socially transformative powers of marital sexual love and seldom missed a chance to thematize this connection in their writings and speeches.

Dissenters' Calls for Women's Equality

Dissenters' calls for women's equality were closely bound up with this passionate defense of marriage, and their glorification of women's special qualities also makes most sense when it is understood as part of this larger project. Ronge, for example, called attention to this connection when he effused that love "has its sacred and divine birthplace especially in the female breast, and inflames and intensifies it ever anew in the male soul." At another point, he intoned that "we believe in the *greatness and dignity of femininity*, in the *redeeming power of love*."[56] In Mannheim, Scholl made similar connections when he criticized Jesus' and subsequent Christians' validation of the celibate life as "this contemptuous view of marriage, of woman."[57] Scholl further opined that the commandment to be celibate

> degrades the entire female sex . . . because in the final analysis it rests on the conviction that *any* association *at all* with a woman in marriage is, seen strictly, a degradation of the man. . . . But this then means nothing other than that through the woman the man is defiled. The woman herself is therefore something unclean, the woman is ungodly. . . . Is not through this church law the whole female sex declared to be a herd of lepers?[58]

As these remarks suggest, dissenters' championing of women's equality—their insistence that women were human beings meriting human rights—grew in large part out of their overriding zeal to defend women as worthy love objects.

To understand what was unique about the dissenters' proposals, it is helpful to review the contemporary options. Cognizant of calls for women's equality in France and Britain, especially those inspired by utopian socialism and radical Benthamite liberalism, German conservatives *and* liberals worked to justify their own hostility to women's emancipation. As with Jews, so also with women, the basic argument put forward was that those who were in some way "different" from the (white, Christian, male) norm, could not be equal. Conservatives were utterly convinced that women were thoroughly different from men, and unapologetically portrayed women as weaker and more susceptible to sin, and therefore more in need of control.[59] This position fit comfortably with their more general demands for a corporatist, hierarchically organized society—in Wilhelm Heinrich Riehl's words, "The recognition of the necessity of inequality must become the cornerstone of a conception of society as an organic entity."[60] Conservatives also openly denounced any efforts to allow women to step out of the private sphere of the home.[61]

Even though they defined women's supposedly distinctive nature much more positively than did conservatives, liberals seemed to need to insist and elaborate on the existence of gender difference more obsessively than conservatives. Above all, liberals had to do more fancy theorizing in order to reconcile their own demands for greater political freedoms for men with their insistence on the exclusion of women from public life. In order to resolve this philosophical dilemma, they, like many of their Enlightenment predecessors, invoked the laws of nature. Thus, for example, Carl Theodor Welcker, in the liberal *Staats-Lexikon*, indicatively asserted in 1838 that "our more perfect present-day natural-rights and Christian theory of state. . . . makes human rights the foundation of citizen rights, thereby founding the equality of the latter on the equality of the former. And yet such manifold inequality between man and woman, such a great difference in their life-tasks and in their strengths, and consequently also in their legal circumstances is already determined by Nature." The health of the state, Welcker insisted, required the maintenance of sexual difference and inequality, for (here he was explicitly attacking the French Saint-Simonians) "those who by unilaterally following an abstract rule of equality ignore the laws and barriers of nature and demand more rights for women than women, according to those laws and barriers, can possibly want, destroy [that Christian and German family life that is] the holiest and most solid foundation of human and civic virtue and happiness."[62] In short, for mainstream liberals, difference and equality were conceived as irreconcilable.

Given this context, it makes sense that the religious dissenters of the 1840s would seem like a marvelous alternative, for they proposed that difference and equality between the sexes were absolutely reconcilable, and their writings were saturated with calls for women's emancipation.[63] So, for example, while on his first missionary travels, Ronge proclaimed that his movement would

> loosen the seal for the free participation of the female sex in public life . . . and the effects which this free participation will call forth—buttressed by the sanctifying and overpowering might of the female spirit in world history—will be unimaginable and immeasurable. Women should not simply and solely be limited to their family, they should cast their gaze also onto

congregational life, and help create and act there, as in a greater family, and they should look out in the even larger circle that is the nation and should awaken and strengthen holy enthusiasm among the youth for the nation's welfare and salvation.[64]

This sort of rhetoric about the redemptive power of womanhood was closely related to dissenters' insistence on equality within marriage. As Ronge put it, a marriage based on love required "equal rights for both spouses, in the family, as well as before the law." Why? Because "a woman held in tutelage cannot satisfy the free man, cannot complete his being."[65]

While at first this may appear as a great contrast to standard liberal views, on second glance it does quickly become evident that the dissenters' vision of gender equality was inextricable from their dream of a romantic partnership—and for this vision the maintenance of gender difference was just as essential as it had been for mainstream liberals, and their ideal of a more patriarchal family. Ronge, indeed, made his distaste for any blurring of gender differences explicit when he contrasted "that beautiful sanctifying femininity" with (what he called) "emancipation mania": those women who thought it was "necessary to take over completely male spheres of activity and imitate . . . male manners."[66]

Similar tendencies were evident among Baden's *Deutschkatholiken*. Stockach preacher Albrecht, for example, declared that "for the concept of marriage as an intimate togetherness . . . only One foundation is decisive and sufficient . . . it is the equal human dignity and the equal human right that the woman deserves just like the man." Yet Albrecht also assured his listeners that "the whole emotional world of the woman . . . the whole breadth of her duties is utterly divergent from the nature and calling of the man." Thus he intoned: "Blessed is the woman, whose husband is a man, courageous, generous, a man who protects her, a man, with whose strength her mildness unites into beautiful harmony."[67] Albrecht believed that it was precisely the difference between the sexes which drew them to each other, so as to produce a more perfect whole; equality between the spouses was necessary because a man needed a woman to come home to who would actually understand him.[68] Joseph Dominik Carl Brugger, preacher to the Heidelberg congregation, also reminded his listeners that "the Eternal did not create the one and fairer half of humanity so that they could be *slaves*, passive tools in the hand of the stronger and power-hungry man, but rather so that they could be *participating* and *equal* companions to the other half."[69] And Heribert Rau, another preacher to the Mannheim congregation, while announcing that men and women were "equally entitled," also rhapsodized about how "the wild lust for deeds in men . . . the lust

for conflict and battle" were "vanquished by the gentleness . . . dili-
gence . . . sense for beauty and propriety in women." He exclaimed:
"How divinely beautiful is a marital life, in which the *man* exists for his
calling and for his family, while in the house the woman is *everything*. . . . She . . . vitalizes and beautifies the homey hearth, the sanctu-
ary for which the man invests his energies in acting and fighting for the
fatherland."[70] In short, the mutual complementarity of men's and
women's different qualities was presented as *the* basis for a sound marriage. Equality between the sexes was possible precisely when gender
difference was maintained; equality was not meant to liberate women
from the family or their nature-ordained tasks within it.[71] Being in a
companionate, egalitarian, loving marriage (preferably with a dissenting
man) was thought to be the highest and most desirable goal a woman
could attain, the pinnacle of female achievement.

Dangerous Orient(alism)

Strikingly, however, dissenters went to extraordinary rhetorical lengths
to reinforce their views on the glories of heterosexual monogamy, as
though somehow worried that these glories were not entirely self-evident. The majority of dissenting speeches, sermons, and articles addressing women's social status couched their arguments in a particular form:
the historical overview, in which changes in women's lot—beginning
with the ancient Hebrews, Greeks, and Romans, through the early
Christians, Germanic peoples, and Muslims, and on into the nineteenth
century—were surveyed. This generic convention, very much in the rationalist, "evolutionary-anthropological" tradition of the Enlightenment, was exceedingly popular also in the nineteenth century.[72] In the
context of religious conflicts this narrative mode took on a particular,
magnified significance.

Numerous dissenting texts spoke of how dreadful life among the ancient Hebrews had been for women. They argued that the Greeks and
Romans had brought some advances, but that Christianity had brought
women the highest dignity and respect. Others stressed that it was only
the blending of Christian and Germanic custom, as the Germanic peoples took over the Roman empire and adopted Christianity, that
brought women genuine progress. Dissenting minister Brugger in Heidelberg, for example, marveled at "what a beautiful lot, what a glorious
sphere of activity women now have within Christianity and in comparison with those in the Orient and outside Christianity."[73] Rau in
Mannheim similarly informed his listeners that in the generations before

Christ, women had been "the slaves of slaves ... like the Turkish women still today.... Among the Greeks and Romans women were treated with a bit more dignity, but only a bit." He declared that "*the dawn of freedom* came to women only with Christianity," for Christianity "abolished polygamy."[74] Unequivocally, then, having a man all to herself was presented as *the* ticket to women's liberation (a message, incidentally, singularly insensitive to the reality that thousands of women in Germany were not finding, or not choosing, husbands, and that the efforts of many women's rights activists of the time to encourage economic self-sufficiency for women were urgently motivated by the realization that many women would never marry).[75]

Dissenters made the unsavory image of polygamous "Orientals" a favorite theme, and continually associated Jews with the hedonistic, misogynist "Orient." Dissenters liked to remind their readers that "a voluptuous life of the senses, like the Orient produced, had to see in *women* only *an object of pleasure.* ... Among the *Jews*, in accordance with Oriental custom, the woman was in general seen as a lesser being than the man."[76] It was only Christ who had, they announced, "released the soul of the woman from the bonds of Judaism and paganism."[77] They further analyzed the "truly Oriental way of enslaving women also in Mosaism"—especially the "Mosaic law of polygamy"—and praised the good effects brought by the "Greek and Roman example."[78] Albrecht too lamented that the Old Testament allowed polygamy, a condition which was "still to this hour allowed among the peoples of the Orient." He further declared that "the Mosaic law did not just allow polygamy, but at times even required it," but assured his listeners that there had been progress since Christ's coming. "Nowhere was the marriage relationship more intimate than among the old Germanic peoples," Albrecht said, celebrating how "the Occidental man brought trophies of victory to pay homage to the woman of his heart, while the Oriental man maintained the woman and maiden under an offensive yoke of slavery and did not allow her to recognize her own dignity."[79] Ronge also urged his faithful to "compare the Jews, where women had no rights, with the Greeks, among whom they had some rights." Like Albrecht, Ronge believed that although "through Christianity their equal rights were declared," it was "among the Germanic peoples women had the most rights."[80]

The disturbing implications of the German-Oriental contrast repeatedly evoked by leading *Deutschkatholiken* have been incisively exposed by historian Hermann Greive; the form in which dissenters presented their preoccupation with women's status, then, must be evaluated as a central component of this problematic theo-political tendency.[81] In unreflectingly denigrating the "Oriental" cultures of Judaism and Islam, dissenters blithely ignored the implicit aspersions their rhetoric was casting also on their Jewish contemporaries.

It was left to Jewish newspapers to identify the danger of such historico-philosophical exercises in exacerbating anti-Judaism. *Der Israelit des neunzehnten Jahrhunderts* analyzed Christian theologians' ahistorical habit of "dating the genealogy of the soul's nobility from the moment of Christ's birth and presenting the countless peoples who had gone before as bereft of all higher qualities," and *Der Orient* criticized the way "the Christian rationalists of the last decades have, misled by the position of women in the *contemporary* Orient, hatched the false view that the position of women was exactly like that among the Hebrews, who were of course also from the Orient, and this lie gets spread so frequently and so boldly, that it has become a stereotype."[82] Furthermore, dissenters' generic survey failed to acknowledge that Judaism too had been "modernizing" itself, both in general and with respect to women's status. Reform Jews, for example, not unlike Christian dissenters, argued for greater equality for women within Jewish religious life and within Jewish marriages and criticized those elements of Talmudic law which were "an insult to the free personality of women, an insult against religion" (so much so that more orthodox Jews ridiculed the reformers' "chivalrous" efforts to "break a Talmudic lance in honor of the Jewess").[83]

A tiny handful of the more theologically radical dissenters told a more differentiated story and questioned whether Christianity represented an improvement over Judaism. However, they did so less in order to defend Judaism than to denigrate Christianity; according to Protestant dissenter Leberecht Uhlich, for example, "not only the Old Testament gives the woman a lower status than the man, also the New Testament does it."[84] The most radical dissenters pointed out that many of the advances credited to Christianity had actually been pioneered by the ancient Hebrews. Scholl, for instance, argued that "the idea that the woman has the same destiny in relation to God as the man, that she was, like the man, made 'in God's image,' that like the man she should become 'holy' and perfect, is not at all a new Christian idea, but an age-old Jewish idea."[85]

No matter what their position on ancient Judaism, however, dissenters concurred in their disdain for the Muslim "harems" still thought to pervade the "Orient" in the nineteenth century. For example, despite his slightly more thoughtful perspective on Judaism, Uhlich did not refrain from using Turks as a rhetorical foil: "The women of many a slavish tribe in Turkey think it is no problem if they are beaten by the man; that is the custom there," he announced, commenting as well that "polygamy is a leaden weight, which handicaps the progress of all Moham-medan peoples."[86] And Heinrich Thiel, generally regarded as one of the most radical defenders of women's emancipation among the dissenters, also used an unflattering reference to Turks to underscore his point. In mocking anti-feminists' reliance on the "state of nature," he declared that "whether the rooster rules the hen, can determine [the actions of] the reasonable person as little as the Christian can be determined by whether the Turk has a harem."[87]

The dissenters' rhetoric served to underscore the superiority of a mo-nogamous marriage in which equality was understood to depend on sex-ual difference and mutual complementarity. The fact that almost no dis-senting text on women's status was without a reminder to its listeners that "Oriental" polygamy was equivalent to slavery also suggests how mutually constitutive gender identity and national identity (or what we might now call ethnicity) are—how inextricable gender relations are from other relations of differentiation and power.[88] Hyperbole about the oppressions of the Orient allowed the dissenters to displace the very real problem of the sexual double standard in nineteenth-century Ger-many onto a culture outside Europe.[89] It also helped them to locate themselves at the center of Christian Germanic middle-class culture—as men fully in tune with the mainstream consensus. Finally, simultane-ously, dissenters' compulsion to repeat this self-congratulatory narrative device gives evidence of their paramount eagerness to present their movement, and themselves, as God's gift to women. As one dissenting newspaper urged its female readers: "Hang on with gratitude to the re-form of our century [i.e., the dissenting movement], it is that which will ransom you."[90]

The Confessional

A further narrative device employed by dissenters when discussing gen-der relations was to invoke the dangers posed to women by the (sup-posedly) only ostensibly celibate priest; anxieties centered on the con-fessional. In his highly charged appeals to the Catholic-born in his audiences, for instance, Ronge asked whether "German mothers" would "sell their daughters as prostitutes for the servants of Rome," and par-ticularly ridiculed "German men" for not defending their "brides and sisters and daughters" against the "idiot servants of Rome, who inso-lently damage their sacred chastity"; "act like *men*," he demanded, "re-ject Rome!"[91] Because, according to Badenese *Deutschkatholiken*, the institution of priestly celibacy was really a "school of lechery," and be-cause the confessional was for too many priests "a place of the most cunning lasciviousness wrapped in the holy cloak of religion," "those parents to whom the purity of their daughters is dear, are forced to *forbid* them to go to confession."[92]

It is possible that in elaborating on the vulnerabilities of women in the confessional, the dissenters were actually thematizing their *own* sense of vulnerability. Certainly the confessional's role in the church's more general enforcement of "servitude of the spirit" was one of the dissenters' main complaints about Roman Catholicism.[93] Badenese dissenters indignantly labeled the confessional "that torture-chamber of the conscience" and argued that the obligation to confess was "a Roman presumption and tyranny" which "made a farce out of the autonomy of thinking people, [and produced] a loss of self, debilitation and desacralizing of the innermost human being, a repression, enslavement and smothering of the free spirit."[94]

But without question the dissenters' biggest fixation centered on the priest's invasion of the heterosexual dyad, his disruption of matrimonial twosomeness. What dissenters refused to name explicitly was the very real emotional support and often quite beneficial counterbalance to their husbands that priests could offer women.[95] Instead, they confined themselves to making lurid charges. Johannes Czerski, for instance, another of the earliest leaders of the dissenting movement and like Ronge an ex-priest, expressed particular outrage over the way "the young hot-blooded doubter, worrying about his capacity for self-denial, is told when he enters the priestly life: 'You will not have one wife, but you will have one thousand!'"[96] Dissenters warned that in the confessional, priests interrogated women about "the secrets of the marriage bed," or, as Scholl railed—reminding his listeners that priests' power over women could destroy marriages—there "the wife is often handled by the priest as though her body and soul belonged to him!"[97]

And it was in this context that the image of woman as seducible and unreliable appeared. As one dissenting newspaper intoned, "If the woman is not so honorable and chaste, then obviously confessions about sexual sins must from the depths of the heart call forth stimulations and consequences on both sides, where youth and warm blood assert their power. . . ."[98] Ronge was most bothered by the way "the priesthood allows the woman to sin and then makes her into its slave through absolution."[99] And as another contributor to the debates put it, "To marry a woman whose soul belongs to another—young man, consider this carefully—that means to marry adultery along with her." For "privy to the innermost secrets of the woman, [the priest] is the master of her soul. Now there is complete sharing between the husbands, for she has two: to one belongs the soul, to the other the body, but whoever owns the soul also in truth owns the body, for thought has the body in its power."[100] Albrecht similarly declared that "many a woman . . . for whom the confessor means more to her than the husband who loves her, thinks she is no adulteress."[101] And yet another contended that it was "deeply wounding for a man's honor and dignity, to have to share the holiest communion of marriage, the exchange of the most secret thoughts and wishes, with another; to see that edifice, which he thought he had built up in the soul of his wife, destroyed in the confessional."[102]

Dissenters' descriptions of the confessional did manage to convey concern for women's vulnerability and that was no doubt the level at which many people interpreted them. But incontrovertibly, the dissenters' imagery also necessarily evoked a sense of threat for their male listeners and readers, and encouraged a sense of competition between husband and priest. Priests were (contradictorily) portrayed by dissenters—depending on whatever larger point they were trying to elaborate—as both undersexed *and* oversexed, as both emasculated *and* predatory (a phenomenon which bore an uncanny resemblance to the contradictory ways homosexual men would be represented just two or three decades later).[103] Criticizing priests was a way for dissenters themselves to assert their own proper—virile but controlled—masculinity; their male listeners and readers were enjoined to define their masculinity in opposition to the symbol of the priest as well. The clearest implication of dissenting rhetoric was that if men wanted happiness in marriage and fidelity from their wives, they would have to break from Catholicism and join the dissenting movement. As the rhetoric also indicated, however, dissenters were a bit worried about whether women would cooperate with this agenda.

Women's Difference

Dissenters' recurrent apprehension about women's unreliability was, crucially, inextricably intertwined with misgivings about precisely that special difference of woman's nature that they elsewhere celebrated. It was most especially women's purported overemotionality which worried them. The editorial staff of the *Deutschkatholisches Sonntags-Blatt*, for example, expressed grave concern about the way "women have largely—given the predominance in them of emotion over reason—turned with visibly greater energy toward the old faith [than men have]." The *Sonntags-Blatt* was clearly speaking of its old enemy, Catholicism, for it argued that

> the priests of this faith have recognized well that they have little support any more from the enlightened men of the new age. . . . That is why they have focused particularly on women; . . . for in them emotion predomi-

nates, an emotion . . . that is easily aroused by images of heaven and hell and . . . that can be led along the path of religious rapture.[104]

Dissenters were also exceedingly concerned about women's potential influence over their children. Again, then, women were posing a danger to men, this time through their weighty roles as mothers. Albrecht, for example, reminded his listeners that "the salvation of the future depends largely on the mothers. But as long as one finds it praiseworthy for the woman to remain caught in external ceremonial service, as long as one praises her religious habits as piety, for so long also the sons will only become free through the most heated inner struggles."[105] Albrecht's poetry left no doubts that what he meant by "external ceremonial service" were the rituals of Catholicism, "that dazzling deception for dull-witted women."[106] Similarly, the *Sonntags-Blatt* announced that "it is well-known that women exert the greatest influence on the views of their husbands and children through their roles as wives and mothers." The paper expressly sought to advance women's emancipation by recommending that women's education be substantially improved, with particular attention to "history, geography and the study of nature . . . , beside a thorough education in German language and literature. Hereby the capacity for reason will above all be formed and the capacity for judgment in the most important matters of life strengthened." Nevertheless, women's education was not just an end in itself. Rather, the paper argued: "If women were led to the same recognition in their youthful schooling as men, the dominion of the priests would surely come to a more rapid end."[107] As all these remarks suggest, the real life-or-death battle dissenters felt they were engaged in was one between male dissenters and priests, and it was precisely women's difference, in particular their emotionality, that was causing dissenters to fear they might lose that battle.

The writings of Mannheim minister Carl Scholl made this connection between women's weakness and dissenters' fear of failure particularly clear. Scholl's retrospective essay on women's role within dissent brought to the surface what was only a veiled subtext in other dissenters' arguments. In his 1875 essay on "*Die Frauen in der Religion*" (Women in Religion), Scholl reflected on the power of women in their roles as mothers, on the intrinsic link he perceived between women and religion due to women's peculiarly emotional nature, and on the dangers which women thus posed to the unceasingly embattled dissenting movement. Looking back on the heady early days of dissent in the 1840s, Scholl reminded his readers that it had

> above all also been the women, who brought their whole ardour and depth of sensibility and good sense to this movement. . . . The same ones, who up until that time had held themselves quietly and shyly within the narrow

confines of their domesticity . . . gained the courage to step into public, found associations, women's clubs, kindergartens, to organize fund drives, lotteries, all for the sole purpose of advancing a reforming movement, in which they with their childlike nature had immediately sensed and recognized the gospel of a new era.[108]

In fact, Scholl continued, all through the course of history women had exercised an "essential, fundamental and encouraging influence" on religious developments.

But at the same time, Scholl warned, women had also had an inhibiting influence "and thereby have *damaged* religion itself":

> They have done this because far too many of them . . . have been and still are the main pillars of the antiquated faith and customs and thereby of the priesthood and of priestly dominion; they have done it by exercising their influence on the family, . . . by knowing how to restrain or divert both [husband and children] from purified, freer religious views.[109]

Scholl accused women of hiding dissenting literature brought by the mailman and of restraining children from attending dissenting religious instruction. On the one hand, there was a kernel of truth to his complaints, for—especially because of the social pressures on women to be the moral guardians of their families—women were indeed more hesitant to break from traditional religious practices than men were, and were often more hesitant than men to leave their traditional churches in the first place.[110] On the other hand, however, many women clearly had been strong supporters of the movement; and as all the energy the dissenters spent in trying to persuade men to support it too suggests, dissenters were not quite so sure whether men were truly—naturally—as "free-thinking" as they liked to claim. Furthermore, most striking is the way Scholl's overarching goal of discrediting Catholicism seemed to depend on a strong disparagement of women's purported peculiarities.

Scholl used an elaboration of women's difference to attack conservative Catholicism—and the women who supported it. He argued that "the main cause of this often so passionately hostile position of many women toward freer religious perspectives . . . lies, in our view, in the peculiar *affinity* between the character of the old *religion* and the character—that is, the peculiar nature—of the *female being*, the female mind. The old religion was based primarily on ominous dark *emotion*, its wishes and desires, and on the *fantasy* that made itself available to those wishes." Clearly then, women's special nature—which so many dissenters, including Scholl, celebrated—also posed an extreme danger to the embattled dissenting movement. Not only did it cause the movement to fail to attract more female members. Nor did it only create problems because of women's powerful roles as mothers. Women's nature also created threatening problems for husbands. This became particularly apparent when Scholl remarked that "the whole external appearance of the [Catholic] religion, the *rituals*, the *architecture* of the churches, and—not to be forgotten—the exceptional position of the *priesthood*, are all designed to captivate and capture the soul of the woman from this [emotional] side."[111] In the same text, then, Scholl could both hail women's distinct nature, the warm enthusiasm and fervent engagement of women which had been so indispensable to the growth and survival power of dissent, *and* decry the dangers brought to dissent by those very same distinctive qualities.

These contradictory views on women did not only emerge in retrospect, however, but were evident already at the height of the movement. In 1848, when Scholl delivered a speech analyzing the appeal religious dissent held for women—to my knowledge the only *deutschkatholische* speech to address this subject exclusively and in detail—all the conflicting elements of male dissenters' attitudes toward women again came to the fore in crystallized form. In "*Unsere Reform und die Frauen*" (Our Reform and the Women), Scholl began by noting that women had indeed been among the first and most eager members of the fledgling congregations. The explanation for this phenomenon lay above all, Scholl argued, in women's emotional (rather than rational) nature, which caused them to be particularly attracted to religious movements. A further explanation derived from the program of equality and dignity for women promoted by the dissenters. He contrasted this program with the oppressive conditions experienced by women in the society at large, conditions he argued were often legitimated and intensified by the doctrines of traditional Roman Catholicism. In particular, Scholl focused on the ways dissenters' challenges to Catholic doctrine about celibacy, and dissenters' encouragement of marriages based above all on mutual love, were central to the appeal which dissent held for women.

Like other dissenters, Scholl stressed the vulnerability of women under Catholicism, arguing that "*celibacy* degrades individual women who secretly fall victim to individual priests, with whom in the best case they are connected by genuine honest love, but which they cannot declare before the world as legitimate wives. How many thousands of the best human lives have been bent, broken, poisoned, murdered in this way!" Scholl sarcastically analyzed the veneration of the Virgin Mary as well, asking whether

> the church thinks it can make up for [the way it degrades women through the institution of celibacy] by elevating at least *one* woman . . . into heaven! But thereby it forgets the main point that this queen of heaven is after all according to its faith herself again a woman like no other, because she is

supposed to be "immaculately conceived," while all others were born in the dirt of sin! The excommunication of the female sex through celibacy therefore remains intact, despite the queen of heaven and her rapturous veneration.[112]

It was his incisive analysis of the institution of celibacy—as well as his defense of divorce and encouragement of love marriages—that earned Scholl particular favor with feminist historians of the 1980s.[113]

But when Scholl turned to a discussion of the confessional, his analysis revealed other concerns: "Already through her coming into the confessional where she communes with the priest all alone," Scholl intoned, "[the woman] encourages him to make use of his spiritual rights all the more audaciously. And how far this audacity goes, this priestly impudence, this holy shamelessness! What gazes, what questions, what half-shy, half-insolent allusions . . . is the maiden, is the wife, subjected to!"[114] Here Scholl was engaging in the standard *deutschkatholische* tactic of working to goad his male listeners.

Scholl made other rhetorical efforts to unnerve his male listeners, and in these cases the logic of his argument depended in part on a strong differentiation between men's and women's character traits, on a differentiation between "man's predominating intellect, and the woman's feeling, fervor and capacity to give of herself." Scholl had begun his speech disingenuously by simply documenting the appeal dissent had held for women: "Since the first emergence of our efforts it was [the women] who with very special warmth and fervor took up our efforts, who with swift decisiveness declared themselves for [our cause], and signed their names to the lists of our new congregations." But as he continued, his method became clearer:

> If [the women] do not find true satisfaction [in the old church], then they feel an emptiness in their hearts. . . . And if then a religious movement arises which proclaims . . . those principles which the woman had silently needed, and in which she sees the yearning of her soul and spirit fulfilled, then she greets the new ideas as a gospel . . . and does not have the many hesitations and considerations, which do not allow the man to reach a firm resolve. She brings her inborn constancy and self-surrender as her most beautiful dowry into our new congregations, she brings her whole heart, her complete love.[115]

Despite the fact that Scholl carefully stayed away from mentioning body parts and instead focused on the needs of the soul, he nevertheless managed to set up a clear atmosphere of competition between two "men": the old church and the new church, each of whom vied to satisfy the yearning bride. He claimed that his church, the new church, could offer women more satisfaction, and that that was in fact why so many women had joined. This was one further way in which Scholl used sexual innuendo to threaten traditional men.

But the innuendo operated on yet another level. This subtext is only self-evident when Scholl's speech is considered in the context of the ever-increasing preoccupation with manliness in left-liberal circles in the late 1840s. In radical tracts from those years, manliness was always coded as decisiveness, willingness to turn ideas into action. Nothing was more scorned than sleepiness, cautiousness, indecision, half-heartedness. By portraying women as those able to give of themselves completely, Scholl offered a provocative contrast to men, who "because of so many hesitancies, considerations, little anxieties, because of this and that, because of relatives, because of business clients, because of their superiors and who knows what all else, persist in their previous untrue, and therefore immoral condition."[116] Decisiveness and masculinity were clearly inextricable for Scholl. It would remain a persistent tenet of his thinking; in a sermon delivered twenty years later, Scholl made the connections especially plain: "Whoever feels too constrained in his church, his synagogue, and whoever yearns for a free space, a free religion, should finally collect his courage and decide to take a manly, a moral, a patriotic action. . . . Each of you should ask himself, if it is not finally time to act, time to put an end to this indecisiveness, this vacillating between church and free congregation, this half-ness?"[117]

In sum, then, Scholl used sexual innuendo as well as certain assumptions about gender difference in order to challenge male listeners with *both* the possibility that they might lose their wives to the priests of the old church, *and* that they might lose them to the manly appeal of the new church—while simultaneously insisting *both* that men not allow women to outdo them in devotion to the dissenting cause, *and* insisting that men prove their difference from women. In all these ways, then, Scholl provoked men to demonstrate their own manliness by entering the ranks of the *Deutschkatholiken*. Along the way, Scholl portrayed women both as objects of male desire and male ownership—the pawns in the larger battles waged between men, and as creatures of pure emotion—vulnerable and ultimately unreliable. Scholl's speech, and the conflicting levels at which it operated, provides a compact synopsis of the web of contradictions evident in so many of the male dissenters' texts about women.

The evident prevalence of concern with women's status and feminine imagery in *deutschkatholische* texts made dissent appear to be *the* forum in 1840s Germany in which gender relations could be contested and reformulated. But the crucial role which dissent most certainly played in the early women's rights movement has obscured the other purposes served by the discussion of gender continually carried on by the dissenters. The dissenters, as it turns out, were in many ways more conventional, in terms of both gender and ethnic politics, than most other scholars of the movement have acknowledged. A distrust of and hostility to women not unlike that of their conservative religious enemies resurfaced with conspicuous frequency in their sermons, tracts, and articles, even as they railed against the effects that that distrust and hostility had had in their own lives. Their rhetorical depictions of Jews and Turks, in pseudohistorical narratives indistinguishable from those written by their mainstream contemporaries, revealed a strong affinity with that mainstream, and a profound lack of thoughtfulness about the very religious tolerance they demanded for themselves. The tiny handful of more radical dissenters and religious critics—to be discussed in chapters 4 and 5— who questioned the prevailing stereotypes about Jews and women, showed up the majority of dissenters' failure of imagination.

The dissenters were most definitely directing themselves to their female listeners and readers, but they were as much, if not more so, concerned to address and engage men. Just as (as the next chapter will show) experiments in philosemitism need to be seen as an integral part of intra-Christian conflict, so also the dissenters' experiment in feminism is most helpfully understood as inextricable from the intra-male conflict out of which it emerged. For a major reason for the dissenters' interest in gender issues lay in the legacy of hostility to conservative Catholicism they inherited—and elaborated. The dissenters' defense of women's equality, and their insistence on women's difference from men, were both deeply embedded in their effort to justify women as worthy love objects, just as their glorification of the power of love itself was an impassioned response to conservatives' privileging of celibacy and pronounced distrust of sexual attraction and love as the bases for a marriage.

The less appealing images of women that dissenters also mobilized revealed deeper anxieties. On the one hand, the writings on women provided male dissenters with an important venue for articulating their own anguish at institutional religion's power to shape individuals' understanding of themselves. On the other hand, and conversely, for both formerly Protestant and formerly Catholic dissenters, attacking institutional Catholicism was also a time-honored way to process generalized male insecurities about one's own sexuality and masculinity. Criticizing Catholicism was the most culturally acceptable mode for naming their own distress. I want to propose, then, that the religious dissenting movement of the 1840s, this largest of all pre-revolutionary German protest movements, this movement so fiercely beloved by Badenese liberals that it caused them to change their minds about Jews and to become the advocates of religious egalitarianism for which they have become renowned, was, most seriously and profoundly, concerned with questions of sexuality and masculinity.

And so, while other recent scholars have praised the male dissenters for their decisive pro-woman stance and for creating the context in which organized feminism was first produced in Germany, I believe a more complex and nuanced picture is needed. Placing the dissenting movement in its proper context—the religious conflicts over sex which spawned it, and which caused sexual matters to become some of its central preoccupations, and taking seriously the ambiguous rhetoric about women that other scholars of the movement have ignored, forces us to rethink the roots of German feminism. The point is certainly not to deny the vital relationship between feminism and dissent, but rather to suggest a more equivocal story of the emergence of feminism: by raising questions about the extent to which the dissenting movement's literature on the emancipation of women was in fact more centrally concerned with the rights, hopes, and fears of men.

4

PROBLEMATICS OF PHILOSEMITISM

THE 1840s were a crucial moment in the development of Jewish-Christian relations in Germany. One reason for this was that the 1840s were a period of tremendous internal struggle within Christianity. On the one hand, this decade saw the successful revival of conservative theological trends within both Protestantism and Catholicism, as well as the politicization of this religious conservatism; the calculated deployment of anti-Jewish rhetoric was an important feature of the new religious right's bid for political influence.[1] On the other hand, specifically in reaction to this rise of neoorthodoxy, the 1840s also witnessed the emergence of the liberal-left Christian dissenting movement; by leaving the traditional Protestant and Catholic churches, the (male) dissenters often lost the political rights they had previously held, and thereby became similar in status to Jews. One of the most important consequences of this combination of changes within Christianity was that Badenese liberals, many of whom had been long-standing opponents of Jewish emancipation, came to make Jewish emancipation a central plank in their political platform. As liberals came to political power in the revolutions of 1848/49, Jewish emancipation was thus partially implemented with the argument that religious differences should be no obstacle to political equality.

A handful of Jewish rights activists and radical liberal Christians, however, recognized already before 1848 that political equality for Jews, while crucial, would not be adequate to end anti-Jewish prejudices—particularly in an atmosphere in which conservatives were reiterating and elaborating on those prejudices with ever-greater impunity, and presenting anti-Judaism as an essential element of devout Christianity. They therefore identified the reformulation of Christianity in more humanist and less exclusivist terms, and the development of greater social intimacy between Christians and Jews, as urgently necessary supplements to campaigns for political equality. Most Christian dissenters were certainly invested in advancing a more humanist understanding of Christianity, one in which reason and faith could be combined and individual subjectivity (particularly in matters of the heart) validated. They thus generally favored religious tolerance and the separation of church and state, and hence also, on principle, favored Jewish political equality. But most of them were not particularly concerned with advancing social integration between Jews and Christians, and many of them (however unreflectingly) shared mainstream liberals' condescending attitudes toward Judaism as a historically backward religion inferior to Christianity.[2] The most radical Christian dissenters, however, saw the development of greater intimacy between Christians and Jews as a central, essential part of their religious and political agenda.

The Mannheim Monday Club

The two best examples of this philosemitic phenomenon within Baden were dissenting preacher Carl Scholl and radical liberal lawyer and journalist Gustav von Struve (soon to be one of Germany's leading revolutionaries), both active in the city of Mannheim. In February of 1847, the two men (together with medical doctor Adam Hammer) founded a club, the Mannheim Monday Club, named for the day of the week on which it usually met, with the express goal of bringing together Jews and Christians, women and men. The club's purpose was to be "mutual discussion and instruction" on the subject of religion, so that its members could develop "a more thorough and deeper understanding of the religious movements in the midst of which we are."[3] The Mannheim Monday Club was patterned after similar clubs dedicated to religious discussion in Frankfurt, Offenbach, Wiesbaden, and Leipzig.[4] The Frankfurt Monday Club's inclusion of both Jews and Gentiles (indeed, "it was the first social club in Frankfurt that allowed Jews in") clearly provided the primary inspiration for the Mannheim club.[5] But both the Monday Club's overall agenda of "making its members come of age in religious terms, and making those who are already of age and free, completely and thoroughly aware of their freedom," and its explicit effort to encourage Jewish-gentile cooperation, were logical extensions of Scholl's and Struve's particular brand of theological radicalism.[6] Indeed, these two elements of their vision continuously fed and reinforced each other.

Not coincidentally, the Monday Club was born out of a schism within Mannheim's *deutschkatholische* congregation, for already since the fall of 1846 many members had been growing uncomfortable with Scholl's ever more radical departures from traditional Christian teachings and practices. Indeed, conservative critics mistakenly assumed that a new, even more freethinking congregation was being founded.[7] In fact, however, although Scholl withdrew from the position of preacher in light of the intra-congregational tensions his tenure had induced, both he and his supporters Struve and Hammer remained members of the congregation. For them, the club provided a supplement rather than a replacement to the work of the congregation. For Scholl and Struve, who became the group's leaders, the club provided an opportunity to implement more concretely the commitment both of them felt to both Jewish rights and women's rights.

The Mannheim Monday Club's at the time nearly unique inclusion of women (only in Hamburg was there a comparable phenomenon) was certainly part of all three men's specific interest also in advancing women's rights, in addition to being a more general element of many dissenting congregations' agendas.[8] Already a few months earlier, for example, although the authorities largely blocked their efforts, Scholl, Struve, and Hammer, together with liberal diet delegate Karl Mathy, had tried to launch a lecture series in Mannheim on religious, legal, medical, and economic topics which would "be designed so that women also can take part."[9] In addition, Hammer in particular was well known in Mannheim for his leadership role in founding a women's athletic club. He was also renowned for his defense of female midwives against the encroachment of male doctors, for his criticism of overreliance on forceps, and for his pioneering efforts to introduce the use of chloroform in childbirth (with a view to expediting the female sex's "hour of deliverance from the most painful agonies").[10] In subsequent months, moreover, the Monday Club became an important forum for discussing women's issues. In early May 1847, Scholl and Struve brought autodidact philosopher Louise Dittmar from Darmstadt to address the club on the subjects of religious dissent and women's rights.[11] The event went so successfully that Dittmar finally gained the courage publicly to acknowledge authorship of her previous writings, thus preserving for posterity one of the most brilliant feminist voices of the nineteenth century. In late May and June 1847, the Monday Club served as the main locus for organizing an (albeit ultimately vain) opposition to the *deutschkatholische* congregation's decision to retract women's previously granted right to vote on congregational matters—a conflict conservatives sarcastically sought to minimize by labeling it the "world-historical women's-emancipation-question of the local *Deutschkatholiken*."[12] And in his post-revolutionary exile in the United States, Struve, together with his wife and constant companion Amalie Dusar Struve, would become an even more indefatigable defender of women's equality and a cutting analyst of male revolutionaries' masculinism.[13]

But the Monday Club's inclusion of women needs to be understood as an important aspect of Scholl and Struve's philosemitic project as well. As Jewish rights activist Anton Rée, leader of the similarly interethnic club in Hamburg whose purpose was to encourage "intimate be-friending" between Gentiles and Jews, put it, "If we want to win fruits in social life, then we cannot exclude those who in this respect have such an unending influence."[14] By including women, then, the efforts to break down social barriers were expressly extended into the familial, personal sphere.[15] This enthusiasm for intergroup intimacy was in many ways a logical extension of liberals' and dissenters' long-standing conviction that it was precisely in the personal, private realms of marriage and inter-familial friendship that social hostilities based in religious differences could be most effectively overcome—a conviction neatly encapsulated by the slogan popularized during the mixed marriages controversy: "Love unites what faith divided."

The conservative response to the Monday Club's further development of this agenda was, in turn, predictably venomous. One newspaper, for example, declared that "*it is simply not tolerable that entire societies of the most motley mixtures are literally seduced to faithlessness, and if any club pursues tendencies dangerous to the state, then it is the local so-called Monday Club.*"[16] This remark suggests how strongly sexual impropriety, the dissolution of social boundaries, and threats to established authority were interlinked in conservative concerns, as well as the potency of the challenge generated by the Monday Club's very existence.

Although very few individual names are known, the Monday Club did apparently attract a significant number of both Jews and Christians, both women and men.[17] For example, the *Mannheimer Abendzeitung* announced that "immediately at the first founding of the local club more than 40 members, single people as well as entire families, and certainly from all walks of life, signed on." Discussing the first official meeting on March 1, 1847, the *Abendzeitung* reported proudly that "*Deutschkatholiken*, Jews, Roman Catholics and Protestants had taken part as members," while the conservative *Mannheimer Morgenblatt* snidely announced that "approximately 80 people attended, for the most part Jews." Reporting on the second official session on March 8, the *Morgenblatt* informed its readers that "a large audience had turned up this time, among them also a number of ladies. Approximately 50 new members joined, among them 19 Israelites." At least at one point attendance at the Monday Club reached 600, "of every confession."[18] The club also met fairly regularly for a full year, from February 1847 to February 1848, alternating between "discussions," guest lectures, and talks delivered by Scholl or Struve on such subjects as "the relationship of religion to the natural sciences," "the unique and the borrowed in religions," and "the meaning of Christmas."[19] To encourage the discussions, a "question urn" was established, "in which every club member can place his doubts or views in question form," and according to the *Abendzeitung*, "every member has the right to express his views freely in the discussions, and everyone who is capable can do so in a lecture."[20]

Dissolved in March 1848 in response to the news that revolution had broken out in Paris, the Mannheim Monday Club's brief existence gave testimony to the crucial significance of specifically *religious* radicalism in opening a space in which new, experimental visions of social interaction could be formulated. As the club's executive committee put it in announcing that "until further notice" there would be "no more gatherings": "The urgency of the most serious political questions makes calm attention to religious ones impossible now."[21] The shift from religious to political radicalism had unfortunate consequences. As more strictly political concerns superseded religious ones, Jewish and women's issues were pushed to the margins. A proliferation of clubs open to men only supplanted the heterosocial club life represented by the Monday Club.[22] Furthermore, while women across Baden participated in revolutionary activities, their goal was to further the revolution, not advance women's rights.[23] And while Jews were members of the various new clubs, the need to improve Jewish-gentile relations was no longer discussed.[24] As Scholl noted sadly, "The political revolt pushed these efforts directed chiefly toward spiritual and personal closeness into the background, and contented itself with the inclusion of equal state-citizen rights also for Jews in the '*German Basic Rights*' [developed at the Frankfurt Parliament]."[25]

The revolution did indeed technically introduce political equality between Christians and Jews when the Frankfurt Parliament announced the irrelevance of religious differences for state citizenship in its declaration of Basic Rights. This principle became law in Baden in February 1849 as well, and it was certainly no small matter (although Jews in Baden would not be granted complete equality—including the right to move from one town to another—until 1862, and although the decade of post-revolutionary repression significantly hampered the implementation of the new law). Nevertheless, the revolution in Baden also began with outbreaks of fierce anti-Jewish violence, and the revolutionary years even saw some Badenese petitioners demand "total removal" of the Jews from Baden.[26] The contradictory consequences of the revolution for Jews confirmed that the betterment of Jewish-Christian relations in daily social life can usefully be seen as an indispensable supplement to political equality. And it was this project that was advanced most insistently by the more radical religious dissenters.

While much has been written about the rise of German antisemitism and about the history of efforts for Jewish emancipation—and, to a lesser extent, about the relationship of the institutional Christian churches to both those phenomena—almost nothing has been written about the attitudes toward Jews of radical Christians who left the established churches.[27] Although too little is known about the Monday Club's lived practice to evaluate definitively its contributions to the advancement of Jewish rights and interethnic cooperation, an examination of Scholl and Struve's many writings on Jewish-Christian relations sheds a great deal of light on what was imaginable to the most theologically and politically critical Gentiles.

Furthermore, there is very little scholarly literature on the subject of German philosemitism, and certainly there is none on the philosemitism of the 1840s. In part this is because, as Hans Joachim Schoeps once pointed out, the proportional relationship between philo- and antisemitism is "like that of a sluggish little trickle to a broadly flowing stream."[28] In part, too, it is because philosemitism, it seems, is so often in some way problematic. For example, as Michael Brenner has eloquently argued, philosemites of the Kaiserreich "put themselves on the line for that which they themselves identified as being in the Jews' interest," and their defense of Jews was above all "a means to advance their own urgent concerns."[29] And Frank Stern's incisive analysis of the self-serving, guilt-induced philosemitism of the post-1945 period suggests that rhetorical overelaborations of what Jews could offer German culture—politically, economically, and culturally—were simply the instrumentalizing flip sides of old antisemitic stereotypes.[30] Nonetheless, as the recent studies by Brenner and Stern show, it is precisely the problematic aspects of philosemitism—as well as the very divergent forms it has taken over the centuries—that make it such an important phenomenon to investigate. Finally, not least among the reasons for examining the philosemitism of the 1840s lies in how intensely this disturbingly small phenomenon was followed by progressive German Jews. An exploration of contemporaneous reactions in the Reform Jewish press to the sort of gentile agenda Scholl and Struve represented shows that it was not just with the benefit of hindsight that the problematic aspects of 1840s Christian humanists' philosemitism became apparent.

Carl Scholl

Both Scholl and Struve came to the founding of the Mannheim Monday Club out of a long-standing interest in improving Jewish-Christian relations. Scholl (1820–1907), a native of Karlsruhe, had been raised in an atmosphere of religious tolerance, and had Jewish friends and classmates throughout his adolescence.[31] He believed that the impressions left on him by these early experiences were simply intensified by his theological studies (he went on to become a Protestant pastoral candidate), and particularly his preoccupation with the historical personality of Jesus. Scholl came to know many more Jewish families in the 1840s. By his own account, he "*deliberately* and *in principle nurtured* my personal relations with Jews *in particular*," and he credited precisely these personal acquaintanceships with having expanded his horizons and having led him gradually to develop his idea of a "religion of humanity" uniting and transcending all confessions.[32] In addition, there were rumors circulating in 1846 that Scholl was going to marry a Jewish woman. While it was not until 1862 that Scholl married a (different) Jewish woman— Regine Eller, daughter of a rabbi in Celle—this "philo" factor in his philosemitism should probably not be underestimated.[33] Indeed, from the 1870s on, as virulent antisemitism became more widespread across Germany, Scholl became even more devoted to the anti-antisemitism cause. He went on to publish numerous, often quite clever and provocative, critiques of antisemitic sophistries, culminating in his 1893 collection, *Hundert Jahre nach Lessings Nathan* (One Hundred Years after Lessings Nathan), the title of which clearly indicates the legacy in which Scholl felt he was working.[34]

Furthermore, already in his youth, Scholl was strongly critical of traditional Christianity. He was variously accused in the 1840s of "pantheism" and "Hegelianism," and of spreading "young-Hegelian philosophy."[35] Scholl had studied in Tübingen with Ferdinand Christian Baur, founder of the critical "Tübingen School" and teacher of many Hegelians. Scholl's debt to Left Hegelian Ludwig Feuerbach's *Das Wesen des Christenthums* (The Essence of Christianity, 1841) would also be implicitly evident in the title of his first collection of sermons, *Das Wesen des Deutschkatholicismus* (The Essence of *Deutschkatholizismus*), and in the tendency of those sermons to redefine Christianity in humanized terms.[36] Suspended by the Protestant church authorities in January 1845 for having preached a sermon considered theologically unacceptable because of its humanist and relativist perspective and its questioning of various traditional dogmas, Scholl hoped the concurrently emerging dissenting movement would provide him with a new field of endeavor and a means of subsistence.[37] Since no Free Protestant congregations were being founded in Baden, but interest in *Deutschkatholizismus* was proliferating, Scholl gladly accepted an invitation to hold a trial sermon for the fledgling *deutschkatholische* congregation in Mannheim, which in January 1846 was actively looking for a permanent preacher.

Already this first sermon made clear how Scholl's humanist reconceptualization of Christianity necessarily held implications for Jews. In the sermon, entitled "*Was wollen die Deutschkatholiken?*" (What do the *Deutschkatholiken* want?), Scholl first explained dissenters' dissatisfactions with both the Catholic and the Protestant churches and dissenters' yearning to unite across the Catholic-Protestant divide. He also elaborated that dissenters would take as the basis of their faith nothing but "*the historical documents of the holy scriptures and EVERY ERA'S RIGHT TO A REASONABLE-HISTORICAL INTERPRETATION of these.*" Scholl's own "reasonable-historical" interpretation of Christ saw him

> as the founder—not of the Christian church—for he couldn't have cared less about just a church—but as the founder of the whole new world of the spirit, the savior from the shackles of falsehood, superstition and slavery . . . , the herald of peace and love. . . . But through this free consideration of views on the person of Christ . . . a whole new perspective opens up.[38]

This perspective, according to Scholl, was the added possibility of reunification between Christians and Jews.

In his reflections on the mission implied in the *deutschkatholische* name, Scholl told his listeners that the name referred to both the Greek root of "catholic," meaning all-encompassing, and to the project of German national unity: "*all Germans united . . . Germany united, strong, free and great, Germany above all!*" Scholl thus strategically worked to merge aspirations for national unity (such a central component of the progressive agenda in the 1840s) with his program for overcoming the barriers between Christians and Jews by identifying Germany as the first place in which the union between Catholics, Protestants, and Jews could be made a reality: "And should our hearts not beat higher at this thought: *The brothers who 300 years ago, the brothers who 1800 years ago, went their separate ways, ALL TOGETHER AGAIN, ALL AGAIN UNITED!!*"[39]

But Scholl was not only urging greater openness on the part of his gentile listeners; he also had recommendations to make to Reform Jews. Thus, for example, Scholl expressed the hope that "*these enlightened ones within Jewry*" would soon acknowledge that in

> their *INNERMOST BEING they already long since are standing on Christian ground,* and like so many Catholics and Protestants, remain *Jews* in *name* alone! Through this avowal they then profess themselves, as we do, to him, whose personal appearance, whose life, teaching and martyr death is the *irrefutable historical starting-point of our common spiritual and moral development.*[40]

In the 1840s, like so many of his contemporaries, Scholl was convinced that human history was a history of continual progress, with Christianity providing an inevitable advance over its chronological antecedents, and that the issue at hand was to shape the future. Scholl believed that the union between Christians and Jews he was advocating would grow into an even more wonderful religion than Christianity had been, a religion that encompassed all others within it. Thus, and despite his explicit advocacy of freedom of belief for all, Scholl's goal was not only greater unity between those who were from different groups, but also the ever-increasing erasure of group differences. This element of his vision retrospectively reveals the authoritarian underside shared by so many "enlightened" projects in the early nineteenth century.

Nonetheless, Scholl's visionary message and charismatic style clearly appealed to the congregation. Scholl was hired immediately on the basis of this first sermon, making him—at age twenty-six—the first official *deutschkatholischer* preacher in Baden. The congregation was initially quite satisfied with Scholl's leadership, and his popularity contributed both to the dynamic growth of the congregation and to the appeal *deutschkatholische* services had also for outside visitors.

The inclusion of Jews was an indispensable component of Scholl's humanist redefinition of Christianity.[41] By his own account already in 1846, his decision to join the *deutschkatholische* movement was in part motivated by the prospect of reunification between Christians and Jews that the movement opened up. Also in retrospect, Scholl would argue that "in none of our free congregations has [the idea of reunification between Christians and Jews] been expressed with such warmth and enthusiasm as it has been so particularly in ours;—it is this idea, as you know, for whose realization I have, from the first hour of my entrance into the Mannheim congregation, invested my whole being in word and deed." Looking back on the early days of 1846 and "my very first lecture that I delivered . . . in Mannheim," Scholl confirmed how inseparable his theological radicalism and his commitment to Jewish-Christian union were: "As [the *deutschkatholische* congregations'] most immediate task I designated the renunciation of all coercion in matters of faith and participation in a further development of religion based on reason and scholarship, but the next task I declared to be the working-toward a 'union with the like-minded of all confessions,' and also very particularly with our fellow citizens in *Jewry*."[42]

Given Scholl's vocal interest in Jewish-Christian relations, it was perhaps no coincidence that—although none became official members in the 1840s—Jewish men and women did regularly attend his services, and this fact no doubt encouraged him to persevere in his mission of Jewish-Christian union. Scholl used the Jewish presence in the Sunday services to reinforce his own arguments, frequently calling his listeners' attention to the fact that there were Jews in their midst.[43] In a sense, perhaps, Scholl was instrumentalizing them—using their presence as markers of his own humanism—as living proof, as it were, of how radical he was. On the other hand, their attendance also suggests that the survival of Christian humanism was not a matter of indifference to at least part of Mannheim's Jewish community; in this context it seems relevant that two Jewish banking establishments in Mannheim committed themselves to giving the *deutschkatholische* congregation donations of 100 florins every year.[44] That a few years later Jews attended *deutschkatholische* services in Heidelberg and Pforzheim as well seems also to indicate the significance some saw in the Christian experiment of dissent.[45]

One of the most urgent tasks Scholl set himself was to undermine Christians' sense of superiority over Jews by continually stressing the Jewish roots of Christianity as a whole, and especially the Jewish roots of precisely those rituals considered peculiarly Christian: baptism and communion. For example, he argued that baptism, far from having been a Christian invention, was in fact "a *Jewish* ceremony," "a Jewish custom already long before developed by the prophets of the old covenant and by the requirement of cleansings or washings in the [Jewish] law." At the same time, Scholl tried to redefine baptism in more humanist and less exclusivist terms, assuring his listeners that the crucial thing was to be "baptized with [Christ's] spirit,—the baptism by water does not determine the Christian!"[46] To give his ideas practical form, Scholl also expressly urged the congregation to drop the requirement of baptism for non-Christians interested in becoming congregation members.[47] Similarly, Scholl reminded his listeners about the origins of communion in the Jewish feast of Passover, even as he sought to transform communion into "a love-meal, a brotherly meal" so that Jews could participate in it as well—which they did.[48] Throughout his 1846 sermons (or "Sunday lectures," as he preferred to call them), Scholl also repeatedly stressed Jesus' own Jewishness. As he explained retrospectively, if Christians could only "imagine Jesus as a real flesh-and-blood *Jew*"—or (as he in subsequent decades provocatively put it) as "a member of the Semitic race"—it would "rip out the strongest and deepest root of the anciently-embedded Jew-hatred."[49]

Scholl's insistence on Christianity's Jewish roots attains even greater significance in light of the prevailing theological and philosophical climate. As Amy Newman has recently shown, Kant, Schleiermacher, Fichte, and Hegel all rejected the notion that Christianity was built on Judaism and had close affinities with it. Kant, for example, claimed that early Christianity "'arose suddenly,' 'completely forsaking the Judaism from which it sprang.'" Schleiermacher stressed that "'Christianity cannot in any wise be regarded as a remodeling or a renewal and continuation of Judaism,'" while establishing as a rule for the study of the Old Testament that "'whatever is most definitely Jewish has least value.'" Fichte even tried to show that Jesus "could not have been of Jewish descent at all," while Hegel, by contrast, made a much more sophisticated (and insidious) argument, one which, as Newman notes, was "a brilliant reversal of the antisemitic harangue that portrays the Jews as the murderers of Christ":

> Using the dialectical model, God *had* to become incarnate within Judaism itself (the universal *must* particularize itself), because this was the only way that universal Christianity could effectively and conclusively sublate particularistic Judaism. This approach had the additional advantage of answering the question of why God had become incarnate as a Jew: this was in fact a shrewd strategic move devised to destroy Judaism from within.[50]

In such a context, Scholl's views clearly were unusual.

And yet, as his rhetorical flourishes showed, Scholl's efforts to combat anti-Jewish prejudice, and to recall his listeners to Christ's original, profoundly humanist message, were frequently inextricable from an unexamined implication that to be a true humanist one had to embrace at least some aspects of Christianity. Throughout all his efforts, Scholl moved awkwardly back and forth between a redefinition of Christianity that could incorporate Jews and an assumption of Christian superiority over Judaism. A classic example is provided by his 1846 lecture on "The Development of Faith." There Scholl described Christianity as a synthesis of the best elements within Greek paganism and Judaism, arguing that "the peculiarity of Christianity is therefore this, that in it, in contrast to paganism and Judaism, we first came to consciousness of the immanence of God in the human being, or the oneness of God and the human being. Whoever therefore carries this consciousness within himself,—whatever name he may have,—he is in his innermost spirit a Christian!—Baptismal and confirmation certificates are not necessary!"[51]

It is possible that Scholl's insistence on linking humanism with Christianity was partially a response to attacks by religious conservatives, and the insecurity these induced in other dissenters. Across Germany, as Scholl reported, "again and again we are accused of no longer being Christians."[52] (Indeed, some Protestant opponents of dissent said it was nothing but a "modern Judaism.")[53] And in their own city of Mannheim, dissenters suffered from "constant police harassment, the ridicule and slander of unprincipled opponents, the 'chasing and sticking-out-of-tongues' from well-trained Romish street urchins."[54] The sense of being under siege intensified particularly during the petition storm of

early 1846. In this situation, many dissenters clung to their self-definition as Christians.[55] Although Scholl (as became apparent at the latest
by the fall of 1846) was rather impatient with more traditionalist congregation members, the religious right's success in discrediting the dissenters' faith forced him to negotiate quite cautiously in his efforts simultaneously to reassure and to transform his listeners—to discredit
the Christian credentials of his opponents while working to redefine
the content of Christianity.[56] Scholl therefore worked hard to appeal
to both more religious and more rationalist listeners, often sliding from
a traditional Christian formulation immediately into a humanist varia-
tion of the same idea, as though they were interchangeable—speaking,
for example, of "being like Christ, that is, to have God in one's
heart."[57] Another strategy he used to reassure the congregation was to
turn the persecution into a virtue by comparing dissenters to Christ
and to the early Christians: Scholl called dissent "the Messiah of this
century" and argued that Christ had returned *"in these days. . . .*
He has returned, and thus he strides through our lands, *crying woe to
the pharisees and the scribes! . . . The same ones,* who nailed him to the
cross back then as a *revolutionary and a heretic, the same ones* want to
crucify him again!"[58] All these strategies, of course, however inadvertently, once again had the effect of reinforcing the superior value of
Christianity.

Scholl's fierce resistance to the religious right's deliberate divisiveness
also had another ambiguous effect for Jews. In response to conservatives' exclusivist insistence on a church-defined faith, Scholl, like many
of his fellow dissenting preachers, stressed the superiority of human love
over faith, arguing that "our era wants. . . . love that reaches further
than faith, love that unites what faith has divided. . . . love which creates
heaven on earth."[59] Or again at another point Scholl argued: "We want
to unite what the previous confessions have divided. . . . We have made
love our very first principle, the love that extends equally to all people
regardless of differences in religion."[60] Reinterpreting Christ's dictum
that "I have not come to bring peace, but a sword"—a message that
could easily be interpreted in conservative terms—Scholl assured his listeners that the love practiced by dissenters could defeat particularly
Catholic conservatives' efforts to reassert sharper boundaries. To this
end, Scholl invoked the power of "the sword of love," which could
"shatter the barriers" caused by "the damning and hereticization . . .
practiced by the holy fathers of Rome." Scholl elaborated:

> These barriers must be shattered by the sword of love, these barriers must
> fall,—and this sword is particularly given into our hand! We must demon-
> strate over and over again, that in all confessions there is something true,

that they are all only the different lightrays of one and the same truth. . . . This we must demonstrate for as long as it takes, till we have won people's hearts, till we have removed the prejudices, shattered the barriers and united the confessions![61]

Again, despite the ostensible beauty of this vision, the authoritarian undertone often characteristic of universalizing projects was evident as well. Also in his other lectures of 1846, Scholl moved back and forth between an unambiguous advocacy of freedom of belief for "each confession, . . . even if it is one we must consider regressive" and an explicit anticipation of the erasure of all differences—the "final unification" of "all confessions."[62] Scholl, in short, not only wanted "*all confessions united*" but also "*no confessions anymore.*"[63] The barriers Scholl wanted shattered too often resembled floodgates that opened in one direction only. But it was precisely the religious right's insistence on barriers and on insurmountable difference that might have led someone like Scholl to reject difference in his effort to reject those barriers.

In sum then, as the months passed, Scholl increasingly tried to push the congregation toward what he called a "freer" stance. As he explained a year later, the lectures he delivered in 1846 were deliberately designed to wean the congregation gradually, "step by step," away from traditional Christianity, and making room for Jews within the dissenting movement was clearly an important component of this project.[64] In fact, whatever problems there were with his vision, his opponents understood him all too well. Because of Scholl's humanist redefinition of baptism, for example, "fanatical Christians called me the 'Jew-pastor'" and plastered the windows of his home with manure.[65]

More traditionalist members of the congregation also became increasingly resistant to Scholl's innovations, and from November 1846 on, the conflict was carried on openly in a series of heated congregational meetings. Scholl twice tried to resign, but "*Gustav von Struve*, my personal friend" led the campaign to keep Scholl as the congregation's preacher. Many more conservative members also felt Scholl should stay on, if only he would stay away from criticism of dogma and attacks on the sacraments, and instead devote himself to the congregation's spiritual edification. Finally, however, realizing Scholl was inflexible, the congregation let him go on February 21, 1847. Scholl's first plan (although the project ultimately fell through) was to coedit a new journal, the *Reformblatt*, with the Jewish intellectual Raphael Loewenthal in Frankfurt who was also a friend of Struve's. In addition, he traveled to Hamburg and Berlin in order to help launch clubs there in which Jews and non-Jews could work together "to combat anti-Jewish prejudice" and to "bring about greater personal intimacy." Above all, however,

Scholl—while remaining a member of the congregation—turned his attention to the Monday Club he had helped to create a few weeks earlier, hoping to find in it "my next forum of activity."[66]

Gustav von Struve

In Gustav von Struve (1805–70), Scholl had found a friend and fellow activist who shared many of his convictions. Despite the signal role he has played in histories of German liberalism, Struve's ideas about Jews have never been discussed by historians. Yet throughout the 1840s, Struve wrote scathing critiques of mainstream liberals' ambivalence about emancipation, and continually sought ways to bring Christians and Jews together socially.

Struve's religious attitudes in general have received only cursory, and often inaccurate, attention in the massive literature devoted to his political efforts.[67] Yet religious issues were of primary concern to Struve in the years before the Badenese revolutions, and continued to be an important preoccupation throughout his post-revolutionary exile in the United States. If we do not accept the narrow definition of religious faith conservatives ultimately succeeded in establishing, but rather remember that the 1840s were a time of intense conflict over what constituted "true Christianity," it becomes apparent that (contrary to most historians' assumptions) Struve was quite a religious man. In 1847, for example, Struve delivered a sort of statement of faith:

> *Religion* is nothing external, but rather internal, a feeling, that the Creator placed in the heart of the human being, and which not only makes him attracted to all that is true, beautiful and good, but also drives him forcefully to achieve all those things and give them practical reality. . . . Therefore every human being has religion, no matter how very different the *form* is, in which it is individually expressed.[68]

Likewise, in subsequent years, Struve would repeatedly criticize self-proclaimed atheists, arguing that "it is of course very easy to say that religion is nonsense and church is in bad taste, but with that [attitude] neither the nonsense in the field of religion nor the bad taste in the church are driven out." Struve instead believed that "beside the many religions advocated by the clergy there is one that lives in the hearts of human beings. . . . It is a secret urge, which lifts people above the base passions of this earth, steels them in danger and gives them courage in suffering. . . . [It is] the religion of human love, of freedom and a sense for justice."[69]

Many of Struve's writings from the 1840s reveal a man for whom, like

Scholl, reconceptualizing Christianity was inseparable from his efforts to encourage Jewish-Christian cooperation. The shifts in his thinking from his fictional work in the 1830s to his political journalism in the 1840s reveal how the emergence of Christian dissent, the radicalization of dissent encouraged by Scholl in Mannheim, and a personal process of political radicalization, affected Struve's attitudes toward Jews in complex ways. On the one hand, Struve was increasingly able to give his vision concrete form. While Struve's writings reveal that he had been concerned about breaking down the barriers of prejudice between Jews and Christians already long before the advent of Christian dissent, it was only the emergence of dissent in 1845, and particularly its radical outgrowth of 1847, the Monday Club, that provided him with an opportunity to turn his theoretical commitment into practical reality. In the 1840s, Struve was involved in a number of clubs that had Jewish as well as gentile members, for example, the Mannheim *Turnverein* and the "Club for the Advancement of the Welfare of the Laboring Classes."[70] But only the religious forums of the *deutschkatholische* congregation and the Monday Club made closer relations between Jews and Christians one of their explicit goals, and only these two groups addressed the problem of religious differences, which was after all one of the main ostensible reasons given at that time for Jews' exclusion from political rights. Nevertheless, there was also in the 1840s a shift in Struve's attitude from respect for and celebration of religious difference to a rather more authoritarian demand that Jews give up their difference and join radical Christian humanists in a common project.

Struve was a liberal lawyer of aristocratic background.[71] He began his activity as a political journalist in 1843, when he joined Berthold Auerbach and Gabriel Riesser—two of Germany's most famous Jewish publicists and intellectuals—in publishing the *Konstitutionelle Jahrbücher* in Stuttgart.[72] His first organizational activism came in 1843 as well, when he became the mentor for a number of progressive and nationalist fraternities at the University of Heidelberg, as well as the editor for the first nationalist-oriented student newspaper. Believing that work on a daily newspaper could bring him broader influence, Struve took over the editorship of the *Mannheimer Journal* in 1845, and having lost that position due to his political views at the end of 1846, he launched a new, independently financed newspaper, the *Deutscher Zuschauer*. The years 1845 and 1846 also saw the publication of numerous political essays in book form.[73] Constantly at war with Mannheim's archconservative and ultramontane censor, Mariano Freiherr von Uria-Sarachaga, in and out of jail for his written attacks on the unconstitutionality of the political system that had evolved after the Congress of Vienna, Struve was gradually politically radicalized. Married in 1845 to Amalie Dusar, "the sharer of both his opinions and his perils" and a coauthor of many of his works, Struve found all the personal support he needed to be unshakeable in his commitment to political reform, though he often felt alienated from other radicals as much as from mainstream liberals and conservatives—differing from them not only in his (lawyerly) preoccupation with constitutional questions, but also in his belief in "utopian principles of humanity."[74] But as Struve explained in a letter to his fictional friend "Waldemar": "You don't seem to know that it is exactly this spiritual battle that constitutes my actual happiness in life. I would not want to exist without it. If I thought I would have to return to the same dreamy speculative and spectating life I was leading for the last fifteen years—excepting the very last six months—it would be unbearable for me. . . . You know that there is only one thing that I'm afraid of: to do the wrong thing."[75]

Struve's first effort to do the right thing with respect to Jewish-Christian relations appeared in fictional form; already this very first text insisted on the link Struve was continually to establish between criticizing Christianity and advancing greater intimacy between Christians and Jews. The text, published under the pseudonym Gustav Carl, was a five-act tragic drama he had been working on throughout the 1830s.[76] Entitled *Die Verfolgung der Juden durch Emicho* (The Persecution of the Jews by Emicho), it was set in the city of Trier in the year 1096. The story was based on a real event that occurred in the midst of the First Crusade—the slaughtering of Jews in Trier and other Rhenish cities by a band of German crusaders on their way to Jerusalem, a band led by Count Emicho of Leiningen.[77]

Die Verfolgung began by telling of the cruel crusader Emicho, and his even more fanatic lover, Leontine, who together with the soldiers under Emicho's command, were trying to kill all the Jews in Trier. The persecuted Jews therefore sought refuge with the archbishop, but he followed the cautious, "pious" route and told them he would only protect them if they converted to Christianity.[78] This in turn led to a debate among the Jews about whether or not to convert, a debate that allowed Struve to address the complexities facing Jews in their efforts to be treated as equals without having to assimilate. In a related subplot, a Jewish brother and sister, Israel and Selma, were busy falling in love with a gentile sister and brother, Thusnelda and Herrmann, and vice versa. Filled with political intrigues, mistaken identities, and a wise and decent fool, the tale was relentlessly melodramatic and sentimental. Yet it also offered an excellent vehicle for Struve to present not only encapsulated versions of nineteenth-century debates about Jewish-Christian relations, but of debates between neoorthodox and humanist Christians as well, replete with references to the conflicts about celibacy and mixed marriages that so exercised Badeners in the 1830s and 1840s.

It was no coincidence that Struve chose a medieval theme, for the focus on the crusades allowed him to emphasize the link between intolerant medieval Christianity (which was, obviously, Catholic) and persecution of Jews, thereby establishing a connection between conservative Catholicism and anti-Judaism in his own day. Indeed, in his later writings as well, Struve would repeatedly call both conservative Catholic and anti-Jewish attitudes "medieval."[79] Having established fanatical Christianity as the problem, Struve offered various responses and solutions. Among these were an insistence on solidarity with the persecuted—including a willingness to become one of the persecuted oneself, a willingness literally to place one's own body on the line between the Jews and the crusaders' knives—as well as a responsibility to criticize the complicity of those who did not intervene against the violence.[80] Another response was an insistence on religious tolerance, including full respect for the Jewish faith. As Struve has the Jewish character Abraham say to the archbishop: "Consider my lord, that our faith is anchored just as tightly in our hearts, as your faith is in yours. . . . Who on this earth may insist that he alone possesses the truth?"[81] But the most important solutions involved the creation of new, "recombined" families by adoption and marriage—an intriguing inversion of G. E. Lessing's use of the familial metaphor in *Nathan the Wise*—as well as the need radically to reconceptualize Christianity.

Besides its obvious appeal as a motor for the plot, Struve's focus on interconfessional marriage allowed him to make several points. One of these was that in light of violent persecution, tolerance was insufficient. What was required was the building of new alliances between people who were different. Furthermore, the remarkable thing about this early Struve text is that at this point he was not interested in achieving homogeneity in society—he wanted people to be allowed to preserve their differences. Thus, one of the important agreements the interconfessional lovers come to is that no one will try to convert the other away from his/her heritage. The focus on marriage also let Struve insist on the transformative power of romantic love—again, literally the "philo" element of philosemitism—a love that could make people undertake the personal changes Struve felt were the prerequisite to societywide changes. While both the Jewish and the gentile siblings had to give up some of their prejudices, Struve made it clear that the Christians, the privileged ones, had to give up more.

In Struve's fictional presentation, it was precisely the persecution of Jews that forced Christians to rethink Christianity. Most dramatically, the young Christian Herrmann told the evil Dean of the Cathedral, while "removing the cross that he had always worn," that "Because this cross has been the signal, For base pillage and cold slaughter, I must give it back to you. . . . I wore it chastely on my breast, For the cause of pious deeds, This defiled thing take it back, I lay it at your feet."[82] While Struve's critique of institutional Christianity was sharp, the point was to redefine—not reject—Christianity. So that his message could not possibly be misunderstood, Struve let the fool proclaim:

> Christ . . . planted pure love In the human spirit. Therefore whoever is driven by hate, Is not aglow for Christ's teachings. Whoever persecutes his brothers, Persecutes our Lord, Whoever returns hate for hate, Is far from Christ's paths. Yet for many hundred years, Ever since Christ was resurrected, Fanatical hordes veil themselves, In the cloak of Christianity. With hate in their wild hearts, rudely spiting Christ's own words, They sow the seeds of anguish, Calling this religion.[83]

Even more strongly than dissenting preacher Scholl, then, the fool made his disgust at the maltreatment of Jews central to his overall critique of Christianity, while—like Scholl—advancing his own version of Christ's original purpose. But in the play as a whole, Struve went far further than Scholl. Unlike Scholl, Struve was attentive to the debates *within* Judaism, and he clearly validated those Jewish characters who refused to convert. Also unlike Scholl, Struve was far more critical of social circumstances, letting the fool say, in a barely veiled reference to Struve's own role in the nineteenth century: "Wretched land and wretched time, Where only covered in fool's garb, Can one dare to speak the truth!"[84] And finally, when Struve had the Jewish youth Israel deliver a concluding speech to the audience, the difference between his own and Scholl's perspective emerged once more: "Unhappy members of my tribe, As if by God you'd been cast out! When will your misery cease? And when will God send you assistance? Will not one day the children's children Of those who ridicule you now, Begin to recognize that they Must strive, atoning for historical injustice?"[85] In an age devoted to the celebration of progress, and the conviction that Christianity was already a major advance over Judaism, Struve was unusual in stressing the need for Christians to take responsibility for the dark sides of Christian history.

A decade later, in his journalistic writings devoted explicitly to Jewish themes, the consistency of Struve's concerns for both equality and integration were evident, as well as the consistency of his efforts to contrast a loving Christianity that could accept difference with an intolerant Christianity seeking only to harm or convert. By 1845–46, Jewish emancipation had become a "*Tagesfrage*," a "question of the day," whose significance was indicated by the many German diets that were debating it. In the running commentary Struve kept up on these debates, he devoted particular attention to those who defended their oppression of Jews by reference to their own Christianity. Thus, for example, he pointed out that Christianity "is the religion of love and not of persecution," that Christianity "commands love, gentleness, and justice," and that "it contradicts the spirit of Christianity to impose political disadvantages on a religious association because of its religious convictions."[86]

Struve, a liberal himself, staunchly dedicated to the concept of constitutional rights, was also particularly disgusted with the extent of liberals' ambivalence about Jewish emancipation. Struve in general found most liberals appallingly weak-kneed. His writings from the mid-1840s are marked by an obsession with countering the effects of "false liberalism," with resisting "the halves" (in contrast to the "wholes"), the "heroes of the word" (rather than of the "deed").[87] Struve repeatedly suggested that most liberals were "unmanly men," "political hermaphrodites" who "use all the liberal slogans" but basically "wriggle their way through between the demands of the people and the wishes of the government." In this spirit, he insisted that "whoever bows down before the narrow-minded views of [anti-Jewish] zealots, who does not have the courage to resist them without being worried about endangering his own popularity, he may be a good party-man, a man of freedom and justice he will never be."[88]

Struve also strategically contended that liberals' recalcitrance vis-à-vis Jews hampered their achievement of other goals. Thus, for example, he suggested in 1845 that "whoever disputes the Jews' right to the civic improvement that was promised them, must then put up with the way his own claim to constitutionality, religious equality among Christians, freedom of the press and freedom of trade and shipping are disputed." But Struve was alert as well to the psychological dynamics keeping liberals and others from accepting the rational logic of his argument. For example, Struve noted that if one kept pressing those who wanted to keep Jews in an unequal position, if one countered their objections one by one,

> then at the end one arrives at the point where the opponent of the Jews cries out: "I don't like Jews, I don't want them to have the same rights as me." So then we have the old slogan, just in new words. . . . "I want it and I command it, and that is reason enough." When a government relies on this reason, of course, everybody yells about it; but the spirit of self-interest thinks it can use this argument well and still simultaneously present itself as extremely liberal. There again we have the false liberalism, which itself wants to have all possible freedom, but wants to concede as little as possible to one's neighbor, that is, one's rival.

This point was made even more succinctly in an essay critically analyzing the culture of Frankfurt, a city that had long prided itself on the egalitarianism of its civic institutions: "The Frankfurter will tolerate none of his fellow citizens in a position above him, but to see the Jews under him is his joy, a joy in which everyone—from the bootwiper to the banker—can take part."[89]

In light of all these circumstances, Struve was convinced that greater social integration between Jews and Christians was the most immediate task. As he put it sadly, "An *equalization* of Jews and Christians in political terms can hardly come to pass as long as their *equalization* in social terms has not yet happened."[90] And crucially, at all points, Struve argued that the burden was on Gentiles to change themselves. Struve was particularly distressed, for example, that Jews were excluded from Mannheim's main social club, the *Harmonie* (whose members were drawn from the ranks of the town's liberal bourgeoisie), and had thus been forced to start their own club. Struve wrote: "It is not the Jews' fault, that in our day, in the highly cultured city of Mannheim, there is a Jewish social club. Rather, we Christians must take responsibility for this. . . . It goes without saying that just as the fault that is here criticized has been committed by the Christians, so also only these can make up for it."[91]

Similarly, Struve was outraged by reports in the early summer of 1846 that Jewish girls were being denied the right to enroll in Mannheim's several girls' schools. Challenging his fellow Gentiles "to prove that they are free of prejudices . . . through the *deed*," he called on them to boycott the existing schools and found a new, non-discriminatory one—since "all those who wish that their children might not be imprinted with prejudice—already in their earliest education—against those who believe differently, cannot put them into institutes which discriminate against children on the basis of their faith."[92] Obviously not in a position to start his own school, Struve sought other ways to express his growing conviction that legal and political equality would not be enough, and would never succeed in diminishing group prejudice. His leadership in the Monday Club was to be one expression of this impulse.

There were, however, definite limitations to Struve's analysis of Jewish-Christian relations, and these emerged more frequently in essays that were *not* explicitly devoted to Jewish concerns, but rather addressed other issues. An examination of these limitations reveals that it was precisely Struve's growing radicalization and growing frustration with the lack of progressive political engagement among his fellow citizens that led him to reflect ever more critically about the power of conservative religion to restrain progressive social change. Struve's growing impatience with conservative Christianity expanded to include a disgust with orthodox Judaism as well. Thus, for instance, in 1846, in an essay entitled "*Polizeistaat, Priesterstaat und Rechtsstaat*" (Police State, Priests' State, and State of Law), Struve articulated his religious vision of "a more beautiful future" which entailed "a union of the better ones among all the religious confessions."[93] But the flip side of this inclusiveness was a hatred of all authoritarianism: "Jesuits, Pietists and rabbis are all more or less on the same level. All of them want to secure their own dominion, also in earthly matters, by leading their people on the leash with the fear of a higher world order."[94] This preoccupation with the ideological power of traditional religion proved to be of major importance in complicating Struve's previously stated commitment to the acceptance of religious difference.

From the moment of its emergence, Struve closely followed the development of *deutschkatholischer* dissent. He repeatedly used the lead editorial in the *Mannheimer Journal* to report and comment on the *Deutschkatholiken*, or to defend the cause of dissent in general, and he continued this practice in editorial essays in his *Deutscher Zuschauer*, the paper he launched in November 1846.[95] His interest in dissent grew out of his disrespect for the traditional churches. Struve shared all the standard liberal prejudices against the Catholic church, calling priestly celibacy "that school of lechery," confession "the means of pandering to [the priest's] lusts," and the pope "that worst enemy of the German nation."[96] But he also hated institutional Protestantism and its subservience to state authority, and in December 1846, he and his wife Amalie—both raised as Protestants—joined the local *deutschkatholische* congregation.[97]

Clearly, Scholl's presence in that congregation was part of the appeal for Struve, for the two men had many convictions in common. Like Scholl, Struve claimed to defend "the purified gospel" while redefining Christian concepts in earthly terms:

> We understand church to mean the visible home of the heavenly kingdom; we understand church life and religious scholarship . . . not as a pushy and self-aggrandizing, un-Christian phariseeism, but rather as thorough unprejudiced research on all parts, an examination and evaluation of . . . the rich and marvelous *material given to* us in the *holy scripture*, . . . always keeping in mind the goal, that in and through the church the kingdom of God, that is, the kingdom of truth, justice and peace, is meant to be realized ever more extensively, more surely and more blessedly.[98]

Also like Scholl, in face of the persecution dissenters were experiencing, Struve strategically presented dissent as ultra-Christian: "Whoever resists this movement, battles with Christ himself, for it is He, freshly vitalized, who is to be returned to us through the Reformation of the nineteenth century."[99] And like Scholl, Struve rapidly grew impatient with more conservative dissenters, accusing most of them of failure to "accomplish the great work of internal liberation on themselves," of being still caught in an "unclear halfness."[100]

Struve's redefinition of Christianity in human terms was not only related to his dislike of neoorthodox Catholicism and state-controlled Protestantism, but also, predictably, held implications for Jews. Through most of 1846, Struve's attitudes toward Judaism were consistent with his attitudes toward Christianity. Thus, for example, he expressed appreciation for "the lively movement that is now emerging in the lap of Judaism," while criticizing "the so-called conservative party" among Jews, "that is, the party that clings to the old, and multiplies in opposition to the spirit of the time."[101] But by November 1846, on the eve of his conversion to *Deutschkatholizismus*, Scholl's rhetoric had made its mark on him. Thus, for example, in one essay, Struve took the opportunity to redefine Christianity in a way that reminded his readers of its Jewish roots—while also insisting on the need for Jews to join the dissenting movement. The echoes with Scholl's sermons were unmistakable. Struve wrote:

> Reform Jewry is realizing ever more clearly that the concept of Christianity held by *consistent Deutschkatholizismus*, is the one to which finally every still so-called Israelite who makes a claim to be spiritually educated, however much he has till now resisted this admission to himself, must own up, since it does not require anything more than the recognition that the Judaism of the Old Testament was *thoroughly reformed* and—in combination with the truth of paganism—transformed, into the general religion of humanity by the appearance of the carpenter's son from Nazareth. This is a fact of history which cannot be denied![102]

Here the authoritarian underside of Christian humanism came to the fore, even more forcefully than it had in Scholl's proclamations. Even though Struve was not demanding anything of Jews that he did not also demand of Christians, it was clear that the emergence of dissent, together with his increasing frustration over the resilience of traditional religiosity—with all the obstacles that implied for his efforts to overcome prejudice and to advance social change in general—had led Struve to lose sight of the respect for Jewish difference he had shown in his fiction and in his early journalism.[103]

The Reform Jewish Response

Scholl's and Struve's reflections on Jewish-Christian relations can be better understood when placed in the context of contemporaneous debates within German Jewry. A wide range of Jewish journalists and activists addressed the dilemmas of Jewish-Gentile integration in the 1840s. In pamphlets, and in newspapers such as the well-established *Allgemeine Zeitung des Judenthums*, *Der Orient*, the *Zeitschrift für die religiösen In-*

teressen des Judenthums, and *Der Israelit des neunzehnten Jahrhunderts,* as well as more short-lived efforts such as *Die Reform des Judenthums, Reform-Zeitung, Der Jude in Deutschlands Gegenwart,* and *Der Phönix,* they debated amongst themselves and reported on and responded to gentile treatment of Jews. These debates intensified after 1845. One reason was that German Jewry was experiencing a theological polarization parallel to the growing polarization of German Christians. For example, one newspaper analyzed the situation of Badenese Jewry thus: "For some time now already . . . a vital active interest in efforts to reform the synagogue is unmistakable," but at the same time, "the *stable* party, hostile to all innovation . . . has likewise awakened from its deep sleep, has been jolted out of its indolence."[104] Another reason was that religious matters of all sorts had become increasingly hot political topics. In part this was because of the emergence of Christian dissent. But it was also due to a more general interpenetration of religious and political matters—as the relationship between the states and the Catholic church became more combative, political bodies like parliaments and cabinets debated religious matters, the political press addressed religious topics, and the outcomes of elections, petition campaigns, political demonstrations, and other forms of popular political life were in part determined by religious hostilities.

Just as the 1840s saw serious contests over the content of Christianity, so also it was in the 1840s that Reform, Conservative, and Neo-Orthodox Judaism defined themselves in relation to each other. Already since the 1810s, reformers had sought to change Jewish worship services in keeping with the spirit of the times. The purpose was not only to meet Christian observers' objections to the purported unseemliness of Jewish services—the accusation that the synagogue was, in J. H. Campe's words, a place where people are "unruly" and "mumble in an unlovely manner."[105] The goal was also to revitalize Judaism, to combat the growing estrangement from traditional Judaism that many educated Jews in particular were feeling. Strict decorum, an abbreviated liturgy and edifying sermon, prayers in German, and choral music thus replaced the traditional chanting and exposition of the Torah. Rabbis interested in religious reform gathered at conferences repeatedly in the 1840s (at Brunswick in 1844, Frankfurt in 1845, and Breslau in 1846) in order to consult with one another and to formalize Reform's precepts. Alarmed by too many departures from inherited practice and a zeal for acculturation that could not but offend the still incompletely assimilated overwhelming majority of German Jews, Rabbi Zecharias Frankel broke from the Reform project he too had been involved in in 1845, advocating instead a "positive-historical Judaism" (which would ultimately become known as Conservative Judaism).[106] Meanwhile, also in the

1840s, even more outraged by what Frankel called Reform's "Jew-hating" tendencies, orthodox rabbis led by Samson Raphael Hirsch developed the movement of Neo-Orthodoxy. This movement, while accused of being nothing but "Jewish ultramontanism" by its Reform opponents and while certainly attached to traditional forms of worship and Jewish life, soon proved to be no less modernized and adaptive to its non-Jewish environment than the more liberal movements it opposed.[107]

In part because internal divisions within German Jewry were just sorting themselves out in the 1840s, there was still a great deal of fluidity between the different groups. Furthermore, any discussion of Jewish reform efforts in the 1840s must attend to three clearly distinct but nonetheless interconnected concerns: the reform of Jewish religious life (with its various divergent directions), the struggle for formal political equality, and the struggle to overcome the barriers of prejudice in daily social interaction with Gentiles. These concerns were intertwined in various complicated ways. Thus, for example, theologically conservative Jews might resist religious reform efforts and yet wish and work for formal political equality. Or, for example, impoverished rural Jews might actually oppose the introduction of political equality because they feared a concomitant upsurge in prejudice and violence in daily social interaction. Some groups might simply work for all three goals, while explicitly seeking to incorporate Jews from different theological perspectives; the Badenese *Verein zur Verbesserung jüdischer Zustände* (Club for the Improvement of Jewish Conditions), for example, set itself precisely this task.[108] Alternatively, Jews and concerned Gentiles might identify a need to overcome social barriers before there could be any hope for the introduction of political equality. Or finally, well-intentioned Gentiles could mistake Jewish efforts at social integration for a readiness to leave behind all religious differences as well. In all probability, it was these final two possibilities that were operative in Scholl's and Struve's efforts on behalf of Jewish-Christian integration.

Meanwhile, it was not at all clear that Conservative or Neo-Orthodox Jews were the only ones attached to the Jewish faith or to a Jewish identity in general; one of the great developments of the 1830s and 1840s had been the growth of a sort of "Jewish pride" movement in Germany. While a fair number of educated and assimilated Jews in the first years of the nineteenth century had converted to Christianity—the famous "ticket of admission to European culture"—it was precisely reform activists in the 1830s and 1840s who eloquently recalled their fellow Jews to the value of Judaism.[109] As one Jewish newspaper put it in 1848, for a few decades conversion had seemed like an easy option—"a little bit of baptismal water in order to wash away all political obstacles." But recently, "Jews have become a bit more *difficult* on this point . . . a certain sense of honor . . . has developed."[110] In part this phenomenon was an enraged response to the way German monarchs had developed the notion of a "Christian state" in their eagerness to stave off potential revolutionary upheaval; however patently this motive revealed a cynical instrumentalizing of religion, the inevitable effect—as liberal, nationally identified Jews in particular would find offensive—was to reinforce an identification between Germanness and Christianity.[111] In part, too, the "growing strengthening of self-esteem among the Jews" was simply a result precisely of many educated Jews' greater assimilation into gentile society.[112] And finally, the move to reclaim Jewish identity was partially also a response to the distressing fact that the era of Enlightenment and partial emancipation had not done away with anti-Jewish prejudice; in many ways it seemed that such prejudice was once again on the rise.

Struve's friend Gabriel Riesser—although based in Hamburg, he was constantly in dialogue with Badeners and closely monitored developments there—was the most eloquent (and prominent) Jewish rights activist of the 1830s and 1840s, and the most sophisticated analyst of anti-Judaism. In his journal, *Der Jude*, Riesser in 1833 called on Jews to have a "dignified pride" and "a feeling of independence": While for a time many educated Jews had "sought all salvation in saying the name 'Jew,' and everything connected with it, only very softly, and ever more softly, till one could not hear it at all—as if thereby in the end one could make forgotten all the injustice, all the suffering, all the hate that had been attached to it," this, Riesser felt, was a "useless striving." Instead, he stressed that while "forgiveness and forgetting may heal wounds after victory has been won," as long as the injustice lasted "the oppressor must be sternly and seriously reminded of his wrong, so that he stops committing it." In an essay from 1831, Riesser had also dissected Gentiles' "craven arrogance" and "pleasure in oppressing": "Only a slave-people," he remarked, "can take delight in the greater enslavement of a few; only a feeble cowardly nation can find in the contrast of a tiny number of oppressed a means for rousing its sense of self-worth, a means for stimulating it in its sickly impotence."[113]

But all this insight and pride could not stop the revival of anti-Judaism in the 1840s in both respectable and popular circles; the battle for self-respect continually had to be fought anew. Anton Rée, for example, the leader of the interethnic Hamburg club, struggled in 1846 over what caused such ferocious anti-Jewish sentiment to persist—could it possibly be, he tentatively proposed in an awkwardly circumlocutory formulation, the "screaming [differences] of blood and popular custom," a "racial or tribal hostility" more deep-seated than religious fanaticism? Utterly clear that this was "a wrong . . . *others* must make up for," he nonetheless acknowledged how extraordinarily difficult it was to maintain "cheerfulness and life-courage" in the face of hate, and pleaded with his fellow activists to remember that "one's own consciousness is still rich enough in true manly defiance, still strong enough to carry us over the deepest abyss that opens up before our feet."[114] And meanwhile, as the Jewish historian Adolf Jellinek put it in 1845, Jews in so many communities still had "no inkling of what they—by their human dignity and as sons of the state—deserve."[115]

In this complex context, the growth of Christian dissent—both of the *deutschkatholische* and the Free Protestant variety—was of the greatest interest to Jewish observers. Not only were Jewish rights activists forced to confront the question of Christian dissent for political reasons—because German governments repeatedly elaborated a comparison between dissenters and Jews—but there were religious ramifications as well.[116] For in face of the rise of an avowedly anti-Jewish religious right, members of the Jewish community pinned great hopes on the possibility of a less hateful Christianity. As a Baden-based paper explained,

> The old Christian church wanted to be the sole source of salvation, and we Jews were damned in its eyes; now a daughter is emerging from the lap [of this church], that teaches, just as Judaism does, that all virtuous people are qualified to be saved—can one hold it against the Jew, if the progress of the daughter is not a matter of indifference to him?[117]

At the same time, as one commentator suggested, "the religious movements within Christianity also have a mighty influence over those within Judaism."[118] Some Jewish commentators worried about the atmosphere of religious hostility and polarization exacerbated by the emergence of dissent.[119] Others challenged dissenters' supporters to be consistent: "If concern for [*deutschkatholische* movement founder Johannes] Ronge and his church springs from the pure source of love and toleration [rather than simply from disgust at Catholicism], then that same concern will become no less loud in face of this question of humanity"— that is, "the Jewish question."[120] Yet others simply praised the effect dissent had on gentile attitudes toward Jews. As one report from Mannheim to *Der Israelit des Neunzehnten Jahrhunderts* put it, "Thereby now, that the Christian confessions are being brought closer to each other, thereby, that in more recent times one hears less about the *one and only truth*, the step has been taken which opens people's hearts to a truly humane religion."[121] Many Jewish observers were clearly hopeful that sympathetic Gentiles would help to break down the barriers of prejudice between the two groups, and they saw Christian dissenters as likely contributors to this process.

Jewish rights activists were convinced that only practical efforts to bring Jews and Gentiles together socially could diminish prejudice. For example, the anonymous author of *Eine deutsch-jüdische Kirche: Die nächste Aufgabe unsrer Zeit* (A German-Jewish Church: The Next Task of Our Time)—probably the Berlin reform activist Sigismund Stern—explained in 1845 that "the German governments are not showing any signs of willingness to emancipate us, whether this is in deference to an unfavourable public mood, or out of other reasons, in any case we can expect our equalization only from a befriending of the people."[122] *Der Jude in Deutschlands Gegenwart* insisted that "associations for the purpose of eliminating social barriers and prejudices must be formed among Jews and non-Jews."[123] And *Der Israelit des neunzehnten Jahrhunderts* suggested that

> while up till a few years ago the question of emancipation was preoccupying people almost exclusively, and one anticipated all salvation for Israel from the practical resolution of the same, . . . one is nowadays . . . arriving more and more at the conviction that with the external emancipation very little would as yet be accomplished for the desired transformation of Jewish conditions. One is therefore conceptualizing this question in its deeper sense, in its social and religious aspects, and the more external, legislative-political aspect is retreating more into the background.[124]

The difference between Jewish and gentile perspectives on Jewish-gentile relations, however, was this: Even the most reform-minded Jews, in other words, even those who urged their fellow Jews to assimilate completely in social terms, almost always refused to let go of Jewish religious difference. Thus, for example, the author of *Eine deutsch-jüdische Kirche* argued that "we must therefore give up all that is unnecessary and repelling, that obstructs a more intimate civic amalgamation [*Verschmelzung*]," but he was equally adamant that "the *truths* of Judaism, its whole spiritual content, this we want to hold fast to and will not give it up at any price."[125] Typically, Jewish commentators simply did not see a conflict between religious difference and social integration. As Rée put it: "We want a political and social equalization *in spite of* confessional difference." Rée could thus have been speaking directly to Scholl and Struve when he added: "Also with respect to the general Jewish question we thus strive in opposition to those Christians who say there shall be no longer any difference whatsoever between you and us; but, *nota bene*: you must also for your part give up something, and confess yourselves to—Christianity. (!)"[126] In a related vein, the *Allgemeine Zeitung des Judenthums* defended "the *truth* that is in Judaism" and reported with scorn on the way dissenting leaders "just love to add in 'the free Jews' with the 'free Protestants' and 'free Catholics.'"[127]

And Rée's colleague Eduard Cohn criticized efforts "to homogenize the confessions," calling instead for "separation of church and state, so that every individual can live according to his conscience."[128] Finally, Scholl and Struve's friend Raphael Loewenthal, more theologically radical than Rée and Cohn—he was disgusted with (what he called) Judaism's "shipwreck of rotten, used-up institutions"—nonetheless had absolutely no intention of leaving the Jewish faith itself behind. Rather, "the innermost kernel of Judaism, the great unclouded idea of God must be preserved for the people in living immediacy. . . . We must leave behind a pure, noble religion . . . for our children and grandchildren." Far from wanting to join the Christian dissenting movement, then, Loewenthal instead saw in it an inspiring example to emulate *within* his own religion.[129]

While none of these comments were directed explicitly at Scholl and Struve and their Monday Club, the implications of the Reform Jewish perspective for understanding the strengths and weaknesses of Scholl's and Struve's vision are evident. On the one hand, Scholl, and most especially Struve, seemed to have come to the conclusion that social rapprochement was a necessary precondition for reducing prejudice and achieving political equality. On this point, many Jews agreed. On the other hand, Scholl persistently, and Struve increasingly, seemed to have misinterpreted both Jews' efforts to achieve social integration and political equality, *and* efforts at religious reform *within* Jewry, as signs of many Jews' willingness to leave behind the Jewish religion entirely. On this point, Jews of almost all political and religious persuasions disagreed most strenuously. The Monday Club was clearly designed to contribute to breaking down the barriers of prejudice that still divided the people of Mannheim, and Scholl's inclusive worship services and Struve's calls for mixed-confessional schools and mixed-confessional social clubs likewise represented important steps in that direction. But Scholl's and Struve's insistence that Jews give up their religious difference met with sustained opposition from all but a tiny minority of Jews (either those who were entirely antireligious or those who were converts to Christianity).

That Jews in Mannheim were just as appalled by gentile insensitivity as Rée and Cohn were in Hamburg, emerged from a report sent from Mannheim to the *Allgemeine Zeitung des Judenthums* in May 1847. The Mannheim correspondent reported on an article that had been published in the *Mannheimer Abendzeitung*:

> How far the radical press goes with its delusions and contradictions one can occasionally see in the local *Abendzeitung*. [This paper], which has often enough supported the rights to, and debates about, the emancipation of the Jews, in these days has made the declaration: educated Jews should no

longer concern themselves with emancipation, but rather should convert *en masse* to the "free congregation," and thereby bring a satisfactory sacrifice for "humanity". . . . What egoism!

Furthermore, as the *Allgemeine* brilliantly observed, since the dissenters' religious ideals were nothing other than what "Judaism had already, in Mosaism, proclaimed and taught," then why should Jews convert to dissent? The dissenters, it suggested, "should much rather come to Judaism!"[130] While the original article in the *Mannheimer Abendzeitung* carried a Hamburg by-line, it was clear that the editors of the *Abendzeitung* had either not distanced themselves from its content, or had themselves added the offending commentary to their Hamburg staffer's report. The *Abendzeitung* had been a longtime supporter of Scholl, reporting frequently in glowing detail on his and the *deutschkatholische* congregation's activities. The timing of the article's publication suggests that (like Struve in November 1846) now also the most prominent liberal newspaper in town (in April 1847) was falling for the seductive reasoning represented by Scholl and others like him. Certainly, some Jews must have continued to attend *deutschkatholische* services and the Monday Club.[131] But other Mannheim Jews quite apparently saw where ex-Christian religious humanism was leading, and strove to spell out the dangers.

Jewish activists had repeatedly stressed that religious humanism could also be formulated in terms accepting of diversity rather than tending toward absorption or erasure of differences; Moses Mendelssohn had argued already in 1783 that *"religious union is not toleration;* it is diametrically opposite to it."[132] But Christians, no matter how philosemitic they felt themselves to be, apparently could not hear this. The tragedy of Scholl's and Struve's efforts on behalf of Jews in the 1840s was that their "sword of love" did not only seek to shatter barriers, but also to destroy the identity of those on the other side. What was meant to be a democratic dialogue too soon turned into a highly problematic monologue.

5

THE FEMINIST CONUNDRUM

ALTHOUGH some contemporary feminists insist that women are fundamentally different from men, and that the goal of feminism is to reorganize society in line with "female values," many of the most sophisticated feminist theorists of the 1980s and 1990s have challenged the "commonsense" notion that differences between men and women are self-evident or grounded in nature. They argue that the meanings we attach to biological sexual difference, and even the very notion of biological sexual difference itself, are preeminently social constructions.[1] But to almost all political and religious activists of the 1840s, no matter what their ideological point of view, no difference seemed more natural, more incontrovertible, than the difference between the sexes. Nonetheless—inadvertently proving just how unstable gender categories actually are—contemporaries put forward quite conflicting accounts of what exactly women's difference consisted. They argued, for example, over whether women were more susceptible to sin, or more moral, than men, or whether women were by nature unreliable or by nature faithful—and often, quite unself-consciously, they made antithetical claims concurrently. Increasingly, there was also a spirited controversy over whether women's difference justified their political disenfranchisement and legal, economic, and social subjection, or whether it might not be possible for women to have greater equality and yet maintain their difference; the male leaders of the religious dissenting movement of the 1840s were the most vocal and widely publicized advocates of this latter position. But the notion that women as a group simply were naturally different from men, and that such difference was a good thing and, indeed, needed urgently to be preserved, went largely unchallenged.[2]

Also most female feminists and political activists of the day, like Louise Otto, Fanny Lewald, Johanna Küstner, and Kathinka Zitz-Halein, continually linked their demands for greater equality, and/or their efforts to expand women's sphere of activity, with concern about retaining women's femininity and difference from men.[3] They distanced themselves from "those who have brought the phrase 'emancipation of women' into discredit by degrading the woman into a caricature of the man," as Otto put it in the opening issue of her *Frauen-Zeitung*.[4] Even the writings of Louise Aston, despite their critique of loveless marriages and despite Aston's own short-lived but much-mythologized experiment in free love, atheism, and cigar-smoking, rarely called into question standard conceptions of gender roles.[5] Indeed, so pervasive was the consensus about women's nature and its essential difference from men's that recent feminist scholars of German feminism have asserted that a critique of this consensus would have been unimaginable in the 1840s.[6] The views advanced by autodidact philosopher Louise Dittmar, however, who came to public attention through a speech she delivered to Carl Scholl and Gustav von Struve's Mannheim Monday Club in 1847, constitute a sharp and startling contrast to the perspectives on gender relations prevailing in her day.[7]

What distinguished Dittmar (1807–84) from her contemporaries was neither her political persuasion—her political writings clearly place her within the camp of "radical liberals" or "radical democrats" (to use the terms of the time) to which many 1848 revolutionaries also belonged, nor her close ties to the religious dissenting movement, nor her advocacy of women's rights per se. Rather, what distinguished Dittmar was, first, her extraordinarily unusual willingness to question the notion of sexual difference. What also differentiated her from her contemporaries was the theoretical and philosophical quality of her analysis of the female condition, and the ways her efforts to work within the ideological frameworks available to her—particularly liberalism and religious criticism—exposed the contradictions and limitations of those frameworks, despite their seeming coherence and universal applicability.

Dittmar had no problem articulating precisely what she thought was wrong with her society. "Since my earliest youth," she wrote in 1849, "I found nothing more painful than the lack of respect for and devaluation of my sex. . . . All the conditions in which women find themselves seemed to me insulting and inadmissible."[8] The problem, as she pointed out, was how hard it was to engender change, and so she tried to tackle the dilemma from many different angles: "I seize upon whatever can help me with this, thus I seized upon the social movement, thus the religious movement."[9] Dittmar here clearly stated her method: to appropriate anything from the conceptual frameworks available in her day that could assist her in making sense both of the female condition and the possibilities for social transformation. The difficulty was that women's concerns did not easily fit within either of the available frameworks. This was because of the specific historical circumstances under which both the liberal and the radical religious projects had evolved.

Liberalism, like the Enlightenment from which it grew, offered a vision of equality and free self-determination for all individuals, but—as Joan Scott in particular has pointed out—the universal, abstract, rights-bearing individual was initially imagined as a man. Presenting itself as gender-neutral, the liberal project was exclusionary and self-contradictory from the first. The crucial irony for women was that the very same "state of nature" to which Enlightenment-inspired philosophers and policy-makers referred in proclaiming the equality of all (white, Christian) men, the very starting-point from which they derived their own "natural rights," also offered them the most seemingly incontrovertible proof of the difference between men's and women's bodies and the different traits, tasks, and spheres "naturally" appropriate to each.[10] Anyone seeking to advance women's rights was thus left with a peculiar dilemma—stymied by the seeming opposition that had been established between equality and difference. Would-be feminists could either try to extend the seemingly universal, seemingly gender-neutral language of equality, liberty, and happiness also to women; or they could try to develop the notion of difference assigned to women into an insistence on women's special needs and/or capacities. But, as Denise Riley has most eloquently elaborated, neither approach is fully satisfactory. However much gender may be a social construction rather than a biological verity, simply to claim inclusion in the gender-neutral category of "human being" threatens to make invisible precisely those very specific ways those human beings labeled "women" have been oppressed. Conversely, to concur that women have different needs and capacities from men threatens to lock them into that difference, to reinforce the notion that they do not deserve equality.[11]

Radical religious criticism too had its roots in the Enlightenment, with its insistence on human autonomy and reason and—simultaneously, paradoxically—its rage at the ideological power churches had over the hearts and minds of their members. The defense and validation of individual human subjectivity vis-à-vis institutional religious authority thus became a cornerstone of religious critics' project, and the revival of a militant Catholic neoorthodoxy in the supposedly so enlightened nineteenth century made institutional Catholicism a particular target of progressives' hostility. But another crucial element in religious reformers' and radicals' battles with the Catholic church in the first half of the nineteenth century had to do with sexuality and marriage. Whether defending priests' rights to marriage in the anti-celibacy campaigns of the late 1820s and early 1830s, or individuals' rights to free choice in love in the mixed marriage controversies of the 1830s and 1840s, critics of the Catholic church expended a great deal of energy defending the claims of the (male) body to (legitimate) sexual pleasure, and glorifying the power and moral value of married love—all the while unreflectingly merging sexuality, marriage, reproduction, and domesticity. Circumscribing a private sphere free from the control of religious authorities in particular, and celebrating marriage as the site of untrammeled bliss and individual self-development and perfectibility, became articles of faith for religious reformers and liberals alike, as well as for their dissenting heirs in the 1840s. Because of this specific context of conflicts in which the religious dissenting movement evolved, the dissenters' defense of women's equality proved to be inextricable from their effort to justify women as worthy love objects, and to defend the idea of a romantic partnership.

Louise Dittmar was the most important contemporary critic of mainstream Badenese liberals' views on gender relations—particularly as those views were summarized in Carl Theodor Welcker's famous essay on the subject in the *Staats-Lexikon* (discussed in detail below). Dittmar was also the only women's rights activist of the 1840s whose work called into question—however tentatively or implicitly—the masculinism at the heart of religious dissenters' defenses of individual subjectivity and sexuality. What makes her work especially intriguing is the way she pushed against the limits of the available systems of meaning, exposing the inadequacies of the extant philosophical frameworks even as, seeking to make them work for her, she remained entangled within them. Her writings reveal just how radical a critique of conventional gender arrangements was imaginable in her day, even as she ended up reproducing some of her contemporaries' most problematic assumptions. An analysis of the evolution of her thought from 1845 to 1849 shows how difficult it was to sustain a critique of her contemporaries' notions of gender difference in face of the persistence of women's concrete disenfranchisement in economic, legal, and political terms. It reveals as well the near-impossibility, in view of her contemporaries' profound investment in marital bliss, of finding a language capable of communicating the limitations of the marital ideal, while nonetheless insisting on every individual's rights to love and personal happiness.

Louise Dittmar

Dittmar was born in Darmstadt—the seventh child of ten—into the family of a higher treasury official and thus into the comfortable ranks of the German Protestant bourgeoisie. Although Dittmar's father worked at the court of Hessen-Darmstadt's grand duke, the family did not have conservative leanings. At least two of her brothers had ties to leftist circles. One was a friend of Georg Büchner's, and one married the daughter of C. W. Leske (Karl Marx's Darmstadt publisher) in whose home many radicals gathered. These familial ties presumably reinforced Dittmar's own political leanings. As the one unmarried daughter, she was weighed down by many domestic duties and was unable to receive any formal education. But after her parents' death, when Dittmar was thirty-eight years old, she began to publish, producing nine books in the space of five years. The first two, *Bekannte Geheimnisse* (Open Secrets, 1845) and *Skizzen und Briefe* (Sketches and Letters, 1845) covered a wide range of political and social issues and addressed women's disenfranchisement in scathing terms. Four books on religious topics followed: *Der Mensch und sein Gott* (The Human Being and his God, 1846), *Lessing und Feuerbach* (1847), *Vier Zeitfragen* (Four Timely Questions, 1847), and *Zur Charakterisierung der nordischen Mythologie* (Characterization of Nordic Mythology, 1848). *Vier Zeitfragen* was a reprint of the lecture she delivered to the Mannheim Monday Club. The applause and encouragement she received from the club (and especially from Scholl and Struve) gave her the impetus finally to acknowledge authorship of her previous books, which had appeared anonymously, and thus it is this group which has ensured her place within historical memory.[12] Two poetry collections followed: *Wühlerische Gedichte* (Subversive Poems, 1848) and *Brutus-Michel* (1848), both celebrating leading revolutionaries and criticizing the Frankfurt Parliament.[13] Dittmar also delivered further lectures—to audiences in Mainz, Hanau, and Darmstadt—in the course of 1848.[14]

In January of 1849 Dittmar founded the journal *Soziale Reform*, one of the five feminist journals launched in Germany during the revolutionary years. In it she printed not only her own essays, but also articles by others, the majority of which addressed women's concerns. Contributors included Ludwig Bamberger, Karl Fröbel, Claire von Glümer, Johanna Küstner, Malwida von Meysenbug, Louise Otto, and Otto Wigand.[15] The journal folded after only four issues, but the essays in it were reprinted, along with some new ones, in a book entitled *Das Wesen der Ehe nebst einigen Aufsätzen über die soziale Reform der Frauen* (The Essence of Marriage, Along with Some Essays about Women's Social Reform, 1849). The essays on marriage in this book, collectively entitled *Das Wesen der Ehe*, were republished separately in 1850, and this is the last book Dittmar ever managed to publish. Notwithstanding the fact that her theological writings had been favorably reviewed by newspapers not only in Darmstadt and Mannheim, but also in towns as far away as Halle, Berlin, and Hamburg, and that her own journal had attracted contributions from some of the leading democrats and women's rights advocates of her day, she was unable (despite repeated efforts) to find a publisher in the post-revolutionary years.[16] During the years of reaction, publishers probably found the causes Dittmar advocated simply too risky to take on.[17] Indeed, with the exception of Louise Otto's *Frauen-Zeitung*, which was not forced to shut down until 1852, no women's newspaper outlasted the revolution.[18] Criticized (as less than appropriately feminine) also by other women's rights advocates, Dittmar eventually grew discouraged and stopped writing. She died in obscurity three decades later. The obituary her nieces issued did not mention that their "good aunt" had also been a writer.[19]

A close examination of Dittmar's writings from 1845 to 1849 reveals her to be one of the foremost German spokespersons for that international phenomenon of utopianism, that mixture of radical liberalism, progressive Christianity, and various strands of early socialism, that (as Barbara Taylor has most persuasively argued) was so frequently more attentive to women's rights than later "scientific" socialism was.[20] Like Gustav Struve, Dittmar was enraged by the halfheartedness and inconsistency of Germany's most prominent liberal leaders, and called for the extension—to women, to Jews, and to the poor—of such classic liberal goals as education, free self-determination, and self-development. Like Carl Scholl, she was fascinated by Lessing and Feuerbach and the forms of religious criticism and religiously inflected humanism they advanced. She was also as familiar with the work of Rousseau, Voltaire, Montesquieu, and Diderot as with that of Goethe and Schiller, and she was equally well versed in the classics and the Bible; all her writings built on, and commented critically upon, this legacy. Like utopians elsewhere, Dittmar was as concerned to criticize the role of the military, the death penalty, the incitement to national and tribal hatreds (*Völkerhass*), the mishandling of industrial development, and the growing poverty of her day, as well as the hypocrisy of a Christianity which intolerantly denied rights to Jews, as to expound on the oppression of women. She thus embedded her critique of the extant gender relations in a critical analysis of all social injustice, both along class and religious lines, calling for a redistribution of wealth and for a radical humanism that considered Jews to be Christians' moral equals. Also like other utopians, Dittmar moved back and forth between demands for reform and calls for a complete social revolution, between invocations of the need for individual responsibility and an insistence on the necessity for structural change, between a belief that extending love and charity to the oppressed was an important political task, and a Left Hegelian conviction that things needed to get worse before they would get better, and that a violent solution was inevitable. Above all, like most radical humanists, Dittmar continually struggled with the problem that the object of her solicitude—the human being—treated itself and others so badly. As a result, her writings moved back and forth between agonized acknowledgments of the mess human beings had made of the world, the persistence of their selfishness, stupidity, and cruelty—accompanied by an (almost Foucauldian) despair over the ways the physical torturings of the past had simply given way to more subtle but no less controlling psychological repression—and declarations that progress was constant and inevitable, and that the reign of justice and human love and decency was at hand.[21]

Just as the philosemitism Struve and Scholl advanced necessarily involved a multifaceted engagement with the legacy of Christianity, so too did Dittmar's efforts to develop a feminist analysis inevitably carry her onto religious ground. This was not only because it was specifically the religious dissenting movement of the 1840s that most actively promoted greater equality for women. Dittmar was also concerned to engage critically with Christianity because of her preoccupation with two other issues. Over and over again, Dittmar was drawn to a study of Christianity because of her interest in the workings of ideology, in the powerful hold it had on individuals' souls, and the difficulties individuals invariably encountered in constructing a self unbeholden to any higher authorities. Equally important, though harder to pinpoint, was Dittmar's persistent interest in the Christian legacy of disdain for the body and its claims and pleasures. In an era when most of her progressive male contemporaries invariably veiled (however flimsily) their defense of men's sensual enjoyment in odes to domesticity, to refer to women's sexuality in any way without immediately assuming its purpose was reproductive would have been quite scandalous; criticizing Christian devaluation of the body was one way to approach the unmentionable without mentioning it outright. But finally, one of the most important reasons for Dittmar's engagement with Christianity is that it offered not only a legacy of psychological and physiological oppression and one of human history's most successful excuses for earthly inequality. There was also a submerged strand within the Christian tradition that Dittmar could and did draw on: one that emphasized the equal dignity and worth of every individual and the transformative power of human love—a tradition of prophetic denunciation of injustice and a vision of human liberation for the future. This version of Christianity offered faith that a complete transformation and renewal of the world—the creation of justice on earth—was actually eminently, indeed imminently, possible.

The Thorny Crown of Femininity

Dittmar's earliest writings were in many ways her most innovative ones.[22] The format of her first two books, *Bekannte Geheimnisse* and *Skizzen und Briefe*, was essential to her method and message. Both consisted of a large number of very short items (ranging in length from one paragraph to five or six pages), each of which developed one or two ideas. *Bekannte Geheimnisse* was a political satire loosely in the tradition of Voltaire's *Candide*, which followed the travels and travails of one "Juste Milieu," a muddle-headed German male of the middle strata, whose stuffiness, passivity, affable hypocrisy, political indifference, and lack of imagination, made him, in the view of Dittmar's narrative persona, a perfect representative of his class and nation. Juste Milieu was a sort of everyman, at times a bumbling bourgeois, at times Germany itself. As the book's title suggests, German middle-class life was full of dirty secrets, blatantly obvious to everyone and yet utterly taboo to discuss. Juste Milieu's episodic adventures gave the author the opportunity to poke fun at diverse institutions of German life: particularly the self-serving civil service, the military, the all-pervasive surveillance and censorship, the indecisive liberals in the parliaments, the churches—and the suffocating life-circumstances of far too many middle-class women. *Skizzen und Briefe* was even more fragmentary, offering reflections on economic, political, religious, aesthetic, and philosophical questions, and interspersing these essays with historical anecdotes, parables, and letters to various interlocutors. Breaking up the book in this way allowed Dittmar to play with point of view, speaking, alternately, in first and third person, as a man and as a woman, at times in a scholarly tone, at times addressing a personal friend, at times directing herself to the reader, a strategy whose effectiveness was enhanced by the author's anonymity.

Dittmar's anonymity gave her not only strategic flexibility, but also more authority, and made it less likely that the books would be written off as products of personal bias or a single agenda. Because of the way the different pieces of each text were juxtaposed with one another, each piece could be interpreted in multiple ways. A tale in which gender relations seemed to figure not at all, for example, turns out upon closer inspection to have much to say on the topic, once the metaphorical allusions have been decoded by reading the surrounding items. And yet each item's message was clearly meant to resonate on broader levels as well. Furthermore, in both books, gender relations did not become an explicit and constant theme until two-thirds of the way through. This may have been because Dittmar was always more than "just a feminist," and felt she had as much to say about other aspects of human relations as about gender—as indeed she did. Although not all her writing was equally eloquent, she did manage extraordinarily well to capture the complex mood of Restoration Germany—the anxiety, the yearning hopefulness and, above all, the sense of claustrophobia—with, by turns, exceptional sensitivity and biting sarcasm. It is also possible that the deferral of explicit engagement with gender relations was a ploy to draw in antifeminist readers in particular, and gain their interest and respect, before she presented insights to which she knew many of them would be vehemently resistant. Another reason for this structural strategy may have lain in Dittmar's conviction that the arrangement of gender relations in her society was inextricably intertwined with other social arrangements and could not be tackled in isolation. In all likelihood, all of these impulses were factors in her choice of organization.

The juxtaposition of diverse points of view in Dittmar's texts was also essential because of what she felt to be the near-impossibility of communicating persuasively the urgent need for a fundamental transformation in her society's gender relations. Especially in *Skizzen und Briefe* there is a painful self-consciousness that its author will be dismissed as subjective and partial, even as she tries to document the powerful investments that make it possible for the subjectivity and partiality of her opponents to be passed off as neutral, objective, and universally valid.[23] As she put it: "If I had the most incontrovertible certainties to say about the female sex, I would still be preaching to deaf ears; because those certainties, especially when they are presented as demands, are assigned to the realm of speculation rather than provable fact." She then went on to give a concrete example of her dilemma:

> How would I have to proceed, if I wanted to make the false position of the woman visible to the man? I would necessarily have to prove it in relationship *to him*. . . . I would have to move in real close: since the woman is forced to get married *at any cost*, so it is rarely important to her, to whom she gets married. So if you, dear man, would like a woman who likes you, you will seldom find one [under the current conditions]. You expect to have a compliant spouse, and she turns out to be willful; you wish for a wife who will be sweet to you, but she bestows her sweetness only on others; you want a rich one, but you find out that she is rich only in faults, etc. etc.

Most enraging to Dittmar was that, after she had logically demonstrated that each of these unpleasant scenarios derived directly from the grossly unfair expectation on women to marry themselves off at all costs, her interlocutor would still be incapable of seeing why women's status needed to change: "On the contrary, he would say: the *man's* status needs improving. He must be able to choose freely, he must be able to give his children a secure and independent lot so that they are not forced to enter a loveless marriage.—In short, he would turn everything upside down."[24] It was this state of affairs that explains the multiplicity of lines of attack Dittmar employed in seeking to persuade her readers.

One of Dittmar's earliest and most persistent concerns had to do with the difficulty of being a woman in her society. On the one hand, to be a woman meant that one would not be taken seriously, would be subjected to male authority, would not be seen as an individual in one's own right, and would not be able to participate usefully in public life. On the other hand, there was intense pressure on women to behave in properly feminine ways, to not step out of the ascribed gender role. It was, in short, an impossible conundrum. To be a woman was not desirable, but not to be a woman (i.e., not "womanly") was in some ways worse. Dittmar sought to communicate the anguish this conundrum caused in a variety of ways.

One task Dittmar set herself was to detail the social mechanisms by which women were kept in line. In a sketch entitled "Preconditions for Women's Human Rights," for example, she cuttingly observed that "to be charming is women's obligation . . . if charm is lacking, the salary is cut off." A woman could not even define for herself what femininity should mean: "Womanliness is not even recognized as such, unless it conforms to the fabricated requirements of the man." Women were not granted the status of subject, but only of object, and even that only if they were well behaved: "Let's call a spade a spade. A man never recognizes a woman as created for her own sake, and therefore allows her no free development. . . . If *he* can love her, she has fulfilled all conditions; if he does not love her, she loses all rights and therefore all recognition." Already as a child a woman was taught that she would get neither affection nor respect unless she was beautiful, and these lessons persisted into adulthood, for—she continued—despite efforts to improve German men's manners, there were still "gentlemen" in "so-called society" who "turn away mockingly if an unattractive, ungraceful woman enters." Counterbalancing such painful bluntness was the gentle humor of *Bekannte Geheimnisse*, and its description of Juste Milieu's search for the perfect wife: Juste Milieu's

> demands did not exceed those of any other man. All he wanted was a simple, modest, virtuous, lovable, cooperative, domestic, educated, sensible, talented, beautiful and wealthy wife, whose entire heart he would fill, who would be eternally devoted to him and who would have no other thought but him. If these conditions were fulfilled, Juste Milieu promised himself occasionally to look on her as his equal—provided that she never ever questioned his authority.[25]

Another strategy Dittmar experimented with was to suggest that the category "woman" needed to be expanded—that what constituted proper femininity should not be too narrowly defined. This strategy was implicitly evident in the ways she described heroic women of the past. Dittmar was, for example, especially intrigued by the figure of Charlotte Corday, arguing that male writers had misunderstood her, portraying her either as a woman vengeful because she had been scorned in love, or as a daydreaming virgin like Joan of Arc. Whereas, Dittmar said, "if I were a poet. . . . I would portray her as standing in the midst of life, . . . driven only by the power of an idea." Just as Dittmar praised the mytho-logical character Galathea for devoting her life to a higher love than love for a man while being no less a woman, so also she felt Corday was best explained as an individual whose greatest passion lay in "*helping*," whose "whole soul consisted of a struggling for liberty, which is the absolute opposite of *self-involved* love." According to Dittmar, Corday believed (however deluded this proved to be in hindsight) that killing Marat would bring an end to the ways the French Revolution—"whose sig-nificance lay in the *establishment of human rights*"—had turned into des-potism and violent anarchy. Corday was thus, in Dittmar's view, just like so many heroic men, a complex human being capable of extraordinary self-sacrifice. But Dittmar insisted she was also very much a woman: "adorned with all the advantages of her sex." In short, Dittmar found it offensive that "when it's a man they recognize that concern with love can give way to higher goals . . . when it's a woman they think that's unnatural, degenerate." But she clearly also rejected the notion that anyone should have to choose between love and those "higher goals": In a related tale, Dittmar explored the figure of Aspasia in ancient Greece, admiring how "Aspasia's character was incompatible with . . . every demand the Greeks made of *their* women." Yet Dittmar nonethe-less contended that "she was nothing so little as unfeminine, just be-cause she was a more talented and more demanding woman," while also reporting proudly that "the greatest man of her age found her to be exactly the kind of woman he was looking for."[26]

At yet other times, Dittmar tried simply to lay claim to being a human being and, accordingly, to deserving human rights. ("Let us say it loud and clear," she would write in 1847, "we *demand* happiness; we con-sider it our *right*.")[27] And yet already in her earliest writings there was a clear recognition that there was nothing simple about trying to include women in the category of "human beings."[28] This was partially because men often made "these traditional tragicomic mistakes—this position-ing of women above and below the human being."[29] But the most im-portant cause of the difficulty lay in the way Enlightenment narratives of human freedom and equality had not been designed to include women in the first place. Referring to those thinkers who theorized an original state of nature on the basis of which Germans could press their claims for greater democracy, Dittmar pointed out in *Skizzen und Briefe* that "they search about in all of existence to find an unconditionally free sit-uation for the human being [*Mensch*] but strictly speaking, they only understand that to mean the man [*sie begreifen im eigentlichsten Sinn nur den Mann darunter*]."[30]

Inserting women into the story of the social contract was not a smooth operation, for, as feminist theorists like Carole Pateman have pointed out in the 1980s, the implicit supplement to the social contract was always the sexual contract; from the outset, women's relationship to the body politic was meant to be mediated through her male partner, and only men were imagined as citizens.[31] Dittmar made quite similar points: "If only one would allow women their full human rights without preconditions, without making it necessary for them to buy into them with a marriage contract. Woman alone is not treated in accordance with universal contracts; she must offer more and receives less." Dittmar particularly singled out the self-contradiction of liberals, especially the way "they insist that before God and the world the human being is entitled to its rights and may make demands, while they cannot resist positioning the man vis-à-vis the woman as voluntary benefactor."[32]

The call for women to be treated in accordance with universal contracts might seem, on the surface, easy to implement—the circle of those who are considered citizens could simply be expanded to include women. But it was not so. For many political theorists of Dittmar's day, putting a woman into the category of equally entitled human being was perceived to be fundamentally disruptive of the social order, for the social contract's viability was felt to *depend* on the maintenance of the sexual contract. As Joan Landes has explained in discussing the effects of the French Revolution, the extension of equality to ever more men rested on the reformulation and exacerbation of women's inequality, particularly expressed through the formal exclusion of women from the political public sphere and their relegation to the realm of the family.[33] This inequality was justified by reference to the difference between the sexes supposedly inscribed in the laws of nature. In these matters, German liberals followed faithfully in the footsteps of their French predecessors.[34]

In light of these circumstances, another important strategy for Dittmar involved calling into question whether women really were, by nature, so very different from men. "I am suspicious of all characterizations of women that start from their antipodes, the men," she wrote. "They are not fair enough to acknowledge that there could be a life that is more beautiful and more appropriate for women without fearing that their male nature has been violated." In *Skizzen und Briefe* Dittmar still entertained the idea that perhaps a man and a woman might have different mental skills, but she was nonetheless convinced that with those different skills a woman could arrive at "exactly the same intellectual results." And furthermore, she insisted, "just because in the past woman could not do this or that, does not prove that this or that is impossible for her. . . . In short, I simply cannot admit that woman in any way at all is inferior to man."[35] This is a case Dittmar would later make more forcefully.

In her writings during the revolutionary years, Dittmar explicitly called attention to the ways in which that which was deemed natural was really the result of social conditioning. For example, in her essays on marriage, she pointed out that to provide no educational opportunities for a woman—to educate her for nothing else but domesticity—"and then to say, 'that is her destiny,' does that not mean that she is being *pre*destined?" In the concluding article in her journal *Soziale Reform*, Dittmar was even more direct in attacking the way "nature" was used to limit women's possibilities:

> What is nature, what is destiny? Is nature not itself changeable? Is the destiny of humans not something arbitrary? Truly, to legislate here is to be very presumptuous or very narrow-minded. It is possible that women will occasionally fail against nature, but who will have to suffer for it? Against their destiny? Who is insolent enough to force one onto them?

Dittmar argued that given the freedom to develop themselves, women could develop all the same talents as men. She insisted that no sphere need be closed to women:

> There is almost no field of social life which could then not be cultivated by and for [the woman]. For example the immense kingdom of natural science, chemistry, mechanics and their multitude of practical applications; psychology, medicine, from doctoring the soul down to physical nursing; intellectual and physical education, from poetry, philosophy and mathematics down to ABC and one times one; from the practicing of artistic poses down to athletics; the field of art . . . from the nurturing of creative genius down to mechanical copying.

All that was needed, Dittmar reasoned, was an equal opportunity for women to acquire an education. In this spirit she recommended the establishment of polytechnical institutes for women, and a "grand interlocking set of institutions," financed by the state but run by women, that would prepare women for the careers of their choice. And meanwhile, she observed, "I just don't see that . . . men . . . are all such geniuses."[36]

Most important, and this tendency was already evident in *Skizzen und Briefe*, Dittmar explored a different way to understand the lessons offered by nature. She proposed a view of nature that emphasized the differences between all individuals, irrespective of sex, and argued that what was natural was whatever was peculiar to a given individual. Rejecting the primacy of gender difference, she focused on differences *among* women and, indeed, among men. For example, in commenting on the plethora of prescriptive texts for women circulating in her day (one of the most famous of which was entitled *Elisa, Or Woman as She Should Be*), Dittmar declared pointedly: "There are no more and no fewer women as they should be than there are men as they should be."[37] In the same vein, she argued that "only that which contradicts the nature of a being, is unnatural, aside from that everything that is, is natural. Whether it contradicts the external demands on it or not, in no way diminishes its inner legitimacy." Over and over again, throughout the years, with ever more confidence, Dittmar would extol "*individual peculiarity*, without which people themselves and all of life are *without charm*," and insist that every individual "must be understood and treated as an end in himself, *as he is*, while the purpose of the whole must be directed toward transforming unity into the greatest possible diversity."[38]

Religious Criticism

It was no coincidence, then, that Dittmar's next four books addressed religious topics, for Dittmar found the strongest support for her emphasis on individual peculiarity and diversity and the need to encourage individual self-development in the rhetoric of religious criticism—even as her critical engagement with theology also helped her to articulate just how difficult achieving autonomous selfhood was. *Der Mensch und sein Gott* was in many ways a classic example of the standard rationalist religious criticism of her day. Positioning herself as a man—the title page said the anonymously authored book was "*von einem Weltlichen*" (by a man of the world, by a secular man)—Dittmar also clearly identified herself as a "theologically-untrained layperson," and indicated that the book was meant to provide an introductory overview of religious history and religious phenomena of the present for the educated, but not expert, public. *Lessing und Feuerbach* (her last anonymous work) simply reproduced hundreds of quotes from the writings of Lessing and Feuerbach, intercut with her own exegetical commentary on them. Dittmar's main goal in this text was to show how Feuerbach had improved on Lessing's ideas. Lessing's "fundamental mistake," according to Dittmar, was to assume the existence of a "personal God," a concept she felt was "absolutely irreconcilable with the independence of the human spirit"; his other error lay in seeking to portray "*Christian love*" as the "*true, universal love*," whereas, Dittmar felt, it really was only "a *conditional, exclusivist* love."[39] *Vier Zeitfragen*, the lecture she delivered to the Monday Club in 1847, represented an attempt to translate the insights she had gained from the study of religious criticism and history (and particularly her new fascination with the notion of the dialectic) to an analysis both of the economic and political tensions of her day, and of the psychological damage all political and religious systems of the past had done to human beings in general, and to women in particular. Dittmar clearly anticipated the revolution that would break out less than a year later, and her most urgent concern in *Vier Zeitfragen* was to awaken a feeling of self-worth in women so that the restructuring of society she felt was impending might include a revolution in gender relations as well. And finally, *Charakterisierung der nordischen Mythologie* ventured onto the terrain of paganism, with particular attention to the old Germanic gods; like *Der Mensch und sein Gott*, it represented a synthetic, popularized overview of others' research.

Der Mensch und sein Gott and *Charakterisierung der nordischen Mythologie* in particular also contained some rather problematic elements. Much of *Der Mensch und sein Gott* presented the familiar survey of developments from the ancient Greeks and Hebrews to the appearance of Jesus of Nazareth and the early Christian communities, then through the Middle Ages (with the obligatory excursus discussing the conjunction of Christian and Germanic traditions), and on to the Reformation and Enlightenment. Dittmar's analysis of each stage of historical development, however, was more radical than most. Dittmar judged each stage of human evolution as wanting because—while each held out the promise of a union between the human and the divine, a union of mind and body, a focus on earthly justice and human autonomy and reason—each time the promise had remained unfulfilled. Moses, Jesus, Luther, rational deism—each time humanity had moved a bit closer to God, a bit closer to recognizing its own worth. And yet each new progress had also brought with it a regress of sorts, either a new authoritarianism to which humans were subject, and/or a new level of self-denial and repressiveness toward the body. Over and over again, Dittmar defended "the guiltless body" and criticized how both Jewish and Christian teachings had demanded "voluntary *renunciation* of earthly satisfaction," and had "opposed sensuality, treating it as the root of all vices," while particularly the medieval, pope-run church "tore soul and body further and further apart."[40]

Dittmar's criticism of ancient Judaism as well as Christianity for its anti-sensuality marked a departure from other accounts of ancient Judaism (for example, those by Lessing or by most male dissenters of her day) which stressed the sensuality of the Hebrews.[41] This was hardly, however, a laudable difference; it simply shows how everyone filled out the contours of the generic narrative of historical evolution with his or her own pet concerns. (Indeed, in *Vier Zeitfragen* Dittmar would contradict herself by linking Jews and pagans with sensuality and the early

Christians with overweening spirituality.) Furthermore, despite the fact that when Dittmar turned to a discussion of her own era she uncompromisingly defended not only Jewish political equality, but also Jewish moral equality with Christians, her descriptions of ancient Hebrews nonetheless played into contemporaries' anti-Jewish stereotypes just as much as male dissenters' renditions had. Thus, for example, in *Der Mensch und sein Gott* she criticized the "pettiness" and "severity" of Jewish law, implicitly contrasted "Jewish stubbornness" with "Christian humility," and identified the persistence of belief in a domineering, punitive, and distant God as "the legacy of Judaism within Christianity."[42]

In a related vein, in *Charakterisierung der nordischen Mythologie*, Dittmar uncritically adopted the prevailing stereotypes of a fundamental Oriental-Germanic opposition. Once again, she inserted her own concerns into an otherwise unimaginative replication of the now increasingly standard narrative of the dialectical interaction of opposites—railing, for example, against the suppression of "misunderstood sensuality" and calling for "free *self-determination*" for all individuals. But she also contrasted the "fatalism" and "raw pleasure-seeking" of the Orientals with the "strength" and "higher self-esteem" of the Germanic peoples. Furthermore, in stark contrast to the cutting criticisms of German boorishness and mediocrity evident in her earlier writings, Dittmar now, in 1848, sought to flatter Germans for living in the "land of the dialecticians."[43] She also strategically announced both that Christianity and Germanicness were so compatible because Christ best represented the ideal of spiritual independence so central to the Germanic tradition, and that Germany was the land in which the reconciliation of age-old oppositions (including that between man and woman) could most happily be resolved.[44]

In many ways, then, these four texts are Dittmar's least successful writings. This was not only because the overt and obviously unreflected contradictions in her stereotypical representations could not minimize the ugliness of those stereotypes. It was also because her effort to reach a wider audience by appropriating popular analytic frameworks meant the texts largely consisted of reductionist summaries of others' ideas. *Vier Zeitfragen*, for instance, because of its more explicit focus on women's lot, did have some unique perspectives to offer, but it too frequently deteriorated into a potpourri of popular truisms.

Nonetheless, despite the fact that her four forays into religious criticism were largely unoriginal, taken together they do offer insight into what it was that attracted Dittmar to theological questions in the first place. First and foremost was her obsession with the difficulty of achieving a sense of self-worth in a hostile society—particularly for women. As Dittmar had put it already in 1845, "I know what a Sisyphus-task one burdens oneself with, when one espouses the cause of the female sex. . . . Since [the woman] has no sense of self-esteem, or rather has a limitless self-contempt, she must necessarily assume that he who takes on her cause is her enemy."[45] It was this concern that made Feuerbach's work so intriguing to Dittmar. From Feuerbach, Dittmar adopted the idea that what people worshipped as a God was really only the projected image of their own potential perfection; in projecting perfection onto a fictive being, they denied their own worth. As Feuerbach himself had put it in 1841 in *The Essence of Christianity*: "Man in relation to God denies his own knowledge, his own thoughts, that he may place them in God. Man gives up his personality."[46] This particular idea of Feuerbach's occurred in endless variations in Dittmar's work. In *Der Mensch und sein Gott* Dittmar wrote that "the evils of our time lie precisely in that lack of thinking-for-oneself which is a result of faith, for the faith in a power that takes care of us leads to faith in [a power] that does our thinking for us." In *Lessing und Feuerbach* she again argued that "as long as we assume the existence of a 'higher' reason, so long must we naturally despise our own [reason]." And in *Vier Zeitfragen*, Dittmar announced that "no God can make up for the loss of our self-esteem and there is no higher task than to wake this feeling in ourselves and others." Defending the legitimacy of each and every individual's "*YEARNING for happiness*," she thus demanded the encouragement of "a sense of self-worth for *every* person, for each *sex* equally."[47]

The study of theology clearly helped Dittmar think critically about ideology more generally, and many of her remarks about religion are only thinly veiled references to gender ideology: "You must believe, what you do not know; you dare not ask, how did this or that come to be . . . you must simply blindly obey." Dittmar, indeed, explicitly credited Feuerbach with helping her to see the links between divine authority and all other authorities and social pressures that kept women in mental bondage. "Feuerbach's *Essence of Christianity* gave me the courage," she would write in *Soziale Reform* in 1849,

> in battling the highest authority [i.e., God] simultaneously to battle against every *authority imposed from above* . . . Without smashing the last hidden fetter, the most hidden little thread that so mysteriously creeps over, we can not free ourselves from the after-effects of a morality that entangles us from earliest adolescence on and that particularly for the female sex becomes a practically impenetrable web.[48]

And yet, Dittmar's vision of a just society not only demanded an attack on conventional Christianity, but also drew on the Christian tradition. As she explained in *Vier Zeitfragen*: "When I candidly say: I am not religious, all I am saying is I am not that, indeed I hate that, which one usually takes it to mean; my nature consists in *resistance against injustice*, not in *pious tolerance* of the seemingly inescapable. And I believe that only the *misunderstanding* of the truly religious (*that* which was *the basis* of all reforming efforts) interprets spiritual independence as irreligiosity." On the one hand, Dittmar would go to the extreme in denying the existence of divinity outside of humanity, for in her time no one could know what perfection human beings were capable of once the authorities of state and church had been removed. *Der Mensch und sein Gott*, for example, concluded on this note:

> Our era no longer wants to honor a dead biblical literalism; what is at stake is to shape life newly out of itself. [The era] struggles for fulfillment of a dream, that it has sought for millenia in heaven, it is searching for peace of mind. It wants to establish a new idea, . . . a bible which declares human beings as an association in the here and now, and that awakens the powers of the inexhaustible *human* spirit for *this* life. To create this living bible is the task of all thinking and truthful people; it is their divine calling to let the new *savior* be resurrected, to realize the miracles, to raise the dead, to heal the sick, to multiply loaves and make fire from water. . . . Our church is the world, our religion is reason, our Christianity is Humanity, our statement of faith is freedom, our worship service is the truth.[49]

On the other hand, however, as this quote indicates, no other language but religious language could express the urgency with which Dittmar felt a total transformation of individual souls and social structures was necessary and legitimate, and no other language could properly convey her sense of the sacredness of each individual's right to self-determination.

In short, there is an unresolved tension in Dittmar's writing between scathing attacks on the hypocrisy and oppressiveness of the Christian churches and a reliance on a language and a conceptual framework that can only be described as profoundly religious. For example, in *Skizzen und Briefe* she told the story of Beate, a woman burned at the stake for heresy and witchcraft in the seventeenth century. In her final words to the townspeople, Beate said: "I had no God and no faith, for I had your God, and I cursed Him because He could not unite the spirit and the bodily senses, because He directed the striving soul only toward heaven and filled it with scorn and loathing for earthly needs. . . . Desist from the God who does not comfort the penitent and take in the lost!" Both anti-Christianity and deep religiosity are evident here (as is, again, the concern with the claims of the body). Similarly, to underscore the legitimacy of her demand for justice for women, Dittmar concluded an essay on women's rights in her newspaper *Soziale Reform* with a passage which, for readers schooled in the New Testament, created clear echoes between women and the early Christian disciples:

Poor and without rights, oppressed legally and in principle, physically un-
suited for battle, intellectually deprived, . . . limited in her means, scorned,
ridiculed, repressed and persecuted with the full weight of a life-ethic that
is hostile to her—where should she gather strength, where should she plow
and sow without land? . . . And yet, she will plow and sow and reap a thousand times over, like no other worker in the vineyard of the Lord!

This passage reverberates with and reformulates at least two biblical passages: one from the Apostle Paul's Second Letter to the Corinthians,
and one from the Gospel of Matthew about God's just treatment of laborers in His vineyard.[50] Dittmar thereby laid claim to an ancient language of justice and reinterpreted it to incorporate women.

The Trouble with Love

That Dittmar's angry references in her religious criticism to the repression of the body and the bodily senses need also to be read as references
to women's sexuality in particular becomes clear in light of her writings
on love and marriage, especially her final book, *Das Wesen der Ehe*. With
this book, she returned to the problem of liberalism. *Das Wesen der Ehe*
was a lengthy response to Carl Theodor Welcker's 1838 essay on gender
relations in the *Staats-Lexikon* he edited together with Karl von Rotteck.
The response suggests how intensively Dittmar was in dialogue with
Badeners, and with the liberalism they supposedly represented so impressively. Dittmar was, in general, disgusted with "these liberals of
1830" (a reference to the French July Revolution and the subsequent
onset of the glory days of Badenese liberalism) because, as she announced, "they do not even concern themselves with finding the causes
of social abuses, but rather only prove their historical necessity and development." Indeed, as she pointed out, Welcker's whole article simply
"starts from the premise and the endeavour to subordinate the woman
to the man and to justify all the already existing legal and moral conditions relating to the woman."[51]

Welcker's essay, "*Geschlechtsverhältnisse*" (Relations between the
Sexes), does indeed provide an illustrative summary of mainstream liberals' various views on gender, and the subtle ways these were interconnected with one another. The *Staats-Lexikon* represented the cumu-
lative and synthetic statement of southwest German liberalism in the
pre-revolutionary years. As Leonard Krieger has noted, it was "the most
influential organ of political liberalism in pre-March Germany," and
Karin Hausen and Carola Lipp have specifically demonstrated how representative Welcker's ideas on gender were.[52] A brief look at Welcker's

arguments helps to explain the difficulties Dittmar ran into when she tried to refute them.

Welcker could imagine women only in relation to men. Women, he believed, were (or at least should be) fundamentally different from men, and it was precisely that difference that both made love between the sexes possible and delightful, *and* made women's equality utterly undesirable. "Most women," he asserted, "either are wives, or want to become such." Women who demanded equality, however, forfeited that option, because (Welcker was sure) a pleasant family life "with such unfeminine men-women [*Mannweiber*] would be impossible." (Indeed, nothing—except for an "effeminate man"—was "as repugnant and perverted as the man-woman.") Meanwhile, to reject equality for women, as he reassured his readers, "does not in the least impair the principle of the social contract or consensus, but rather is appropriate to it"; giving women equality, by contrast, would not only "contradict human destiny and happiness and destroy the dignity of family life," but would also constitute "the overthrow of our prevailing social order."[53] On women's difference and subordination, then, both happy family life, *and* a healthy, stable social order depended.

Welcker's social vision was grounded in (his interpretation of) biology; the starting-point for his philosophical reflections on the political rights of women was the sexual act—in which men naturally played the "active" role and women naturally assumed the "passive" one. After intercourse, he assured his readers, man (who was naturally rational) was "*freer*" to take responsibility for "other *external* activity"; woman was naturally emotional, and her purpose was "*the lasting maintenance of the species through inner development.*" Woman's "life-goal is love," Welcker announced, but, as he repeatedly made clear, he could not conceive of any purpose for (proper) women's sexuality besides reproduction, a task for which he found women's bodies particularly well designed. Indeed, he argued (in a classically unreflected merging of marriage, sexuality, and reproduction) that "reproduction is more of a need for the woman than for the man; the woman suffers more from being unmarried than he does"—while also implying that lack of love could lead women into "mental derangement." In sum, as Welcker put it, "the woman's entire being is directed toward the familial and sexual relationship, and the fulfillment of her duties in this respect constitute her whole worth." Yet Welcker at certain moments also worried that women might not be quite as passive as he hoped; he thus announced that women needed to dedicate themselves to "self-sacrifice, self-restraint and purity" rather than "selfish drives and passions"—for, as he warned, "where women become degenerate, there civic virtue and strength also disappear."[54]

Throughout, then, Welcker moved back and forth between an insistence that nature itself guaranteed women's difference and women's proper place, and an apparent anxiety that "the voice of nature does not speak quite so intelligibly to everyone"—and thus that the views he was advancing needed to be ensconced in law and buttressed by continual admonitions to women to conform.[55] And throughout, Welcker also worked to portray marriage as the greatest goal a woman could achieve, revealing *en route*, once again, liberal men's keen investment in couple-dom and domesticity. While liberals would fight fiercely to wrest marriage away from church control in an era of rising religious conservatism, the idea of civil marriage was sacred. As Dittmar once remarked wryly to a fellow feminist, to be an overt atheist in her society was easier than to challenge the concept of civil marriage.[56]

In her response to Welcker, Dittmar struggled to expose the gaps in his reasoning, while simultaneously building on certain elements of his argument. Thus, for example, Dittmar unequivocally demanded equality for women within marriage, and—a logical move in 1849—sought to portray that equality as an inevitable and necessary concomitant to political democracy. "True democrats," Dittmar strategically stressed, would "carry the democratic principle, the full granting of rights and the full enjoyment of personal freedom, also into this realm [of marriage]. . . . It is therefore a logical consequence that, as soon as the democratic principle has achieved victory, the essence of marriage will undergo a complete transformation." But Dittmar also sought to build on Welcker's assumptions about women's difference from men. Thus, for instance, at one point she accepted his identification of women with emotion and men with reason, while seeking to turn this association to women's advantage by arguing that

> if we want to make life more human, and not only more manly, then the man seems to be just as un-self-sufficient as the woman. . . . Just as the eye and the ear perceive in different ways, and one can measure and weigh the same things in different ways using either size or scales, and every narrowing or limiting, every subordination of these absolutely valid assessments must lead to wrongheadedness, mistake, deceit, and confusion; so also with the subordination and limitation of the female judgment and its influence on the shaping of life.[57]

Notions of women's difference also surfaced at moments when Dittmar was calling attention to women's specific vulnerabilities as women. This was especially apparent when Dittmar criticized the humiliating invasion particularly of women's privacy in divorce courts, or when she called for the state to take responsibility for childcare, or when she insisted that the state provide recourse for women against domestic abuse. In general, notions of women's difference emerged most clearly when Dittmar was seeking to elaborate her rather utopian notions of the role of the state. (The state, she thought, should get out of the business of regulating marriage and divorce entirely; couples in love could choose to live together and could choose to sanctify their union in a religious ceremony if they wished; those no longer in love could separate.) Rather than dedicating its laws to enforcing women's sexual fidelity, economic dependence, and political invisibility, Dittmar maintained, the state "should be the representative of female rights":

> It should understand the woman as woman, understand her not only in her right to be human but also in her entitlement as a female, and not let the latter lead to an impairment of her personal freedom; it should guard this [personal freedom] doubly, against the encroachments of the external world and against the world of men, and thereby protect her against her husband as against every other man.

In a related vein, Dittmar strategically suggested that the reason why women needed to participate in making and administering the laws that affected women was because women's perspective was different from men's. Similarly, she tactically contended that it was precisely because women had for so long been deprived of an education and a means of self-support that the state should finance institutions of higher education specifically for women, and assist women in establishing a variety of institutions "which would provide [women] the means to their economic freedom."[58] (She particularly recommended institutions which would combine theory and practice, such as teaching hospitals and polytechnical institutes which were also producers' cooperatives.) All these arguments fit neatly into *Das Wesen der Ehe*'s overall point: that the happy marriages Welcker wanted would only be possible if women had political representation and, above all, economic independence. In sum, in her eagerness to name more specifically what women needed in order to be more capable of achieving equality with men, Dittmar inevitably fell into assuming that very difference between the sexes she elsewhere criticized.

Dittmar got into a similar conundrum when she attacked Welcker's notions about marriage. She fiercely disputed his glorification of coupledom and domesticity; yet she just as fervently insisted that every individual deserved love and happiness, that love and happiness, indeed, were "the purpose of life."[59] One strategy Dittmar used was to deromanticize domesticity, reminding her readers of the mind-numbing tedium of most domestic tasks and the profound sense of claustrophobia that the much-vaunted familial togetherness could produce. While Welcker had rhapsodized about "happy family life. . . . this Christian and German family life—the greatest and most hopeful progress in the whole history of humanity," Dittmar declared that "we would like to hurl this happy family life into the deepest abyss," and wished "that this current family life could be rotted out root and branch!"[60] Another tactic Dittmar used was to reject Welcker's assumption that women were fixated on love, arguing in *Das Wesen der Ehe* that "women are capable of and interested in other things besides domesticity" and that there simply was "no proof that a woman has a stronger need for love [than a man]."[61] Also in her other writings, Dittmar expressed fundamental annoyance at the notion that "people like so much to identify woman's only role as to be that dependent creature, incapable of a single autonomous thought, who takes no *freely active* part in the higher development of humanity; whose only motivation is love." "There could come a time," she declared, "when more than one woman renounces that kind of love, in order to consecrate herself to a higher one."[62] At another point in *Das Wesen der Ehe*, Dittmar stressed that love was not just the property of married couples. Calling love "the driving force of life," an "earthshaking power" with "a great role to play in world history," Dittmar imagined a grand "coalition" of lovers of all sorts against the corruptions and oppressions of the sick society ("*Afterkultur*") she felt she lived in. This coalition would be composed of "men and women, the married and the unmarried, old and young . . . for father and mother, brother and sister, spouses and lovers are all part of it with their whole being." And at yet another point, Dittmar simply argued: "We call attention to the contradiction which lies in assuming such a need for love in a woman that failure to satisfy it causes mental disturbances, and yet wanting to force the woman to remain locked within the current arrangement"—in other words, within a marriage in which she was economically, legally, and politically dependent.[63]

But finally, Dittmar's most fully developed and yet also most elusive strategy involved her efforts to expose the disjunctions between sexual love and actual marriages. Part of this involved calling attention to those (buried) moments in Welcker's essay when he himself had allowed that desire and domesticity could sometimes be at odds. For although the bulk of his essay had pretended that love, sexuality, marriage, reproduction, and cozy familialism were inextricably fused, he had concluded his essay on a rather different note. In view of the fact that "the sexual drive" was "the strongest human drive," Welcker did feel that it "might become necessary in larger cities" to provide some (state-regulated) prostitutes. Not that he used the word prostitution, or even mentioned that actual women participated in the activity. Rather, invoking the classic nineteenth-century concept of the prostitute as society's sewer, Welcker delicately proposed that it might be necessary "to provide a latrine [*Abtritt*] for the otherwise uncontrollable, depraved drives . . . in the greatest possible concealment and yet well supervised by the police."[64] In her response, Dittmar expressed particular exasperation at Welcker's insensitivity to the plight of unmarried women, who, as she fumed, "have according to the author's theory the choice, either to go crazy, or——[*sic*] the farthinking statesman does, in point of fact, find certain state-run arrangements fully necessary, notwithstanding the fact that these arrangements also demand their willing victims."[65]

But another part of Dittmar's response involved reminding readers, however elliptically, of the gap between female desires and what most men actually provided. The challenge was to find a way to criticize her society's marital arrangements without implying that emancipated women had no interest in love. Already in her tale about the seventeenth-century witch Beate, in *Skizzen und Briefe*, Dittmar had sought tentatively to communicate what to most of her contemporaries obviously seemed like a paradox: that Beate was repulsed by the man who sought her hand ("she acknowledged to herself that she was more than devoid of feeling, for the love of this man only filled her with horror"), while at the same time "the strangest thing in her mysterious nature was an indescribable yearning for love." In *Das Wesen der Ehe* Dittmar took a somewhat different tack. There she remarked that "not just being deprived of love, but also a marriage which conflicts with a certain kind of individuality is the cause of many spiritual and physical disturbances and abnormalities." Or again at another point, she contended that within marriages as they were currently arranged, people were "physically and spiritually lacerating themselves, wearing themselves away."[66]

The combination of vagueness and fervor in these remarks stood in sharp contrast to the explicitness of her other demands, and their meaning is harder to read; but other comments were more direct. Already in *Skizzen und Briefe* Dittmar had spoken of "that which grows in the innermost essence of a woman's soul: love, the love which they so selfishly and narrow-mindedly imprison, which they violently suppress into impotence and unconsciousness." Now too in *Das Wesen der Ehe* Dittmar rhetorically asked:

> And for love, that springs out of the most heated yearning for satisfaction, for this thirst of the soul, to which asylum does he [the stupid Philistine—i.e., Welcker] direct it? To the prison of civil marriage, this economic and political asylum of unfreedom. Love is something he does not know, it is not listed in his *Staats-Lexikon*, he only knows "relations between the sexes," legitimate and illegitimate.

Although (by her own account) tempted to spend a larger part of her argument criticizing Welcker's claim that women needed love more than men did, Dittmar instead decided to build her case on his claim by showing how women's capacity for love was systematically distorted by her society's socialization of women. "We are ashamed of the bodily senses," Dittmar averred in disgust, going on to argue that "the disrespect for woman, her social repression, is most closely linked with the disrespect for and repression of the senses." Among the middle and upper classes in particular, she reported, "every natural feeling is systematically dissolved, chemically decomposed, as it were, through the lye of conventional prejudices":

> Especially in the case of women this desire is suppressed, weakened and clouded through an unnatural upbringing, through moral thumbscrews and through the most clever principle of deadening. We must therefore not . . . let ourselves be persuaded into the assumption that the love of women can be awakened by a command here, be held in check there, be bought with a position, a provision here, be banned with an external necessity there, in short, that it could be, according to inclination, allowed to develop so and so many degrees of warmth, and then soon be turned down under the freezing point. And we may just as little think ourselves wiser and better than those who—in spite of all thumbscrews and cooling-down devices that we call a good upbringing, propriety, morality—every now and then explode the whole distillation-apparatus into smithereens.[67]

Far from being the embodiment of passivity, interested only in reproduction, as Welcker proposed (decent) women were, women, Dittmar here again implied, were not so very different from men: just as fully human, just as passionate, just as multifaceted. Not only did they have the capacity and yearning to participate in a multitude of publicly useful activities; they had the right to private pleasure as well. Instead of seeing sexual difference as a justification for inequality, Dittmar suggested that it was only social and marital inequality that kept men from recognizing the similarities between the sexes: "The barbarism that makes the woman the man's possession allows . . . only the woman in the woman to be visible; . . . the woman's human nature . . . cannot express itself. That is why the woman remains a slave . . .; that is why love remains the man's monopoly . . . and that is why woman, marriage and love bear the brand of slavery." It was not that women had no sexual desire, it was that social conditions (the fear of pregnancy and pressures for propriety) limited its expression: "The man can satisfy the urge for love, at least in the physical sense, very easily, while the woman is forced to resist that urge for physical and moral reasons."[68]

In an era when "speaking of the body" (in feminist critic Mary Poovey's words) was considered utterly unacceptable for honorable middle-class women, and in which (as Thomas Laqueur has documented) a great many medical professionals and social theorists alike believed that proper women had no sexual feeling, Dittmar's indirection is understandable, even as her boldness is remarkable.[69] In both her indirect and explicit remarks, Dittmar offered a challenge to those liberals *and* dissenters who too easily ignored women's sexuality and emotions despite all their invocations of the glories of sexual love. *Das Wesen der Ehe*, however obliquely, pointed toward a third alternative, one that would take women's sexual and emotional perspectives seriously on their own terms—even as her other writings strove to show just how constricting and oppressive to women assumptions about women's difference from men could be.

That Dittmar had the courage to venture such views at all was in part due to the fact that the revolutionary years were a sort of millenial moment, in which the upending of all inequalities seemed possible. Dittmar's goal was to make sure that women were included in any project of social transformation. In 1849, she wrote in her newspaper:

> For [the female sex] the "self-purpose of the human being" must become the female gospel. With social reform the Reformation-story of [women] begins. More than a female Huss and Luther will rise and press for the letter of the gospel, and hammer her articles against the indulgences. The truth, that the human being only exists for his own sake is written too deeply into the human heart to fail to catch fire, as soon as life itself throws in the spark. And it did that.

And, she concluded, "the liberation of women will be the greatest revolution, not only of our time, but of all times, for it will break chains that are as old as the world."[70] The defeat of the revolution brought an end to such dreams. But already in her own day, Dittmar did not have much success.

In particular, her frequent rejection of the notion that there were natural differences between the sexes was not a popular position. Johanna Küstner, for instance, expressly castigated Dittmar for pursuing a path "hostile to female nature." Kathinka Zitz-Halein went further, explaining that Dittmar found little support among other women because "a true woman cannot agree with teachings that strip her of all femininity, that make her into a man-woman, a hermaphrodite."[71] And indeed, even in Dittmar's own journal, other feminists (both male and female) obsessively reiterated their beliefs in natural differences. Ludwig Bamberger, for example, while on the one hand arguing that "the restriction of women to the life of feeling only is nothing but a perfumed slavery, a Christian-Germanic harem-theory," also insisted that "the *equal* participation of both sexes in public life [that he had been advocating] does not mean the *same* participation." For, he inquired rhetorically, "who would want to efface differences that are given in nature?" Louise Otto also announced that "I start from the view that the nature of woman is different than that of the man," while Claire von Glümer expressed particular pity for "those sad creatures that one calls emancipated women . . . the ones that have stopped being a woman and yet cannot change their innermost being, cannot remake themselves into a man."[72]

Nonetheless, despite her isolation (or maybe because of it) Dittmar's writings are important both for the history of German feminism and for the histories of German liberalism and religious dissent. Not only does her existence teach us that the history of German feminism was not simply one of unrelenting accommodation to a philosophy of sexual difference.[73] Even though she was never able satisfactorily to resolve the tension between equality and difference that liberal theory had established, nor ever found a way to talk with adequate explicitness about the moral legitimacy of women's sexual desire and pleasure, Dittmar's writings also served to lay bare some of the unacknowledged investments and exclusionary foundations upon which both the liberal and the religious dissenting projects of her day were built.

The variety of generic forms with which Dittmar experimented—political satire, cultural criticism in allegorical and epistolary form, religious and mythological history, philosophical and theological exegesis, public speech, poetry, and journalism—gives evidence not only of her intellectual range, and the ways she struggled (despite the inevitable contradictions and setbacks) to evolve as a thinker and an activist. It also suggests something about the extraordinary difficulty of finding a language capable of convincing others that justice, pleasure, and a society in which individual peculiarity is valued were goals worth fighting for . . . especially when one's efforts were continually invalidated as signs of overemotionality, or insufficient femininity, while the goals themselves were deemed either sentimental, shocking or, simply, impossible to achieve.

CONCLUSION

DEVELOPMENTS in 1830s and 1840s Baden reveal that neither secularization nor religious revival were straightforward processes. Instead, the pre-revolutionary era brought an everincreasing interpenetration of religious and political matters, as religious reformers turned to political authorities for redress of their grievances, as the political left and middle made the demands of religious reformers their own, and as the religious right came to adapt political methods for its own ends and to gain greater influence in political life. Religious conservatism was clearly central to the early emergence of organized political conservatism; by representing themselves as more in touch with "the people" than their liberal counterparts, religious conservatives successfully put liberals on the defensive. Political liberals, whose faith in progress was profound, were utterly unprepared for the emergence of such a modernized conservatism; neoorthodoxy was a phenomenon they could only understand as a regression to medieval times. Meanwhile, both liberals' and radicals' resistance to the religious right was by no means antireligious. As Hermann Greive once perceptively remarked, "The release and self-liberation of the individual from institutional bonds entailed a growing emotional, internalized attachment to religion. . . . The very critique of religion was instrumental in saving religion."[1] But it was not only the sincerity of their own beliefs that caused progressives to insist on their own religiosity; the felt need to resist the religious right on its own terms also led many to appropriate religious discourse to justify their own goals. Simultaneously, however, religious conservatives adopted the language of progressives and laid claim to such ideals as "freedom" and "tolerance" for themselves.

On the one hand, a reentry into the imaginative universe of the 1830s and 1840s reminds us of the powerful sense of possibility which existed in an only partially modernized society poised on the eve of a revolution.[2] It shows that the 1830s and 1840s were not only a time of intense battle over the content of "true Christianity," but that these decades also saw a major conflict over the content of "true liberalism." For many radical democrats of the day firmly identified themselves also as liberals, and would have been quite distressed to find that the more moderate liberals they saw as traitors to the liberal cause have subsequently frequently come to be seen as representing liberalism as a whole. The history of nineteenth-century Germany would be impoverished indeed, then, without a reconstruction of the visions (however fragile *and* inadequate they proved to be) of those pre-Marxist forms of radicalism which both depended on a humanized form of religiosity and insisted on a more comprehensive interpretation of the Enlightenment legacy. In particular, Scholl, Struve, and Dittmar's hybrid blend of radical liberalism, unorthodox Christianity, and early forms of socialism suggests that there did exist a German variant to that utopianism which was found in France and Britain in the 1830s and 1840s, and which also in those lands was concerned with the opening of new avenues of Jewish-Gentile cooperation and the critical interrogation of gender relations.[3] Their examples highlight the similarities between German utopianism and its French and British counterparts, but also make clear that it was a truly indigenous creation, an outgrowth of specifically German religious conflicts, and inspired more by Lessing and Feuerbach than by Fourier, Saint-Simon, or Owen.

On the other hand, a reexamination of the pre-revolutionary years also illuminates the origins of later tragic developments. Focusing on the conflicts of this era, for example, shows how central the aggressive deployment of anti-Jewish rhetoric was to the formation of a successful conservative Catholic populism, a phenomenon that would only intensify in later decades. It reveals as well how much difficulty mainstream liberalism intrinsically had with the tension between equality and difference—the conflict over who should be included and who excluded from the realm of formal politics—from its beginnings as a political movement. Reconstructing the religious conflicts of the 1830s and 1840s also foregrounds the central significance of anticlericalism to the formation of liberal thought and thereby helps to make greater sense of German liberalism's post-revolutionary history in another way. It helps to explain how, through a complicated process, liberals came to be bearers of the ideals of secularization and the separation of church and state (for they were not always that), *and* how their seemingly inconsistent animus toward Catholicism came simultaneously to be embedded in this new commitment from its inception. It helps to illuminate, in short, how German liberals would later get caught in that near-fatal alliance with the authoritarian Prussian state against the Catholic church called the *Kulturkampf*.[4]

Integrating the religious and political histories of the pre-revolutionary period also suggests the need for a new framework for the much-debated question of whether German liberalism differed substantially from its western counterparts.[5] There is a puzzling lack of attention to the "Jewish question" in most standard studies of German liberalism, a lack evident as well in the extant efforts to analyze German and western liberalisms—and the Enlightenments from which they grew—comparatively. This is all the more peculiar since it was primarily the Nazis' genocidal war against the Jews that led to the historiographical preoccupation with German liberalism in the first place, and also since Jewish studies scholars have produced extensive commentary on the relationship between liberalism and Jewish emancipation. Surely, attitudes about minorities—attitudes about "difference," as it were—are as crucial an indicator of the quality of a nation's liberalism as its (much more frequently studied) attitudes about suffrage, economic conflict, or state authority, and the anti-Jewish attitudes of leading liberals should be taken seriously as part of the history of German liberalism, and not just of the history of antisemitism. Simultaneously, however, the recent burgeoning of critiques of the western Enlightenments for their antisemitisms and racisms also suggests the need to interrogate some of the premises underlying another extant historiographical consensus—the consensus that the ultimately tragic trajectory of German history was somehow due to an "inadequate" spread of western Enlightenment ideals. Perhaps, then, as Claudia Koonz put it recently, the point might be not so much "to debate whether Germans absorbed too much or too little Enlightenment, but to emphasize, in the tradition of the Frankfurt School, the Enlightenment's dual legacy: on the one hand, the 'emancipatory project' of increasing human equality, and on the other, a totalizing Utopian vision."[6]

In neglecting the role of religion, and particularly in neglecting the interplay between religious conservatives and political liberals and radicals, many historians have also missed an opportunity to notice just how politically volatile debates about such seemingly private matters as individual subjectivity, sexuality, love, and marriage were. For numerous reasons, attention to these kinds of "personal politics" is crucial for a full understanding of politics in general. For one thing, it was on the ground of religious conflict that activists of the 1830s and 1840s sought to negotiate the "irrational" aspects of political life: to come to terms with intergroup prejudice and sexual desire, the power of ideology, and the complexities of individual psychology. Only against this background, for example, can we understand both liberals' and dissenters' rage at religious conservatives' unabashed efforts to invade individual souls—conservatives' efforts to be, in Alban Stolz's unapologetic phrasing, "a saw in the conscience [*eine Säge in das Gewissen*]."[7] And only against this background does utopian radicals' insistence that social transformation needed to be rooted in interpersonal encounters and self-transformation make sense. This is also the relevant context for understanding both Jewish rights and women's rights activists' interest in analyzing their opponents' psychological investments in oppressive practices, the difficulties in developing self-esteem that subordinated groups experienced, and the near-impossibility of exposing how ideology could make unjust relations seem "natural" without getting written off as biased oneself.

Furthermore, while most scholars treat hostilities between progressives and religious conservatives as self-evident rather than inquiring into their sources, a close examination of the roots of these hostilities in the 1830s and 1840s reveals that they had a great deal to do with the opposing sides' fierce battle for control of the private realm, and above all with their conflicting conceptions of sexuality. Liberals' and radicals' near-hysterical fury at the invasion not only of individual psyches, but also of the marital pair and its bedroom—represented by the Catholic priest and the practice of the confessional—was the preeminent cause for their inability to be tolerant of Catholicism. Theodore Zeldin eloquently made this point for nineteenth-century France over two decades ago.[8] It holds no less true for nineteenth-century Germany.

Finally, the religious conflicts of the pre-revolutionary era in Germany offer insight into an understudied area in the history of sexuality. The history of sexuality is a relatively new field; one of its major contributions has been to show that while human beings have engaged in and discussed sexual activities for all of human history, it was the turn from the eighteenth to the nineteenth century, and even more the course of the nineteenth century, that brought a particular conception and systematization of "sexuality" as an overwhelmingly important area of human experience separable from, and yet interconnected with, all the rest. It was in this time period that sexuality increasingly was thought to constitute an individual's innermost essence, and it was in this era that sexuality became a prime focus of social concern, with debates about sexuality frequently becoming debates about society as a whole—developments that have only intensified up to the present day. Throughout this time period, furthermore, the dialectical interaction between efforts to control sexual expression, and efforts to liberate it—along with the incitements, and pressures to conform, paradoxically generated by those respective efforts—continually produced new understandings of what exactly sexuality was.[9] But while scholars have noted that one fundamental aspect of modern notions of sexuality is the near-religious fervor with which Europeans and Americans of the twentieth century celebrated the transformative and redemptive qualities of sexual activity, they have not adequately made clear how this phenomenon emerged. Paying attention to the circumstances that caused sexual relations to become a major terrain upon which religious conservatives and their various critics sought to work out the proper relationship between individual subjectivity and religious authority, and to the ways conservatives' assaults on dissenters in particular for their supposed sexual immorality led dissenters to portray sexual love as not only natural but also divine, offers a symptomatic glimpse of how the more widespread spiritualization of sexuality might have come to be.

Part of my purpose, then, has been to experiment with integrating the study of interethnic and sexual relations into the study of questions more typically raised in traditional German historiography. The study of the interaction of race and gender, or of ethnicity and sexuality, remains only in its infancy in European historiography in general, and in scholarship on Germany in the eighteenth and nineteenth centuries in particular. One way these concerns have been brought in is through the analysis of Jewish women's doubly burdened lives; Deborah Hertz's and Marion Kaplan's elegant studies are excellent examples of this trend.[10] But recent developments in U.S. scholarship suggest that the racial and gender identities of white men—and the ways they imagined both blacks and women—can be important areas of study as well.[11] This is the approach I have tried to adapt in critically analyzing both the self-understandings of Christian German men, and the ways they conceived of Christian-Jewish and male-female relations.

Differentiations along ethnic and sexual lines, however, are by no means parallel phenomena; the dynamics of "othering" functioned entirely differently for Jews and women and require different conceptual apparatuses in order to be understood. Not only were Jews a tiny minority, while women constituted half of society, but the rejection of their equality on the basis of their "difference" from the Christian male norm worked differently for each group: Jews were constantly enjoined to become less different, while women were insistently told to retain their difference. And meanwhile, the mutual embeddedness of assumptions about gender and assumptions about sexuality—what Nancy Armstrong has called "the turn of cultural logic that both differentiates the sexes and links them together by the magic of sexual desire"—tremendously complicated women's ability to claim equality.[12]

Furthermore, conflicts over Christian-Jewish relations and over male-female relations intersected in complex ways. Liberals' anger at the Catholic hierarchy's response to the anti-celibacy campaigns and its intervention in mixed marriages, for instance, contributed decisively to liberals' eventual defense of Jewish rights to political equality. Efforts to encourage Christian-Jewish intimacy, in turn, both depended on the participation of women, and drew on the rhetoric of the campaign to defend mixed Protestant-Catholic marriages. Furthermore, gendered language provided a way to process matters quite unrelated to gender relations, while "ethnicized" language formed a recurrent motif within intra-Christian conflicts over sexuality. Conservatives' assaults on dissenters relied on both sexual innuendo and vituperative anti-Judaism, for example, while both male dissenters and Dittmar's explorations of sexuality relied in part on German-Oriental contrasts and implicitly anti-Jewish rhetoric.

In order to make sense of these phenomena, I drew on insights recently developed in the fields of critical race studies, postcolonial theory, feminist theory, and the history of sexuality.[13] Much of this scholarship begins from the assumption that there is nothing natural or inherently obvious about the definition of an ethnic group and the relations of ethnic groups to each other, the traits assigned to each gender and the ways gender relations are thought properly to occur, or the ways human sexuality is understood and organized, but that these are all preeminently social constructions whose formation is profoundly implicated in relations of power. These scholars have particularly worked to expose what strenuous ideological labor goes into the upholding and "naturalization" of such seemingly self-evident binary oppositions as white/nonwhite, Occident/Orient, man/woman, heterosexual/homosexual, and (as my own work suggests) Christian/Jewish. Repeatedly, they have pointed out how important it is to attend to the dynamics of power by which the second half of each conceptual pairing continually gets subordinated to the first, which is presented as normative. But they have also stressed that these hierarchically organized pairings are not stable. For one thing, the seeming opposites actually have much in common with one another. Moreover, each half of the pairing is itself internally divided, crosscut by other categories of knowledge. And finally, the seemingly normative category in each pairing is actually dependent for its existence and meaning on the subordinated one. One corollary of this conceptual dependence is that obsession with the marginalized, subordinated group often lies at the heart of the more dominant group's self-understanding.

In Germany in the first half of the nineteenth century, what it meant to be a Jew, and what it meant to be a Christian, was indeed only seemingly self-evident. The meaning, or identity, of each term was recurrently debated and elaborated. Thus, for example, contemporaries continually worried over whether Jews' difference from Christians resided in their distinctive nationality, religious views, or social behavior. At the same time, there was growing intra-Christian conflict, as humanist and inclusive forms of Christianity vied for supremacy with hierarchical and exclusivist varieties. In the course of these conflicts over Jewish and Christian identity, especially as ever more radical forms of Christian humanism proliferated, it became increasingly unclear where exactly the boundary between Jews and Christians lay. Fights over the political enfranchisement of Jews and over the disenfranchisement of Christian splinter groups in particular exposed the instability of this boundary. Also in this context, conservative Christians began to use anti-Jewish rhetoric against other Gentiles as a way to mark the borders between acceptable and unacceptable forms of Christianity, again demonstrating the metaphoric potential of apparently literal categories. Disputes over what precisely constituted the differences between Christians and Jews also necessarily involved conflicts over what the proper relations between those groups should be, as evidenced especially in the heated controversies over philosemitic efforts to encourage greater intergroup intimacy and familiarity. In short, then, although Jews were a marginalized minority in nineteenth-century German society, Jewish-Christian relations formed a central concern in Christian self-understanding.

Also striking is how frequently battles among men over the terms of Christianity involved an intense preoccupation with women. In these disputes women sometimes went unnamed, but they were implicitly present at every point, as men fought with one another over the legitimacy of sex and love, and over who should control marriage and family life. These conflicts concerned whether or not men had a fundamental right to sexual relations (as in controversies over priestly celibacy), whether or not men should be able to choose freely who they would love and marry (as in disputes over mixed Catholic-Protestant marriages), and whether husbands or clergymen were the final arbiters of what went on in the familial sphere. Contemporaries also put forward quite conflicting opinions on what properly constituted masculine and feminine nature. Progressives of all stripes, for instance, urgently defended every man's natural need and right to couple with a woman and enjoy domestic bliss with her, while conservatives treated bodily urges and emotional attractions with deep suspicion. The political explosiveness of these conflicts should not be underestimated; they shaped the evolution of key political alliances and hostilities, and they determined the relationship between state governments and the institutional churches. Matters involving the most intimate reaches of individuals' psyches, and their most intimate interpersonal relations, were also the highest matters of state, forming the subject of stormy parliamentary debates and diplomatic correspondence with the Holy See alike. In all this urgency to defend domesticity, however, women themselves were rarely granted the status of individual political subjects, but rather functioned primarily as the objects fought over; those who styled themselves as progressives but nonetheless wanted to restrict women to the private sphere sought the justification for this restriction in the notion that women were "by nature" different from men. Nevertheless, the intensity of attachment men so clearly had to the domestic realm, and especially the very fact that conflicts over familial life formed such a prominent component of political debate, exposed the fictionality both of the public/private divide and of its gendered connotations. Meanwhile, even among those men styling themselves as women's rights advocates, the constantly recurring image of priest and woman together in the confessional pointedly revealed the depth of male anxieties about the vulnerability of the private sphere, the instability of the heterosexual pairing, and the potential unreliability of (the otherwise so celebrated) women.

In sum, then, what it meant to be a Jew, a Christian, a woman, or a man were all matters of repeated contest in the 1830s and 1840s; the identities of each term were continually renegotiated. Becoming alert to the instability of these only seemingly self-evident terms helps make sense of such peculiar but pervasive phenomena as the coexistence of pro- and anti-Jewish arguments in a parliamentary speech, the coexistence of glorifying and denigrating remarks about women in a dissenting sermon, the deployment of anti-Jewish rhetoric against other Christians in the Catholic press, or the prevalence of sexual innuendo in a tract explicitly criticizing sexual immorality. It helps us, in short, to think in new ways about the relationships between the ambiguity of individual and group identities and the complexities of ideological conflict.

ABBREVIATIONS USED IN NOTES

AlZJu	*Allgemeine Zeitung des Judenthums*
Bgf	*Der Bürgerfreund*
BK	*Badische Kirchenzeitung*
BuFra	Bundesarchiv (Aussenstelle) Frankfurt
DkSB	*Deutschkatholisches Sonntags-Blatt*
DtZus	*Deutscher Zuschauer*
ErzFrei	Erzbischöfliches Archiv Freiburg
EwL	*Es werde Licht!*
FJour	*Frankfurter Journal*
FrGM	Archiv der Freireligiösen Gemeinde Mannheim
GlaKa	Generallandesarchiv Karlsruhe
IsJa	*Der Israelit des neunzehnten Jahrhunderts*
JuDeuGe	*Der Jude in Deutschlands Gegenwart*
KKr	*Katholische Kirchenreform*
KR	*Kirchliche Reform*
LakiKa	Landeskirchliches Archiv Karlsruhe
LBIYB	*Leo Baeck Institute Year Book*
Lbote	*Der Landbote*
MAb	*Mannheimer Abendzeitung*
Mbote	*Der Morgenbote*
MJour	*Mannheimer Journal*
MMorg	*Mannheimer Morgenblatt*
OberZ	*Oberrheinische Zeitung*
Ori	*Der Orient*
Phö	*Der Phönix*
RefJu	*Die Reform des Judenthums*
RZ	*Reform-Zeitung*
Seebl	*Seeblätter*
SocRep	*Sociale Republik*
StaFrei	Stadtarchiv Freiburg
StaHei	Stadtarchiv Heidelberg
StaPreu	Staatsbibliothek Preussischer Kulturbesitz, Berlin
SZKS	*Süddeutsche Zeitung für Kirche und Staat*
UBGie	Universitätsbibliothek Giessen
ZrelInt	*Zeitschrift für die religiösen Interessen des Judenthums*

NOTES

INTRODUCTION

1. Friedrich Hecker, *Die staatsrechtlichen Verhältnisse der Deutschkatholiken mit besonderem Hinblick auf Baden* (Heidelberg: Groos, 1845), p. 17.

2. See ibid., pp. 23–24 and 58–59; Hecker, in *Verhandlungen der Stände-Versammlung des Grossherzogthums Baden* (II. Kammer), 22 Aug. 1842, 4. Protokollheft, pp. 128–30; and id., "Weiblichkeit und Weiberrechtelei," in Helmut Bender (ed.), *Aus den Reden und Vorlesungen von Friedrich Hecker* (Waldkirch: Waldkircher Verlagsgesellschaft, 1985).

3. Valuable recent studies in the field of German religious history include Helmut Walser Smith, *German Nationalism and Religious Conflict: Culture, Ideology, Politics, 1870–1914* (Princeton: Princeton Univ. Press, 1995); Thomas Mergel, *Zwischen Klasse und Konfession: Katholisches Bürgertum im Rheinland, 1794–1914* (Göttingen: Vandenhoeck und Ruprecht, 1994); David Blackbourn, *Marpingen: Apparitions of the Virgin Mary in Bismarckian Germany* (New York: Oxford Univ. Press, 1993); Wolfgang Altgeld, *Katholizismus, Protestantismus, Judentum: Über religiös begründete Gegensätze und nationalreligiöse Ideen in der Geschichte des deutschen Nationalismus* (Mainz: Matthias-Grünewald, 1992); Sylvia Paletschek, *Frauen und Dissens* (Göttingen: Vandenhoeck und Ruprecht, 1990); Wolfgang Schieder (ed.), *Volksreligiosität in der modernen Sozialgeschichte* (Göttingen: Vandenhoeck und Ruprecht, 1986); Jonathan Sperber, *Popular Catholicism in Nineteenth-Century Germany* (Princeton: Princeton Univ. Press, 1984); Wilfried Loth, *Katholiken im Kaiserreich: Der politische Katholizismus in der Krise des wilhelminischen Deutschlands* (Düsseldorf: Droste, 1984); Werner K. Blessing, *Staat und Kirche in der Gesellschaft: Institutionelle Autorität und mentaler Wandel in Bayern während des 19. Jahrhunderts* (Göttingen: Vandenhoeck und Ruprecht, 1982); and Margaret Lavinia Anderson, *Windthorst: A Political Biography* (New York: Oxford Univ. Press, 1981).

4. Lothar Gall, *Der Liberalismus als regierende Partei: Das Grossherzogtum Baden zwischen Restauration und Reichsgründung* (Wiesbaden: F. Steiner, 1968), pp. xi–xii.

5. For the best introductions to the problem of German liberalism in general, see James J. Sheehan, *German Liberalism in the Nineteenth Century* (Chicago: Univ. of Chicago Press, 1978); David Blackbourn and Geoff Eley, *The Peculiarities of German History: Bourgeois Society and Politics in Nineteenth-Century Germany* (Oxford: Oxford Univ. Press, 1984); Dieter Langewiesche, *Liberalismus in Deutschland* (Frankfurt a. M.: Suhrkamp, 1988); Wolfgang Schieder (ed.), *Liberalismus in der Gesellschaft des deutschen Vormärz* (Göttingen: Vandenhoeck und Ruprecht, 1983); and Konrad H. Jarausch and Larry Eugene Jones (eds.), *In Search of a Liberal Germany: Studies in the History of German Liberalism from 1789 to the Present* (Oxford: Berg, 1990).

6. Useful discussions of Baden's development from 1803 to 1848 can be found in Gall, *Liberalismus*, pp. 1–57; Loyd E. Lee, *The Politics of Harmony:*

Civil Service, Liberalism and Social Reform in Baden, 1800–1850 (Newark: Univ. of Delaware Press, 1980); Norbert Deuchert, *Vom Hambacher Fest zur badischen Revolution: Politische Presse und Anfänge deutscher Demokratie 1832–1848/49* (Stuttgart: Theiss, 1983); Hans-Peter Becht, *Die badische zweite Kammer und ihre Mitglieder, 1819 bis 1841/42: Untersuchungen zu Struktur und Funktionsweise eines frühen deutschen Parlaments* (Ph. D. diss., Univ. of Mannheim, 1985); and Paul Nolte, *Gemeindebürgertum und Liberalismus in Baden, 1800–1850: Tradition—Radikalismus—Republik* (Göttingen: Vandenhoeck und Ruprecht, 1994); as well as Wolfram Fischer, "Staat und Gesellschaft Badens im Vormärz," in Werner Conze (ed.), *Staat und Gesellschaft im deutschen Vormärz: 1815–1848* (Stuttgart: Ernst Klett, 1962); Josef Becker, *Liberaler Staat und Kirche in der Ära zwischen Reichsgründung und Kulturkampf* (Mainz: Matthias-Grünewald, 1973), pp. 11–15; Rainer Wirtz, *"Widersetzlichkeiten, Excesse, Crawalle, Tumulte und Skandale": Soziale Bewegung und gewalthafter sozialer Protest in Baden 1815–1848* (Frankfurt a. M.: Ullstein, 1981), pp. 38–51; Willy Real, *Die Revolution in Baden 1848/49* (Stuttgart: W. Kohlhammer, 1983), pp. 11–43; and Werner Schubert (ed.), *Verhandlungen der Stände-Versammlung des Grossherzogtums Baden in den Jahren 1847 bis 1849* (Vaduz, Liechtenstein: Topos, 1989), pp. ii–xv.

7. See Berthold Rosenthal, *Heimatgeschichte der badischen Juden seit ihrem geschichtlichen Auftreten bis zur Gegenwart* (Bühl/Baden: Konkordia, 1927), pp. 241–47; *Die politischen, Kirchen- und Schul-Gemeinden des Grossherzogthums Baden mit der Seelen- und Bürgerzahl vom Jahr 1845* (Karlsruhe: C. F. Müller, 1847), p. 202; Karl Otto Watzinger, *Geschichte der Juden in Mannheim 1650–1945* (Stuttgart: W. Kohlhammer, 1984), pp. 13–26; Adolf Lewin, *Geschichte der badischen Juden seit der Regierung Karl Friedrichs (1738–1909)* (Karlsruhe: Braun, 1909), pp. 1–51; *RZ*, April 1847, pp. 30–31; Jonathan Sperber, *Rhineland Radicals: The Democratic Movement and the Revolution of 1848–1849* (Princeton: Princeton Univ. Press, 1991), p. 50; Thomas Nipperdey, *Deutsche Geschichte 1800–1866: Bürgerwelt und starker Staat* (Munich: C. H. Beck, 1983), pp. 248–51.

8. See Monika Richarz, "Emancipation and Continuity: German Jews in the Rural Economy," in Werner E. Mosse et al. (eds.), *Revolution and Evolution: 1848 in German-Jewish History* (Tübingen: J.C.B. Mohr, 1981); Michael Anthony Riff, "The Anti-Jewish Aspect of the Revolutionary Unrest of 1848 in Baden and its Impact on Emancipation," *LBIYB*, XXI (1976), pp. 27–28; Reinhard Rürup, "Jewish Emancipation and Bourgeois Society," *LBIYB*, XIV (1969), p. 82; and Wirtz, *"Widersetzlichkeiten,"* pp. 48 and 60–87.

9. For particularly helpful and historically grounded discussions of the workings of ideology, and of how discourses of resistance can produce unintended side effects, see Mary Poovey, *Uneven Developments: The Ideological Work of Gender in Mid-Victorian England* (Chicago: Univ. of Chicago Press, 1988); and most especially Judith Walkowitz, "Male Vice and Female Virtue: Feminism and the Politics of Prostitution in Nineteenth-Century Britain," in Ann Snitow et al. (eds.), *Powers of Desire: The Politics of Sexuality* (New York: Monthly Review Press, 1983); and Judith Walkowitz, "The Making of an Outcast Group: Prostitutes and Working Women in Nineteenth-Century Plymouth and

Southampton," in Martha Vicinus (ed.), *A Widening Sphere: Changing Roles of Victorian Women* (Bloomington: Indiana Univ. Press, 1977). Poovey and Walkowitz are both inspired by *and* modify the arguments of Michel Foucault. See esp. the material collected in Michel Foucault, *Power/Knowledge: Selected Interviews and Other Writings 1972–1977* (New York: Pantheon, 1980).

CHAPTER ONE
BODIES AND SOULS

1. For interesting earlier perspectives on the sources of liberal-Catholic hostilities in Baden, see Gert Zang, "Die Bedeutung der Auseinandersetzung um die Stiftungsverwaltung in Konstanz (1830–1870) für die ökonomische und gesellschaftliche Entwicklung der lokalen Gesellschaft: Ein Beitrag zur Analyse der materiellen Hintergründe des Kulturkampfes," and Werner Trapp, "Volksschulreform und liberales Bürgertum in Konstanz: Die Durchsetzung des Schulzwangs als Voraussetzung der Massendisziplinierung und -qualifikation," both in the imaginative collectively produced regional study, Gert Zang (ed.), *Provinzialisierung einer Region: Regionale Unterentwicklung und liberale Politik in der Stadt und im Kreis Konstanz im 19. Jahrhundert. Untersuchungen zur Entstehung der bürgerlichen Gesellschaft in der Provinz* (Frankfurt a. M.: Syndikat, 1978).

2. Neoorthodox Protestantism, while strong, for example, in Prussia, did not gain much of a following in pre-revolutionary Baden in any event. See Hermann Rückleben, "Theologischer Rationalismus und kirchlicher Protest in Baden 1843–49," in *Pietismus und Neuzeit* (1979).

3. Franz Schnabel, *Deutsche Geschichte im neunzehnten Jahrhundert*, vol. 4 (Freiburg i. B.: Herder, 1937), p. 159.

4. [Franz Rosshirt], *Beleuchtung und actenmässige Ergänzung der Karlsruher Schrift: "Der Streit über gemischte Ehen und das Kirchenhoheitsrecht im Grossherzogthum Baden"* (Schaffhausen: Hurter, 1847), p. iv.

5. Franz Christoph von Wamboldt, Joseph Anton Helfferich, and Karl Schies, memorandum to the Congress of Vienna, in Ernst Rudolf Huber and Wolfgang Huber (eds.), *Staat und Kirche im 19. und 20. Jahrhundert: Dokumente zur Geschichte der deutschen Staatskirchenrechte*, vol. 1 (Berlin: Duncker and Humblot, 1973), pp. 105 and 107.

6. For a helpful reinterpretation of Wessenberg which seeks to rescue him from cooptation by political liberals, and restore a more balanced understanding also of his many loyalist qualities, see Karl-Heinz Braun, "Hermann von Vicari und Ignaz Heinrich von Wessenberg: Zwei Prälaten im kirchenpolitischen Vergleich," in *Freiburger Diözesan-Archiv*, vol. 107 (1987), esp. pp. 213–30.

7. *Worte der Wahrheit an das katholische Volk in Baden und Süddeutschland von einem Freunde der christlich-katholischen Kirche und der deutschen Eintracht* (Basel: J. C. Schabelitz, 1846), pp. 13–14.

8. Professor Leonhard Hug to Pope Gregory XVI, 4 Oct. 1833, quoted in Heinrich Maas, *Geschichte der katholischen Kirche im Grossherzogthum Baden* (Freiburg i. B.: Herder, 1891), p. 47.

9. Schreiber's slogan quoted in ibid., p. 52.

10. Petition by Professors Heinrich Amann and Karl Zell, 21 Apr. 1828, reprinted in *Verhandlungen der Stände-Versammlung des Grossherzogthums Baden* (II. Kammer), 9 May 1828, 4. Protokollheft, pp. 59–73.

11. Ibid.

12. Herr, in *Verhandlungen* (II. Kammer), 27 Oct. 1831, 28. Protokollheft, p. 73.

13. A classic compendium of such "data" can be found in Johann Anton Theiner and Augustin Theiner, *Die Einführung der erzwungenen Ehelosigkeit bei den christlichen Geistlichen und ihre Folgen* (Altenburg: Verlag der Hofbuchdruckerei, 1828).

14. Cover epigraphs on *Unterricht für das katholische Volk in Deutschland über die Aufhebung der Ehelosigkeit seiner Priester* (no place, no publisher, 1803). Cf. I Corinthians 7, 9.

15. [Benedikt Maria von Werkmeister], *Vorschlag, wie in der deutschen katholischen Kirche die Priesterehe allmählich eingeführt werden könnte* (no place, no publisher, 1803), pp. 3 and 7–9.

16. Joseph Theodosius Abs, *Das Cölibatgebot, im Widerspruche mit Bibel, Kirche und Staat* (Halberstadt and Heiligenstadt: J. C. Dölle, 1813), the unpaginated preface and p. 89. Here, as elsewhere in this chapter, the emphasis was in the original.

17. See Christoph Trefurt, *Der Zölibat aus dem Gesichtspunkte der Moral, des Rechts und der Politik betrachtet* (Heidelberg and Leipzig: Groos, 1826), pp. 36–37 and 47.

18. Cf. *Verhandlungen* (II. Kammer), 13 May 1828, 4. Protokollheft, p. 192; and Duttlinger, in *Verhandlungen* (II. Kammer), 27 Oct. 1831, 28. Protokollheft, pp. 70–71.

19. See Franz Josef Mone, *Die katholischen Zustände in Baden* (Regensburg: G. J. Manz, 1841), p. 63.

20. Mittermaier, in *Verhandlungen* (II. Kammer), 16 Dec. 1831, 35. Protokollheft, p. 19; Bader, p. 22; Merk, p. 17; Rotteck, pp. 60–61; Welcker, pp. 17–19.

21. Merk, in ibid., p. 16; Seltzam, p. 20; Itzstein, p. 15; Rotteck, p. 24.

22. The goal of population growth was at this time beginning to receive criticism as concerns about potential "overpopulation" emerged. The literature of the day thus reveals the coexistence of plans to expand and plans to curtail population growth. In this context, advocates of priestly celibacy often stressed how well-positioned clergymen in particular were to raise their children to be upstanding, productive, and self-supporting citizens.

23. Compare the reports in Karl Alexander von Reichlin-Meldegg, *Das Leben eines ehemaligen römisch-katholischen Priesters: Eine Jubelschrift* (Heidelberg: F. Bassermann, 1874), pp. 41, 74, and 109; Maas, *Geschichte*, pp. 47 and 58; and Hermann Lauer, *Geschichte der katholischen Kirche im Grossherzogthum Baden* (Freiburg i. B.: Herder, 1908), p. 145.

24. See seminary director Dürr's interviews with the seminarians, 6 July 1831; and the reports made for the Archdiocesan Office by Archbishop Bernhard Boll's then-assistant Hermann von Vicari, 6 July 1831 and 15 July 1831, all in ErzFrei B2–32/512.

25. Schippel, in *Verhandlungen* (II. Kammer), 13 May 1828, p. 4. Protokollheft, pp. 184–85.

26. Winter's remarks are paraphrased by Mone, *Zustände*, p. 63. See also the letter from Professor Hug to Archbishop Boll, 23 Apr. 1828, which alludes to *raisons d'état* preventing the abolition of celibacy, in ErzFrei NL Bernhard Boll Nb 1/1.

27. August Franzen, "Die Zölibatsfrage im neunzehnten Jahrhundert. Der 'Badische Zölibatssturm' (1828) und das Problem der Priesterehe im Urteile Johann Adam Möhlers und Johann Baptist Hirschers," in *Historisches Jahrbuch* 91 (1971), pp. 361–62. On the various anti-celibacy campaigns, see also "Der Cölibat," *DkSB*, 28 Nov. 1852, p. 191.

28. Letter from Professor Hug to Archbishop Boll, 23 Apr. 1828, in ErzFrei NL Bernhard Boll Nb 1/1; and letter from Vicar-General Egger in Augsburg to Vicari, 22 Nov. 1829, quoted in Maas, *Geschichte*, pp. 48–49.

29. Mone, *Zustände*, pp. 88–94. Despite Rome's and conservatives' strong opposition to synods, however, the idea of synods did also appeal to some less radical Catholics, who saw in them the possibility for renewal of religious life and/or even the potential for resisting *Staatskirchentum*; the call for synods thus cannot be read simply as an anti-church demand. See Josef Becker, *Liberaler Staat und Kirche in der Ära von Reichsgründung und Kulturkampf* (Mainz: Matthias-Grünewald, 1973), p. 20.

30. Johann Adam Möhler, "Beleuchtung der Denkschrift für die Aufhebung des den katholischen Geistlichen vorgeschriebenen Cölibates. Mit drei Actenstücken" (1828), in Johann Josef Ignaz Döllinger (ed.), *Dr. J. A. Möhler's gesammelte Schriften und Aufsätze*, vol. 1 (Regensburg: G. J. Manz, 1839), pp. 180, 183, 185, and 190–91.

31. *SZKS*, 25 Dec. 1847, p. 1366. Cf. also Boll's own remarks: Calling attention to the biblical passages "which so strongly recommend fighting the natural drives," Boll poignantly described how "for 1800 years millions of human beings like us, of both sexes, have lived without marriage, and dedicated themselves to the welfare of humanity and the propagating of holy religion, and for the sake of the heavenly kingdom have courageously battled with and conquered the sensuous drives." Archbishop Boll to his staff, 9 Aug. 1831, in ErzFrei NL Bernhard Boll Nb 1/1.

32. Adolf Strehle in his anonymously edited *Die gemischten Ehen in der Erzdiöcese Freiburg* (Regensburg: G. J. Manz, 1846), pp. 43–44.

33. Johann Baptist von Hirscher, "Erklärung des Professors Dr. von Hirscher zu Freiburg, veranlasst durch einen gegen ihn gerichteten Artikel . . ." (1843), reprinted in Hubert F. Schiel, *Johann Baptist von Hirscher: Eine Lichtgestalt aus dem deutschen Katholizismus des XIX. Jahrhunderts* (Freiburg i. B.: Caritasverlag, 1926), p. 85.

34. Matthias Häusler, *Noch ein nachdrückliches Wort über das ernstliche letzte Wort eines Cölibat-Feindes und eines würdigen Consortens, der um die hohe Erlaubniss des Rücktrittes in den Laienstand wehmüthig flehet* (no place, no publisher, 1815), pp. 8–9, 48, 50, 55, 60, 64–65, and 76.

35. Seminary director Dürr's report to Archbishop Boll, 9 July 1831, and the seminarians' response after the archbishop ordered an investigation, quoted and discussed in Maas, *Geschichte*, pp. 55–56.

36. Letter from Wessenberg to Karl Mittermaier, 1 Nov. 1845, quoted in Ferdinand Strobel, *Der Katholizismus und die liberalen Strömungen in Baden. Teildruck: Der Kampf mit dem kirchlichen Liberalismus* (Speyer: Pilger-Druckerei, 1938), p. 120. Cf. also Franzen, "Zölibatsfrage," pp. 349–50.

37. On the older negative views of sexuality and of womanhood, see Jean Delumeau, *Sin and Fear: The Emergence of a Western Guilt Culture, 13th–18th Centuries* (New York: St. Martin's Press, 1990); and Georg Denzler, *Die verbotene Lust: 2000 Jahre christliche Sexualmoral* (Munich: Piper, 1988), pp. 267–330. On the new "individualization" of conservative Catholic teachings on women in the first half of the nineteenth century—the insistence that women in particular needed to engage in continual self-monitoring of their own bodies and imaginations, see Edith Saurer, " 'Bewahrerinnen der Zucht und der Sittlichkeit': Gebetbücher für Frauen—Frauen in Gebetbüchern," in *L'Homme: Zeitschrift für Feministische Geschichtswissenschaft* 1/1 (1990).

38. *Die Musterehe und die Nothwendigkeit einer Wiederherstellung der Ehe nach der Musterehe* (Freiburg i. B.: Herder, 1850), p. 18.

39. Johann Baptist von Hirscher, *Die christliche Moral als Lehre von der Verwirklichung des göttlichen Reiches in der Menschheit*, 5th ed., vol. 2 (Tübingen: H. Laupp, 1851), pp. 418–20.

40. Alban Stolz, "Weibervolk," *ABC für grosse Leute: Kalender für Zeit und Ewigkeit 1864; mit groben Bildern*, 4th ed. (Freiburg i. B.: Herder, 1864), p. 111.

41. For details on Archbishop Boll's transformation under pressure, see Boll's letter to his archdiocesan office, 20 July 1831, in ErzFrei B2–32/512; and Reichlin-Meldegg, *Leben*, pp. 81 and 85–95.

42. Letter from Archbishop Boll to Pope Gregory XVI, 26 Oct. 1832, quoted in Maas, *Geschichte*, pp. 52–53.

43. For example, compare the contrasting views in Clemens Rehm, *Die katholische Kirche in der Erzdiöcese Freiburg während der Revolution 1848/49* (Munich: Karl Alber, 1987), p. 13; and Karl-Heinz Braun's review of Rehm's book in *Freiburger Diözesan-Archiv*, vol. 107 (1987), pp. 365–70, esp. p. 366.

44. Archbishop Boll to Grand Duke Leopold, Oct. 1831, quoted in Maas, *Geschichte*, p. 51.

45. Pastoral letter from Archbishop Boll to all priests in his archdiocese, 13 July 1832, in ErzFrei library.

46. Encyclical of 15 Aug. 1832, in Claudia Carlen (ed.), *The Papal Encyclicals 1740–1878* (Wilmington, N.C.: McGrath, 1981), p. 237.

47. Bernetti to Baden's Minister of Foreign Affairs, von Türckheim, 5 Oct. 1833, in Huber and Huber, *Staat und Kirche*, p. 485.

48. Papal brief of 4 Oct. 1833, in ibid., pp. 480–82.

49. Grand Duke Leopold to Archbishop Boll, 6 Aug. 1830, quoted in Maas, *Geschichte*, p. 50.

50. Becker, *Liberaler*, p. 20.

51. Maas, *Geschichte*, p. 52.

52. See Friedrich von Weech, *Badische Biographien*, vol. 1 (Heidelberg: F. Bassermann, 1875), p. 5; and Huber and Huber, *Staat und Kirche*, p. 486.

53. Strobel, *Katholizismus*, p. 87.

54. Welcker, in *Verhandlungen* (II. Kammer), 21 Feb. 1844, 2. Protokoll-heft, p. 155; cf. Sander, pp. 158–59; Zittel, pp. 161–62.

55. Carl Theodor Welcker, "Verbotene Ehen, insbesondere Priester-Cölibat," in Carl Theodor Welcker and Karl von Rotteck (eds.), *Das Staats-Lexikon*, 1st ed., vol. 15 (Altona: J. F. Hammerich, 1843), pp. 665–66 and 674.

56. *Der Streit über gemischte Ehen und das Kirchenhoheitsrecht im Grossher-zogthum Baden* (Karlsruhe: G. Braun, 1847), pp. xviii and xxxi. Also cf. *KKr*, July 1845, p. 220.

57. Q., "Gemischte Ehen," in Rotteck and Welcker, *Das Staats-Lexikon*, 1st ed., vol. 6 (Altona: J. F. Hammerich, 1838), p. 475–76. "Q." was well known to be Amann, for the essays he wrote for the *Staats-Lexikon* under this by-line, especially one on the confessional, were another factor contributing to the arch-bishop's insistence that the government fire him. See Strobel, *Katholizismus*, p. 86.

58. *SZKS*, 29 Nov. 1846, p. 1077.

59. Karl von Rotteck, "Familie, Familienrecht," in Rotteck and Welcker, *Das Staats-Lexikon*, 1st ed., vol. 5 (Altona: J. F. Hammerich, 1837), pp. 386–87.

60. Carl Theodor Welcker, "Geschlechtsverhältnisse," in Rotteck and Welcker, *Das Staats-Lexikon*, 1st ed., vol. 6, pp. 648–49.

61. For another contemporary liberal articulation of the significance of hap-piness in marriage, see Karl von Rotteck's afterword to Q., "Gemischte Ehen," in Welcker and Rotteck, *Das Staats-Lexikon*, 1st ed., vol. 6, p. 481. For a con-temporary liberal articulation of the relationship between marriage and specifi-cally bourgeois class-consciousness, see *MAb*, 28 Jan. 1847, p. 97. Also see Karin Hausen, "'. . . eine Ulme für das schwanke Efeu'. Ehepaare im deutschen Bildungsbürgertum," in Ute Frevert (ed.), *Bürgerinnen und Bürger: Geschlech-terverhältnisse im 19. Jahrhundert* (Göttingen: Vandenhoeck und Ruprecht, 1988), esp. pp. 89–92; Peter Borscheid, "Geld und Liebe: Zu den Auswir-kungen des Romantischen auf die Partnerwahl im 19. Jahrhundert," in Peter Borscheid and Hans J. Teuteberg (eds.), *Ehe, Liebe, Tod: Zum Wandel der Fa-milie, der Geschlechts-und Generationsbeziehungen in der Neuzeit* (Münster: F. Coppenrath, 1983); and Nancy Kaiser, "Marriage and the Not-So-Simple Life in the 1840s," in Jost Hermand and Reinhard Grimm (eds.), *From the Greeks to the Greens: Images of the Simple Life* (Madison: University of Wisconsin Press, 1990).

62. See esp. Borscheid, "Geld," pp. 130–34; and Marion A. Kaplan, *The Making of the Jewish Middle Class: Women, Family and Identity in Imperial Ger-many* (New York: Oxford Univ. Press, 1991), pp. 85–116.

63. See Borscheid, "Geld," p. 113.

64. See *Der Streit*, pp. 80–81: "In no other land do we find the Catholic and Protestant populations mixed in the same way and [in no other land] are there proportionately so numerous familial connections between the inhabitants of both confessions as in the Grand Duchy." Compare also the documents col-lected in GlaKa 233/32303; and cf. Grand Duke Leopold's remarks: "The many hundreds of mixed marriages [among my subjects] are testimonies to har-mony and love" (quoted by Minister of the Interior Karl Friedrich Nebenius in conversation with Archbishop Demeter, 19 Mar. 1839, in [Strehle], *Die ge-*

mischten Ehen, p. 38). Finally, see Archbishop Demeter's comment in his "Bemerkungen des Erzbischofs von Freiburg" (30 Jan. 1839) that every twentieth marriage in Baden was a mixed one (ErzFrei NL Demeter Nb 2–8). By 1864, the first year for which systematic statistics are available, 11,772, or 5.6 percent, of all marriages in Baden were mixed. Almost half of these were in the northernmost quarter of Baden, in the area surrounding Mannheim and Heidelberg. See Badisches Statistisches Landesamt (ed.), *Die Religionszugehörigkeit in Baden in den letzten 100 Jahren* (Freiburg i. B.: Herder, 1928), pp. 220–21.

65. Letter from the Ministry of the Interior's Catholic Church Section to Archbishop Demeter, 16 Nov. 1838, in GlaKa 233/32303. See also Q., "Gemischte Ehen," p. 479; and Schnabel, *Deutsche Geschichte*, p. 126.

66. See the letter from Nebenius to Vicari, 5 Dec. 1845, in [Strehle], *Die gemischten Ehen*, p. 71.

67. Ludwig Buchegger, "Widerlegung der wichtigsten Gründe, welche man gegen die kirchlichen Vorschriften in Betreff der gemischten Ehen anführt" (29 Jan. 1839), in [Strehle], *Die gemischten Ehen*, p. 78; and Strehle's own editorial remarks, p. 8. Buchegger was a member of Archbishop Demeter's staff; his original memorandum, under the title "Gutachten über die gemischten Ehen im Grossherzogthum Baden," is in ErzFrei B2–18/25. Cf. also Demeter's "Bemerkungen" in ErzFrei NL Demeter Nb 2–8.

68. Third Organizational Edict, 11 Feb. 1803, in [Strehle], *Die gemischten Ehen*, p. 6.

69. First Constitutional Edict, 14 May 1807, and Marriage Order, 15 July 1807, in ibid., pp. 6–7.

70. Pius VIII's papal brief, 25 Mar. 1830, in Huber and Huber, *Staat und Kirche*, p. 319. Also see Schnabel, *Deutsche Geschichte*, p. 132.

71. It had been possible to sign a premarital contract stating that girls be raised in the faith of the mother and boys in the faith of the father, but it was very difficult to raise all the children in the mother's faith. Only in the rare instance that a couple was to live in a town in which education was only available in the mother's religion, could children of both sexes be raised in that religion. Such an arrangement was therefore impossible in a town with a mixed-confessional population. See the details in the First Constitutional Edict of 14 May 1807, in Huber and Huber, *Staat und Kirche*, p. 83.

72. Archdiocesan Office's directive to the *Dekanat* M. in Z., 27 Feb. 1830, in [Strehle], *Die gemischten Ehen*, p. 16.

73. Minister of the Interior Ludwig Winter to the Archdiocesan Office, 30 Oct. 1832, and Ministry of State resolution, 17 Apr. 1833, both in GlaKa 234/1571.

74. See Raymund Kottje and Bernd Moeller (eds.), *Ökumenische Kirchengeschichte*, vol. 3 (Mainz: Matthias-Grünewald, 1974), pp. 162–65; and Schnabel, *Deutsche Geschichte*, pp. 121–43 and 153.

75. Johann Joseph Görres, *Athanasius*, 2d ed. (Regensburg: G. J. Manz, 1838), pp. 102–3 and 151–53.

76. Archdiocesan Office to the Ministry of the Interior's Catholic Church Section, 22 June 1838, in GlaKa 233/32303 (the letter is written by Vicari on Demeter's behalf). It was widely understood that it was Gregory XVI and his

immediate predecessor Pius VIII, and not the bishops of Germany, who were the main initiators of the stricter praxis in mixed marriages. See ibid., as well as Maas, *Geschichte*, p. 176.

77. Archdiocesan Office to the Ministry of the Interior's Catholic Church Section, 22 June 1838, in GlaKa 233/32303. Cf. Boll's pastoral letter, 13 July 1832, in ErzFrei library.

78. Demeter's speech to his Cathedral Chapter, 20 Apr. 1838; Archdiocesan Office to Priest Anton Nägele in Dingelsdorf, 15 June 1838; and Cathedral Chapter resolution, 22 Mar. 1839; all in ErzFrei B2–18/25.

79. See the letter from the Catholic High Church Council to the Archdiocesan Office, 25 Nov. 1845, in [Strehle], *Die gemischten Ehen*, p. 62.

80. Vicari's general directive, 9 Aug. 1845, in ErzFrei B2–18/26.

81. Vicari to the Ministry of the Interior, 24 Nov. 1845, in GlaKa 233/32303.

82. Ministry of the Interior to the Catholic clergy of Baden, 21 Nov. 1845, in [Strehle], *Die gemischten Ehen*, pp. 57–58.

83. Friedrich Hecker, *Die staatsrechtlichen Verhältnisse der Deutschkatholiken mit besonderem Hinblick auf Baden* (Heidelberg: Groos, 1845), p. 28.

84. *Mbote*, 15 Oct. 1845, p. 16.

85. *Mbote*, 12 Nov. 1845, pp. 35–36.

86. See *Verhandlungen* (II. Kammer), 17 July 1846, 6. Protokollheft, p. 35.

87. Vicari to Catholic High Church Council, 3 Dec. 1845, in [Strehle], *Die gemischten Ehen*, p. 67.

88. Gregory XVI's papal brief, 23 May 1846, in Huber and Huber, *Staat und Kirche*, pp. 516–18.

89. Cf. Strehle's editorial remarks in *Die gemischten Ehen*, pp. 3–4, as well as the footnotes on pp. 36 and 67. The press had, however, kept the reading public notified about the various stages of the conflict. Thus, for example, the public was told about the state's initial intransigence toward Vicari, and about Vicari's decision to turn to the pope for assistance in resolving the conflict. See *MAb*, 1 Dec. 1845, p. 1396; and 16 Dec. 1845, p. 1475.

90. [Strehle], *Die gemischten Ehen*, pp. 67, 84, and 86–87.

91. "Gesetz, die Eingehung einer Ehe von Staatswegen bei einem vorhandenen anerkannten kirchlichen Hindernisse betreffend" (Law about entering into marriage under state auspices when there is a recognized church obstacle), 6 Nov. 1846, in Huber and Huber, *Staat und Kirche*, pp. 518–19.

92. The November 1846 law still insisted that if the Protestant clergyman had no objections to a particular marriage (and Protestant clergymen usually did not), then he would have to perform the religious marriage ceremony. Ibid., p. 519. Not until October 9, 1860 was it really possible for couples freely to choose a civil marriage. See Maas, *Geschichte*, p. 513. The marriage of Carl Scholl, preacher to the dissenting congregation in Mannheim, and Regine Eller, daughter of a rabbi from Celle, in 1862, was "the first civil marriage in our Grand Duchy," according to Georg Schneider, who delivered the eulogy at Regine Scholl's graveside, quoted in *Es werde Licht!*, Aug. 1902, p. 166. Civil marriage was not made compulsory in Baden until December 21, 1869. See Karl

Kah, *Die Ehe und das bürgerliche Standesamt nach badischem Recht* (Heidelberg: Selbstverlag, 1870).

93. See Lauer, *Geschichte*, p. 193.

94. See Maas, *Geschichte*, p. 176. This development was also confirmed by observers at the time. See *SZKS*, 4 Dec. 1846, p. 1094.

95. See *SZKS*, 4 Dec. 1846, p. 1094; and 6 Dec. 1846, p. 1102.

96. The weekly *Süddeutsche Katholische Kirchenzeitung* first appeared in 1841 for the purpose of encouraging greater ultramontanism and theological conservatism among Baden's Catholic clergy and interested laypeople. Its primary editor was Professor Staudenmaier, though a number of other well-known conservative Catholic leaders were involved. In 1845, in direct response to the emergence of the *Deutschkatholiken*, the paper was transformed into a daily, expressly political paper, the *Süddeutsche Zeitung für Kirche und Staat*. This new paper explicitly set itself the task of spreading political as well as theological conservatism as it attacked liberalism in all its forms, and soon gained a reputation for its virulent and strident tone. Franz Josef Buss was clearly the guiding spirit behind this venture, though again the editorship was collective, and Buss's participation waned as he became absorbed in his parliamentary activities. See Wilhelm Hubert Ganser, *Die Süddeutsche Zeitung für Kirche und Staat* (Berlin: E. Ebering, 1936), esp. p. 15; and Julius Dorneich, *Franz Josef Buss und die katholische Bewegung in Baden* (Freiburg i. B.: Herder, 1979), pp. 107–26.

97. For example, see Alban Stolz, *Mixtur gegen die Todesangst, zusammengesetzt von einem badischen Jesuiten: Kalender für Zeit und Ewigkeit 1843* (Villingen: F. Förderer, 1842), the first of eighteen such almanacs. During the early 1840s, Stolz was teacher, and then director, at the theological college (*Theologenkonvikt*) in Freiburg. See Weech, *Badische Biographien*, vol. 4 (Karlsruhe: G. Braun, 1891), pp. 454–61.

98. Quoted in Dorneich, *Franz Josef Buss*, p. 128. While new volumes were published each year, the old ones (continually reprinted) also continued to sell over the succeeding years, often reaching distribution levels between 100,000 and 300,000. Dorneich also points out, in discussing Stolz's impact, that "precisely because in these [rural] circles so few things were read, almanacs had the greatest influence in shaping the opinions of the simple *Volk*." See pp. 127 and 129. Compare as well *MAb*, 28 Oct. 1845, p. 1269: Almanacs "are carried also into the poorest huts and for a great part of the *Volk* during the winter they [are] almost the only reading material."

99. See Maas, *Geschichte*, pp. 141 and 144–47; and Lauer, *Geschichte*, p. 178. Vicari, together with Franz Josef Buss, was also instrumental in bringing the first female religious order (the Sisters of Mercy) back into Baden since all the orders had been secularized in the wake of the French Revolution. See Lauer, p. 180; and Franz Josef Buss, *Der Orden der barmherzigen Schwestern* (Schaffhausen: Hurter, 1844). This was considered a great triumph for the ultramontanists, because liberals were very afraid of the proselytizing influence the nuns would exert as they worked in hospitals and other charitable institutions. For example, see *Verhandlungen* (II. Kammer), 24 July 1846, 6. Protokollheft, pp. 174–215; and cf. *Verhandlungen* (I. Kammer), 14 Sept. 1846, 2. Protokollheft, pp. 450–54.

100. See Dorneich, *Franz Josef Buss*, pp. 133–47. This growing conservative control over the education of the clergy also alarmed liberal observers, who worried, for example, over how Catholic doctrine would be interpreted and put into practice by men who, from the time they were little boys, had been raised in ultramontane institutions, "inaccessible to the general enlightenment—stifled through monkish religious exercises." *Mbote*, 19 Nov. 1845, p. 42.

101. Cf. Strobel, *Katholizismus*, p. 168; Maas, *Geschichte*, pp. 176–77; Ganser, *Süddeutsche*, p. 78; and [Rosshirt], *Beleuchtung*, p. 12. The National Union Catalogue lists Nebenius as author, but probably the author was in fact Beck, working under Nebenius's supervision.

102. *Der Streit*, pp. 77 and 82.

103. Ibid., pp. xxviii, xxx, and 82.

104. Ibid., pp. xvii and 79–80. Compare also Nebenius's argument that mixed marriages were "an essential foundation for the harmonious coexistence of the members of both confessions." Nebenius to Vicari, 5 Dec. 1845, in [Strehle], *Die gemischten Ehen*, p. 74.

105. *Der Streit*, pp. xxix–xxxi.

106. Buchegger, "Widerlegung," p. 77; and Franz Josef Buss, "Aufgabe der Zeitschrift," in *Capistran: Zeitschrift für die Rechte und Interessen des katholischen Teutschlands* 1/1 (Schaffhausen: Hurter, 1847), p. 8. See also the approving commentary on Buchegger's memorandum by other members of the Archdiocesan Office in February and March 1839, in ErzFrei B2-18/25.

107. Mone, *Zustände*, pp. 15–16.

108. Buchegger, "Widerlegung," pp. 79 and 82.

109. [Rosshirt], *Beleuchtung*, pp. 44–45.

110. Buchegger, "Widerlegung," pp. 76–77.

111. Alban Stolz, "Amulett gegen die jungkatholische Sucht" (1845), reprinted in Alban Stolz, *Gesammelte Werke*, 3d ed., vol. 8 (Freiburg i. B.: Herder, 1913/14), p. 23.

112. Buchegger, "Widerlegung," pp. 79 and 82.

113. Alban Stolz, "April," *Mixtur gegen Todesangst: Kalender für Zeit und Ewigkeit Erster Jahrgang 1843. Für das gemeine Volk und nebenher für geistliche und weltliche Herrenleute*, 16th ed. (Freiburg i. B.: Herder, 1868), pp. 44–45.

114. Buss, "Aufgabe," *Capistran*, vol. 1, no. 1, pp. 4–5, 7, and 9.

115. *Musterehe*, pp. 10, 16, and 21.

116. *SZKS*, 29 Nov. 1846, p. 1077.

117. See Denzler, *Lust*, p. 332; and Joseph Renker, *Christliche Ehe im Wandel der Zeit: Zur Ehelehre der Moraltheologen im deutschsprachigen Raum in der ersten Hälfte des 19. Jahrhunderts* (Regensburg: Friedrich Pustet, 1977), esp. pp. 89 and 103. Examples of explicit contemporary assertions of this belief can be found in G. M. Dursch, *Katholisch-dogmatische Predigten*, vol. 1 (Tübingen: H. Laupp, 1852), p. 173; and Joseph Dürr, *Predigten auf alle Sonn- und Festtage des katholischen Kirchenjahrs*, vol. 1 (Villingen: F. Förderer, 1841), p. 68.

118. Alban Stolz, "Sechstes Gebot: Du sollst nicht ehebrechen," in *Essig und Oel (Dritter Theil vom Vaterunser): Kalender für Zeit und Ewigkeit Fünfter Jahrgang 1847*, 14th ed. (Freiburg i. B.: Herder, 1870), pp. 37–38; cf. I Corinthians 3, 16; and Stolz, "April," pp. 36–37.

119. Hirscher, *Die Christliche Moral*, vol. 3, pp. 513–16. *Die christliche Moral* was first published in 1835, and then revised in four subsequent editions, as Hirscher became increasingly conservative, but it is unlikely that the passages on marriage changed, since the portions the *Süddeutsche Zeitung für Kirche und Staat* reprinted in 1846 are identical with the 1851 versions. Hirscher was considered more moderate about sexual matters than many of his conservative contemporaries because, for example, he contended that sex within a Christian marriage could be acceptable also after a woman had conceived, and after menopause. But he too, like his contemporaries, considered "the deliberate prevention of conception . . . said to occur not infrequently" to be deeply sinful (see p. 577; and cf. pp. 451 and 562), and he was obviously no friend of mixed marriages.

120. Hirscher, *Die christliche Moral*, vol. 3, pp. 507–9; reprinted in *SZKS*, 12 Jan. 1846, p. 25.

121. *SZKS*, 2 Dec. 1846, p. 1085. Cf. Stolz's related remarks from the 1860s: "Civil marriage originated in a land and in a time, when a frenzy of wickedness and rebellion against all divine and natural order had broken out; it originated in a revolution that beheaded the king and queen, forbid faith in God, and flooded the land with the blood of innocents." See Alban Stolz, "Der Wechselbalg, womit Baden und Österreich aufgeholfen werden soll" (1868), in *Gesammelte Werke*, p. 531.

122. *Musterehe*, pp. 17 and 21. The footnote on p. 17, added in 1850, notes that "our premonitions in 1847 unfortunately did not deceive us," and another footnote (p. 21) notes that "the deterioration of family life was considered by the author in 1847 an omen of the impending outbreak."

CHAPTER TWO
JEWISH EMANCIPATION AND JEWISH DIFFERENCE

1. Groundbreaking early efforts to document liberal ambivalence and/or hostility toward Jews can be found in Eleonore Sterling, *Judenhass: Die Anfänge des politischen Antisemitismus in Deutschland (1815–1850)* (Frankfurt a. M.: Europäische Verlagsanstalt, 1969); and Reinhard Rürup, "German Liberalism and the Emancipation of the Jews," *LBIYB*, XX (1975).

2. Werner E. Mosse, "Introduction: German Jewry and Liberalism," in Friedrich-Naumann-Stiftung (ed.), *Das deutsche Judentum und der Liberalismus—German Jewry and Liberalism* (Sankt Augustin: COMDOK-Verlagsabteilung, 1986), pp. 22–23. Although a number of essays in the collection do refer to the problems in liberals' attitudes toward Jews, the collection's overall message is that there was a natural affinity between the two groups which, on the whole, made for a productive partnership.

3. See Loyd E. Lee, *The Politics of Harmony: Civil Service, Liberalism, and Social Reform in Baden, 1800–1850* (Newark: Univ. of Delaware Press, 1980), p. 145.

4. Because of the progressive new local ordinance, Jews actually faced a further setback, for the legal improvements in the status of many Gentiles affected

the relative status of Jews as well. By removing the distinction between "*Ortsbürger*," "*Gemeindebürger*," or "*Vollbürger*" (local citizen, communal citizen, or full citizen, respectively) on the one hand, and "*Schutzbürger*" (protected citizen, tolerated citizen) on the other, 80,000 gentile Badeners abruptly became full citizens. Jews were suddenly the only "*Schutzbürger*" left, and as the pro-emancipationist Lorenz Brentano would later put it, this was "a snub which did not exist earlier": Jews were "no longer in the same, but rather in a disadvantaged position." The disenfranchisement of Jews was further exacerbated by Paragraph 13 of the communal order in which "electability to the office of mayor or into the town council was now explicitly tied to the Christian statement of faith, and even those Jews who had already achieved 'local citizen' status were denied any participation in the self-government of the community." Also, before the new communal order, Catholics were not able to achieve "local citizen" status in towns where only Protestants had such status; since the law change, all differentiations between Christians had ceased, and only Jews were excluded from free settling in a new community. See Brentano, in *Verhandlungen der Stände-Versammlung des Grossherzogthums Baden* (II. Kammer), 7 Aug. 1846, 7. Beilagenheft, pp. 336–37; and Reinhard Rürup, *Emanzipation und Antisemitismus: Studien zur "Judenfrage" der bürgerlichen Gesellschaft* (Göttingen: Vandenhoeck und Ruprecht, 1975), pp. 56–58.

5. Sander, in *Verhandlungen* (II. Kammer), 27 Sept. 1833, 14. Protokollheft, p. 308.

6. Rotteck, in ibid., pp. 353–54; Sander, p. 305.

7. Sander, in ibid., p. 305. Even Carl Theodor Welcker, who later became one of the most vocal supporters of emancipation, in 1831 confidently asserted that "if we are talking about insults, about rejection and disdain, then this in no way describes Christians' attitudes toward Jews, but certainly does describe the reverse." Quoted in Gabriel Riesser, "Betrachtungen über die Verhandlungen der 2. Kammer des Grossherzogtums Baden über die Emanzipation der Juden" (1832), in *Eine Auswahl aus seinen Schriften und Briefen* (Frankfurt a. M.: J. Kauffmann, 1913), p. 47.

8. A member of Baden's Jewish High Council, quoted by Bekk, in *Verhandlungen* (II. Kammer), 27 Sept. 1833, 14. Protokollheft, p. 291.

9. Hecker, in *Verhandlungen* (II. Kammer), 22 Aug. 1842, 4. Protokollheft, pp. 128 and 130.

10. Rindeschwender, in *Verhandlungen* (II. Kammer), 27 Sept. 1833, 14. Protokollheft, p. 329.

11. For excellent discussions of Jews' economic roles, and contemporaries' distorted interpretations of them, see Monika Richarz, "Emancipation and Continuity: German Jews in the Rural Economy," in Werner E. Mosse et al. (eds.), *Revolution and Evolution: 1848 in German-Jewish History* (Tübingen: J.C.B. Mohr, 1981); and Jacob Toury, *Soziale und politische Geschichte der Juden in Deutschland 1847–1871: Zwischen Revolution, Reaktion und Emanzipation* (Düsseldorf: Droste, 1977), pp. 371–81.

12. Merk, in *Verhandlungen* (II. Kammer), 27 Sept. 1833, 14. Protokollheft, pp. 283 and 285. This tendency put Badenese liberals in a direct lineage

with C. W. Dohm's Enlightenment-era writings. Cf. the useful analysis of Dohm in Robert Liberles, "Dohm's Treatise on the Jews: A Defence of the Enlightenment," *LBIYB* XXXIII (1988).

13. Kuenzer, in *Verhandlungen* (II. Kammer), 17 July 1840, 14. Protokollheft, pp. xix–xx.

14. Bassermann, in *Verhandlungen* (II. Kammer), 22 Aug. 1842, 4. Protokollheft, p. 117.

15. Gerbel, in *Verhandlungen* (II. Kammer), 27 Sept. 1833, 14. Protokollheft, p. 392.

16. Mez, in *Verhandlungen* (II. Kammer), 18 Feb. 1845, 12. Protokollheft, p. 78. Here, as elsewhere in this chapter, the emphasis was in the original.

17. Feminist scholars have done the most important pioneering work in identifying the "double" quality of Enlightenment and liberal projects. For an excellent example, see Joan W. Scott, "French Feminists and the Rights of 'Man': Olympe de Gouges's Declarations," *History Workshop* 28 (Autumn 1989).

18. Bekk, in *Verhandlungen* (II. Kammer), 27 Sept. 1833, 14. Protokollheft, p. 293; cf. also p. 295.

19. Bader, in ibid., pp. 319 and 320.

20. Merk, in ibid., pp. 281 and 286.

21. See *MJour*, 13 Jan. 1846, p. 49.

22. See *JuDeuGe*, 6 Jan. 1846, p. 5; cf. the similar sentiments (copied from the *Deutsche Allgemeine Zeitung*) in *ZrelInt*, 1845, p. 195.

23. For background on the founding of the *deutschkatholische* congregation in Mannheim, see GlaKa 213/3597, report of 2 Aug. 1845; and *Die Feier des ersten Gründungsfestes der Deutschkatholischen Gemeinde in Mannheim* (Basel: Schnabelitz, 1846), p. 6. In 1846/47, the congregation had over 200 adult members. See *MAb*, 3 June 1846, p. 590; and 5 Jan. 1847, p. 15. By May of 1847, the congregation had 230 adult members, along with 76 children: a total of 306 members. See the "Rechenschafts-Bericht pro 1846/47" in FrGM, *Rechnungs-Vorlage nebst Rechenschafts-Berichte, Budgets, Vorstandswahl 1846/ 59–60*. For background on the Heidelberg congregation, see GlaKa 213/3597, reports of 15 Aug. 1845 and 18 Aug. 1845. In 1846, the congregation had 136 official members (see the membership list in GlaKa 356/566). The Pforzheim congregation had 102 members (of whom 50 were children); the Durlach congregation had 17 (of which 7 were children). The Stockach congregation reached a peak of 46 members in 1850; and the Constance congregation claimed to have 38 members in 1845, though official membership rolls never reached more than about 20. See the reports of the Ministry of the Interior on the Pforzheim and Durlach congregations, 17 Nov. 1846 and 30 Apr. 1847, respectively, in GlaKa 233/32307; the Stockach membership list, 20 Dec. 1850, in GlaKa 379/1934/2/147; the Constance congregation's letter, 24 Oct. 1846, and the supplementary membership list, 3 Dec. 1847, both in GlaKa 359/1906/20/1163; and cf. *MAb*, 24 Oct. 1845, p. 1253. No other membership statistics are known, though it is clear that large numbers of nonmembers attended services whenever possible as well. The ten congregations I list are the only Badenese congregations I could identify with certainty. Most of them re-

ceived newspaper coverage; others I discovered only because they sent petitions to the Lower Chamber. For example, the *deutschkatholische* congregations in Mannheim, Heidelberg, Pforzheim, Stockach, and Durlach sent petitions to the Lower Chamber in the spring and summer of 1846. See GlaKa 233/32307, 26 Aug. 1846. The *deutschkatholische* congregations in Mannheim, Heidelberg, Stockach, Constance, Waldshut, Neukirch, Bonndorf, and Hüfingen sent petitions to the Lower Chamber in January and February of 1848. See *Verhandlungen* (II. Kammer), 31 Oct. 1848, 8. Protokollheft, p. 7; and GlaKa 231/1436, petition of 30 Jan. 1848. Interest in establishing a congregation was shown in other towns as well, for example in Achern, Kippenheim, Furtwangen, Freiburg, and Wertheim. See *KKr*, Jan. 1846, pp. 235 and 237; Alfred Diesbach, *Die deutschkatholische Gemeinde Konstanz 1845–1849* (Mannheim: Freireligiöse Verlagsbuchhandlung, 1971), p. 44; Karl Weiss, *125 Jahre Kampf um freie Religion*, ed. and completed by Lilo Schlötermann (Mannheim: Freireligiöse Verlagsbuchhandlung, 1970), p. 54; and *Lbote*, 23 Oct. 1847, p. 551. One historian has claimed that small congregations emerged also in Ladenburg and Weinheim, but I have found no further evidence of this. See Hermann Lauer, *Geschichte der katholischen Kirche im Grossherzogthum Baden* (Freiburg i. B.: Herder, 1908), p. 182. By the 1860s, only the congregations in Mannheim, Heidelberg, and Pforzheim had survived. See *Bundesblätter* (Nordhausen), vol. XXI, Dec. 1868, pp. 10–11. Some congregations had dissolved due to their small size, while others were disbanded by the government in the wake of the 1849 revolution in Baden, on account of the radical political activities of their leading members. See especially the government reports on revolutionary politics and sexual misconduct in the Stockach congregation in GlaKa 233/32307, report of 23 Dec. 1851; 379/1934/2/147, reports of 13 Sept. 1849, 8 July 1851, and 21 Aug. 1861; and 231/1436, letter of 14 Jan. 1852. See also Gustav Tschirn, *Zur 60jährigen Geschichte der freireligiösen Bewegung* (Gottesberg: Hensel, 1904/5), p. 80. Nevertheless, by 1914, congregations existed not only in Mannheim, Heidelberg, and Pforzheim, but also in Freiburg, Karlsruhe, and Aue bei Durlach. See Erzbischöfliches Ordinariat Freiburg i. Br., *Die rechtliche Stellung der Freireligiösen im Grossherzogtum Baden* (Freiburg i. Br.: Verlag und Druck des Pressvereins, 1914), p. 1.

24. See Wolfgang Schieder, "Kirche und Revolution: Sozialgeschichtliche Aspekte der Trierer Wallfahrt von 1844," in *Archiv für Sozialgeschichte* XIV (1974); Rudolf Lill's critique of Schieder, "Kirche und Revolution: Zu den Anfängen der katholischen Bewegung im Jahrzehnt vor 1848," *Archiv für Sozialgeschichte* XVIII (1978); and Sylvia Paletschek, *Frauen und Dissens* (Göttingen: Vandenhoeck und Ruprecht, 1990), pp. 19–23.

25. See StaHei UA, 155/2; Gustav von Struve, *Briefe über Kirche und Staat* (Mannheim: J. Bensheimer, 1846), pp. 56–59; *Seebl*, 26 Aug. 1845, p. 521; Carl Scholl, *Das Wesen des Deutschkatholicismus oder die Versöhnung des Glaubens und der Wissenschaft* (Mannheim: F. Bassermann, 1846), p. 134; and Ernst Rudolf Huber, *Deutsche Verfassungsgeschichte seit 1789*, vol. 2 (Stuttgart: Kohlhammer, 1960), pp. 266–67. In addition, the Generallandesarchiv in Karlsruhe has ample documentation on the authorities' treatment of the congregations in general (233/32307, 213/3597, 231/1436) and also in particular:

Mannheim (233/32307, 362/1342); Heidelberg (356/566); Pforzheim (369/2431); Stockach (379/1934/2/147); and Constance (359/1906/20/59, 359/1906/20/1163). The Erzbischöfliches Archiv in Freiburg has substantial documentation on the Catholic hierarchy's response to the *Deutschkatholiken* in B2–17/22; B2–17/23; and B2–17/24.

26. The best book on dissent is Paletschek, *Frauen*; it offers the most up-to-date general history of the movement, as well as the fullest discussion of dissent's role in launching the first German women's rights movement. Also important is Catherine M. Prelinger, *Charity, Challenge and Change: Religious Dimensions of the Mid-Nineteenth-Century Women's Movement in Germany* (New York: Greenwood, 1987). Earlier works that are still useful include: Friedrich Wilhelm Graf, *Die Politisierung des religiösen Bewusstseins. Die bürgerlichen Religionsparteien im deutschen Vormärz: Das Beispiel des Deutschkatholizismus* (Stuttgart-Bad Cannstatt: Frommann-Holzboog, 1978); and (on the Protestant dissenters) Jörn Brederlow, *"Lichtfreunde" und "Freie Gemeinden": Religiöser Protest und Freiheitsbewegung im Vormärz und in der Revolution von 1848/49* (Munich: R. Oldenbourg, 1976). The next chapter will analyze the complex relationship between dissenters' women's rights and men's rights agendas.

27. See *Deutschlands zweites Ostern oder die Auferstehung der Kirche* (Stuttgart: J. B. Metzler, 1845); *Die neue Reformation oder die deutschkatholische Bewegung* (Leipzig: C.W.B. Naumburg, 1845); *Das neue Jerusalem oder die Zukunft der christlichen Kirche* (Darmstadt, 1845); Heinrich Schreiber, *Deutsch-Katholisches* (Freiburg i. B.: A. Emmerling, 1846), esp. p. 31. Also contrast the sarcastic remarks by Ullrich, in *Verhandlungen* (II. Kammer), 13 Aug. 1846, 8. Protokollheft, p. 115; and in Heinrich von Treitschke, *Deutsche Geschichte im Neunzehnten Jahrhundert*, vol. 5 (Leipzig: G. Hirzel, 1914), pp. 338–39.

28. Bassermann, in *Verhandlungen* (II. Kammer), 15 Dec. 1845, 1. Protokollheft, pp. 139–40; Welcker, p. 145; Georg Gottfried Gervinus, *Die Mission der Deutsch-Katholiken*, orig. ed. 1845, reprinted and ed. by Eckhart Pilick (Mannheim: Freireligiöse Verlagsbuchhandlung, 1982), pp. 13 and 30–31.

29. Friedrich Hecker, *Die staatsrechtlichen Verhältnisse der Deutschkatholiken mit besonderem Hinblick auf Baden* (Heidelberg: Groos, 1845), pp. 2–3, 8, and 28; Bassermann, in *Verhandlungen* (II. Kammer), 15 Dec. 1845, 1. Protokollheft, p. 139; Schreiber, *Deutsch-Katholisches*, p. 33.

30. Zittel, in *Verhandlungen* (II. Kammer), 15 Dec. 1845, 6. Beilagenheft, p. 42.

31. Ibid., p. 39.

32. Ibid., p. 37.

33. Ibid., p. 43.

34. Bassermann, *Verhandlungen* (II. Kammer), 15 Dec. 1845, 1. Protokollheft, p. 140; cf. Welcker's call for "the whole motion," followed by a "general bravo," p. 145.

35. Hecker, in ibid., p. 147.

36. Cf. Trefurt, in ibid., p. 143; Bader and Platz, p. 146; Schaaf, p. 148.

37. For an overview of its attacks on the *Deutschkatholiken*, see Wilhelm

Hubert Ganser, *Die Süddeutsche Zeitung für Kirche und Staat* (Berlin: E. Ebering, 1936), pp. 24–46.

38. Aside from the ones to be quoted below, typical examples include Wilhelm Stern, *Antrag auf Glaubensfreiheit* (Karlsruhe: Macklot, 1846); Franz Anton Staudenmaier, *Das Wesen der katholischen Kirche: Mit Rücksicht auf ihre Gegner dargestellt* (Freiburg i. B.: Herder, 1845), esp. pp. 177–93; and Franz Josef Mone, *Beleuchtung der Zittelschen Motion über Religionsfreiheit* (Bonn: Wittmann, 1846).

39. Ludwig Castorph, *Sendschreiben als unterthänigste Petition an die Allerhöchste Badische Staatsregierung und Hohe Badische Ständekammer hervorgerufen durch die Motion des Herrn Abgeordneten Zittel* (Baden-Baden: Scotzniovsky, 1846), p. 30.

40. Johann Baptist Hirscher, *Beleuchtung der Motion des Abgeordneten Zittel* (Freiburg i. B.: Herder, 1846), p. 21.

41. Franz Joseph Buss, *Das Rongethum in der badischen Abgeordnetenkammer* (Freiburg i. B.: Herder, 1846), p. 70. "Friends of Light" (*Lichtfreunde*) was the sarcastic term applied to formerly Protestant dissenters by their opponents. Soon, however, dissenters proudly adopted the term to describe themselves.

42. Alban Stolz, "Landwehr gegen den badischen Landstand" (1845), reprinted in Alban Stolz, *Gesammelte Werke* (ed. Julius Mayer), 3d ed., vol. 8 (Freiburg i. B.: Herder, 1913/14), pp. 7–14. The information about the public readings comes from editor Julius Mayer's introduction (p. vii) and his editorial footnote on p. 14.

43. "In many towns two churches would have to be built. . . . For the *Rongeaner* fit just as poorly into a Catholic church as Jews or Turks, because probably the majority of them, and especially their main founders, believe just as little in Jesus Christ, the Son of God, even though they won't admit it." Stolz, "Landwehr," p. 9.

44. Alban Stolz, "Amulett gegen die jungkatholische Sucht" (1845), reprinted in *Gesammelte Werke*, pp. 30, 32–33, and 43.

45. Alban Stolz, "Der neue Kometstern mit seinem Schweif, oder Johannes Ronge und seine Briefträger" (1846), reprinted in *Gesammelte Werke*, pp. 56–58 and 60.

46. Buss, *Rongethum*, pp. 8–9, 21, 63, 72, and 75.

47. Ibid., pp. 90–91.

48. Ibid., p. 74.

49. Quoted in Karl Zittel, "Die politischen Partheiungen in Baden," *Jahrbücher der Gegenwart* 1847, p. 358.

50. The petition from the city of Constance, for example, argued that the *Deutschkatholiken*'s "divergence in matters of faith will logically not encourage the unity of the German people, but rather will paralyze its strength through internal divisiveness, because it consumes its life-marrow, which is the Christian principle." See GlaKa 231/1436, petition of 8 Jan. 1846. The petition from the town of Wiesloch, however, was most concerned that the *Deutschkatholiken* should be denied "those same state-citizen rights which the members of the Roman Catholic and Evangelical Protestant church are allowed, that they

should thereby not be granted . . . the right to state financial support of their potential future parsonages and schools, etc." Quoted by Junghanns in *Verhandlungen* (II. Kammer), 23 Jan. 1846, 2. Protokollheft, p. 74.

51. Bassermann, in *Verhandlungen* (II. Kammer), 3 Feb. 1846, 2. Protokollheft, pp. 205–6. The stenographer noted that this speech was met by a "deep impression" among the listeners (p. 206).

52. Junghanns, *Verhandlungen* (II. Kammer), 23 Jan. 1846, 2. Protokollheft, p. 75.

53. Weizel, *Verhandlungen* (II. Kammer), 3 Feb. 1846, 2. Protokollheft, pp. 207–8.

54. See GlaKa 231/1436.

55. See Josef Becker, *Liberaler Staat und Kirche in der Ära von Reichsgründung und Kulturkampf* (Mainz: Matthias-Grünewald, 1973), p. 21; Kurt Kluxen, "Religion und Nationalstaat im 19. Jahrhundert," in Julius H. Schoeps (ed.), *Religion und Zeitgeist im 19. Jahrhundert* (Stuttgart and Bonn: Burg, 1982), p. 41.

56. Cf. Norbert Deuchert, *Vom Hambacher Fest zur badischen Revolution: Politische Presse und Anfänge deutscher Demokratie 1832–1848/49* (Stuttgart: Theiss, 1983), p. 201; and Manfred Hörner, *Die Wahlen zur badischen zweiten Kammer im Vormärz (1819–1847)* (Göttingen: Vandenhoeck und Ruprecht, 1987), pp. 454–68. For contemporaries' contrasting views, see Zittel, "Die politischen Partheiungen," pp. 352–53 and 358–61; and *SZKS*, 9 Apr. 1846, p. 292; 15 Apr. 1846, p. 308; and 24 June 1846, pp. 542–43.

57. Rindeschwender, in *Verhandlungen* (II. Kammer), 26 June 1846, 7. Beilagenheft, p. 135.

58. Ibid., pp. 149–50.

59. Kapp, in *Verhandlungen* (II. Kammer), 13 Aug. 1846, 8. Protokollheft, p. 63.

60. Rindeschwender, in ibid., p. 155; cf. Mathy, p. 118; and Bassermann, in *Verhandlungen* (II. Kammer), 12 Aug. 1846, 8. Protokollheft, p. 50.

61. The Evangelical-Reformed and Lutheran churches in Baden were not united with each other until 1821, and thus in 1818 when the constitution was being formulated, it had been necessary to say that members of all three Christian churches in the land (the two Protestant ones and the Catholic church) would be guaranteed equal political rights. The original recognition that there were three fully legitimate forms of Christianity gave liberals the opening for arguing that newly emergent forms of Christianity should also be legitimated.

62. Hecker, in *Verhandlungen* (II. Kammer), 13 Aug. 1846, 8. Protokollheft, p. 103.

63. Welcker, in ibid., p. 139; Zittel, p. 148. Cf. also Soiron's remarks a few weeks earlier: "I too am a Catholic, but certainly not a member of that Catholic church of which Representative *Buss* says, 'that's *my* church.'" *Verhandlungen* (II. Kammer), 24 July 1846, 6. Protokollheft, p. 212.

64. For example, cf. Kapp, in *Verhandlungen* (II. Kammer), 13 Aug. 1846, 8. Protokollheft, pp. 74–75; and Weller, p. 141.

65. Ibid., p. 160.

66. Hecker, in ibid., p. 106.

67. *MAb*, 20 Aug. 1846, p. 898; *MMorg*, 14 Apr. 1847, p. 491.

68. Fauth, in *Verhandlungen* (II. Kammer), 19 Feb. 1845, 13. Beilagenheft, p. 362.

69. Christ, in *Verhandlungen* (II. Kammer), 21 Aug. 1846, 9. Protokollheft, pp. 47–48.

70. Hecker, in ibid., p. 63.

71. Brentano, in his report to the chamber, in *Verhandlungen* (II. Kammer), 7 Aug. 1846, 7. Beilagenheft, p. 341. This report served as the basis for the August 21 discussion.

72. Bassermann, *Verhandlungen* (II. Kammer), 21 Aug. 1846, 9. Protokollheft, p. 61.

73. Soiron, in ibid., p. 62.

74. Kapp, in ibid., p. 67.

75. For examples, see Stolz, "Kometstern," p. 58; Buss, *Rongethum*, p. 75; Franz Josef Buss, "Aufgabe der Zeitschrift," *Capistran: Zeitschrift für die Rechte und Interessen des katholischen Teutschlands*, vol. 1, no. 1 (1847), pp. 15–16; [Franz Rosshirt], *Beleuchtung und actenmässige Ergänzung der Karlsruher Schrift: "Der Streit über gemischte Ehen und das Kirchenhoheitsrecht im Grossherzogthum Baden"* (Schaffhausen: Hurter, 1847), p. 19; and Amts-Assessor Herterich in Weinheim, "Die Judenemancipation und ihre beiden Geschwister, der Deutschkatholicismus und der Radicalismus," *MMorg*, 26 Feb. 1847, p. 269.

76. Soiron, in *Verhandlungen* (II. Kammer), 21 Aug. 1846, 9. Protokollheft, p. 62.

77. Brentano, in *Verhandlungen* (II. Kammer), 7 Aug. 1846, 7. Beilagenheft, p. 342.

78. Kapp, in *Verhandlungen* (II. Kammer), 21 Aug. 1846, 9. Protokollheft, pp. 66 and 69.

79. Weller, in ibid., p. 65.

80. Kapp, in ibid., pp. 66, 67, and 68.

81. Hecker, in ibid., p. 64.

82. Buss, in ibid., pp. 69–70.

83. *Die Reform des Judenthums* reported that of the delegates missing on the day of the vote, "five as well as the president of the chamber had already earlier expressed their support for [Jewish] equalization; thus, forty-two members, i.e., exactly two-thirds of the chamber, have voted for emancipation, surely a happy outcome" (26 Aug. 1846, p. 176).

84. *AlZJu*, 14 Sept. 1846, p. 549. Also cf. *RefJu*, 26 Aug. 1846, p. 176; *ZrelInt*, 1846, p. 389; *RZ*, Apr. 1847, p. 30; and the enthusiastic report on the Badenese vote squeezed into the index of Isaak Markus Jost's about-to-be-published *Culturgeschichte zur neueren Geschichte der Israeliten von 1815 bis 1845* (Berlin: Schlesinger, 1847), p. 283.

85. On the Ministry of State's and the Upper Chamber's deliberate obstructionism, see the detailed report in Berthold Rosenthal, *Heimatgeschichte der badischen Juden seit ihrem geschichtlichen Auftreten bis zur Gegenwart* (Bühl/ Baden: Konkordia, 1927), pp. 285–88.

86. See Franz Hundsnurscher and Gerhard Taddey, *Die jüdischen Gemein-*

den in Baden: Denkmale, Geschichte, Schicksale (Stuttgart: Kohlhammer, 1968), p. 16; and Adolf Lewin, *Geschichte der badischen Juden seit der Regierung Karl Friedrichs (1738–1909)* (Karlsruhe: G. Braun, 1909), p. 277.

87. *SZKS*, 16 Sept. 1846, p. 822.

88. *SZKS*, 13 Sept. 1846, p. 815; and 16 Sept. 1846, p. 822. See also the even more aggressively anti-Jewish remarks in the *Süddeutsche* in 1848 in Dagmar Herzog, "Anti-Judaism in Intra-Christian Conflict: Catholics and Liberals in Baden in the 1840s," *Central European History* 27/3 (1994).

89. For examples, see *MAb*, 25 Dec. 1846, p. 1405; 8 Mar. 1847, p. 259; 14 Oct. 1847, pp. 1118–19; 9 Mar. 1848, p. 271; Brentano, in *Verhandlungen* (II. Kammer), 9 Mar. 1848, 3. Protokollheft, p. 108; Hecker, in *Verhandlungen* (II. Kammer), 7 Apr. 1848, 4. Protokollheft, p. 45; and *DkSB*, 7 Aug. 1853, p. 125.

90. Joan Wallach Scott, *Gender and the Politics of History* (New York: Columbia Univ. Press, 1988), p. 7.

91. Overviews of the evolution of anti-Jewish racism can be found in George Mosse, *Toward the Final Solution: A History of European Racism* (New York: H. Fertig, 1978); Werner Conze, "Rasse," in Otto Brunner et al. (eds.), *Geschichtliche Grundbegriffe: Historisches Lexikon zur politisch-sozialen Sprache in Deutschland*, vol. 5 (Stuttgart: Klett-Cotta, 1984), pp. 135–78; and Jacob Katz, *From Prejudice to Destruction: Anti-Semitism, 1700–1933* (Cambridge: Harvard Univ. Press, 1980).

92. Sander Gilman, *The Jew's Body* (London: Routledge, 1991); Yosef Hayim Yerushalmi, *Assimilation and Racial Anti-Semitism: The Iberian and the German Models* (New York: Leo Baeck Institute, Inc., 1982).

93. For a few more examples of recognizably racial language in the first half of the nineteenth century, see Deborah Hertz, *Jewish High Society in Old Regime Berlin* (New Haven: Yale Univ. Press, 1988), pp. 259–64; and Rainer Erb and Werner Bergmann, *Die Nachtseite der Judenemanzipation: Der Widerstand gegen die Integration der Juden in Deutschland 1780–1860* (Berlin: Metropol, Veitl, 1989), pp. 48–52.

94. See Lee, *Politics*, p. 144. The only reason I have singled out this tiny moment in Lee's otherwise excellent book is that it so perfectly encapsulates the general consensus.

95. For the best critical analysis of the problematic suppositions underlying many historians' assumptions about German exceptionalism and Germany's purportedly peculiar propensity to illiberalism, see David Blackbourn and Geoff Eley, *The Peculiarities of German History: Bourgeois Society and Politics in Nineteenth-Century Germany* (Oxford: Oxford Univ. Press, 1984).

96. For example, in addition to the texts mentioned below, see Henry Louis Gates, Jr., "Writing 'Race' and the Difference it Makes," in Henry Louis Gates, Jr. (ed.), *"Race," Writing and Difference* (Chicago: Univ. of Chicago Press, 1986); Carroll Smith-Rosenberg, "Dis-Covering the Subject of the 'Great Constitutional Discussion,' 1786–1789," *Journal of American History* 79/3 (Dec. 1992); Peter Hulme, "The Spontaneous Hand of Nature: Savagery, Colonialism and the Enlightenment," in Peter Hulme and Ludmilla Jordanova (eds.), *The Enlightenment and its Shadows* (New York: Routledge, 1990); Mary Louise Pratt, *Imperial Eyes: Travel Writing and Transculturation* (New York: Rout-

ledge, 1992); Bryan Cheyette, *Constructions of "the Jew" in English Literature and Society* (New York: Cambridge Univ. Press, 1993); and especially Vincent P. Pecora, "Habermas, Enlightenment, and Antisemitism," in Saul Friedlander (ed.), *Probing the Limits of Representation: Nazism and the "Final Solution"* (Cambridge, Mass.: Harvard Univ. Press, 1992).

97. Arthur Hertzberg, *The French Enlightenment and the Jews* (New York and London: Columbia Univ. Press, 1968), p. 266.

98. Shmuel Trigano, "The French Revolution and the Jews," *Modern Judaism* 10 (1990), p. 178.

CHAPTER THREE
(WO)MEN'S EMANCIPATION AND WOMEN'S DIFFERENCE

1. See esp. Sylvia Paletschek, *Frauen und Dissens* (Göttingen: Vandenhoeck und Ruprecht, 1990); Catherine M. Prelinger, *Charity, Challenge and Change: Religious Dimensions of the Mid-Nineteenth-Century Women's Movement in Germany* (New York: Greenwood, 1987); and Alexandra Lotz, " 'Die Erlösung des weiblichen Geschlechts': Frauen in Deutschkatholischen Gemeinden," in Carola Lipp (ed.), *Schimpfende Weiber und patriotische Jungfrauen: Frauen im Vormärz und in der Revolution 1848/49* (Moos and Baden-Baden: Elster Verlag, 1986).

2. For example, see the Mannheim *Deutschkatholiken* membership list, 26 May 1846, in GlaKa 362/1342; and the Heidelberg *Deutschkatholiken* membership list, probably from May 1846, in GlaKa 356/566; and cf. Paletschek, *Frauen*, p. 244.

3. Karl Kleinpaul, in *KR*, Feb. 1847, p. 14. Emphasis here, as elsewhere in this chapter, was in the original.

4. Louise Otto, "Die Teilnahme der weiblichen Welt am Staatsleben," in *Vorwärts! Volkstaschenbuch für das Jahr 1847*, quoted in Margrit Twellmann, *Die Deutsche Frauenbewegung: Ihre Anfänge und erste Entwicklung. Quellen 1843–1889* (Meisenheim am Glan: Anton Hain, 1972), p. 5.

5. With the exception of one anonymous woman, whose views did not particularly distinguish her from her male contemporaries (indeed she was more conservative in both her theology and her ideas about gender than most of the men), all the (published) contributors to the debates about women's rights among dissenters in the 1840s were male. In 1850, a few more women's voices joined the fray. See the texts reprinted in the "Anhang" to Sylvia Paletschek, "Die Stellung der Frau im Deutschkatholizismus und in den freien Gemeinden im ausgehenden Vormärz und zu Beginn der Reaktionszeit" (M.A. Thesis, Univ. of Hamburg, 1983).

6. See Gustav von Struve, *Politisches Taschenbuch für das deutsche Volk* (Frankfurt a. M.: Literarische Anstalt, 1846), p. 287. Two more of the many contemporary articulations of this point can be found in *Mbote*, 19 Nov. 1845, p. 43; and *Lbote*, 7 Apr. 1847, pp. 171–72.

7. For background on the feminization of religion, see Hugh McLeod, "Weibliche Frömmigkeit—männlicher Unglaube? Religion und Kirchen im bürgerlichen 19. Jahrhundert," in Ute Frevert (ed.), *Bürgerinnen und Bürger:*

Geschlechterverhältnisse im 19. Jahrhundert (Göttingen: Vandenhoeck und Ruprecht, 1988), pp. 134–56; as well as the outstanding essay by Edith Saurer, "'Bewahrerinnen der Zucht und der Sittlichkeit': Gebetbücher für Frauen—Frauen in Gebetbüchern," *L'Homme: Zeitschrift für Feministische Geschichtswissenschaft* 1/1 (1990). Also cf. the remarks by a conservative and a radical contemporary: Ludwig Castorph, bemoaning the state of secularization, contrasted "the still Christian lady wife" with "so many *gentlemen, etc.* that one sees in church maybe four times in the course of the year, usually on high holidays," while Louise Dittmar, bemoaning the oppressive conditions for women within the traditional churches, asked rhetorically: "Who else still went to church, but the unenlightened *Volk* and the female sex, that still believed itself forced to sacrifice its own convictions to the tyranny of convention?" See Ludwig Castorph, *Sendschreiben als unterthänigste Petition an die Allerhöchste Badische Staatsregierung und Hohe Badische Stände-Kammer hervorgerufen durch die Motion des Herrn Abgeordneten Zittel* (Baden-Baden: Scotzniovsky, 1846), p. 45; and [Luise Dittmar], *Der Mensch und sein Gott in und ausser dem Christenthum* (Offenbach a. M.: G. André, 1846), p. 67.

8. Johannes Ronge, *Zuruf* (Dessau: H. Neubürger, 1845), p. 12.

9. Johannes Ronge, "Letter to the Inferior Clergy," in anon., *John Ronge, the Holy Coat of Treves and the New German-Catholic Church* (New York: Harper and Bros., 1845), pp. 129, 130, 131, 134, and 135.

10. See *Trau-Rede, am 21. Februar 1845 bei der kirchlichen Trauung des katholischen Predigers Czerski in Schneidemühl gehalten von dem evangelischen Ortspfarrer Grützmacher* (Berlin: W. Hermes, 1845), pp. 4 and 6.

11. *Seebl,* 21 May 1846, p. 257.

12. Cf. Norbert Deuchert, *Vom Hambacher Fest zur badischen Revolution: Politische Presse und Anfänge deutscher Demokratie 1832–1848/49* (Stuttgart: Theiss, 1983), p. 201.

13. *OberZ,* 5 July 1846. The *Mannheimer Abendzeitung* also praised Schreiber's marriage (26 May 1846, p. 562).

14. *Unsre Antwort: Abgedrungene Erklärung der Mannheimer Deutsch-Katholiken auf das Manifest des erzbischöflichen Ordinariats in Freiburg* (Belle-Vue: Verlags-Buchhandlung, 1846), p. 16.

15. "Die Ehe, vom bürgerlichen und kirchlichen Standpunkte aus betrachtet," *KKr,* June 1845, p. 165.

16. Johannes Ronge, *Maria, oder: Die Stellung der Frauen der alten und neuen Zeit* (Hamburg: G. W. Niemeyer, 1849), p. 8.

17. Eduard Baltzer, "Die Ehe," in *Das Menschenleben in seinen Hauptbeziehungen* (Nordhausen: F. Förstemann, 1851), p. 160; *Trau-Rede,* p. 4; Leberecht Uhlich, *Die Ehe: Eine Erörterung* (Magdeburg: Selbstverlag, 1857), pp. 10 and 15–16.

18. See the song "Gemischte Ehen" in *Rongelieder: Die religiösen Ideen der Gegenwart* (Stuttgart: E. Theiner, 1845), pp. 67–70; and cf. the songs "Unsere Braut" and "Klage eines katholischen Geistlichen, oder: Der Cölibat."

19. Albrecht was best known as the preacher to the *deutschkatholische* congregation in Ulm, in the neighboring state of Württemberg. But from March to November 1847 (and again in 1850 and 1851), he also actively ministered to

the Stockach congregation. See the letter from the Badenese Ministry of the Interior to the Regierung des Seekreises, 5 Feb. 1847; the letter from Sebastian Gulde (leader of the Stockach congregation) to the Regierung des Seekreises, 9 Nov. 1847; the notations on the back of the order from the Landeskommissar for the Seekreis to the Bezirks-Amt Stockach, 13 Dec. 1850; and the letter from the Stockach *Deutschkatholiken* to the Ministry of the Interior, 10 Mar. 1851, all in GlaKa 379/1934/2/147. See also the petition from the Stockach *Deutschkatholiken* to the Lower Chamber, 14 Jan. 1852, in GlaKa 231/1436. In addition, see Hans Wagner, *Aus Stockachs Vergangenheit* (Singen/Hohentwiel: Verein für Geschichte des Hegaus, 1967), pp. 384–85; *Mbote*, 9 May 1847, pp. 151–52; *SZKS*, 15 May 1847, pp. 569–70; 31 May 1847, pp. 635–36; 29 June 1847, p. 754; 14 July 1847, pp. 805–6; and 24 Sept. 1847, pp. 1050–51; *Lbote*, 13 Mar. 1847, p. 123; 27 Mar. 1847, p. 152; 11 Sept. 1847, p. 471; 29 Sept. 1847, pp. 505–6; 20 Oct. 1847, p. 545; 17 Nov. 1847, p. 591; 22 Dec. 1848, pp. 831–32; *DkSB*, 12 Oct. 1851, p. 44 (this report also indicates that in 1850–51, Albrecht ministered to Baden's Constance congregation as well); and 17 Apr. 1853, p. 64.

20. Friedrich Albrecht, "Ave Maria," in *Religion: Eine Sammlung von Predigt-Vorträgen im Geiste des neunzehnten Jahrhunderts*, vol. 1 (Ulm: Gebr. Rübling, 1857), p. 181. Albrecht had already delivered at least one version of this sermon in 1847; his views on Mary garnered particular venom from his ultramontane opponents. See *SZKS*, 15 May 1847, p. 569; and 29 June 1847, p. 754.

21. Friedrich Albrecht, "Erbsünde," *Religion*, vol. 1, pp. 290 and 292.

22. Friedrich Albrecht, *Glaube, Hoffnung, Liebe: Ein Glaubensbekenntniss in drei Sonettenkränzen* (Ulm: Selbstverlag, 1856), pp. 39 and 48.

23. Friedrich Albrecht, "Ueber die Ehe," *Predigten, Aufsätze, Mittheilungen*, no. 5 (Ulm: G. P. Geuss, 1846), p. 8. The marriage service was held in Ulm on May 17, 1846; it was the first marriage sermon Albrecht had delivered since joining the dissenting movement.

24. See Georg Denzler, *Die verbotene Lust: 2000 Jahre christliche Sexualmoral* (Munich: Piper, 1988).

25. For example, see "Familie," in Hermann Rolfus and Adolph Pfister (eds.), *Real-Encyclopädie des Erziehungs- und Unterrichtswesens nach katholischen Prinzipien: Unter Mitwirkung von geistlichen und weltlichen Schulmännern für Geistliche, Volksschullehrer, Eltern und Erzieher*, vol. 1 (Mainz: Florian Kupferberg, 1863), pp. 562–63; and *Die Musterehe und die Nothwendigkeit einer Wiederherstellung der Ehe nach der Musterehe* (Freiburg i. B.: Herder, 1850).

26. Joseph Dürr, *Predigten auf alle Sonn- und Festtage des katholischen Kirchenjahrs und bei besonderen Anlässen* vol. 2 (Villingen: F. Förderer, 1843), pp. 246–47. See also the discussion of this general phenomenon in chapter 1.

27. See, for example, Wilhelm Hubert Ganser, *Die Süddeutsche Zeitung für Kirche und Staat: Freiburg 1845–1848* (Berlin: E. Ebering, 1936), pp. 31–32, which lists all the issues of the *Süddeutsche* which sought to defame the *Deutschkatholiken* in sexual terms—thirty-six issues in 1845–46 alone.

28. Franz Josef Buss, *Das Rongethum in der badischen Abgeordnetenkammer* (Freiburg i. B.: Herder, 1846), pp. 21, 67, and 72.

29. Declaration of the archbishop's office with respect to the Badenese *Deutschkatholiken*, 3 Apr. 1846, reprinted in Georg Schneider, *50 Jahre freireligiösen Gemeindelebens: Festschrift zur Feier des fünfzigjährigen Bestehens der freireligiösen Gemeinde in Mannheim* (Mannheim: Mannheimer Aktiendruckerei, 1895), p. 47.

30. See Franz Anton Staudenmaier, *Das Wesen der katholischen Kirche: Mit Rücksicht auf ihre Gegner dargestellt* (Freiburg i. B.: Herder, 1845), p. 184.

31. Alban Stolz, "Amulett gegen die jungkatholische Sucht" (1845); and Alban Stolz, "Der neue Kometstern mit seinem Schweif oder Johannes Ronge und seine Briefträger" (1846), in *Gesammelte Werke*, vol. 8 (Freiburg i. B.: Herder, 1913/14), pp. 43 and 60.

32. Report from the Catholic parish office in Heidelberg to Archbishop Vicari, 29 July 1845, in ErzFrei B2–17/24.

33. The accusations involved not only adultery and concubinage, but also rape and seduction between children. See the letter from Hummelsheim (the local Catholic priest) et al. to the Bezirks-Amt, 21 Aug. 1851, and the Bezirks-Amt's interviews with Hummelsheim and with schoolteacher Nepomuk Haitz, both 12 Nov. 1851, all in GlaKa 379/1934/2/147. As part of the authorities' larger effort to shut down the Stockach congregation in the post-revolutionary years, Albrecht was ordered to stop preaching in Stockach on February 7, 1851. In 1852, all congregational gatherings were forbidden, the congregation's right to religious tolerance was withdrawn, and the youth of the congregation were forced to attend Catholic religious education classes. All children that had been baptized as *Deutschkatholiken* had to be rebaptized as Catholics. Whoever did not officially return to the Catholic church, became—as dissenting historian Karl Weiss put it—"unemployed and breadless." See the petition of the Stockach congregation to the Lower Chamber of the Badenese diet, 14 Jan. 1852, in GlaKa 231/1436; the letter from the Landeskommissar to the Bezirks-Amt in Stockach, 16 Sept. 1851; the decree of the Ministry of State, 26 Feb. 1852, and the accompanying letter of the Ministry of the Interior to the Regierung des Seekreises, 2 Mar. 1852, all in GlaKa 379/1934/2/147. See also the letter from the archbishop's office to the Catholic parish office in Stockach, 26 Sept. 1851, in ErzFrei B2–17/24; and Karl Weiss, *125 Jahre Kampf um freie Religion*, ed. and completed by Lilo Schlötermann (Mannheim: Freireligiöse Verlagsbuchhandlung, 1970), p. 64.

34. J. H. Mehlmann, "Einige Worte über deutsch-katholische Praxis," *MMorg*, 20 July 1847, p. 964.

35. Ronge, *Maria*, p. 15.

36. Carl Scholl, "Am Tag der Einweihung der Gemeindehalle (17 Dec. 1848)," in *Aus hohen Tagen: Das Erwachen der Geister in Oesterreich* (Berlin: H. Lüstenöder, 1891), p. 114; Uhlich, *Die Ehe*, p. 16. See also the description of J.D.C. Brugger's sermon in *MAb*, 18 Nov. 1846, p. 1259.

37. Handwritten "Trauungsrede," 14 May 1846, in StaFrei NL Schreiber K1/27 2/9.

38. Uhlich, *Die Ehe*, pp. 6 and 9–10.

39. Johannes Ronge, *Religion und Politik* (Frankfurt a. M.: Literarische Anstalt, 1850), pp. 23–24.

40. Heinrich Loose, "Rede," in *Antritts-Predigt von Friedrich Albrecht, deutsch-katholischem Pfarrer zu Ulm, bei seiner durch Heinrich Loose, deutsch-katholischem Pfarrer in Esslingen vollzogenen Einweihung nebst der Einweihungs-Rede des Letztern* (Basel: Senl und Fischer, 1846), p. 3; the handwritten "Trauungsrede," 14 May 1846, StaFrei NL Schreiber Kl/27 2/9.

41. See Hermann Jellinek, *Die religiösen, socialen und literarischen Zustände der Gegenwart. In ihren praktischen Folgen untersucht. Erster Theil: Die religiösen Zustände der Gegenwart, oder: Kritik der Religion der Liebe* (Zerbst: Kummer, 1847).

42. For explicit attacks on Catholic-induced divisiveness, see *Der Volksführer*, 3 Apr. 1849, pp. 313–14; Carl Scholl, "Der Gottesruf des Frühlings: 'Erwachet!'" in *Das Wesen des Deutschkatholicismus oder die Versöhnung des Glaubens mit der Wissenschaft* (Mannheim: F. Bassermann, 1846), p. 110; *MJour*, 11 May 1846, p. 551.

43. Carl Scholl, "Was wollen die Deutschkatholiken? (B.)" in *Wesen*, pp. 24 and 26–27.

44. Ronge, *Zuruf*, pp. 11–12.

45. *KKr*, Oct. 1845, p. 94. A story in the *Mannheimer Abendzeitung* also argued that the ultramontane attitude toward mixed marriages was leading ever more people across Baden to support the *Deutschkatholiken*. See *MAb*, 25 Nov. 1845, p. 1375.

46. Petition from the Mannheim *Deutschkatholiken* to the Lower Chamber (requesting the introduction of civil marriage), 14 Dec. 1845, reprinted in Schneider, *50 Jahre*, p. 9; *Unsre Antwort*, pp. 14–16. See also the report sent by the Mannheim *Deutschkatholiken* to *KKr*, Dec. 1845, p. 189.

47. See the report from the Catholic parish office in Heidelberg to the archbishop's office, 29 July 1845, in ErzFrei B2–17/24.

48. Of the fourteen couples who had joined the Heidelberg congregation together as couples, nine were mixed. Forty-nine further individuals were married but had joined alone (or were widowed); of these *at least* fourteen lived in mixed marriages. See the Heidelberg *Deutschkatholiken* membership list, probably from May 1846, in GlaKa 356/566.

49. See the Mannheim *Deutschkatholiken* membership list, 26 May 1846, in GlaKa 362/1342.

50. Quoted in E. N. Misch, *Die Ehe zwischen Juden und Christen: Ein Votum mit Bezug auf das preussische Recht und Toleranzedikt* (Leipzig: O. Wigand, 1847), p. 1. Documents concerning the case are collected in Ferdinand Falkson (ed.), *Gemischte Ehen zwischen Juden und Christen: Dokumente* (Altona: J. F. Hammerich, 1845); and in another book also edited by Falkson and with the same title, but with completely different contents, published Hamburg: Hoffmann und Campe, 1847. According to a contemporary, only one German state—Saxony-Weimar—allowed mixed marriages between Jews and Christians without any problems whatsoever, just as England, France, Belgium, Denmark, and Holland did. See J. Kinorhc, "Ueber die Ehe zwischen Juden und Christen," *KR*, Oct. 1846, pp. 3 and 8. But actually, civil marriage was legal in the

Rhineland, because of the legacy of Napoleonic law, and thus in the various Rhenish territories "neither marriage among Jews nor between Jews and Christians presented the special legal problems it did elsewhere." See Jonathan Sperber, *Rhineland Radicals: The Democratic Movement and the Revolution of 1848–1849* (Princeton: Princeton Univ. Press, 1991), p. 50.

51. References to the case can be found, for example, in *KR*, Jan. 1846, p. 26; Mar. 1846, p. 30; and Oct. 1846, pp. 1–8; *AlZJu*, 1 Dec. 1845, p. 731; *JuDeuGe*, 13 Jan. 1846, pp. 14–15; *IsJa*, 28 Mar. 1847, pp. 100–101; 19 Dec. 1847, p. 407; 9 Jan. 1848, p. 14; 23 Jan. 1848, pp. 29–30; and 25 June 1848, pp. 203–6. The *Frankfurter Journal* also reported on the case (see *MAb*, 2 May 1847, p. 470), and the Jewish monthly *Reform-Zeitung* carried detailed analyses of the whole affair. See *RZ*, Feb. 1847, pp. 11–13; and Mar. 1847, pp. 17–20. Even a legal newspaper, Eberty's *Zeitschrift für Recht und Gesetzgebung*, came to Falkson's defense. See *KR*, Mar. 1846, p. 30. Falkson himself reported decades later that his efforts to marry had been "followed no less intently by the French and English press." See Ferdinand Falkson, *Die liberale Bewegung in Königsberg (1840–1848): Memoirenblätter* (Breslau: S. Schottlaender, 1888), p. 170.

52. See *IsJa*, 23 Jan. 1848, p. 29; and *MAb*, 2 May 1847, p. 470.

53. Falkson, *Gemischte Ehen* (1847), pp. viii–ix.

54. See *MAb*, 2 May 1847, p. 470.

55. Kinorhc, "Ueber die Ehe," pp. 1 and 8.

56. Ronge, *Maria*, p. 8.

57. Carl Scholl, "Die Marien-Verehrung: Zur gerechteren Würdigung der katholischen Religion," in *EwL*, 1871, p. 124.

58. Carl Scholl, "Unsere Reform und die Frauen" (12 Nov. 1848), *Aus hohen Tagen*, p. 93.

59. See *SZKS*, 30 Sept. 1847, p. 1069; Denzler, *Lust*, pp. 267–330; and cf. the discussion of conservative Catholic views on women in chapter 1.

60. Wilhelm Heinrich Riehl, "Die Frauen: Eine social-politische Studie," in *Deutsche Vierteljahresschrift* 1852, no. 3, p. 238.

61. For example, cf. Jolly and von Stockhorn's remarks in *Verhandlungen der Stände-Versammlung des Grossherzogthums Baden* (II. Kammer), 30 Apr. 1844, 4. Protokollheft, pp. 241 and 249; and *SZKS*, 30 Sept. 1847, p. 1069.

62. Carl Theodor Welcker, "Geschlechtsverhältnisse," in Karl von Rotteck and Carl Theodor Welcker (eds.), *Das Staats-Lexikon*, 1st ed., vol. 6 (Altona: J. F. Hammerich, 1838), pp. 630 and 645. For a related assertion of contemporaries' fears that "women's emancipation" would necessarily involve both a blurring of gender identities and women's abandonment of familial roles, see *Evangelisches Kirchenblatt zunächst für das Grossherzogthum Baden*, 15 June 1845, pp. 97–98.

63. The only other group of men attempting to implement greater equality for women were left-liberal democrats, but they advanced many of the same ambiguous notions that dissenters did, and indeed, there was tremendous overlap in membership between dissenting circles and democratic ones. On the democrats' gender views, cf. Carola Lipp, "Frauen und Öffentlichkeit: Möglich-

keiten und Grenzen politischer Partizipation im Vormärz und in der Revolution 1848," and id., "Liebe, Krieg und Revolution: Geschlechterbeziehung und Nationalismus," both in Lipp, *Schimpfende*, pp. 295 and 364. On the overlap in membership, see Paletschek, *Frauen*, esp. pp. 11, 13, 52–55, and 144.

64. Johannes Ronge, *Rede, gehalten am 23. Sept. 1845 in der Münsterkirche zu Ulm* (Ulm: E. Rübling, 1845), p. 12.

65. Ronge, *Maria*, p. 12.

66. Ibid., p. 10.

67. See Friedrich Albrecht, "Mann und Weib," *Religion* vol. 2 (Ulm: Gebr. Rübling, 1866), p. 470; id., "Ave Maria," p. 181; and id., "Das rechte Band der Ehe," *Religion*, vol. 2, p. 479.

68. Albrecht, "Ueber die Ehe," pp. 4–5 and 11.

69. Joseph Dominik Carl Brugger, "Martha und Maria," *Das Christenthum im Geiste des neuenzehnten Jahrhunderts* (Heidelberg: Hoffmeister, 1847), p. 145.

70. Heribert Rau, "Die Stellung der Frauen in der Christenheit," *Worte zum Herzen des deutschen Volkes: Vorträge und Gebete* (Stuttgart: Franckh, 1848), pp. 147, 149, and 152.

71. Ronge again made matters explicit: "Women should by no means leave the spheres of activity to which nature has directed them; at the hearth of the family in particular they should awaken and nourish the holy flame of humanity." Although Ronge was insistent that women "should neither be sold into marriage, nor, as so often happens, should coercion and fear be the bonds of marriage," he was nonetheless equally insistent that "neither should they renounce the sanctifying relationship of marriage." Johannes Ronge, "Die Stellung der Frauen," in *Für christkatholisches Leben* VI (1848), p. 354.

72. Julius Carlebach, "The Forgotten Connection: Women and Jews in the Conflict between Enlightenment and Romanticism," *LBIYB*, XXIV (1979), p. 128.

73. Joseph Dominik Carl Brugger, "Die Frauen vor und in dem Christenthum," *DkSB*, 12 Mar. 1854, p. 39.

74. Rau, "Die Stellung der Frauen," pp. 145–46.

75. See Riehl, "Die Frauen," pp. 287–88 and 295; Louise Dittmar, *Das Wesen der Ehe* (Leipzig: O. Wigand, 1850), p. 73; Ignaz Demeter, "Bemerkungen des Erzbischofs von Freiburg" (30 Jan. 1839), in ErzFrei NL Demeter Nb 2–8; *SZKS*, 28 Sept. 1847, p. 1061; and Renate Möhrmann (ed.), *Frauenemanzipation im deutschen Vormärz: Texte und Dokumente* (Stuttgart: Reclam, 1978), p. 10. Despite the phenomenon of widespread singlehood, and despite the fact that many unmarried women joined the dissenting congregations, most male dissenters ignored the issue of unmarried women entirely. The only exception I have been able to find is Ronge. Characteristically, his unquestioning advocacy of marriage went so far that he exclaimed about "how dangerous . . . our social conditions [are], where so many are forced by external circumstances to remain unmarried," and worried about what effects this had "on female morality and thereby on the happiness of families and nations." See Ronge, "Stellung," p. 354.

76. Heinrich Thiel, "Die deutsch-katholische Frau," *Der Inhalt des Deutsch-Katholizismus* (Dessau, 1846), pp. 72–73.

77. "Die Frau im Alterthume und die christliche Frau," in *KKr*, Oct. 1845, p. 77. This was the one female-authored dissenting text of the 1840s.

78. "Die Ehe," *KKr*, June 1845, p. 162.

79. Albrecht, "Mann und Weib," p. 467; id., "Das rechte Band," p. 474; id., "Ave Maria," p. 182.

80. Ronge, "Stellung," p. 352; Ronge, *Maria*, p. 9.

81. Hermann Greive, "Religious Dissent and Tolerance in the 1840s," in Werner E. Mosse et al. (eds.), *Revolution and Evolution: 1848 in German-Jewish History* (Tübingen: J.C.B. Mohr, 1981), pp. 347–51. Cf. also the important pioneering text by Edward Said, *Orientalism* (New York: Pantheon, 1978); and (for useful discussions of the ongoing tendency in self-identified feminist Christian theology to make anti-Jewish arguments) Hanneke van der Sluis, "Eine Ladung Dynamit: Antijüdische Tendenzen in der feministischen Theologie," in Marion Th. Kunstenaar (ed.), *Der eigene Freiraum: Frauen in Synagoge und Kirche* (Offenbach a. M.: Burckhardthaus-Laetere Verlag, 1989); Susannah Heschel, "Anti-Judaism in Christian Feminist Theology," *Tikkun* 5/3 (1990); and Judith Plaskow, "Feminist Anti-Judaism and the Christian God," *Journal of Feminist Studies in Religion* 7/2 (Fall 1991).

82. *IsJa*, 21 Dec. 1845, p. 414; and *Der Orient. Literatur-Blatt* 20 Aug. 1846, p. 540. (Notably, the latter remark also gives evidence of anti-Muslim stereotypes.)

83. *RefJu*, 2 Dec. 1846, p. 285; and the highly critical review of Reform rabbi Samuel Holdheim's *Die religiöse Stellung des weiblichen Geschlechts im talmudischen Judenthume* (Schwerin, 1846) in *Der Orient. Literatur-Blatt*, 20 Aug. 1846, pp. 538–42. For further examples of Reform Jewish feminism from the 1840s, see *IsJa*, 30 Mar. 1845, pp. 98–99; *RefJu*, 27 May 1846, pp. 65–69; 3 June 1846, pp. 73–75; and 2 Sept. 1846, pp. 177–78; *Eine deutsch-jüdische Kirche: Die nächste Aufgabe unserer Zeit. Von einem Candidaten der jüdischen Theologie* (Leipzig: O. Wigand, 1845), p. 9; Samuel Holdheim, *Das Religiöse und Politische im Judenthum: Mit besonderer Beziehung auf gemischte Ehen* (Schwerin: C. Kürschner, 1845), pp. 50–54; id., *Vorschläge zu einer zeitgemässen Reform der jüdischen Ehegesetze* (Schwerin: C. Kürschner, 1845), esp. pp. 16–20; and W. Gunther Plaut, *The Rise of Reform Judaism: A Sourcebook of its European Origins* (New York: World Union for Progressive Judaism, 1963), pp. 252–55.

84. Uhlich, *Die Ehe*, p. 3.

85. Scholl, "Die Marien-Verehrung," p. 124. On the whole, Scholl was not impressed with either Judaism or Christianity, and whatever comparisons he advanced between the two religions, and their treatment of women, were generally designed to demonstrate the failings of both. For example, see Carl Scholl, *Hundert Jahre nach Lessings Nathan* (Bamberg: Handels-Druckerei, 1893), pp. 8–9.

86. Uhlich, *Die Ehe*, pp. 4 and 6.

87. Thiel, "Die deutsch-katholische Frau," p. 72. Thiel also used a transcontinental contrast to reinforce his militant critique of European men: "Yes, women are slaves, but they have the misfortune that their men have less empathy for them, than for the black slaves of the American planters. Most blacks suffer more physical maltreatment than most women, but they are coarse, insensible to the finer sufferings of the soul; our women have . . . a more delicate, higher life of feeling, the wounding of which . . . makes their lives to a worse hell, than the bodily pains of the crude, strong Negro" (p. 69).

88. For an introduction to the relevant theoretical considerations, see Evelyn Brooks Higginbotham, "African-American Women's History and the Metalanguage of Race," in *Signs* 17/2 (Winter 1992); Gail Bederman, " 'Civilization,' the Decline of Middle-Class Manliness, and Ida B. Wells's Antilynching Campaign (1892–94)," in *Radical History Review* 52 (Winter 1992); and Pamela Scully, "Rape, Race, and Colonial Culture: The Sexual Politics of Identity in the Nineteenth-Century Cape Colony, South Africa," *American Historical Review* 100/2 (Apr. 1995).

89. Cf. the related points made in Joyce Zonana, "The Sultan and the Slave: Feminist Orientalism and the Structure of *Jane Eyre*," in *Signs* 18/3 (Spring 1993), esp. pp. 592–605. On the prevalence of the double standard in nineteenth-century Germany, see Welcker, "Geschlechtsverhältnisse," pp. 660 and 665; Stanley Zucker, *Kathinka Zitz-Halein and Female Civic Activism in Mid-Nineteenth-Century Germany* (Carbondale and Edwardsville: Southern Illinois University Press, 1991), pp. 14–16, 158 and 184–85; and Ute Frevert, *Women in German History: From Bourgeois Emancipation to Sexual Liberation* (Oxford: Berg, 1989), pp. 48 and 133. It also seems important to point out here that I am not trying to minimize the oppression of women in non-European cultures (as Gayatri Spivak put it in her at once feminist and postcolonial/ anti-racist reading of *sati*, "Obviously I am not advocating the killing of widows"). See Gayatri Chakravorty Spivak, "Can the Subaltern Speak?" in Cary Nelson and Lawrence Grossberg (eds.), *Marxism and the Interpretation of Culture* (Urbana: Univ. of Illinois Press, 1988), p. 301. What I am trying to say is that criticizing the gender arrangements of other cultures is somewhat more complicated than criticizing our own (particularly when there is a power differential between the two cultures); we urgently need to find ways to talk about the complexity of discourses which, while they have liberatory potential for one oppressed group, simultaneously encourage discrimination against another. For subtle and thoughtful examples of how this might be done, see Susan Pedersen, "National Bodies, Unspeakable Acts: The Sexual Politics of Colonial Policy-making," in *Journal of Modern History* 63 (Dec. 1991); and Ania Loomba, "Dead Women Tell No Tales: Issues of Female Subjectivity, Subaltern Agency and Tradition in Colonial and Post-colonial Writings on Widow Immolation in India," in *History Workshop* 36 (Autumn 1993).

90. "Die Frau des Christenthums," in *Der fränkische Morgenbote*, 24 July 1851, p. 66.

91. Ronge, *Zuruf*, pp. 12–13; id., *An meine Glaubensgenossen und Mitbürger* (Altenburg: Schnuphase, 1845), pp. 9–10; id., "Letter to the Inferior

Clergy," p. 143. Cf. the similar concerns in "Der Cölibat," in *DkSB*, 28 Nov. 1852, pp. 190–91.

92. Gustav von Struve, *Briefe über Kirche und Staat* (Mannheim: J. Bensheimer, 1846), p. 53; *Unsre Antwort*, p. 16.

93. Badenese dissenting preacher Gottfried Scheibel's letter to Catholic priest Schindler in Pforzheim, reprinted in *SZKS*, 1 Aug. 1846, p. 673.

94. Struve, *Briefe über Kirche*, p. 53; *Unsre Antwort*, p. 23.

95. Cf. on this point Jeffrey R. Watt, *The Making of Modern Marriage: Matrimonial Control and the Rise of Sentiment in Neuchâtel, 1550–1800* (Ithaca: Cornell Univ. Press, 1992), p. 11.

96. Johannes Czerski, *Rechtfertigung meines Abfalles von der römischen Hofkirche* (Bromberg: L. Levit, 1845), p. 14.

97. "Die Ehe," *KKr*, Apr. 1845, p. 87; and Scholl, "Unsere Reform," pp. 94–95.

98. "Die Ehe," *KKr*, June 1845, p. 167.

99. Ronge, *Maria*, p. 7.

100. "Der katholische Priester in seiner Stellung zum Weibe und zur Familie von J. Michelet: Aus dem Französischen," *KKr*, May 1845, pp. 140 and 142. After establishing the compatibility between Michelet's views and those of the *Deutschkatholiken* ("The author [Michelet] seems . . . to want nothing but what the *deutschkatholische* church has already done. . . . France will and must sooner or later follow the path of our new church" [p. 139]), the reviewer primarily confined himself to quoting or paraphrasing Michelet's own words. Cf. also the quite similar remarks in Friedrich Albrecht, "Die Trauung," in *Religion*, vol. 2, p. 498.

101. Friedrich Albrecht, "Du sollst nicht ehebrechen," in *Religion*, vol. 2, p. 505.

102. *Keine Ohrenbeichte mehr! Zeitgemässes Wort eines Rhein-Hessischen Katholiken an seine Glaubensgenossen* (Frankfurt a. M.: C. Körner, 1845), p. 7.

103. See John C. Fout, "Sexual Politics in Wilhelmine Germany: The Male Gender Crisis, Moral Purity, and Homophobia," in *Journal of the History of Sexuality* 2/3 (January 1992), pp. 404, 413, and 416. Cf. John D'Emilio, "The Homosexual Menace: The Politics of Sexuality in Cold War America," in Kathy Peiss and Christina Simmons (eds.), *Passion and Power: Sexuality in History* (Philadelphia: Temple Univ. Press, 1989), p. 232.

104. *DkSB*, 5 March 1854, p. 39. Cf. the very similar sentiments in "Die Frau des Christenthums" (*Der fränkische Morgenbote*), p. 65.

105. Albrecht, "Ave Maria," p. 185.

106. Albrecht, *Glaube*, pp. 4, 5, and 16.

107. *DkSB*, 12 Mar. 1854, pp. 39–40.

108. Carl Scholl, "Die Frauen in der Religion," *EwL*, Oct. 1875, p. 4.

109. Ibid., p. 4; cf. p. 1.

110. See Paletschek, *Frauen*, pp. 149–52.

111. Scholl, "Die Frauen," pp. 5–6.

112. Scholl, "Unsere Reform," pp. 92–94.

113. See Gerlinde Hummel-Haasis (ed.), *Schwestern zerreisst eure Ketten: Zeugnisse zur Geschichte der Frauen in der Revolution von 1848/49* (Munich:

DTV, 1982), p. 145; Paletschek, "Stellung," pp. 79 and 82; Prelinger, *Charity*, p. 65.

114. Scholl, "Unsere Reform," p. 94.

115. Ibid., pp. 88, 91, and 98.

116. Ibid., p. 90.

117. Carl Scholl, *Ein Gruss in die Heimath: Vier Vorträge aus Anlass meines Wegzugs von Mannheim nach Nürnberg* (Mannheim: Schneider, 1869), pp. 26–27.

CHAPTER FOUR
PROBLEMATICS OF PHILOSEMITISM

1. Classic examples are provided by (in Prussia) Friedrich Julius Stahl, *Der christliche Staat und sein Verhältniss zu Deismus und Judenthum* (Berlin: L. Oehmigke, 1847); and (in Bavaria) "Die Juden," *Historisch-politische Blätter für das katholische Deutschland* 22 (1848), pp. 617–19. See also the discussions of Hermann Wagener and his *Kreuzzeitung* in Prussia and Ernst Zander and his *Volksbote* in Bavaria, in James F. Harris, *The People Speak!: Anti-Semitism and Emancipation in Nineteenth-Century Bavaria* (Ann Arbor: Univ. of Michigan Press, 1994). Characteristic examples of the phenomenon in Baden include Alban Stolz, *Landwehr gegen den badischen Landstand* (Freiburg i. B.: Herder, 1845), as well as other writings by Stolz; Franz Josef Buss, *Das Rongethum in der badischen Abgeordnetenkammer* (Freiburg i. B.: Herder, 1846), as well as other writings by Buss; and numerous essays appearing in the *Süddeutsche Zeitung für Kirche und Staat* from 1846 to 1848. See Dagmar Herzog, "Anti-Judaism in Intra-Christian Conflict: Catholics and Liberals in Baden in the 1840s," *Central European History* 27/3 (1994).

2. See Hermann Greive, "Religious Dissent and Tolerance in the 1840s," in Werner E. Mosse et al. (eds.), *Revolution and Evolution: 1848 in German-Jewish History* (Tübingen: J.C.B. Mohr, 1981), pp. 337–52; as well as the section on "Dangerous Orient(alism)" in chapter 3.

3. See the club founders' flyer dated February 8, 1847, reprinted in *MMorg*, 7 Mar. 1847, pp. 315–16; and *OberZ*, 8 Mar. 1847, p. 288. Cf. also *MAb*, 25 Feb. 1847, p. 213; *FJour*, 26 Feb. 1847; *OberZ*, 27 Feb. 1847, p. 248; *MJour*, 26 Feb. 1847, p. 249; and *Lbote*, 3 Mar. 1847, p. 101.

4. See *MAb*, 25 Feb. 1847, p. 213.

5. *Die Gegenwart*, vol. 5, 1850, p. 378. Cf. *MAb*, 2 Dec. 1846, p. 1313; the letter from Minister Bekk to the city government in Mannheim, 27 Feb. 1847, in GlaKa 233/1864; and Carl Scholl, "Meine ersten Kämpfe, nach meinem Anschluss an die freien Gemeinden," *EwL*, Feb. 1901, p. 71.

6. Flyer of 8 Feb. 1847, reprinted in *MMorg*, 7 Mar. 1847, pp. 315–16.

7. See *MMorg*, 14 Feb. 1847, title page; *SZKS*, 16 Feb. 1847, p. 200; *MJour*, 16 Feb. 1847, p. 215; *FJour*, 17 Feb. 1847; and *Mbote*, 18 Feb. 1847, p. 60.

8. Women were not included, for example, in the Frankfurt club; wives were only invited to attend special gala events. See *MAb*, 28 Dec. 1846, p. 1413. Although heterosocial clubs devoted to leisure activities already existed in Mannheim and elsewhere, to my knowledge no other club besides the

Mannheim one sought to contribute to the advancement of *both* Jewish *and* women's rights, with one important exception: a cluster of clubs in Hamburg (some composed purely of women, both Jewish and gentile, one both interethnic and heterosocial—the Society for Social and Political Interests of the Jews) that have been documented by Catherine Prelinger in *Charity, Challenge and Change: Religious Dimensions of the Mid-Nineteenth-Century Women's Movement in Germany* (New York and Westport, Conn.: Greenwood Press, 1987), esp. pp. 60–63 and 87–88; cf. on the Society also Mosche Zimmermann, *Hamburgischer Patriotismus und deutscher Nationalismus: Die Emanzipation der Juden in Hamburg 1830–1865* (Hamburg: Hans Christians Verlag, 1979), pp. 109–26. Only in April 1848 was a comparable "Religious Club for Members of all Confessions," explicitly including both women and men, started in Leipzig. See *IsJa*, 28 May 1848, pp. 174–75.

9. See *MAb*, 8 Oct. 1846, p. 1095; along with *MAb*, 18 Oct. 1846, p. 1135; *MJour*, 5 Dec. 1846, p. 1459; *MAb*, 9 Dec. 1846, p. 1337; and the letter from the Ministry of the Interior to the Ministry of State, 10 Nov. 1846, and the directive from the Ministry of State to the Mannheim municipal office, 18 Nov. 1846, both in GlaKa 233/18587.

10. See *MAb*, 26 Apr. 1846, p. 447; 29 May 1846, p. 575; and 19 Feb. 1847; as well as Adam Hammer, *Die Anwendung des Schwefeläthers im Allgemeinen und insbesondere bei Geburten* (Mannheim: Selbstverlag, 1847).

11. See Luise Dittmar, *Vier Zeitfragen: Beantwortet in einer Versammlung des Mannheimer Montag-Vereins* (Offenbach a. M.: G. André, 1847).

12. *Bgf*, 6 June 1847, p. 43. For details on the conflict, see FrGM, *Rechnungs-Vorlage nebst Rechenschafts-Berichte, Budgets, Vorstandswahl 1846/59–60*; *MJour*, 1 June 1847, p. 667; 6 June 1847, p. 682; 13 June 1847, p. 715; 15 June 1847, p. 727; 16 June 1847, p. 731; 17 June 1847, p. 735; 19 June 1847, p. 743; *MAb*, 14 June 1847, p. 631; and 19 June 1847, p. 651; and *MMorg*, 15 June 1847, p. 792.

13. For example, see Amalie Struve, "Die Frauen," *DtZus*, 9 July 1851, pp. 2–3: id., "Die Feinde weiblicher Freiheit," *DtZus*, 16 July 1851, p. 18; id., "Die Frauen und die Revolution," *DtZus*, 31 Dec. 1851, p. 207; Gustav Struve, "Die Stellung der Frauen im Leben," *DtZus*, 24 Dec. 1851, p. 199; id., "Mann und Frau," *SocRep*, 1 May 1858, p. 3; and id., *Die Zeit von 1848 bis 1863: Nachtrag zu G. Struve's Weltgeschichte* (Coburg: F. Streit, 1864), esp. pp. 891–93.

14. Anton Rée, *Erster Jahresbericht der Gesellschaft für sociale und politische Interessen der Juden der Generalversammlung den 23. Oct. 1847 von Dr. Anton Rée als d. Z. Präses abgestattet* (Hamburg, 1847), p. 5.

15. Cf. on this point also Carola Lipp, "Frauen und Öffentlichkeit: Möglichkeiten und Grenzen politischer Partizipation im Vormärz und in der Revolution 1848/1849," in Carola Lipp (ed.), *Schimpfende Weiber und patriotische Jungfrauen: Frauen im Vormärz und in der Revolution 1848/49* (Moos and Baden-Baden: Elster Verlag, 1986), pp. 272–73.

16. *Bgf*, 30 May 1847, pp. 39–40; reprinted in *MMorg*, 2 June 1847, Beilage, p. 797. Emphasis here, as elsewhere in this chapter, was in the original. For further examples of hostile coverage, see *MMorg*, 6 Mar. 1847, p. 311; and

16 June 1847, p. 797; *BK*, 29 July 1847, p. 88; *SZKS*, 5 Sept. 1847, p. 990; *Bgf*, 16 May 1847, p. 29; 13 June 1847, p. 44; 20 June 1847, p. 52; 11 July 1847, p. 62; 6 Nov. 1847, p. 156; 19 Nov. 1847, p. 160; and 20 Nov. 1847, p. 171.

17. No membership lists are available, and the only members named in the press were Carl Scholl, Gustav von Struve, Adam Hammer, J. Schoeninger, Johann Peter Grohe, and Friederike Cohen.

18. *MAb*, 25 Feb. 1847, p. 213; and 2 Mar. 1847, p. 234; *MMorg*, 6 Mar. 1847, p. 311; and 11 Mar. 1847, title page; *MAb*, 28 Apr. 1847, p. 455. Cf. also *MAb*, 14 Mar. 1847, p. 276; *OberZ*, 30 Apr. 1847, p. 517; and *Bgf*, 16 May 1847, p. 29.

19. A total of twenty-one meetings were held between March 1 and August 2, 1847. Then it seems that no meetings were held for two months, though two important political events involving Monday Club members filled the newspapers during that time: On August 29, Friederike Cohen was arrested for distributing the radical tract "German Hunger and German Princes" (see esp. *SZKS*, 5 Sept. 1847, p. 990). And on September 12, there was the liberal demonstration in Offenburg led by Struve together with Elias Eller and Friedrich Hecker, the demonstration thought by many to be the harbinger of the coming revolution (see esp. *SZKS*, 24 Sept. 1847, pp. 1049–50). Announcements for the Monday Club resumed with the November 8 meeting; seven meetings were held between November 8, 1847 and February 14, 1848. On February 14, a new executive committee was to be elected, indicating that the club had every intention of continuing business as usual. See *MAb*, 13 Feb. 1848, p. 171.

20. See *MMorg*, 11 Mar. 1847, title page; *MAb*, 14 Mar. 1847, p. 276; and see also Carl Scholl, *Einleitende Worte, gesprochen im Mannheimer Montags-Verein: Montag den 1. März 1847* (Mannheim, 1847), p. 9; and *BK*, 29 July 1847, p. 88.

21. See *MAb*, 5 Mar. 1848, p. 245. The notice was dated March 3.

22. Already the fall of 1847 saw a proliferation of political clubs in Mannheim, as radicals increasingly tested the boundaries of how much organized political activity the government would allow (since October 1833, explicitly political clubs had been outlawed in Baden). While the Monday Club continued to exist until March 1848, increasingly announcements appeared indicating that a Monday Club meeting would be canceled because the assembly room in the *Badener Hof*, the club's usual meeting place, was to be used by another group. These other groups, the "Temperance Club, Workers' Club, Singing Club, Athletic Club, . . . Citizens' Club" were often composed of the same individuals as were involved in the Monday Club, as one conservative paper noted: "Always the same names, always the same business" (*Bgf*, 20 Nov. 1847, p. 171). There was one important exception to this rule, however: all the other groups were composed of men only.

23. During and immediately after the revolution in Baden, there were at least ninety-six women who were arrested for revolutionary activities. They were prosecuted for such diverse crimes as storming an armory, manufacturing ammunition, participating in battle, taunting local citizens' militias into fighting on the revolutionary side, assisting in jailbreaks, decorating revolutionaries' graves,

and—in four cases—giving inflammatory public speeches as they presented red flags to the revolutionary troops. (Supporting documentation is in the General-landesarchiv in Karlsruhe.) In addition, there were at least seventeen "demo-cratic" or "patriotic" clubs in the Grand Duchy. These clubs usually confined their activities to collecting and distributing money, food, clothes, and ban-dages. See Gerlinde Hummel-Haasis (ed.), *Schwestern zerreisst Eure Ketten: Zeugnisse zur Geschichte der Frauen in der Revolution von 1848/49* (Munich: DTV, 1982), pp. 47–48, 86–100, 137, 302–4, 318–19, and 322–24. While all this engagement was no doubt politicizing and empowering for the women who participated in it, none of it reflected an explicit concern with advancing women's rights—an assessment scholars working on other parts of Germany confirm. See Hummel-Haasis, esp. p. 144; Sylvia Paletschek, *Frauen und Dissens* (Göttingen: Vandenhoeck und Ruprecht, 1990), esp. pp. 235 and 251; and Lipp, "Frauen und Öffentlichkeit," p. 298.

24. At least fourteen Badenese Jews were prominently involved in revolu-tionary activities, and there were surely more, despite the fact that most Jews were politically moderate and loyal to the Grand Duke. See Adolf Lewin, *Ge-schichte der badischen Juden seit der Regierung Karl Friedrichs (1738–1909)* (Karlsruhe: G. Braun, 1909), pp. 279–82. But, as was the case with women, none of the revolutionary activities these Jewish radicals were engaged in con-cerned the effort to advance Jewish rights.

25. Similarly, Scholl's friend Benda from Berlin, describing the impact of the outbreak of revolution on a club dedicated to increasing social interaction be-tween Jews and Christians—the *"Reform-Verein"*—told him that "because of the advent of *political* matters the '*Reform-Verein*' [was] recently dissolved." See Carl Scholl, *Hundert Jahre nach Lessings Nathan* (Bamberg: Handels-Druckerei, 1893) pp. v–vi.

26. For example, see the petition from Boxberg to the Lower Chamber, 1 Apr. 1848, in GlaKa 231/2086. See also the discussions of the violence in Lewin, *Geschichte*, pp. 280–81; and Michael Anthony Riff, "The Anti-Jewish Aspect of the Revolutionary Unrest of 1848 in Baden and its Consequences for Emancipation," *LBIYB*, XXI (1976).

27. Two excellent exceptions to this rule are Greive, "Religious Dissent"; and Prelinger, *Charity*, esp. pp. 55–104.

28. Hans Joachim Schoeps, *Philosemitismus im Barock: Religions- und gei-stesgeschichtliche Untersuchungen* (Tübingen: J.C.B. Mohr, 1952), p. 1.

29. Michael Brenner, "'Gott schütze uns vor unseren Freunden'—Zur Am-bivalenz des Philosemitismus im Kaiserreich," *Jahrbuch für Antisemitis-musforschung* 2 (1993), p. 175. Brenner's essay also includes an important and persuasive critique of G. E. Lessing's Enlightenment-era philosemitism. For a related critical analysis of Weimar-era philosemitism, see "Philosemitismus," *Jüdisches Lexikon* IV/I (Berlin: Jüdischer Verlag, 1927), pp. 910–14.

30. See Frank Stern, *The Whitewashing of the Yellow Badge: Antisemitism and Philosemitism in Postwar Germany* (Oxford: Pergamon Press, 1992).

31. For biographical information, see Carl Scholl, "Durch! Erinnerungen aus meinen eigenen Leben," in *EwL*, 1871, pp. 129–60; id., "Das Friedensamt des deutschkatholischen Geistlichen. (Antrittsrede.)," in *Das Wesen des*

Deutschkatholicismus oder die Versöhnung des Glaubens und der Wissenschaft (Mannheim: F. Bassermann, 1846), pp. 32–35; and Scholl's handwritten autobiography in outline form, in StaPreu NL Brümmer, Briefe I, Karl Scholl.

32. See Scholl, *Hundert Jahre*, pp. iii–iv and vi–vii; and id., "Durch!" pp. 132–33.

33. For the initial rumors, see *SZKS*, 30 Dec. 1846, p. 1169 (this item was copied from the *Mannheimer Journal*); *SZKS*, 4 Jan. 1847, p. 14; and 6 Jan. 1847, p. 24; *Lesehalle*, Feb. 1847, p. 54; and cf. Carl Scholl, *Paulus und die Galater* (Hamburg: Berendsohn, 1847), p. 42. The woman's name was never mentioned (but it cannot be Regine Eller, for Scholl did not meet her until the 1860s). Scholl instead ended up a few years later marrying Charlotte Sattler, a member of the dissenting congregation in Schweinfurt, which he served as a preacher in 1849. Sattler divorced her husband and went with Scholl to London; there they married in 1851. She subsequently accompanied him to Zurich, where they lived until at least 1860. See Paletschek, *Frauen*, p. 142. It is unknown what became of her and, strikingly, Scholl suppresses all references to her in his autobiographical writings, even though he mentions his marriage to Eller. See Scholl, *Hundert*, pp. vii and 18; and Scholl's handwritten autobiography in outline form, in StaPreu NL Brümmer, Briefe I, Karl Scholl. It is likely that Scholl's marriage to Eller colored his retrospective narratives of the continuity of his commitment to Jewish concerns.

34. See Carl Scholl, "Christliche Schacherjuden," in *EwL*, May 1874, pp. 119–28; id., *Das Judenthum und die Religion der Humanität* (Leipzig: Friese, 1879); id., *Das Judenthum und seine Weltmission* (Leipzig: R. Friese, 1880); id., "Moses Mendelssohn," in *EwL*, Mar. 1886, pp. 77–88; id., *Zwei Antisemiten. Ein Freidenker und ein Hofprediger. Nebst einem Anhang: Die wirkliche semitische Unmoral oder Grundsätze der jüdischen Sittenlehre* (Nürnberg and Leipzig: Friese, 1890); id., "Der Antisemitismus vom sittlichen Standpunkt aus betrachtet," in *EwL*, June 1894, pp. 129–44 and July 1894, pp. 145–60; and id., *Hundert Jahre*.

35. See Scholl, *Paulus*, pp. 46, 50, 57, and 59; cf. *Bgf*, 6 Nov. 1847, p. 156.

36. For more information on the atmosphere of theological criticism that shaped Scholl's choices, see John Edward Toews, *Hegelianism: The Path Toward Dialectical Humanism, 1805–1841* (New York: Cambridge Univ. Press, 1980).

37. See the report from Scholl's superiors (Stadtdecanat Karlsruhe) to the Protestant Church Division of the Ministry of the Interior, 9 Jan. 1845, that led to Scholl's suspension, in LakiKa PA 252. See also Carl Scholl, *Meine Suspension* (Leipzig: O. Wigand, 1846); and id., "Durch!" pp. 159–60.

38. Scholl, "Was wollen die Deutschkatholiken? (A.)," in *Wesen*, pp. 6 and 9–10.

39. Ibid., pp. 11 and 13.

40. Ibid., pp. 10–11.

41. See Scholl, *Das Judenthum und die Religion*, p. 15.

42. Scholl, "Friedensamt," p. 35; id., *Das Judenthum und die Religion*, p. 22; id., *Hundert Jahre*, p. iv.

43. See Carl Scholl, "Vorwort," in *Wesen*, p. ix; id., "Eins ist Noth!" in

Wesen, pp. 120–21; id., "Die Frauen in der Religion," *EwL*, Oct. 1875, p. 4; and id., *Das Judenthum und die Religion*, pp. 4 and 15; cf. also id., "Christus Todesweihe. (Palmsonntag.)," in *Wesen*, p. 148; id., "Das Pfingstfest. (Nebst den Vorbereitungsworten zum 'Brudermahl.')," in *Wesen*, pp. 240–42; and *KR*, Nov. 1846, p. 31.

44. See *KKr*, Mar. 1846, p. 45.

45. See *DkSB*, 2 May 1852, p. 72; and report of 17 June 1851, in GlaKa 369/2431, pp. 1–27.

46. Scholl, "Christus Todesweihe," p. 146; id., "Eins ist Noth!" p. 120; and id., "Pfingstfest," p. 242.

47. See the minutes of the congregational meeting, 30 May 1847, in FrGM, *Rechnungs-Vorlage nebst Rechenschafts-Berichte, Budgets, Vorstandswahl 1846/59–60*. The *Kirchliche Reform* was already in February 1847 under the impression that Jews were allowed to join the *deutschkatholische* congregation in Mannheim without undergoing baptism (see *KR*, Feb. 1847, p. 14), an indication that at the very least this possibility was being repeatedly entertained by the congregation.

48. Scholl, "Christus Todesweihe," p. 146; and id., "Pfingstfest," pp. 233 and 242. Cf. *KR*, Nov. 1846, p. 31; id., "Die Frauen," p. 4; and id., *Das Judenthum und die Religion*, p. 4.

49. Scholl, *Das Judenthum und die Religion*, pp. 14–15; and id., *Hundert Jahre*, p. vii. Cf. id., "Christus, der Galiläer," in *Wesen*, pp. 217–27; and id., "Jesus von Nazareth auch ein Semite," in *Hundert Jahre*, pp. 65–88.

50. Amy Newman, "The Death of Judaism in German Protestant Thought from Luther to Hegel," *Journal of the American Academy of Religion* LXI/3 (1993), pp. 460, 465, 474, and 475.

51. Carl Scholl, "Die Entwicklung des Glaubens," in *Wesen*, p. 57.

52. Carl Scholl, *Ein Opfer der Ueberzeugung! Für die Mundhelden des Christenthums und der Freiheit überhaupt* (Mannheim: J. Bensheimer, 1846), p. 4; the same remark is in *Die Feier des ersten Gründungsfestes der Deutschkatholischen Gemeinde in Mannheim* (Basel: Schnabelitz, 1846), p. 15.

53. Conservative Protestant clerics in the Grand Duchy of Posnania, quoted in *KKr*, Mar. 1846, p. 41.

54. Scholl, *Paulus*, p. 19.

55. See Scholl, *Das Judenthum und die Religion*, p. 18.

56. For example, see Scholl, *Ein Opfer*, pp. 4–7; and *Die Feier*, p. 15.

57. Carl Scholl, "Das Seesturm-Wunder," in *Wesen*, p. 83.

58. Carl Scholl, "Flammenworte aus dem Scheiterhaufen des Johannes Huss an unsere Zeit," in *Wesen*, p. 279; and id., "Petrus verleugnet," in *Wesen*, pp. 70–71.

59. Carl Scholl, "Was wollen die Deutschkatholiken? (B.)," in *Wesen*, pp. 26–27.

60. Carl Scholl, "Worauf ruht unsre Hoffnung?" in *Wesen*, p. 136.

61. Scholl, "Friedensamt," pp. 43–44.

62. Ibid., p. 39.

63. Scholl, "Was wollen die Deutschkatholiken? (A.)," p. 13.

64. Scholl, *Paulus*, p. 16.

65. This was in response to a November 1846 lecture on baptism. See Scholl, *Paulus*, p. 30; id., *Hundert Jahre*, p. v; and id., "Meine ersten Kämpfe," *EwL*, Nov. 1900, p. 28.

66. See Scholl, *Paulus*, pp. 52–53; id., "Meine ersten Kämpfe," *EwL*, Dec. 1900, p. 40, and Feb. 1901, p. 71; id., *Hundert Jahre*, p. v; and (on Struve's friendship with Loewenthal) Levin, *Geschichte*, p. 281. For details on Scholl's professional activities for the rest of his long life, see the handwritten autobiography in outline form, in StaPreu NL Brümmer, Briefe I, Karl Scholl.

67. Some historians have claimed that Struve joined the *deutschkatholische* movement for opportunistic reasons—i.e., in order to use it as a base for radical political organizing. Others, especially historians who are dissenters themselves, are pleased to consider Struve's interest in *Deutschkatholizismus* as genuine, but they inaccurately cite his participation in launching the Monday Club in February 1847 as evidence that he had left the congregation soon after he joined it (an argument that the former group of historians uses as further evidence that he discarded dissent as soon as it no longer served his political purposes). These various arguments are in part based on the false notion that Struve was not a religious man, and/or in part based on the false notion that the Monday Club was a competing congregation. (A number of these historians are also under the false impression that the battle over women's right to vote in the Mannheim congregation was one of the causes of the creation of the Monday Club, when in fact the Monday Club was founded several months *before* the fight over women's rights erupted). Cf. Karl Ackermann, *Gustav v. Struve mit besonderer Berücksichtigung seiner Bedeutung für die Vorgeschichte der badischen Revolution* (Ph.D. diss., Univ. of Heidelberg, 1914), pp. 66–68; Jürgen Peiser, *Gustav Struve als politischer Schriftsteller und Revolutionär* (Ph.D. diss., Univ. of Frankfurt, 1973), pp. 31 and 73; Friedrich Walter, *Mannheim in Vergangenheit und Gegenwart*, vol. 2 (1907, reprinted Frankfurt a. M.: W. Weidlich, 1978), p. 298; Karl Weiss, *125 Jahre Kampf um freie Religion*, ed. and completed by Lilo Schlötermann (Mannheim: Freireligiöse Verlagsbuchhandlung, 1970), p. 49; Alfred Diesbach, *Die deutschkatholische Gemeinde Konstanz 1845–1849* (Mannheim: Freireligiöse Verlagsbuchhandlung, 1971), p. 40; Norbert Deuchert, *Vom Hambacher Fest zur badischen Revolution: Politische Presse und Anfänge deutscher Demokratie 1832–1848/49* (Stuttgart: Theiss, 1983), p. 357. (Most of the later texts simply copied the information from earlier ones.) To the contrary, however, both of the Struves considered themselves *Deutschkatholiken* as late as September 1848 (see the report from the *Bezirks-Amt* Müllheim, 27 Sept. 1848, in GlaKa 241/110).

68. *DtZus*, 9 Jan. 1847, p. 12.

69. See Gustav Struve, "Die soziale Reform der Kirche," *DtZus*, 10 Sept. 1851, p. 77 (see also p. 78); and id., *Zeit*, p. 871. See also the other essays on religion that Struve published in New York in his *Deutscher Zuschauer* and *Sociale Republik*: "Christenthum und Pfaffenthum," *DtZus*, 23 July 1851, pp. 19–20; "Religion und Staat," *DtZus*, 13 Aug. 1851, pp. 43–44; "Die Gebetkrankheit," *SocRep*, 24 Apr. 1858, p. 3; "Die Nachwehen der Gebetkrankheit,"

SocRep, 8 May 1858, p. 3; "Die Quellen des Aberglaubens," *SocRep*, 5 June 1858, p. 1; "Religionsfreiheit," *SocRep*, 12 June 1858, p. 2; as well as id., "Wissenschaft und Religion," in Struve, *Zeit*, pp. 894–904.

70. For evidence of Jewish-gentile cooperation in the *Turnverein* and the "Club for the Advancement . . .," see *MAb*, 16 Nov. 1846, pp. 1250–51; 24 Nov. 1846, pp. 1282–83; and 25 Dec. 1846, p. 1405. For further examples of interreligious cooperation in Mannheim's civic life, see *MAb*, 1 Feb. 1847, p. 115 (on a politically moderate women's charitable club with an interreligious constituency); Karl Otto Watzinger, *Geschichte der Juden in Mannheim 1650–1945* (Stuttgart: Kohlhammer, 1984), esp. pp. 24–46; and Friedrich Teutsch, "Geschichte der jüdischen Gemeinde vom Westfälischen Frieden bis zur Weimarer Republik im Spiegel des Quadrats F 3," in Oberrat der Israeliten Badens et al., *Jüdisches Gemeindezentrum Mannheim F 3: Festschrift zur Einweihung am 13. September 1987, 19. Ellul 5747* (Mannheim: Verlagsbüro v. Brandt, 1987), esp. pp. 28–53.

71. For an overview of the massive literature on Struve, and for biographical information, see what is still the best available political-philosophical biography on him (covering the time up to and including 1849): Peiser, *Gustav Struve*, esp. pp. 1–25.

72. See the discussion of both Riesser and Auerbach in David Sorkin, *The Transformation of German Jewry, 1780–1840* (Oxford: Oxford Univ. Press, 1987), pp. 140–55. Riesser and Struve became friends in their student days in Heidelberg in the 1820s; from the 1840s on, Auerbach was a friend of Scholl's as well. See Peiser, *Gustav Struve*, pp. 10 and 18; and Scholl, *Hundert Jahre*, p. iv.

73. See esp. Gustav von Struve, *Briefwechsel zwischen einem ehemaligen und einem jetzigen Diplomaten* (Mannheim: Bensheimer, 1845); id., *Briefe über Kirche und Staat* (Mannheim: Bensheimer, 1846); id., *Politische Briefe* (Mannheim: Bensheimer, 1846); and id., *Politisches Taschenbuch für das deutsche Volk* (Frankfurt a. M.: Literarische Anstalt, 1846). See also id., *Aktenstücke der Zensur des grossherzoglich-badischen Regierungsrats v. Uria-Sarachaga, eine Rekursschrift an das Publikum* (Mannheim: Verlag des Herausgebers, 1845).

74. Obituary for "Gustave Struve," *New York Times*, 31 Aug. 1870, p. 8; Struve, *Briefe über Kirche*, p. 123.

75. Struve, *Briefe über Kirche*, pp. 125–26. Struve wrote a number of books in which he corresponded with "Waldemar," using Waldemar's cautiousness and greater conservatism as a foil against which to elaborate his own ideas.

76. See the typed copy of Struve's handwritten autobiography (written between 1863 and 1868), BuFra NL Struve FN 17/16, Book 1, chapter 11, pp. 34 and 41; and Book 2, chapter 2, p. 42.

77. For details on the effects which the First Crusade (whose goal was to take Jerusalem back from the Muslims) had on European Jewry, see Shlomo Eidelberg (ed.), *The Jews and the Crusaders: The Hebrew Chronicles of the First and Second Crusades* (Madison, Wisc.: Univ. of Wisconsin Press, 1977); and Robert Chazan, *European Jewry and the First Crusade* (Berkeley: Univ. of California Press, 1987), esp. "The Violence of 1096" (pp. 50–84).

78. Cf. Chazan, *European Jewry*, pp. 95–96.

79. For example, see *MJour*, 25 July 1845, p. 797; 31 Mar. 1846, p. 377; 11 May 1846, p. 551; and 26 May 1846, p. 609.

80. The latter point was a clear reference to the complicity of educated and bourgeois Gentiles in the anti-Jewish violence carried out by plebeians in 1830s Baden, a complicity that has been well documented and analyzed in Rainer Wirtz, *"Widersetzlichkeiten, Excesse, Crawalle, Tumulte und Skandale": Soziale Bewegung und gewalthafter sozialer Protest in Baden 1815–1848* (Frankfurt a. M.: Ullstein, 1981), esp. pp. 76 and 82–87.

81. Gustav Carl [von Struve], *Die Verfolgung der Juden durch Emicho* (Mannheim: Götz, 1841), p. 12.

82. Ibid., p. 85.

83. Ibid., pp. v–vi.

84. Ibid., p. 170.

85. Ibid., p. 180.

86. Struve, *Taschenbuch*, p. 123; id., "Ueber die Rechtsverhältnisse der Bekenner des mosaischen Glaubens," in *MJour*, 25 July 1845, p. 797; and 26 July 1845, p. 801.

87. For just a few examples of this phenomenon, see Struve, *Taschenbuch*, pp. 34–39, 53–57, 81, 195–200, and 245–48; and id., *Briefe über Kirche*, pp. 13, 45, and 126. For confirmation that it was Struve who introduced the contrasts "halves"/"wholes" and "men of the word"/"men of the deed" into public debate, and for a discussion of the conflicts he thereby provoked, see Deuchert, *Hambacher*, pp. 200–203.

88. *MJour*, 11 May 1846, p. 551; Gustav von Struve, "Das Juden-Casino zu Mannheim," in *MJour*, 31 Mar. 1846, p. 377.

89. Struve, "Ueber die Rechtsverhältnisse," *MJour*, 26 July 1845, p. 801 (cf. the similar arguments in Struve's editorial remarks added to anon., "Die badische zweite Kammer und die Gleichstellung der Juden," *MJour*, 3 Jan. 1846, p. 49; and *MJour*, 31 Mar. 1846, p. 377); id., "Ueber die Rechtsverhältnisse," *MJour*, 25 July 1845, p. 797; *DtZs*, 3 Dec. 1847, p. 394.

90. Struve, "Juden-Casino," p. 377.

91. Ibid. While surely right to criticize the exclusivism of the gentile clubs, Struve obviously could not imagine that Mannheim's Jews might actually want to have their own separate club as well (believing instead that if the *Harmonie* decided that "difference of religion cannot be an issue in the admission of new members, and then really acted in this spirit in the admission of new members, then the Jewish social club would soon become superfluous and would have to dissolve itself"). The Jewish social club was called the *Ressource*, was founded in 1829 (although there had been a Jewish club of some sort since 1817), and, as of 1843, had over one hundred members; it was a primary forum for the Jewish community's social life. See Watzinger, *Geschichte*, pp. 31 and 36; Walter, *Mannheim*, pp. 243 and 346–47; and *AlZJu*, 4 Dec. 1843, p. 723.

92. *MJour*, 29 July 1846, p. 907; and 26 May 1846, p. 609.

93. Struve, *Taschenbuch*, p. 77.

94. Ibid., pp. 75–76.

95. See also Gustav Struve, "Rechtsverhältnisse der Deutsch-Katholiken,

ihre Verhältnisse zu den katholischen Gemeinden und zur katholischen Kirche überhaupt," in *Taschenbuch*, pp. 148–53.

96. Struve, *Briefe über Kirche*, p. 53; and id., *Taschenbuch*, pp. 273–78.

97. See Gustav and Amalie von Struve's letter to the Protestant *Stadtpfarramt* in Mannheim, announcing and explaining their conversion to *Deutschkatholizismus*, in *DtZus*, 25 Dec. 1846, p. 13; reprinted in *MAb*, 11 Jan. 1847, p. 37; and *Mbote*, 17 Jan. 1847, p. 23. For Struve's attitudes toward institutional Protestantism, see esp. the scathing satire in Struve, *Taschenbuch*, pp. 291–305.

98. *MJour*, 15 Jan. 1846, p. 55. Cf. also the report on Struve's joining of the congregation (December 27, 1846), and Scholl's delighted response, in *MAb*, 30 Dec. 1846, p. 1421.

99. Struve, *Briefe über Kirche*, pp. 54–55.

100. *DtZus*, 1 May 1847, pp. 142–43.

101. See Struve, *Taschenbuch*, p. 123; and *MJour*, 2 June 1846, p. 640.

102. *DtZus*, 21 Nov. 1846, p. 5.

103. A few years later, analyzing the defeat of the revolutions of 1848/49, Struve was to argue even more strongly that conservative religion inhibited progressive social change. For example, see Gustav Struve, "Europa," *DtZus*, 13 Aug. 1851, p. 49; id., "Religion und Staat," p. 44; id., "Die Quellen des Aberglaubens," p. 1; and id., *Zeit*, pp. 921–22.

104. *IsJa*, 21 Dec. 1845, p. 409. For further commentary on the growing theological polarization among German Jews, see *Ori*, 30 Apr. 1846, pp. 35–36; *RefJu*, 1 Apr. 1846, pp. 7–8; 16 Sept. 1846, p. 200; 9 Dec. 1846, p. 294; and *ZrelInt*, 1846, p. 176.

105. Campe quoted in Paul R. Mendes-Flohr and Jehuda Reinharz (eds.), *The Jew in the Modern World: A Documentary History* (New York: Oxford Univ. Press, 1980), p. 142.

106. Frankel explained his break from Reform in *IsJa*, 3 Aug. 1845, pp. 256–57.

107. See Mendes-Flohr and Reinharz, *The Jew*, pp. 140–44; Frankel's remark (directed specifically at the radical Reform rabbi Samuel Holdheim) is in *RefJu*, 22 Apr. 1846, p. 30; the accusation of "ultramontanism" is in Anton Rée, *Aufruf zu einer rascheren Förderung der jüdischen Angelegenheiten im Vaterlande* (Hamburg: H. Gobert, 1846), p. 15. On Neo-Orthodox Judaism's appropriation of progressive strategies, see *RefJu*, 26 Aug. 1846, p. 169. For a nuanced treatment of Hirsch and the emergence of Neo-Orthodoxy, see Robert Liberles, *Religious Conflict in Social Context: The Resurgence of Orthodox Judaism in Frankfurt am Main, 1838–1877* (Westport, Conn.: Greenwood, 1985).

108. Jewish laypeople started the group in Mannheim in July 1845; a Baden-wide umbrella organization of the same name, with one hundred founding members, was launched in Bühl a few months later with a view to catalyzing local clubs all over Baden. See *AlZJu*, 28 July 1845, p. 478; 8 Dec. 1845, pp. 735–37; 13 Apr. 1846, pp. 239–40; 27 July 1846, pp. 449–51; and *IsJa*, 21 Dec. 1845, pp. 410–11.

109. The phrase is Heinrich Heine's. See Michael Werner, "Heinrich Heine—Über die Interdependenz von jüdischer, deutscher und europäischer

Identität in seinem Werk," in Walter Grab and Julius H. Schoeps (eds.), *Juden im Vormärz und in der Revolution von 1848* (Stuttgart and Bonn: Burg, 1983), p. 18.

110. *IsJa*, 23 Jan. 1848, p. 30.

111. This point is made in the editorial remarks by B. May and J. B. Levy in Gabriel Riesser, *Eine Auswahl aus seinen Schriften und Briefen* (Frankfurt a. M.: J. Kauffmann, 1913), p. 10.

112. Ibid. See also Jacob Toury, "Die Revolution von 1848 als innerjüdischer Wendepunkt," in Hans Liebeschütz and Arnold Paucker (eds.), *Das Judentum in der deutschen Umwelt 1800–1850* (Tübingen: J.C.B. Mohr, 1977), p. 360.

113. *Der Jude*, 2 Apr. 1833, pp. 3 and 6–7; Gabriel Riesser, "Über die Stellung der Bekenner des mosaischen Glaubens in Deutschland: An die Deutschen aller Konfessionen" (1831), in Riesser, *Auswahl*, pp. 22–24.

114. Rée, *Aufruf*, pp. 20–21.

115. Jellinek quoted in Toury, "Die Revolution," p. 359.

116. Comparisons between dissenters and Jews were elaborated not only in Baden, but also in Saxony (see *ZrelInt*, 1845, p. 195), in Württemberg (see *Verhandlungen der Württembergischen Kammer der Abgeordneten auf dem Landtage von 1848–49*, 26 June 1849, 5. Protokollband [Stuttgart: J. Kreuzer, 1849], pp. 4408–9), and in Prussia (see Eduard Bleich [ed.], *Der erste Vereinigte Landtag in Berlin 1847* [Berlin: Karl Reimarus, 1847], vol. 3, pp. 865–86, and vol. 4, pp. 1923, 1930, and 2355). Note especially the Prussian edicts of 1847, which granted Christian dissenters the right to civil marriage and soon thereafter forced Jews—whose marriages had always been handled by their religious leaders, just as Protestant and Catholic marriages were—to undergo civil marriage as well. See *Allgemeine Kirchen-Zeitung*, 17 Apr. 1847, pp. 530–39; *RZ*, Sept. 1847, pp. 69–70; *AlZJu*, 13 Sept. 1847, p. 565.

117. *RefJu*, 22 Apr. 1846, pp. 30–31.

118. *IsJa*, 13 Apr. 1845, p. 120.

119. For example, see *AlZJu*, 8 Dec. 1845, p. 737; and *RefJu*, 22 Apr. 1846, p. 30.

120. *ZrelInt*, 1845, p. 195.

121. *IsJa*, 21 Nov. 1847, p. 374 (the same item had appeared in *FJour*, 1 Oct. 1847, Beilage, p. 2). Further analyses of Christian dissent can be found in *IsJa*, 6 Apr. 1845, p. 112; 21 Dec. 1845, pp. 412–13; *ZrelInt*, 1845, pp. 24–25, 234–35, and 426–27; and *AlZJu*, 26 Oct. 1846, pp. 637–40; and 23 Nov. 1846, p. 698.

122. *Eine deutsch-jüdische Kirche: Die nächste Aufgabe unsrer Zeit. Von einem Candidaten der jüdischen Theologie* (Leipzig: O. Wigand, 1845), p. 19. (Stern's authorship is strongly implied by *IsJa*, 6 July 1845, pp. 210–11; and Dolf Michaelis, "The Ephraim Family and their Descendants (II)," *LBIYB*, XXIV (1979), pp. 244–46.) Cf. also the similar arguments made in Rée, *Aufruf*; *Phö*, 3 July 1847, p. 1; and 10 July 1847, p. 2; *IsJa*, 21 Nov. 1847, p. 374; and *Ori*, 17 Dec. 1847, p. 806.

123. *JuDeuGe*, 6 Jan. 1846, p. 6.

124. *IsJa*, 20 Apr. 1845, p. 121.

125. *Eine deutsch-jüdische Kirche*, p. 19.

126. Rée, *Aufruf*, pp. 12–13.

127. *AlZJu*, 8 Sept. 1845, pp. 557–58.

128. *JuDeuGe*, 6 Jan. 1846, p. 3. Cf. the similar sentiment in *ZrelInt*, 1846, p. 106.

129. Dr. Loewenthal, "Die jüdische Reform," *IsJa*, 8 June 1845, pp. 182–83. Similar instances of insistence that Christian dissent should be a model to emulate rather than a movement to join can be found in *Eine deutsch-jüdische Kirche*; *IsJa*, 8 June 1845, p. 181; 6 July 1845, p. 211; and *RZ*, Jan. 1847, p. 2.

130. *AlZJu*, 24 May 1847, pp. 334–35. The article this piece was responding to was in *MAb*, 30 Apr. 1847, p. 462.

131. For example, see *SZKS*, 5 Sept. 1847, p. 990, which reports on Friederike Cohen's ongoing participation in the club.

132. Moses Mendelssohn, excerpt from *Jerusalem* (1783), in Mendes-Flohr and Reinharz, *The Jew*, p. 62.

CHAPTER FIVE
THE FEMINIST CONUNDRUM

1. Some of the most influential examples from the "difference" school include Carol Gilligan, *In a Different Voice: Psychological Theory and Women's Development* (Cambridge, Mass.: Harvard Univ. Press, 1982); Sara Ruddick, *Maternal Thinking: Towards a Politics of Peace* (Boston: Beacon, 1989); and Deborah Tannen, *You Just Don't Understand: Men and Women in Conversation* (New York: Morrow, 1990). Key texts from the "questioning difference" camp include: Judith Butler, "Gender Trouble, Feminist Theory, and Psychoanalytic Discourse," in Linda J. Nicholson (ed.), *Feminism/Postmodernism* (New York: Routledge, 1990); Joan W. Scott, "Gender: A Useful Category of Historical Analysis," in *Gender and the Politics of History* (New York: Columbia Univ. Press, 1988); Anne Fausto-Sterling, *Myths of Gender: Biological Theories about Women and Men*, 2d ed. (New York: Basic Books, 1992); Hazel V. Carby, *Reconstructing Womanhood: The Emergence of the Afro-American Woman Novelist* (New York: Oxford Univ. Press, 1987); Mary Poovey, *Uneven Developments: The Ideological Work of Gender in Mid-Victorian England* (Chicago: Univ. of Chicago Press, 1988); Denise Riley, *"Am I that Name?": Feminism and the Category of "Women" in History* (London: Macmillan, 1988); and many of the essays collected in Judith Butler and Joan W. Scott (eds.), *Feminists Theorize the Political* (New York: Routledge, 1992).

2. Indeed, as numerous historians in recent years have documented, the elaboration of gender difference (with concomitant gender inequality) was utterly central to the nineteenth-century middle classes' self-definition in Germany, Britain, France, and elsewhere. For example, see Ute Frevert (ed.), *Bürgerinnen und Bürger: Geschlechterverhältnisse im 19. Jahrhundert* (Göttingen: Vandenhoeck und Ruprecht, 1988); Poovey, *Uneven*; Leonore Davidoff and Catherine Hall, *Family Fortunes: Men and Women of the English Middle Class, 1780–1850* (Chicago: Univ. of Chicago Press, 1987); and Scott, *Gender*. As even Jürgen

Kocka (long a critic of women's studies) has in the last few years acknowledged, "there is much evidence that beside the social class differences between owners of the means of production and wage laborers, gender difference belongs to this foundation of inequality which constitutes bourgeois society." See Jürgen Kocka, "Vorwort," in Frevert, *Bürgerinnen*.

3. For an overview of nineteenth-century German women writers' views on gender, see the superb study by Katherine Goodman, *Dis/Closures: Women's Autobiography in Germany between 1790 and 1914* (New York: Peter Lang, 1986). For primary documents, see Renate Möhrmann (ed.), *Frauenemanzipation im deutschen Vormärz: Texte und Dokumente* (Stuttgart: Reclam, 1978); Gerlinde Hummel-Haasis (ed.), *Schwestern zerreisst eure Ketten: Zeugnisse zur Geschichte der Revolution von 1848/49* (Munich: DTV, 1982); and Ruth-Ellen Boetcher Joeres (ed.), *Die Anfänge der deutschen Frauenbewegung: Louise Otto-Peters* (Frankfurt: Fischer, 1983). Analyses of individual women are provided by Stanley Zucker, *Kathinka Zitz-Halein and Female Civic Activism in Mid-Nineteenth-Century Germany* (Carbondale: Southern Illinois Univ. Press, 1991); and Hans Adler, "On a Feminist Controversy: Louise Otto vs. Louise Aston," in Ruth-Ellen Boetcher Joeres and Mary Jo Maynes (eds.), *German Women in the 18th and 19th Centuries* (Bloomington: Indiana Univ. Press, 1986). Overviews of women's activity in the *Vormärz* and the revolution are provided by Lia Secci, "German Women Writers and the Revolution of 1848," in John C. Fout (ed.), *German Women in the Nineteenth Century* (New York: Holmes and Meier, 1984); and Carola Lipp (ed.), *Schimpfende Weiber und patriotische Jungfrauen: Frauen im Vormärz und in der Revolution 1848/49* (Moos and Baden-Baden: Elster Verlag, 1986).

4. Louise Otto, "Programm," *Frauen-Zeitung*, 21 Apr. 1849, p. 1.

5. For example, see Louise Aston, *Aus dem Leben einer Frau* (Hamburg: Hoffmann und Campe, 1847).

6. For example, see Ann Taylor Allen, *Feminism and Motherhood in Germany 1800–1914* (New Brunswick: Rutgers Univ. Press, 1991); and Sylvia Paletschek, *Frauen und Dissens* (Gottingen: Vandenhoeck und Ruprecht, 1990), esp. pp. 160 and 249.

7. Until recently, no research had been done on Dittmar, but in the last few years she has become the subject of intensive study. Excerpts from Dittmar's writings were first reprinted in Möhrmann, *Frauenemanzipation*. She was included in the women's history encyclopedia by Daniela Weiland, *Geschichte der Frauenemanzipation in Deutschland und Österreich* (Düsseldorf: ECON Taschenbuch Verlag, 1983). A comprehensive overview of Dittmar's works and a literary analysis were first provided by Ruth-Ellen Boetcher Joeres in "Spirit in Struggle: The Radical Vision of Louise Dittmar (1807–1884)," and a reconstruction of Dittmar's biography was provided by Christina Klausmann in "Louise Dittmar—Ergebnisse einer biographischen Spurensuche," both in Ruth-Ellen Boetcher Joeres and Marianne Burkhard (eds.), *Out of Line/ Ausgefallen: The Paradox of Marginality in the Writings of Nineteenth-Century German Women*, a special issue of *Amsterdamer Beiträge zur neueren Germanistik* 28 (1989). Further analyses of her work include Dagmar Herzog, "Liberalism, Religious Dissent and Women's Rights: Louise Dittmar's Writings from the 1840s," in

Konrad H. Jarausch and Larry Eugene Jones (eds.), *In Search of a Liberal Germany: Studies in the History of German Liberalism from 1789 to the Present* (Oxford: Berg, 1990); and Germaine Goetzinger, "Soziale Reform der Geschlechterverhältnisse im Vormärz: Louise Dittmar's Ehekritik," in Dagmar Reese et al. (eds.), *Rationale Beziehungen? Geschlechterverhältnisse im Rationalisierungsprozess* (Frankfurt a. M.: Suhrkamp, 1993). A number of other scholars—such as Nancy Kaiser, Lynn Abrams, and Bonnie Anderson—are incorporating analyses of portions of Dittmar's work into projects on other subjects.

8. Louise Dittmar, "Erwiderung," in Louise Dittmar (ed.), *Das Wesen der Ehe nebst einigen Aufsätzen über die soziale Reform der Frauen* (Leipzig: O. Wigand, 1849), p. 109. Hereafter, this text will be designated *Soziale Reform*, to distinguish it from the essays on marriage (*Das Wesen der Ehe*), which were reprinted in 1850.

9. Luise Dittmar, *Vier Zeitfragen: Beantwortet in einer Versammlung des Mannheimer Montag-Vereins* (Offenbach a. M.: G. André, 1847), p. ii.

10. See Joan W. Scott, "French Feminists and the 'Rights of Man': Olympe de Gouges's Declarations," in *History Workshop* 28 (Autumn 1989).

11. See Riley, *"Am I"*; and Denise Riley, "Some Peculiarities of Social Policy concerning Women in Wartime and Postwar Britain," in Margaret Randolph Higonnet et al. (eds.), *Behind the Lines: Gender and the Two World Wars* (New Haven: Yale Univ. Press, 1987).

12. See the title page of Dittmar, *Vier Zeitfragen*, as well as pp. i–viii.

13. Louise Dittmar, *Wühlerische Gedichte eines Wahrhaftigen* (Mannheim: Bensheimer, 1848); id., *Brutus-Michel*, 2d ed. (Darmstadt: C. W. Leske, 1848).

14. For the biographical information, see Klausmann, "Louise Dittmar," esp. pp. 19–20 and 28–29; as well as Zucker, *Kathinka Zitz-Halein*, pp. 84–85.

15. Klausmann has identified one of the anonymous pieces as belonging to Malwida von Meysenbug. See Klausmann, "Louise Dittmar," p. 32. Gudrun Wittig has also listed Fanny Lewald, Ida von Düringsfeld, and Ida Frick as Dittmar's collaborators. See Gudrun Wittig, *"Nicht nur im stillen Kreis des Hauses": Frauenbewegung in Revolution und nachrevolutionärer Zeit 1848–1876* (Hamburg: Ergebnisse Verlag, 1986), p. 72.

16. See the reviews of [Luise Dittmar], *Der Mensch und sein Gott in und ausser dem Christenthum: Von einem Weltlichen* (Offenbach a. M.: G. André, 1846), in *KR*, Sept. 1846, pp. 38–39, and in *MAb*, 23 May 1846, p. 550; and the review of [Luise Dittmar], *Lessing und Feuerbach, oder Auswahl aus G. E. Lessing's theologischen Schriften nebst Originalbeiträgen und Belegstellen aus L. Feuerbach's Wesen des Christenthums* (Offenbach a. M.: G. André, 1847) in *KR*, Oct. 1847, pp. 38–39. The inside back cover of *Vier Zeitfragen* advertised *Mensch* and listed further newspapers that favorably reviewed it, among them the *Katholische Kirchenreform* (Berlin), the *Hamburger Telegraph*, the *Hanauer Zeitung*, and the *Vaterland* (Darmstadt).

17. Letters from Dittmar to the writer Lorenz Diefenbach give evidence of her eagerness to keep writing and her difficulties in finding a publisher. See, for example, Dittmar to Diefenbach, 2 Oct. 1852, and 3 Dec. 1852, UBGie, NL Diefenbach.

18. Mathilde Franziska Anneke's *Kölner Frauenzeitung*, founded in Septem-

ber 1848, had to be shut down after the authorities confiscated the third issue. Louise Aston's *Freischärler für Kunst und soziales Leben* lasted for seven issues from November to December 1848. Louise Marezoll's *Frauen-Spiegel*, also begun in 1848, disappeared as well. See Wittig, *"Nicht nur . . .,"* pp. 70–72.

19. See Klausmann, "Louise Dittmar," pp. 22–23, 29, 32, and 37, and Joeres, "Spirit," p. 299. Klausmann and Joeres both suggest that it was this lack of support from other women as well as the unfriendly political climate that led Dittmar ultimately to stop writing.

20. Barbara Taylor, "Socialist Feminism: Utopian or Scientific?" in Raphael Samuel (ed.), *People's History and Socialist Theory* (London: Routledge and Kegan Paul, 1981). For a comparative perspective on how utopian socialism in England and France created the seedbed for feminist activism, see Barbara Taylor, *Eve and the New Jerusalem: Socialism and Feminism in the Nineteenth Century* (New York: Pantheon, 1983), and Claire Goldberg Moses and Leslie Wahl Rabine, *Feminism, Socialism, and French Romanticism* (Bloomington: Indiana Univ. Press, 1993).

21. Cf. Michel Foucault, *Discipline and Punish* (New York: Pantheon, 1977).

22. The "thorny crown of femininity" is Dittmar's phrase. See [Luise Dittmar], *Skizzen und Briefe aus der Gegenwart* (Darmstadt: C. W. Leske, 1845), p. 109.

23. Interestingly, Jewish rights activists of the 1830s and 1840s ran into similar dilemmas in seeking to make their own case persuasively while working to uncover the biases in their supposedly so objective opponents. Cf., for example, Gabriel Riesser's remarks in *Der Jude*, 2 Apr. 1833, p. 4; id., "Über die Stellung der Bekenner des mosaischen Glaubens in Deutschland: An die Deutschen aller Konfessionen" (1831), and "Rede gegen Moritz Mohls Antrag zur Beschränkung der Rechte der Juden" (1848), both in *Eine Auswahl aus seinen Schriften und Briefen* (Frankfurt a. M.: J. Kauffmann, 1913), pp. 13 and 106; and Anton Rée, *Aufruf zu einer rascheren Förderung der jüdischen Angelegenheiten im Vaterlande* (Hamburg: H. Gobert, 1846), pp. 22–23.

24. [Dittmar], *Skizzen*, pp. 106–8. Emphasis here, as elsewhere in this chapter, was in the original.

25. Ibid., pp. 98–100; and [Luise Dittmar], *Bekannte Geheimnisse* (Darmstadt: C. W. Leske, 1845), p. 36.

26. [Dittmar], *Skizzen*, pp. 84, 89, 91, and 96; Louise Dittmar, "Charlotte Corday," *Soziale Reform*, pp. 28, 31–32, 42.

27. Dittmar, *Vier Zeitfragen*, p. 2.

28. For an excellent, historically specific discussion of the perils of choosing to define oneself either as a "woman" or as a "human being," see Riley, "Some Peculiarities."

29. [Dittmar], *Skizzen*, p. 93; for related remarks, see Luise Dittmar, *Zur Charakterisierung der nordischen Mythologie im Verhältniss zu andern Naturreligionen: Eine Skizze* (Darmstadt: C. W. Leske, 1848), p. 32.

30. [Dittmar], *Skizzen*, p. 88. She also formulated the problem this way: "The great riddle 'human being' has been solved, but woman has not dissolved [been resolved?] within it [*das Weib ist nicht darin aufgegangen*]." Ibid., p. 87.

Or, conversely, as she put it in *Bekannte Geheimnisse*, "according to the most up-to-date arithmetic of the perfect state, the whole human being must go into it, indivisibly, nothing may be left over but a zero—and that's the woman." Id., *Bekannte*, p. 31.

31. See Carole Pateman, *The Sexual Contract* (Stanford: Stanford Univ. Press, 1988). See also the remarks of liberal Badenese diet delegate Adolf Sander in 1844 (made in the context of a critique of military officers' enforced celibacy): "It cannot be denied that the right to found a family by marriage is one of the first and most natural rights that the human being does not receive from the state, but rather brings into the world with him as a human being. . . . Every state that is the least bit civilized and cultured must show consideration for this first and most natural right of its members, and if it does not, then it does not deserve to be a state." His liberal colleague Karl Zittel concurred, invoking "the first right of a citizen, to found a family": "I repeat, this is the first state-citizen right of someone who lives in this land, for the whole political life of our state is founded on family life, just as the moral condition of the life of our people is as well." An essential part of the social contract among men, then, was the right of each man to conclude a sexual contract with a woman. However much liberals in this context were not explicitly or even intentionally excluding women from citizenship, that exclusion was integral to the way they formulated their theories. The contract with a woman was the guarantee of the *man's* humanity—one prime expression of *his* entitlement. See Sander, in *Verhandlungen der Stände-Versammlung des Grossherzogthums Baden* (II. Kammer), 21 Feb. 1844, 2. Protokollheft, p. 158; and Zittel, p. 161.

32. [Dittmar], *Skizzen*, pp. 88 and 98–99.

33. Joan Landes, *Women and the Public Sphere in the Age of the French Revolution* (Ithaca: Cornell Univ. Press, 1988). See also the sophisticated and subtle reflections on the relationship between gender difference, sexual love, and the difficulties the French had in imagining women as citizens in the revolutionary era in Geneviève Fraisse, *Reason's Muse: Sexual Difference and the Birth of Democracy* (Chicago: Univ. of Chicago Press, 1994); cf. the important analysis of Rousseau's influential theorizing of the relationship between heterosexuality and the sociopolitical order (and its impact in Germany) in Isabel V. Hull, "'Sexualität' und bürgerliche Gesellschaft," in Frevert, *Bürgerinnen*.

34. Cf. Herzog, "Liberalism," pp. 63–69.

35. [Dittmar], *Skizzen*, p. 94 (indicatively, this sketch was entitled "The Fantasized Nature of Men"), and 104–5.

36. Louise Dittmar, *Das Wesen der Ehe* (Leipzig: O. Wigand, 1850), pp. 40 and 55–56; id., "Aphorismen," *Soziale Reform*, p. 119; id., "Der weibliche Antheil an sozialen Reformen," *Soziale Reform*, p. 16; and id., "Erwiderung," *Soziale Reform*, pp. 112–13.

37. [Dittmar], *Skizzen*, p. 110. On the prescriptive texts, see Volker Hoffmann, "Elisa und Robert oder das Weib und der Mann, wie sie sein sollten: Anmerkungen zur Geschlechtercharakteristik der Goethezeit," in Karl Richter and Jörg Schönert (eds.), *Klassik und Moderne: Die Weimarer Klassik als historisches Ereignis und Herausforderung im kulturgeschichtlichen Prozess* (Stuttgart: Metzler, 1983).

38. [Dittmar], *Skizzen*, p. 96; Dittmar, *Vier Zeitfragen*, p. 6; Dittmar, "Der Selbstzweck der Menschheit," *Soziale Reform*, p. 6.

39. [Dittmar], *Mensch*, p. iv; id., *Lessing*, pp. 42 and 67.

40. [Dittmar], *Mensch*, pp. 15–16 and 31.

41. For example, see Lessing's contrasting of the "sensuous Jew" and the "spiritual Christian," and his portrayal of Christ as a "better teacher" than the rabbis, in [Dittmar], *Lessing*, pp. 20 and 33; cf. the section on "Dangerous Orient(alism)" in chapter 3.

42. Dittmar, *Vier Zeitfragen*, p. 2; and [Dittmar], *Mensch*, pp. 10, 23, and 39.

43. Dittmar, *Charakterisierung*, pp. 4, 19, 23, 35, and 51; and cf., for example, the classic anti-German remarks in [Dittmar], *Skizzen und Briefe*, pp. 61 and 100.

44. Dittmar, *Charakterisierung*, pp. 41, 45, and 49.

45. [Dittmar], *Skizzen*, p. 111.

46. Ludwig Feuerbach, *The Essence of Christianity* (1841, reprinted New York: Harper and Row, 1957), p. 27.

47. [Dittmar], *Mensch*, p. 68; id., *Lessing*, p. 42; Dittmar, *Vier Zeitfragen*, pp. 3, 6, and 11.

48. [Dittmar], *Lessing*, p. 89; and Dittmar, "Erwiderung," p. 110.

49. Dittmar, *Vier Zeitfragen*, p. iii; and [Dittmar], *Mensch*, pp. 81–82.

50. [Dittmar], *Skizzen*, p. 82; Louise Dittmar, "Die männliche Bevormundung," *Soziale Reform*, p. 15; and cf. 2 Corinthians 6: 4–5, 8b-10, and Matthew 20: 1–17.

51. Dittmar, *Wesen*, pp. 6 and 7.

52. See Leonard Krieger, *The German Idea of Freedom* (Boston: Beacon, 1957), p. 31; Karin Hausen, "Family and Role-Division: The Polarization of Sexual Stereotypes in the Nineteenth Century—An Aspect of the Dissociation of Work and Family Life," in Richard J. Evans and W. R. Lee (eds.), *The German Family* (London: Croom Helm, 1981); Carola Lipp, "Frauen und Öffentlichkeit: Möglichkeiten und Grenzen politischer Partizipation im Vormärz und in der Revolution 1848," and Carola Lipp, "Liebe, Krieg und Revolution: Geschlechterbeziehung und Nationalismus," both in Lipp, *Schimpfende Weiber.*

53. Carl Theodor Welcker, "Geschlechtsverhältnisse," in Carl Theodor Welcker and Karl von Rotteck (eds.), *Das Staats-Lexikon*, 1st ed., vol. 6 (Altona: J. F. Hammerich, 1838), pp. 641, 644, 645, 650, and 651.

54. Ibid., pp. 637, 638, 640, 642, and 647.

55. Ibid., p. 630.

56. Dittmar to Malwida von Meysenbug in "Erwiderung," p. 110.

57. Dittmar, *Wesen*, pp. 18 and 29.

58. Ibid., pp. 21 and 72.

59. Ibid., p. 4.

60. Welcker, "Geschlechtsverhältnisse," p. 648; and Dittmar, *Wesen*, pp. 61 and 62.

61. Dittmar, *Wesen*, pp. 6 and 55 (cf. the similar argument on p. 8).

62. Dittmar, "Charlotte Corday," pp. 31–32; and [Dittmar], *Skizzen*, p. 91.

63. Dittmar, *Wesen*, pp. 6 and 24.

64. Welcker, "Geschlechtsverhältnisse," pp. 658 and 665. On the prevalence of the sewer metaphor, see esp. Alain Corbin, "Commercial Sexuality in Nineteenth-Century France: A System of Images and Regulations," in Catherine Gallagher and Thomas Laqueur (eds.), *The Making of the Modern Body: Sexuality and Society in the Nineteenth Century* (Berkeley: Univ. of California Press, 1987).

65. Dittmar, *Wesen*, p. 7.

66. [Dittmar], *Skizzen*, p. 79; and Dittmar, *Wesen*, pp. 10 and 11.

67. [Dittmar], *Skizzen*, p. 91; and Dittmar, *Wesen*, pp. 9–10, 11–12, 28, and 32.

68. Dittmar, *Wesen*, pp. 6 and 12.

69. Cf. Mary Poovey, "Speaking of the Body: Mid-Victorian Constructions of Female Desire," in Mary Jacobus et al. (eds.), *Body/Politics: Women and the Discourses of Science* (New York: Routledge, 1990); and Thomas Laqueur, "Orgasm, Generation, and the Politics of Reproductive Biology," in Gallagher and Laqueur, *The Making*.

70. Dittmar, "Der weibliche Antheil," p. 16; and id., "Aphorismen," p. 119.

71. Küstner in 1849 quoted in Joeres, "Spirit," p. 299; Zitz-Halein in 1853, reminiscing about a talk held by Dittmar in 1848, quoted in Klausmann, "Louise Dittmar," p. 29.

72. Ludwig Bamberger, "Festrede" (15 Aug. 1848); Louise Otto, "Mein Programm als Mitarbeiterin einer Frauenzeitung"; C[laire] v[on] G[lümer], "Ueber Fourier," all in *Soziale Reform*, pp. 21, 85, and 98.

73. The stakes in this debate over German feminism's supposedly peculiar attachment to "difference" theory are high. See Atina Grossmann and Sara Lennox, "The Shadow of the Past," *Women's Review of Books* (Sept. 1987); Allen, *Feminism*; Dagmar Herzog, "Wo liegt der Unterschied? Aufklärung und Frauenrechte in Deutschland," in Hanna Schissler (ed.), *Geschlechterverhältnisse im historischen Wandel* (Frankfurt a. M.: Campus, 1993); and Dagmar Herzog, "New Developments in German Women's History," in *Journal of Women's History* 4/3 (Winter 1993).

CONCLUSION

1. Hermann Greive, "Religious Dissent and Tolerance in the 1840s," in Werner E. Mosse et al. (eds.), *Revolution and Evolution: 1848 in German-Jewish History* (Tübingen: J.C.B. Mohr, 1981), p. 339.

2. Excellent recent regional studies helping to rethink the 1830s and 1840s in Germany include Jonathan Sperber, *Rhineland Radicals: The Democratic Movement and the Revolution of 1848–1849* (Princeton: Princeton Univ. Press, 1991); Mary Lee Townsend, *Forbidden Laughter: Popular Humor and the Limits of Repression in Nineteenth-Century Prussia* (Ann Arbor: Univ. of Michigan Press, 1992); Paul Nolte, *Gemeindebürgertum und Liberalismus in Baden, 1800–1850: Tradition—Radikalismus—Republik* (Göttingen: Vandenhoeck und Ruprecht, 1994); and James F. Harris, *The People Speak!: Anti-Semitism and Emancipation in Nineteenth-Century Bavaria* (Ann Arbor: Univ. of Michigan Press, 1994).

3. Cf. Michael Graetz, *Les Juifs en France au XIXe Siècle: De la Revolution*

Française à l'Alliance Israelite Universelle (Paris: Éditions du Seuil, 1989), esp. pp. 152–93; Claire Goldberg Moses, "Saint-Simonian Men/Saint-Simonian Women: The Transformation of Feminist Thought in 1830s France," *Journal of Modern History* 54/2 (June 1982); and Barbara Taylor, *Eve and the New Jerusalem: Socialism and Feminism in the Nineteenth Century* (New York: Pantheon, 1983).

4. The intensification of liberal-Catholic tensions (particularly around sexuality and marriage) was by no means only a Badenese phenomenon, but occurred across the Central European lands in the 1840s; it manifested itself particularly in the debates and decisions of the Frankfurt Parliament in 1848. See Dagmar Herzog, "Male Fantasies, Male Fears, and the Roots of the *Kulturkampf.*" Paper delivered at the American Historical Association Convention, Chicago, 6 Jan. 1995.

5. For an introduction to a number of the fundamental issues at stake, see David Blackbourn and Geoff Eley, *The Peculiarities of German History: Bourgeois Society and Politics in Nineteenth-Century Germany* (Oxford: Oxford Univ. Press, 1984).

6. Claudia Koonz, "New Germany, Old Wounds: The Fatherland's Heritage Industry," *Village Voice Literary Supplement* (March 1990), p. 17.

7. Alban Stolz, "Der verbotene Baum: Für Katholiken und Protestanten gezeigt (1874)," in *Gesammelte Werke*, vol. 10 (Freiburg i. B.: Herder, n.d.), p. 117.

8. See Theodore Zeldin, "The Conflict of Moralities: Confession, Sin and Pleasure in the Nineteenth Century," in Theodore Zeldin (ed.), *Conflicts in French Society: Anticlericalism, Education and Morals in the Nineteenth Century* (London: Allen and Unwin, 1970). Ralph Gibson has recently reiterated the central significance of conflicts over sexuality to liberal-Catholic hostilities in France. But as Caroline Ford has pointed out, Zeldin's insights—despite their great explanatory potential—have not yet been given the fuller development they deserve. See Ralph Gibson, "Why Republicans and Catholics Couldn't Stand Each Other in the Nineteenth Century," in Frank Tallett and Nicholas Atkin (eds.), *Religion, Society and Politics in France since 1789* (London: Hambledon, 1991), pp. 117–20; and Caroline Ford, "Religion and Popular Culture in Modern Europe," *Journal of Modern History* 65 (March 1993), esp. pp. 159–60.

9. For an elaboration of these points, see Michel Foucault, *The History of Sexuality. Volume I: An Introduction* (New York: Vintage, 1980); Jeffrey Weeks, *Sex, Politics and Society* (New York: Longman, 1981); Stephen Heath, *The Sexual Fix* (New York: Schocken, 1984); Kathy Peiss and Christina Simmons (eds.), *Passion and Power: Sexuality in History* (Philadelphia: Temple Univ. Press, 1989); and Catherine Gallagher and Thomas Laqueur (eds.), *The Making of the Modern Body: Sexuality and Society in the Nineteenth Century* (Berkeley: Univ. of California Press, 1987).

10. See Deborah Hertz, *Jewish High Society in Old Regime Berlin* (New Haven: Yale Univ. Press, 1988); and Marion A. Kaplan, *The Making of the Jewish Middle Class: Women, Family, and Identity in Imperial Germany* (New York: Oxford Univ. Press, 1991).

11. Particularly valuable examples of this more broad-ranging phenomenon

in U.S. scholarship include: David R. Roediger, *The Wages of Whiteness: Race and the Making of the American Working Class* (New York: Verso, 1991); Eric Lott, *Love and Theft: Blackface Minstrelsy and the American Working Class* (New York: Oxford Univ. Press, 1993); Toni Morrison, *Playing in the Dark: Whiteness and the Literary Imagination* (Cambridge, Mass.: Harvard Univ. Press, 1992); and Gail Bederman, *Manliness and Civilization: A Cultural History of Gender and Race in the United States, 1880–1917* (Chicago: Univ. of Chicago Press, 1995). Pathbreaking examples of efforts to bring such concerns into European history, and to look critically at the self-understandings of white men in the British and French contexts, respectively, are provided by Catherine Hall, *White, Male and Middle-Class: Explorations in Feminism and History* (Cambridge, UK: Polity Press, 1992); and Pamela S. Bogart, "La philanthropie et l'idéologie raciale à travers des métaphores familiales 1789–1808" (paper delivered at the African Literature Association Conference, Gosier, Guadeloupe, 17 Apr. 1993); and Pamela S. Bogart, "Eurocentrisme et philanthropie dans les textes antiesclavagistes de l'abbé Grégoire." M.A. Thesis, Univ. of Antilles-Guyane, Schoelcher, Martinique, 1992. The most important new study on the intersecting workings of race, gender, and sexuality in the nineteenth-century European imagination is Ann Laura Stoler, *Race and the Education of Desire: Foucault's History of Sexuality and the Colonial Order of Things* (Durham, N.C.: Duke Univ. Press, 1995).

12. Nancy Armstrong, *Desire and Domestic Fiction: A Political History of the Novel* (New York: Oxford Univ. Press, 1987), p. 24.

13. Important examples include Stuart Hall, "Race, Ethnicity, Nation: The Fateful/Fatal Triangle" (three lectures delivered at Harvard University, 25–27 Apr. 1994); Henry Louis Gates, Jr., "African American Criticism," in Stephen Greenblatt and Giles Gunn (eds.), *Redrawing the Boundaries: The Transformation of English and American Literary Studies* (New York: The Modern Language Association of America, 1992); Homi Bhabha, "The Other Question— The Stereotype and Colonial Discourse," *Screen* 24/6 (1983); Kwame Anthony Appiah, *In My Father's House: Africa in the Philosophy of Culture* (New York: Oxford Univ. Press, 1992); Mary Louise Pratt, *Imperial Eyes: Travel Writing and Transculturation* (New York: Routledge, 1992); Joan Wallach Scott, *Gender and the Politics of History* (New York: Columbia Univ. Press, 1988); Mary Poovey, *Uneven Developments: The Ideological Work of Gender in Mid-Victorian England* (Chicago: Univ. of Chicago Press, 1988); Judith Butler, *Gender Trouble: Feminism and the Subversion of Identity* (New York: Routledge, 1990); and Eve Kosofsky Sedgwick, *Epistemology of the Closet* (Berkeley: Univ. of California Press, 1990).

BIBLIOGRAPHY

UNPUBLISHED PRIMARY SOURCES

Bundesarchiv Aussenstelle Frankfurt

Nachlass Struve (FN 17/16)

Erzbischöfliches Archiv Freiburg

Nachlass Boll (Nb 1/1)
Bolls Hirtenbrief, 13 July 1832 (Archivbibliothek)
Nachlass Demeter (Nb 2–8)
Ronge und Deutschkatholizismus 1845–1864 (B2–17/22)
Rongeanismus. Berichte der Dekane 1845–1847 (B2–17/23)
Übertritt zum Rongeanismus 1845–1866 (B2–17/24)
Generalia Erzbistum Freiburg (B2–18/25, B2–18/26, B2–32/512)

Archiv der Freireligiösen Gemeinde Mannheim

Rechnungs-Vorlage nebst Rechenschafts-Berichte, Budgets, Vorstandswahl
    1846/59–60

Generallandesarchiv Karlsruhe

Stadt Mannheim (213/3597)
Landtag (231/1436, 231/2086)
Staatsministerium (233/1864, 233/18587, 233/32303, 233/32307)
Justizministerium (234/1571)
Landgericht Freiburg (241/110)
Bezirks-Amt Heidelberg (356/566)
Bezirks-Amt Konstanz (359/1906/20/59, 359/1906/20/1163)
Bezirks-Amt Mannheim (362/1342)
Bezirks-Amt Pforzheim (369/2431)
Bezirks-Amt Stockach (379/1934/2/147)

Landeskirchliches Archiv Karlsruhe

Personalakte Carl Scholl (PA 252)

Stadtarchiv Freiburg

Nachlass Schreiber (K1/27 2/9)

Stadtarchiv Heidelberg

Die deutschkatholische Kirchen-Gesellschaft und deren Angelegenheiten be-
    treffend 1848–1855 (UA 155/2)

Staatsbibliothek Preussischer Kulturbesitz, Berlin

Nachlass Brümmer

Universitätsbibliothek Giessen

Nachlass Diefenbach

PUBLISHED PRIMARY SOURCES

Parliamentary Debates

The published minutes of the debates in the Upper Chamber (I. Kammer) of the Badenese diet from 1846, and the Lower Chamber (II. Kammer) from 1828, 1831, 1833, 1840, 1842, 1844–1846, and 1848 can be found in the General-landesarchiv Karlsruhe, the Landesbibliothek Karlsruhe, and the Universitätsbibliothek Heidelberg.

Newspapers

Allgemeine Kirchen-Zeitung (Darmstadt), 1847
Allgemeine Zeitung des Judenthums (Leipzig), 1843, 1845–1847
Badische Kirchenzeitung (Mannheim—supplement to the *Mannheimer Morgenblatt*), 1847
Der Bürgerfreund (Mannheim), 1847
Capistran: Zeitschrift für die Rechte und Interessen des katholischen Teutschlands (Schaffhausen), 1847
Deutscher Zuschauer (Mannheim), 1846–1847; (New York City), 1851
Deutschkatholisches Sonntags-Blatt (Wiesbaden), 1851–1854
Es werde Licht! (Nürnberg and Leipzig), 1871, 1874–1875, 1886, 1894, 1900–1902
Evangelisches Kirchenblatt zunächst für das Grossherzogthum Baden (Freiburg), 1845
Frankfurter Journal, 1847
Frauen-Zeitung (Grossenhain), 1849
Die Gegenwart (Leipzig), 1850
Historisch-politische Blätter für das katholische Deutschland (Munich), 1848
Der Israelit des neunzehnten Jahrhunderts (Meiningen), 1845, 1847–1848
Der Jude (Altona), 1833
Der Jude in Deutschlands Gegenwart (Hamburg), 1846
Katholische Kirchenreform (Berlin), 1845–1846
Kirchliche Reform (Halle), 1846–1847
Der Landbote (Stockach), 1847–1848
Lesehalle (Schkeuditz), 1847
Mannheimer Abendzeitung, 1845–1848
Mannheimer Journal, 1845–1847
Mannheimer Morgenblatt, 1847
Der Morgenbote (Freiburg), 1845, 1847
Oberrheinische Zeitung (Freiburg), 1846–1847
Der Orient (Leipzig), 1846–1847
Der Orient. Literaturblatt (Leipzig), 1846
Der Phönix (Hamburg), 1847
Die Reform des Judenthums (Mannheim), 1846

Reform-Zeitung (Berlin), 1847

Seeblätter (Constance), 1846

Sociale Republik (New York City), 1858

Süddeutsche Zeitung für Kirche und Staat (Freiburg), 1846–1847

Der Volksführer (Heidelberg), 1849

Zeitschrift für die religiösen Interessen des Judenthums (Dresden), 1845;
(Leipzig), 1846

Books and Articles by Contemporaries

Abs, Joseph Theodosius. *Das Cölibatgebot, im Widerspruche mit Bibel, Kirche und Staat.* Halberstadt and Heiligenstadt: J. C. Dölle, 1813.

Albrecht, Friedrich. "Ueber die Ehe." *Predigten, Aufsätze und Mittheilungen.* No. 5. Ulm: G. P. Geuss, 1846.

———. *Glaube, Hoffnung, Liebe: Ein Glaubensbekenntniss in drei Sonettenkränzen.* Ulm: Selbstverlag, 1856.

———. *Religion: Eine Sammlung von Predigt-Vorträgen im Geiste des neunzehnten Jahrhunderts.* 2 vols. Ulm: Gebr. Rübling, 1857 and 1866.

Aston, Louise. *Aus dem Leben einer Frau.* Hamburg: Hoffmann und Campe, 1847.

"Die badische zweite Kammer und die Gleichstellung der Juden." *Mannheimer Journal* (3 Jan. 1846).

Baltzer, Eduard. "Die Ehe." *Das Menschenleben in seinen Hauptbeziehungen.* Nordhausen: F. Förstemann, 1851.

Bamberger, Ludwig. "Festrede." *Das Wesen der Ehe nebst einigen Aufsätzen über die soziale Reform der Frauen.* Ed. Louise Dittmar. Leipzig: O. Wigand, 1849.

Bleich, Eduard, ed. *Der erste Vereinigte Landtag in Berlin 1847.* Vols. 3 and 4. Berlin: Karl Reimarus, 1847.

Brugger, Joseph Dominik Carl. "Martha und Maria." *Das Christenthum im Geiste des neuenzehnten Jahrhunderts.* Heidelberg: Hoffmeister, 1847.

———. "Die Frauen vor und in dem Christenthum." *Deutschkatholisches Sonntags-Blatt* (12 Mar. 1854).

Buss, Franz Joseph. *Der Orden der barmherzigen Schwestern.* Schaffhausen: Hurter, 1844.

———. *Das Rongethum in der badischen Abgeordnetenkammer.* Freiburg i. B.: Herder, 1846.

———. "Aufgabe der Zeitschrift." *Capistran: Zeitschrift für die Rechte und Interessen des katholischen Teutschlands* 1/1. Schaffhausen: Hurter, 1847.

Castorph, Ludwig. *Sendschreiben als unterthänigste Petition an die Allerhöchste Badische Staatsregierung und Hohe Badische Ständekammer hervorgerufen durch die Motion des Herrn Abgeordneten Zittel.* Baden-Baden: Scotzniovsky, 1846.

"Der Cölibat." *Deutschkatholisches Sonntags-Blatt* (28 Nov. 1852).

Czerski, Johannes. *Rechtfertigung meines Abfalles von der römischen Hofkirche.* Bromberg: L. Levit, 1845.

Eine deutsch-jüdische Kirche: Die nächste Aufgabe unsrer Zeit. Von einem Candidaten der jüdischen Theologie. Leipzig: O. Wigand, 1845.

Deutschlands zweites Ostern oder die Auferstehung der Kirche. Stuttgart: J. B. Metzler, 1845.

[Dittmar, Luise]. *Bekannte Geheimnisse.* Darmstadt: C. W. Leske, 1845.

———. *Skizzen und Briefe aus der Gegenwart.* Darmstadt: C. W. Leske, 1845.

———. *Der Mensch und sein Gott in und ausser dem Christenthum. Von einem Weltlichen.* Offenbach a. M.: G. André, 1846.

———. *Lessing und Feuerbach, oder Auswahl aus G. E. Lessing's theologischen Schriften nebst Originalbeiträgen und Belegstellen aus L. Feuerbach's Wesen des Christenthums.* Offenbach a. M.: G. André, 1846.

Dittmar, Luise. *Vier Zeitfragen: Beantwortet in einer Versammlung des Mannheimer Montag-Vereins.* Offenbach a. M.: G. André, 1847.

———. *Zur Charakterisierung der nordischen Mythologie im Verhältniss zu andern Naturreligionen: Eine Skizze.* Darmstadt: C. W. Leske, 1848.

Dittmar, Louise. *Brutus-Michel.* 2d ed. Darmstadt: C. W. Leske, 1848.

———. *Wühlerische Gedichte eines Wahrhaftigen.* Mannheim: Bensheimer, 1848.

———. *Das Wesen der Ehe.* Leipzig: O. Wigand, 1850.

———, ed. *Das Wesen der Ehe nebst einigen Aufsätzen über die soziale Reform der Frauen.* Leipzig: O. Wigand, 1849.

Dürr, Joseph. *Predigten auf alle Sonn- und Festtage des katholischen Kirchenjahrs.* 2 vols. Villingen: F. Förderer, 1841 and 1843.

Dursch, G. M. *Katholisch-dogmatische Predigten.* Vol. 1. Tübingen: H. Laupp, 1852.

"Die Ehe, vom bürgerlichen und kirchlichen Standpunkte aus betrachtet." *Katholische Kirchenreform* (Apr. 1845, June 1845, July 1845).

Falkson, Ferdinand, *Die liberale Bewegung in Königsberg (1840–1848): Memoirenblätter.* Breslau: S. Schottlaender, 1888.

———, ed. *Gemischte Ehen zwischen Juden und Christen: Dokumente.* Altona: J. F. Hammerich, 1845.

———, ed. *Gemischte Ehen zwischen Juden und Christen: Dokumente.* Hamburg: Hoffmann und Campe, 1847.

"Familie." *Real-Encyclopädie des Erziehungs- und Unterrichtswesens nach katholischen Prinzipien: Unter Mitwirkung von geistlichen und weltlichen Schulmännern für Geistliche, Volksschullehrer, Eltern und Erzieher.* Vol. 1. Ed. Hermann Rolfus and Adolph Pfister. Mainz: Florian Kupferberg, 1863.

Die Feier des ersten Gründungsfestes der Deutschkatholischen Gemeinde in Mannheim. Basel: Schnabelitz, 1846.

Feuerbach, Ludwig. *The Essence of Christianity.* Orig ed. 1841. Reprinted New York: Harper and Row, 1957.

"Die Frau des Christenthums." *Der fränkische Morgenbote* (24 July 1851).

"Die Frau im Alterthume und die christliche Frau." *Katholische Kirchenreform* (Oct. 1845).

Gervinus, Georg Gottfried. *Die Mission der Deutschkatholiken.* Orig. ed. 1845. Reprinted and ed. by Eckhart Pilick. Mannheim: Freireligiöse Verlagsbuchhandlung, 1982.

G[lümer], C[laire] v[on]. "Ueber Fourier." *Das Wesen der Ehe nebst einigen Aufsätzen über die soziale Reform der Frauen.* Ed. Louise Dittmar. Leipzig: O. Wigand, 1849.

Görres, Johann Joseph. *Athanasius.* 2d ed. Regensburg: G. J. Manz, 1838.

Gregory XVI. "Mirari vos." (15 Aug. 1832) *The Papal Encyclicals 1740–1878.* Ed. Claudia Carlen. Wilmington, N.C.: McGrath, 1981.

Hammer, Adam. *Die Anwendung des Schwefeläthers im Allgemeinen und insbesondere bei Geburten.* Mannheim: Selbstverlag, 1847.

Häusler, Matthias. *Noch ein nachdrückliches Wort über das ernstliche letzte Wort eines Cölibat-Feindes und eines würdigen Consortens, der um die hohe Erlaubniss des Rücktrittes in den Laienstand wehmüthig flehet.* 1815 (n.p.).

Hecker, Friedrich. *Die staatsrechtlichen Verhältnisse der Deutschkatholiken mit besonderem Hinblick auf Baden.* Heidelberg: Groos, 1845.

———. "Weiblichkeit und Weiberrechtelei." *Aus den Reden und Vorlesungen von Friedrich Hecker.* Ed. Helmut Bender. Waldkirch: Waldkircher Verlagsgesellschaft, 1985.

Herterich, Amts-Assessor in Weinheim. "Die Judenemancipation und ihre beiden Geschwister, der Deutschkatholizismus und der Radicalismus." *Mannheimer Morgenblatt* (Feb. 1847).

Hirscher, Johann Baptist von. "Erklärung des Professors Dr. von Hirscher zu Freiburg, veranlasst durch einen gegen ihn gerichteten Artikel . . ." (1843). Reprinted in Schiel, Hubert F. *Johann Baptist von Hirscher: Eine Lichtgestalt aus dem deutschen Katholizismus des XIX. Jahrhunderts.* Freiburg i. B.: Caritasverlag, 1926.

———. *Beleuchtung der Motion des Abgeordneten Zittel.* Freiburg i. B.: Herder, 1846.

———. *Die christliche Moral als Lehre von der Verwirklichung des göttlichen Reiches in der Menschheit.* 5th ed. Vols. 2 and 3. Tübingen: H. Laupp, 1851.

Holdheim, Samuel. *Das Religiöse und Politische im Judenthum: Mit besonderer Beziehung auf gemischte Ehen.* Schwerin: C. Kürschner, 1845.

———. *Vorschläge zu einer zeitgemässen Reform der jüdischen Ehegesetze.* Schwerin: C. Kürschner, 1845.

Huber, Ernst Rudolf, and Huber, Wolfgang, eds. *Staat und Kirche im 19. und 20. Jahrhundert: Dokumente zur Geschichte der deutschen Staatskirchenrechte.* Vol. 1. Berlin: Duncker und Humblot, 1973.

Jellinek, Hermann. *Die religiösen, socialen und literarischen Zustände der Gegenwart. In ihren praktischen Folgen untersucht. Erster Theil: Die religiösen Zustände der Gegenwart, oder: Kritik der Religion der Liebe.* Zerbst: Kummer, 1847.

Jost, Isaak Markus. *Culturgeschichte zur neueren Geschichte der Israeliten von 1815 bis 1845.* Berlin: Schlesinger, 1847.

"Die Juden." *Historisch-politische Blätter für das katholische Deutschland* 22 (1848).

"Der katholische Priester in seiner Stellung zum Weibe und zur Familie von J. Michelet: Aus dem Französischen." *Katholische Kirchenreform* (May 1845).

Keine Ohrenbeichte mehr! Zeitgemässes Wort eines Rhein-Hessischen Katholiken an seine Glaubensgenossen. Frankfurt a. M.: C. Körner, 1845.

Kinorhc, J. "Ueber die Ehe zwischen Juden und Christen." *Kirchliche Reform* (Oct. 1846).

Loewenthal, [Raphael]. "Die jüdische Reform." *Der Israelit des neunzehnten Jahrhunderts* (8 June 1845).

Loose, Heinrich. "Rede." *Antritts-Predigt von Friedrich Albrecht, deutsch-katholischem Pfarrer zu Ulm, bei seiner durch Heinrich Loose, deutschkatholischem Pfarrer in Esslingen vollzogenen Einweihung nebst der Einweihungs-Rede des Letztern.* Basel: Senl und Fischer, 1846.

Mehlmann, J. H. "Einige Worte über deutsch-katholische Praxis." *Mannheimer Morgenblatt* (July 1847).

Misch, E. N. *Die Ehe zwischen Juden und Christen: Ein Votum, mit Bezug auf das preussische Recht und Toleranzedikt.* Leipzig: O. Wigand, 1847.

Möhler, Johann Adam. "Beleuchtung der Denkschrift für die Aufhebung des den katholischen Geistlichen vorgeschriebenen Cölibates. Mit drei Actenstücken" (1828). Reprinted in *Dr. J. A. Möhler's gesammelte Schriften und Aufsätze.* Vol. 1. Ed. Johann Josef Ignaz Döllinger. Regensburg: G. J. Manz, 1839.

Mone, Franz Josef. *Die katholischen Zustände in Baden.* Regensburg: G. J. Manz, 1841.

———. *Beleuchtung der Zittelschen Motion über Religionsfreiheit.* Bonn: Wittmann, 1846.

Die Musterehe und die Nothwendigkeit einer Wiederherstellung der Ehe nach der Musterehe. Freiburg i. B.: Herder, 1850.

Das neue Jerusalem oder die Zukunft der christlichen Kirche. Darmstadt, 1845.

Die neue Reformation oder die deutschkatholische Bewegung. Leipzig: C.W.B. Naumburg, 1845.

Otto, Louise. "Die Teilnahme der weiblichen Welt am Staatsleben." *Vorwärts! Volkstaschenbuch für das Jahr 1847.* Reprinted in *Die Deutsche Frauenbewegung: Ihre Anfänge und erste Entwicklung. Quellen 1843–1889.* Ed. Margrit Twellmann. Meisenheim am Glan: Anton Hain, 1972.

———. "Mein Programm als Mitarbeiterin einer Frauenzeitung." *Das Wesen der Ehe nebst einigen Aufsätzen über die soziale Reform der Frauen.* Ed. Louise Dittmar. Leipzig: O. Wigand, 1849.

———. "Programm." *Frauen-Zeitung* (21 Apr. 1849).

Die politischen, Kirchen- und Schulgemeinden des Grossherzogthums Baden mit der Seelen- und Bürgerzahl vom Jahr 1845. Karlsruhe: C. F. Müller, 1847.

Q. "Gemischte Ehen." *Das Staats-Lexikon.* 1st ed. Vol. 6. Ed. Carl Theodor Welcker and Karl von Rotteck. With an afterword by Karl von Rotteck. Altona: J. F. Hammerich, 1838.

Rau, Heribert. "Die Stellung der Frauen in der Christenheit." *Worte zum Herzen des deutschen Volkes: Vorträge und Gebete.* Stuttgart: Franckh, 1848.

Rée, Anton. *Aufruf zu einer rascheren Förderung der jüdischen Angelegenheiten im Vaterlande.* Hamburg: H. Gobert, 1846.

———. *Erster Jahresbericht der Gesellschaft für sociale und politische Interessen der Juden der Generalversammlung den 23. Oct. 1847 von Dr. Anton Rée als d. Z. Präses abgestattet.* Hamburg, 1847.

Reichlin-Meldegg, Karl Alexander von. *Das Leben eines ehemaligen römisch-katholischen Priesters: Eine Jubelschrift.* Heidelberg: F. Bassermann, 1874.

Riehl, Wilhelm Heinrich. "Die Frauen: Eine social-politische Studie." *Deutsche Vierteljahresschrift* (1852, no. 3).

Riesser, Gabriel. *Eine Auswahl aus seinen Schriften und Briefen.* Frankfurt a. M.: J. Kauffmann, 1913.

Ronge, Johannes. "Letter to the Inferior Clergy." *John Ronge, the Holy Coat of Treves and the New German-Catholic Church.* New York: Harper and Bros., 1845.

———. *An meine Glaubensgenossen und Mitbürger.* Altenburg: Schnuphase, 1845.

———. *Rede, gehalten am 23. Sept. 1845 in der Münsterkirche zu Ulm.* Ulm: E. Rübling, 1845.

———. *Zuruf.* Dessau: H. Neubürger, 1845.

———. "Die Stellung der Frauen." *Für christkatholisches Leben* VI (1848).

———. *Maria, oder: Die Stellung der Frauen der alten und neuen Zeit.* Hamburg: G. W. Niemeyer, 1849.

———. *Religion und Politik.* Frankfurt a. M.: Literarische Anstalt, 1850.

Rongelieder: Die religiösen Ideen der Gegenwart. Stuttgart: E. Greiner, 1845.

[Rosshirt, Franz]. *Beleuchtung und actenmässige Ergänzung der Karlsruher Schrift: "Der Streit über gemischte Ehen und das Kirchenhoheitsrecht im Grossherzogthum Baden."* Schaffhausen: Hurter, 1847.

Rotteck, Karl von. "Familie, Familienrecht." *Das Staats-Lexikon.* 1st ed. Vol. 5. Ed. Karl von Rotteck and Carl Theodor Welcker. Altona: J. F. Hammerich, 1837.

Scholl, Carl. *Ein Opfer der Ueberzeugung! Für die Mundhelden des Christenthums und der Freiheit überhaupt.* Mannheim: Bensheimer, 1846.

———. *Meine Suspension.* Leipzig: O. Wigand, 1846.

———. *Das Wesen des Deutschkatholicismus oder die Versöhnung des Glaubens und der Wissenschaft.* Mannheim: F. Bassermann, 1846.

———. *Einleitende Worte, gesprochen im Mannheimer Montags-Verein: Montag den 1. März 1847.* Mannheim, 1847.

———. *Paulus und die Galater: Ein warnendes Bild der Vergangenheit für alle Deutschkatholiken und Freiprotestanten.* Hamburg: Berendsohn, 1847.

———. *Ein Gruss in die Heimath: Vier Vorträge aus Anlass meines Wegzugs von Mannheim nach Nürnberg.* Mannheim: Schneider, 1869.

———. "Die Marien-Verehrung: Zur gerechteren Würdigung der katholischen Religion." *Es werde Licht!* (1871).

———. "Durch! Erinnerungen aus meinem eigenen Leben." *Es werde Licht!* (1871).

———. "Christliche Schacherjuden." *Es werde Licht!* (May 1874).

———. "Die Frauen in der Religion." *Es werde Licht!* (Oct. 1875).

———. *Das Judenthum und die Religion der Humanität.* Leipzig: Friese, 1879.

———. *Das Judenthum und seine Weltmission.* Leipzig: Friese, 1880.

———. "Moses Mendelssohn." *Es werde Licht!* (Mar. 1886).

———. *Zwei Antisemiten. Ein Freidenker und ein Hofprediger. Nebst einem An-*

hang: Die wirkliche semitische Unmoral oder Grundsätze der jüdischen Sitten-lehre. Nürnberg and Leipzig: Friese, 1890.

———. *Aus hohen Tagen: Das Erwachen der Geister in Oesterreich.* Berlin: H. Lüstenöder, 1891.

———. *Hundert Jahre nach Lessings Nathan.* Bamberg: Handels-Druckerei, 1893.

———. "Der Antisemitismus vom sittlichen Standpunkt aus betrachtet." *Es werde Licht!* (June 1894, July 1894).

———. "Meine ersten Kämpfe nach meinem Anschluss an die freien Gemein-den." *Es werde Licht!* (Nov. 1900, Dec. 1900, Feb. 1901).

Schreiber, Heinrich. *Deutsch-Katholisches.* Freiburg i. B.: A. Emmerling, 1846.

Stahl, Friedrich Julius. *Der christliche Staat und sein Verhältniss zu Deismus und Judenthum.* Berlin: L. Oehmigke, 1847.

Staudenmaier, Franz Anton. *Das Wesen der katholischen Kirche: Mit Rücksicht auf ihre Gegner dargestellt.* Freiburg i. B.: Herder, 1845.

Stern, Wilhelm. *Antrag auf Glaubensfreiheit.* Karlsruhe: Macklot, 1846.

Stolz, Alban. *Mixtur gegen die Todesangst, zusammengesetzt von einem badischen Jesuiten: Kalender für Zeit und Ewigkeit 1843.* Villingen: F. Förderer, 1842.

———. "April." *Mixtur gegen Todesangst: Kalender für Zeit und Ewigkeit Erster Jahrgang 1843. Für das gemeine Volk und nebenher für geistliche und weltliche Herrenleute.* 16th ed. Freiburg i. B.: Herder, 1868.

———. *Landwehr gegen den badischen Landstand.* Freiburg i. B.: Herder, 1845.

———. "Sechstes Gebot: Du sollst nicht ehebrechen." *Essig und Oel (Dritter Theil vom Vaterunser): Kalender für Zeit und Ewigkeit Fünfter Jahrgang 1847.* 14th ed. Freiburg i. B.: Herder, 1870.

———. "Weibervolk." *ABC für grosse Leute: Kalender für Zeit und Ewigkeit 1864; mit groben Bildern.* 4th ed. Freiburg i. B.: Herder, 1864.

———. "Der verbotene Baum: Für Katholiken und Protestanten gezeigt (1874)." *Gesammelte Werke.* Vol. 10. Freiburg i. B.: Herder, n.d.

———. *Gesammelte Werke.* 3d ed. Vol. 8. Ed. Julius Mayer. Freiburg i. B.: Herder, 1913/14.

[Strehle, Adolf]. *Die gemischten Ehen in der Erzdiöcese Freiburg.* Regensburg: G. J. Manz, 1846.

Der Streit über gemischte Ehen und das Kirchenhoheitsrecht im Grossherzogthum Baden. Karlsruhe: G. Braun, 1847.

Struve, Amalie. "Die Frauen." *Deutscher Zuschauer* (9 July 1851).

———. "Die Feinde weiblicher Freiheit." *Deutscher Zuschauer* (16 July 1851).

———. "Die Frauen und die Revolution." *Deutscher Zuschauer* (31 Dec. 1851).

[Struve], Gustav Carl [von]. *Die Verfolgung der Juden durch Emicho.* Mannheim: Götz, 1841.

Struve, Gustav von. *Aktenstücke der Zensur des grossherzoglich-badischen Regie-rungsrats v. Uria-Sarachaga, eine Rekursschrift an das Publikum.* Mannheim: Verlag des Herausgebers, 1845.

———. *Briefwechsel zwischen einem ehemaligen und einem jetzigen Diplomaten.* Mannheim: Bensheimer, 1845.

———. "Ueber die Rechtsverhältnisse der Bekenner des mosaischen Glaubens." *Mannheimer Journal* (25 July 1845, 26 July 1845).

———. *Briefe über Kirche und Staat.* Mannheim: Bensheimer, 1846.

———. "Das Juden-Casino zu Mannheim." *Mannheimer Journal* (31 Mar. 1846).

———. *Politische Briefe.* Mannheim: Bensheimer, 1846.

———. *Politisches Taschenbuch für das deutsche Volk.* Frankfurt a. M.: Literarische Anstalt, 1846.

Struve, Gustav. "Christenthum und Pfaffenthum." *Deutscher Zuschauer* (23 July 1851).

———. "Die soziale Reform der Kirche." *Deutscher Zuschauer* (10 Sept. 1851).

———. "Europa." *Deutscher Zuschauer* (13 Aug. 1851).

———. "Religion und Staat." *Deutscher Zuschauer* (13 Aug. 1851).

———. "Die Stellung der Frauen im Leben." *Deutscher Zuschauer* (24 Dec. 1851).

———. "Die Gebetkrankheit." *Sociale Republik* (24 Apr. 1858).

———. "Mann und Frau." *Sociale Republik* (1 May 1858).

———. "Die Nachwehen der Gebetkrankheit." *Sociale Republik* (8 May 1858).

———. "Die Quellen des Aberglaubens." *Sociale Republik* (5 June 1858).

———. "Religionsfreiheit." *Sociale Republik* (12 June 1858).

———. *Die Zeit von 1848 bis 1863: Nachtrag zu G. Struve's Weltgeschichte.* Coburg: F. Streit, 1864.

Theiner, Johann Anton and Augustin. *Die Einführung der erzwungenen Ehelosigkeit bei den christlichen Geistlichen und ihre Folgen.* Altenburg: Verlag der Hofbuchdruckerei, 1828.

Thiel, Heinrich. "Die deutsch-katholische Frau." *Der Inhalt des Deutsch-Katholizismus.* Dessau, 1846.

Trau-Rede, am 21 Februar 1845 bei der kirchlichen Trauung des katholischen Predigers Czerski in Schneidemühl gehalten von dem evangelischen Ortspfarrer Grützmacher. Berlin: W. Hermes, 1845.

Trefurt, Christoph. *Der Zölibat aus dem Gesichtspunkte der Moral, des Rechts und der Politik betrachtet.* Heidelberg and Leipzig: Groos, 1826.

Uhlich, Leberecht. *Die Ehe: Eine Erörterung.* Magdeburg: Selbstverlag, 1857.

Unsre Antwort: Abgedrungene Erklärung der Mannheimer Deutschkatholiken auf das Manifest des erzbischöflichen Ordinariats in Freiburg. Belle-Vue: Verlagsbuchhandlung, 1846.

Unterricht für das katholische Volk in Deutschland über die Aufhebung der Ehelosigkeit seiner Priester. 1803 (n.p.).

Verhandlungen der Württembergischen Kammer der Abgeordneten auf dem Landtage von 1848–49. 5. Protokollband. Stuttgart: J. Kreuzer, 1849.

Welcker, Carl Theodor. "Geschlechtsverhältnisse." *Das Staats-Lexikon.* 1st ed. Vol. 6. Ed. Carl Theodor Welcker and Karl von Rotteck. Altona: J. F. Hammerich, 1838.

———. "Verbotene Ehen, insbesondere Priester-Cölibat." *Das Staats-Lexikon.* 1st ed. Vol. 15. Ed. Carl Theodor Welcker and Karl von Rotteck. Altona: J. F. Hammerich, 1843.

[Werkmeister, Benedikt Maria von]. *Vorschlag, wie in der deutschen katholischen Kirche die Priesterehe allmählich eingeführt werden könnte.* 1803 (n.p.).

Worte der Wahrheit an das katholische Volk in Baden und Süddeutschland von einem Freunde der christlich-katholischen Kirche und der deutschen Eintracht. Basel: J. C. Schabelitz, 1846.

Zittel, Karl. "Die politischen Partheiungen in Baden." *Jahrbücher der Gegenwart* (1847).

SECONDARY SOURCES

Ackermann, Karl. *Gustav v. Struve mit besonderer Berücksichtigung seiner Bedeutung für die Vorgeschichte der badischen Revolution.* Ph.D. diss., Univ. of Heidelberg, 1914.

Adler, Hans. "On a Feminist Controversy: Louise Otto vs. Louise Aston." *German Women in the 18th and 19th Centuries.* Ed. Ruth-Ellen Boetcher Joeres and Mary Jo Maynes. Bloomington: Indiana Univ. Press, 1986.

Allen, Ann Taylor. *Feminism and Motherhood in Germany 1800–1914.* New Brunswick: Rutgers Univ. Press, 1991.

Altgeld, Wolfgang. *Katholizismus, Protestantismus, Judentum: Über religiös begründete Gegensätze und nationalreligiöse Ideen in der Geschichte des deutschen Nationalismus.* Mainz: Matthias-Grünewald, 1992.

Anderson, Margaret Lavinia. *Windthorst: A Political Biography.* New York: Oxford Univ. Press, 1981.

Appiah, Kwame Anthony. *In My Father's House: Africa in the Philosophy of Culture.* New York: Oxford Univ. Press, 1992.

Armstrong, Nancy. *Desire and Domestic Fiction: A Political History of the Novel.* New York: Oxford Univ. Press, 1987.

Badisches Statistisches Landesamt, ed. *Die Religionszugehörigkeit in Baden in den letzten 100 Jahren.* Freiburg i. B.: Herder, 1928.

Becht, Hans-Peter. *Die badische zweite Kammer und ihre Mitglieder, 1819 bis 1841/42: Untersuchungen zu Struktur und Funktionsweise eines frühen deutschen Parlaments.* Ph.D. diss., Univ. of Mannheim, 1985.

Becker, Josef. *Liberaler Staat und Kirche in der Ära von Reichsgründung und Kulturkampf.* Mainz: Matthias-Grünewald, 1973.

Bederman, Gail. "'Civilization,' the Decline of Middle-Class Manliness, and Ida B. Wells's Antilynching Campaign (1892–94)." *Radical History Review* 52 (Winter 1992).

———. *Manliness and Civilization: A Cultural History of Gender and Race in the United States, 1880–1917.* Chicago: Univ. of Chicago Press, 1995.

Bhabha, Homi. "The Other Question—The Stereotype and Colonial Discourse." *Screen* 24/6 (1983).

Blackbourn, David. *Marpingen: Apparitions of the Virgin Mary in Bismarckian Germany.* New York: Oxford Univ. Press, 1993.

Blackbourn, David, and Geoff Eley. *The Peculiarities of German History: Bourgeois Society and Politics in Nineteenth-Century Germany.* Oxford: Oxford Univ. Press, 1984.

Blessing, Werner K. *Staat und Kirche in der Gesellschaft: Institutionelle Autorität und mentaler Wandel in Bayern während des 19. Jahrhunderts.* Göttingen: Vandenhoeck und Ruprecht, 1982.

Bogart, Pamela S. "Eurocentrisme et philanthropie dans les textes antiesclavagistes de l'abbé Grégoire." M.A. Thesis, Univ. of Antilles-Guyane, Schoelcher, Martinique, 1992.

———. "La philanthropie et l'idéologie raciale à travers des métaphores familiales 1789–1808." Paper delivered at the African Literature Association Conference, Gosier, Guadeloupe, 17 Apr. 1993.

Borscheid, Peter. "Geld und Liebe: Zu den Auswirkungen des Romantischen auf die Partnerwahl im 19. Jahrhundert." *Ehe, Liebe, Tod: Zum Wandel der Familie, der Geschlechts- und Generationsbeziehungen in der Neuzeit.* Ed. Peter Borscheid and Hans J. Teuteberg. Münster: F. Coppenrath, 1983.

Braun, Karl-Heinz. "Hermann von Vicari und Ignaz Heinrich von Wessenberg: Zwei Prälaten im kirchenpolitischen Vergleich." *Freiburger Diözesan-Archiv.* Vol. 107 (1987).

———. Review of Clemens Rehm, *Die katholische Kirche in der Erzdiöcese Freiburg während der Revolution 1848/49.* Munich: Karl Alber, 1987. In *Freiburger Diözesan-Archiv.* Vol. 107 (1987).

Brederlow, Jörn. *"Lichtfreunde" und "Freie Gemeinden": Religiöser Protest und Freiheitsbewegung im Vormärz und in der Revolution von 1848/49.* Munich and Vienna: R. Oldenbourg, 1976.

Brenner, Michael. "'Gott schütze uns vor unseren Freunden'—Zur Ambivalenz des Philosemitismus im Kaiserreich." *Jahrbuch für Antisemitismusforschung* 2 (1993).

Bundesblätter (Nordhausen) XXI (Dec. 1868).

Butler, Judith. *Gender Trouble: Feminism and the Subversion of Identity.* New York: Routledge, 1990.

———. "Gender Trouble, Feminist Theory, and Psychoanalytic Discourse." *Feminism/Postmodernism.* Ed. Linda J. Nicholson. New York: Routledge, 1990.

Butler, Judith, and Joan W. Scott, eds. *Feminists Theorize the Political.* New York: Routledge, 1992.

Carby, Hazel V. *Reconstructing Womanhood: The Emergence of the Afro-American Woman Novelist.* New York: Oxford Univ. Press, 1987.

Carlebach, Julius. "The Forgotten Connection: Women and Jews in the Conflict between Enlightenment and Romanticism." *Leo Baeck Institute Year Book* XXIV (1979).

Chazan, Robert. *European Jewry and the First Crusade.* Berkeley: Univ. of California Press, 1987.

Cheyette, Bryan. *Constructions of "the Jew" in English Literature and Society.* New York: Cambridge Univ. Press, 1993.

Conze, Werner. "Rasse." *Geschichtliche Grundbegriffe: Historisches Lexikon zur politisch-sozialen Sprache in Deutschland.* Vol. 5. Ed. Otto Brunner et al. Stuttgart: Klett-Cotta, 1984.

Davidoff, Leonore, and Catherine Hall. *Family Fortunes: Men and Women of the English Middle Class, 1780–1850.* Chicago: Univ. of Chicago Press, 1987.

Delumeau, Jean. *Sin and Fear: The Emergence of a Western Guilt Culture, 13th–18th Centuries.* New York: St. Martin's Press, 1990.

Denzler, Georg. *Die verbotene Lust: 2000 Jahre christliche Sexualmoral.* Munich: Piper, 1988.

Deuchert, Norbert. *Vom Hambacher Fest zur badischen Revolution: Politische Presse und Anfänge deutscher Demokratie 1832–1848/49.* Stuttgart: Theiss, 1983.

Diesbach, Alfred. *Die deutschkatholische Gemeinde Konstanz 1845–1849.* Mannheim: Freireligiöse Verlagsbuchhandlung, 1971.

Dorneich, Julius. *Franz Josef Buss und die katholische Bewegung in Baden.* Freiburg i. B.: Herder, 1979.

Eidelberg, Schlomo, ed. *The Jews and the Crusaders: The Hebrew Chronicles of the First and Second Crusades.* Madison: Univ. of Wisconsin Press, 1977.

Erb, Rainer, and Werner Bergmann, eds. *Die Nachtseite der Judenemanzipation: Der Widerstand gegen die Integration der Juden in Deutschland 1780–1860.* Berlin: Metropol, Veitl, 1989.

Erzbischöfliches Ordinariat Freiburg i. B. *Die rechtliche Stellung der Freireligiösen im Grossherzogthum Baden.* Freiburg i. B.: Verlag und Druck des Pressvereins, 1914.

Fausto-Sterling, Anne. *Myths of Gender: Biological Theories about Women and Men.* 2d ed. New York: Basic Books, 1992.

Fischer, Wolfram. "Staat und Gesellschaft Badens im Vormärz." *Staat und Gesellschaft im deutschen Vormärz 1815–1848.* Ed. Werner Conze. Stuttgart: Ernst Klett, 1962.

Ford, Caroline. "Religion and Popular Culture in Modern Europe." *Journal of Modern History* 65 (March 1993).

Foucault, Michel. *Discipline and Punish.* New York: Pantheon, 1977.

———. *The History of Sexuality. Volume I: An Introduction.* New York: Vintage, 1980.

———. *Power/Knowledge: Selected Interviews and Other Writings 1972–1977.* New York: Pantheon, 1980.

Fout, John C. "Sexual Politics in Wilhelmine Germany: The Male Gender Crisis, Moral Purity, and Homophobia." *Journal of the History of Sexuality* 2/3 (January 1992).

Fraisse, Geneviève. *Reason's Muse: Sexual Difference and the Birth of Democracy.* Chicago: Univ. of Chicago Press, 1994.

Franzen, August. "Die Zölibatsfrage im 19. Jahrhundert: Der 'Badische Zölibatssturm' (1828) und das Problem der Priesterehe im Urteile Johann Adam Möhlers und Johann Baptist Hirschers." *Historisches Jahrbuch* 91 (1971).

Frevert, Ute. *Women in German History: From Bourgeois Emancipation to Sexual Liberation.* Oxford: Berg, 1989.

———, ed. *Bürgerinnen und Bürger: Geschlechterverhältnisse im neunzehnten Jahrhundert.* Göttingen: Vandenhoeck und Ruprecht, 1988.

Gall, Lothar. *Der Liberalismus als regierende Partei: Das Grossherzogtum Baden zwischen Restauration und Reichsgründung.* Wiesbaden: F. Steiner, 1968.

Gallagher, Catherine, and Thomas Laqueur, eds. *The Making of the Modern Body: Sexuality and Society in the Nineteenth Century.* Berkeley: Univ. of California Press, 1987.

Ganser, Wilhelm Hubert. *Die Süddeutsche Zeitung für Kirche und Staat.* Berlin: E. Ebering, 1936.

Gates, Henry Louis, Jr. "Writing 'Race' and the Difference it Makes." *"Race," Writing and Difference.* Ed. Henry Louis Gates, Jr. Chicago: Univ. of Chicago Press, 1986.

———."African American Criticism." *Redrawing the Boundaries: The Transformation of English and American Literary Studies.* Ed. Stephen Greenblatt and Giles Gunn. New York: The Modern Language Association of America, 1992.

Gibson, Ralph. "Why Republicans and Catholics Couldn't Stand Each Other in the Nineteenth Century." *Religion, Society and Politics in France since 1789.* Ed. Frank Tallett and Nicholas Atkin. London: Hambledon, 1991.

Gilligan, Carol. *In a Different Voice: Psychological Theory and Women's Development.* Cambridge, Mass.: Harvard Univ. Press, 1982.

Gilman, Sander. *The Jew's Body.* London: Routledge, 1991.

Goetzinger, Germaine. "Soziale Reform der Geschlechterverhältnisse im Vormärz: Louise Dittmar's Ehekritik." *Rationale Beziehungen? Geschlechterverhältnisse im Rationalisierungsprozess.* Ed. Dagmar Reese et al. Frankfurt a. M.: Suhrkamp, 1993.

Goodman, Katherine. *Dis/Closures: Women's Autobiography in Germany between 1790 and 1914.* New York: Peter Lang, 1986.

Graetz, Michael. *Les Juifs en France au XIXe Siècle: De la Revolution Française à l'Alliance Israelite Universelle.* Paris: Éditions du Seuil, 1989.

Graf, Friedrich Wilhelm. *Die Politisierung des religiösen Bewusstseins. Die bürgerlichen Religionsparteien im deutschen Vormärz: Das Beispiel des Deutschkatholizismus.* Stuttgart: Bad Cannstatt: Frommann-Holzboog, 1978.

Grossmann, Atina, and Sara Lennox. "The Shadow of the Past." *The Women's Review of Books* (Sept. 1987).

"Gustave Struve." *New York Times* (31 Aug. 1870).

Hall, Catherine. *White, Male and Middle-Class: Explorations in Feminism and History.* Cambridge, UK: Polity Press, 1992.

Hall, Stuart. "Race, Ethnicity, Nation: The Fateful/Fatal Triangle." Three lectures delivered at Harvard University, 25–27 Apr. 1994.

Harris, James F. *The People Speak!: Anti-Semitism and Emancipation in Nineteenth-Century Bavaria.* Ann Arbor: Univ. of Michigan Press, 1994.

Hausen, Karin. "Family and Role-Division: The Polarization of Sexual Stereotypes in the Nineteenth Century—An Aspect of the Dissociation of Work and Family Life." *The German Family.* Ed. Richard J. Evans and W. R. Lee. London: Croom Helm, 1981.

Heath, Stephen. *The Sexual Fix.* New York: Schocken, 1984.

Hertz, Deborah. *Jewish High Society in Old Regime Berlin.* New Haven: Yale Univ. Press, 1988.

Hertzberg, Arthur. *The French Enlightenment and the Jews.* New York and London: Columbia Univ. Press, 1968.

Herzog, Dagmar. "New Developments in German Women's History." *Journal of Women's History* 4/3 (Winter 1993).

———."Wo liegt der Unterschied? Aufklärung und Frauenrechte in Deutschland." *Geschlechterverhältnisse im historischen Wandel.* Ed. Hanna Schissler. Frankfurt a. M.: Campus, 1993.

Herzog, Dagmar. "Anti-Judaism in Intra-Christian Conflict: Catholics and Liberals in Baden in the 1840s." *Central European History* 27/3 (1994).

———. "Male Fantasies, Male Fears, and the Roots of the *Kulturkampf.*" Paper delivered at the American Historical Association Convention, Chicago, 6 Jan. 1995.

Heschel, Susannah. "Anti-Judaism in Christian Feminist Theology." *Tikkun* 5/3 (1990).

Higginbotham, Evelyn Brooks. "African-American Women's History and the Metalanguage of Race." *Signs* 17/2 (Winter 1992).

Hoffmann, Volker. "Elisa und Robert oder das Weib und der Mann, wie sie sein sollten: Anmerkungen zur Geschlechtercharakteristik der Goethezeit." *Klassik und Moderne: Die Weimarer Klassik als historisches Ereignis und Herausforderung im kulturgeschichtlichen Prozess.* Ed. Karl Richter and Jörg Schönert. Stuttgart: Metzler, 1983.

Hörner, Manfred. *Die Wahlen zur badischen zweiten Kammer im Vormärz (1819–1847).* Göttingen: Vandenhoeck und Ruprecht, 1987.

Huber, Ernst Rudolf. *Deutsche Verfassungsgeschichte seit 1789.* Vol. 2. Stuttgart: Kohlhammer, 1960.

Hulme, Peter. "The Spontaneous Hand of Nature: Savagery, Colonialism and the Enlightenment." *The Enlightenment and its Shadows.* Ed. Peter Hulme and Ludmilla Jordanova. New York: Routledge, 1990.

Hummel-Haasis, Gerlinde, ed. *Schwestern zerreist eure Ketten: Zeugnisse zur Geschichte der Frauen in der Revolution von 1848/49.* Munich: DTV, 1982.

Hundsnurscher, Franz, and Gerhard Taddey. *Die jüdischen Gemeinden in Baden: Denkmale, Geschichte, Schicksale.* Stuttgart: Kohlhammer, 1968.

Jarausch, Konrad J., and Larry Eugene Jones, eds. *In Search of a Liberal Germany: Studies in the History of German Liberalism from 1789 to the Present.* Oxford: Berg, 1990.

Joeres, Ruth-Ellen Boetcher, ed. *Die Anfänge der deutschen Frauenbewegung: Louise Otto-Peters.* Frankfurt a. M.: Fischer, 1983.

Joeres, Ruth-Ellen Boetcher, and Marianne Burkhard, eds. *Out of Line/ Ausgefallen: The Paradox of Marginality in the Writings of Nineteenth-Century German Women.* Special Issue of *Amsterdamer Beiträge zur neueren Germanistik* 28 (1989).

Kah, Karl. *Die Ehe und das bürgerliche Standesamt nach badischem Recht.* Heidelberg: Selbstverlag, 1870.

Kaiser, Nancy. "Marriage and the Not-So-Simple Life in the 1840s." *From the Greeks to the Greens: Images of the Simple Life.* Ed. Jost Hermand and Reinhold Grimm. Madison: Univ. of Wisconsin Press, 1990.

Kaplan, Marion A. *The Making of the Jewish Middle Class: Women, Family and Identity in Imperial Germany.* New York: Oxford Univ. Press, 1991.

Katz, Jacob. *From Prejudice to Destruction: Anti-Semitism, 1700–1933.* Cambridge, Mass.: Harvard Univ. Press, 1980.

Kluxen, Kurt. "Religion und Nationalstaat im 19. Jahrhundert." *Religion und Zeitgeist im 19. Jahrhundert.* Ed. Julius H. Schoeps. Stuttgart and Bonn: Burg, 1982.

Koonz, Claudia. "New Germany, Old Wounds: The Fatherland's Heritage Industry." *Village Voice Literary Supplement* (Mar. 1990).

Kottje, Raymund, and Bernd Moeller, eds. *Ökumenische Kirchengeschichte*. Vol. 3. Mainz: Matthias-Grünewald, 1974.

Krieger, Leonard. *The German Idea of Freedom*. Boston: Beacon, 1957.

Landes, Joan. *Women and the Public Sphere in the Age of the French Revolution*. Ithaca: Cornell Univ. Press, 1988.

Langewiesche, Dieter. *Liberalismus in Deutschland*. Frankfurt a. M.: Suhrkamp, 1988.

Lauer, Hermann. *Geschichte der katholischen Kirche im Grossherzogthum Baden*. Freiburg i. B.: Herder, 1908.

Lee, Loyd E. *The Politics of Harmony: Civil Service, Liberalism, and Social Reform in Baden, 1800–1850*. Newark: Univ. of Delaware Press, 1980.

Lewin, Adolf. *Geschichte der badischen Juden seit der Regierung Karl Friedrichs (1738–1909)*. Karlsruhe: G. Braun, 1909.

Liberles, Robert. *Religious Conflict in Social Context: The Resurgence of Orthodox Judaism in Frankfurt am Main, 1838–1877*. Westport, Conn.: Greenwood, 1985.

———. "Dohm's Treatise on the Jews: A Defence of the Enlightenment." *Leo Baeck Institute Year Book* XXXIII, 1988.

Lill, Rudolf. "Kirche und Revolution: Zu den Anfängen der katholischen Bewegung im Jahrzehnt vor 1848." *Archiv für Sozialgeschichte* XVIII (1978).

Lipp, Carola, ed. *Schimpfende Weiber und patriotische Jungfrauen: Frauen im Vormärz und in der Revolution 1848/49*. Moos and Baden-Baden: Elster Verlag, 1986.

Loomba, Ania. "Dead Women Tell No Tales: Issues of Female Subjectivity, Subaltern Agency and Tradition in Colonial and Post-colonial Writings on Widow Immolation in India." *History Workshop* 36 (Autumn 1993).

Loth, Wilfried. *Katholiken im Kaiserreich: Der politische Katholizismus in der Krise des wilhelminischen Deutschlands*. Düsseldorf: Droste, 1984.

Lott, Eric. *Love and Theft: Blackface Minstrelsy and the American Working Class*. New York: Oxford Univ. Press, 1993.

Maas, Heinrich. *Geschichte der katholischen Kirche im Grossherzogthum Baden*. Freiburg i. B.: Herder, 1891.

Mendes-Flohr, Paul R., and Jehuda Reinharz, eds. *The Jew in the Modern World: A Documentary History*. New York: Oxford Univ. Press, 1980.

Mergel, Thomas. *Zwischen Klasse und Konfession: Katholisches Bürgertum im Rheinland, 1794–1914*. Göttingen: Vandenhoeck und Ruprecht, 1994.

Michaelis, Dolf. "The Ephraim Family and their Descendants (II)." *Leo Baeck Institute Year Book* XXIV (1979).

Mohrmann, Renate, ed. *Frauenemanzipation im deutschen Vormärz: Texte und Dokumente*. Stuttgart: Reclam, 1978.

Morrison, Toni. *Playing in the Dark: Whiteness and the Literary Imagination*. Cambridge, Mass.: Harvard Univ. Press, 1992.

Moses, Claire Goldberg. "Saint-Simonian Men/Saint-Simonian Women: The Transformation of Feminist Thought in 1830s France." *Journal of Modern History* 54/2 (June 1982).

Moses, Claire Goldberg, and Leslie Wahl Rabine. *Feminism, Socialism, and French Romanticism*. Bloomington: Indiana Univ. Press, 1993.

Mosse, George. *Toward the Final Solution: A History of European Racism.* New York: H. Fertig, 1978.

Mosse, Werner E. "Introduction: German Jewry and Liberalism." *Das deutsche Judentum und der Liberalismus—German Jewry and Liberalism.* Ed. Friedrich-Naumann-Stiftung. Sankt Augustin: COMDOK-Verlagsabteilung, 1986.

Mosse, Werner E. et al., eds. *Revolution and Evolution: 1848 in German-Jewish History.* Tübingen: J.C.B. Mohr, 1981.

Newman, Amy. "The Death of Judaism in German Protestant Thought from Luther to Hegel." *Journal of the American Academy of Religion* LXI/3 (1993).

Nipperdey, Thomas. *Deutsche Geschichte, 1800–1866: Bürgerwelt und starker Staat.* Munich: C. H. Beck, 1983.

Nolte, Paul. *Gemeindebürgertum und Liberalismus in Baden, 1800–1850: Tradition—Radikalismus—Republik.* Göttingen: Vandenhoeck und Ruprecht, 1994.

Paletschek, Sylvia. "Die Stellung der Frau im Deutschkatholizismus und in den freien Gemeinden im ausgehenden Vormärz und zu Beginn der Reaktionszeit." M.A. Thesis, Univ. of Hamburg, 1983.

———. *Frauen und Dissens.* Göttingen: Vandenhoeck und Ruprecht, 1990.

Pateman, Carole. *The Sexual Contract.* Stanford: Stanford Univ. Press, 1988.

Pecora, Vincent P. "Habermas, Enlightenment, and Antisemitism." *Probing the Limits of Representation: Nazism and the "Final Solution."* Ed. Saul Friedlander. Cambridge, Mass.: Harvard Univ. Press, 1992.

Pedersen, Susan. "National Bodies, Unspeakable Acts: The Sexual Politics of Colonial Policy-making." *Journal of Modern History* 63 (Dec. 1991).

Peiser, Jürgen. *Gustav Struve als Politischer Schriftsteller und Revolutionär.* Ph.D. diss., Univ. of Frankfurt, 1973.

Peiss, Kathy, and Christina Simmons, eds. *Passion and Power: Sexuality in History.* Philadelphia: Temple University Press, 1989.

"Philosemitismus." *Jüdisches Lexikon* IV/I. Berlin: Jüdischer Verlag, 1927.

Plaskow, Judith. "Feminist Anti-Judaism and the Christian God." *Journal of Feminist Studies in Religion* 7/2 (Fall 1992).

Plaut, W. Gunther, ed. *The Rise of Reform Judaism: A Sourcebook of its European Origins.* New York: World Union for Progressive Judaism, 1963.

Poovey, Mary. *Uneven Developments: The Ideological Work of Gender in Mid-Victorian England.* Chicago: Univ. of Chicago Press, 1988.

———. "Speaking of the Body: Mid-Victorian Constructions of Female Desire." *Body/Politics: Women and the Discourses of Science.* Ed. Mary Jacobus et al. New York: Routledge, 1990.

Pratt, Mary Louise. *Imperial Eyes: Travel Writing and Transculturation.* New York: Routledge, 1992.

Prelinger, Catherine M. *Charity, Challenge and Change: Religious Dimensions of the Mid-Nineteenth-Century Women's Movement in Germany.* New York: Greenwood, 1987.

Real, Willy. *Die Revolution in Baden 1848/49.* Stuttgart: Kohlhammer, 1983.

Rehm, Clemens. *Die katholische Kirche in der Erzdiözese Freiburg während der Revolution 1848/49.* Munich: Karl Alber, 1987.

Renker, Joseph. *Christliche Ehe im Wandel der Zeit: Zur Ehelehre der Moraltheologen im deutschsprachigen Raum in der ersten Hälfte des 19. Jahrhunderts.* Regensburg: Friedrich Pustet, 1977.

Riff, Michael Anthony. "The Anti-Jewish Aspect of the Revolutionary Unrest of 1848." *Leo Baeck Institute Year Book* XXI (1976).

Riley, Denise. "Some Peculiarities of Social Policy concerning Women in Wartime and Postwar Britain." *Behind the Lines: Gender and the Two World Wars.* Ed. Margaret Randolph Higonnet et al. New Haven: Yale Univ. Press, 1987.

———. *"Am I that Name?": Feminism and the Category of "Women" in History.* London: Macmillan, 1988.

Roediger, David R. *The Wages of Whiteness: Race and the Making of the American Working Class.* New York: Verso, 1991.

Rosenthal, Berthold. *Heimatgeschichte der badischen Juden seit ihrem geschichtlichen Auftreten bis zur Gegenwart.* Bühl/Baden: Konkordia, 1927.

Rückleben, Hermann. "Theologischer Rationalismus und kirchlicher Protest in Baden 1843–49." *Pietismus und Neuzeit* (1979).

Ruddick, Sara. *Maternal Thinking: Towards a Politics of Peace.* Boston: Beacon, 1989.

Rürup, Reinhard. "Jewish Emancipation and Bourgeois Society." *Leo Baeck Institute Year Book* XIV (1969).

———. *Emanzipation und Antisemitismus: Studien zur "Judenfrage" der bürgerlichen Gesellschaft.* Göttingen: Vandenhoeck und Ruprecht, 1975.

———. "German Liberalism and the Emancipation of the Jews." *Leo Baeck Institute Year Book* XX (1975).

Said, Edward W. *Orientalism.* New York: Pantheon, 1978.

Saurer, Edith. "'Bewahrerinnen der Zucht und der Sittlichkeit': Gebetbücher für Frauen—Frauen in Gebetbüchern." *L'Homme: Zeitschrift für Feministische Geschichtswissenschaft* 1/1 (1990).

Schieder, Wolfgang. "Kirche und Revolution: Sozialgeschichtliche Aspekte der Trierer Wallfahrt von 1844." *Archiv für Sozialgeschichte* XIV (1974).

———, ed. *Liberalismus in der Gesellschaft des deutschen Vormärz.* Göttingen: Vandenhoeck und Ruprecht, 1983.

———, ed. *Volksreligiosität in der modernen Sozialgeschichte.* Göttingen: Vandenhoeck und Ruprecht, 1986.

Schnabel, Franz. *Deutsche Geschichte im neunzehnten Jahrhundert.* Vol. 4. Freiburg i. B.: Herder, 1937.

Schneider, Georg. *50 Jahre freireligiösen Gemeindelebens: Festschrift zur Feier des fünfzigjährigen Bestehens der freireligiösen Gemeinde in Mannheim.* Mannheim: Mannheimer Aktiendruckerei, 1895.

Schoeps, Hans Joachim. *Philosemitismus im Barock: Religions- und geistesgeschichtliche Untersuchungen.* Tübingen: J.C.B. Mohr, 1952.

Schubert, Werner, ed. *Verhandlungen der Stände-Versammlung des Grossherzogtums Baden in den Jahren 1847 bis 1849.* Vaduz, Liechtenstein: Topos, 1989.

Scott, Joan Wallach. *Gender and the Politics of History.* New York: Columbia Univ. Press, 1988.

———. "French Feminists and the Rights of 'Man': Olympe de Gouges's Declarations." *History Workshop* 28 (Autumn 1989).

Scully, Pamela. "Rape, Race, and Colonial Culture: The Sexual Politics of Identity in the Nineteenth-Century Cape Colony, South Africa." *American Historical Review* 100/2 (Apr. 1995).

Secci, Lia. "German Women Writers and the Revolution of 1848." *German Women in the Nineteenth Century*. Ed. John C. Fout. New York: Holmes and Meier, 1984.

Sedgwick, Eve Kosofsky. *Epistemology of the Closet*. Berkeley: Univ. of California Press, 1990.

Sheehan, James J. *German Liberalism in the Nineteenth Century*. Chicago: Univ. of Chicago Press, 1978.

Sluis, Hanneke van der. "Eine Ladung Dynamit: Antijüdische Tendenzen in der feministischen Theologie." *Der eigene Freiraum: Frauen in Synagoge und Kirche*. Ed. Marion Th. Kunstenaar. Offenbach a. M.: Burckhardthaus-Laetere Verlag, 1989.

Smith, Helmut Walser. *German Nationalism and Religious Conflict: Culture, Ideology, Politics, 1870–1914*. Princeton: Princeton Univ. Press, 1995.

Smith-Rosenberg, Carroll. "Dis-Covering the Subject of the 'Great Constitutional Discussion,' 1786–1789." *Journal of American History* 79/3 (Dec. 1992).

Sorkin, David. *The Transformation of German Jewry, 1780–1840*. Oxford and New York: Oxford Univ. Press, 1987.

Sperber, Jonathan. *Popular Catholicism in Nineteenth-Century Germany*. Princeton: Princeton Univ. Press, 1984.

―――. *Rhineland Radicals: The Democratic Movement and the Revolution of 1848–1849*. Princeton: Princeton Univ. Press, 1991.

Spivak, Gayatri Chakravorty. "Can the Subaltern Speak?" *Marxism and the Interpretation of Culture*. Ed. Cary Nelson and Lawrence Grossberg. Urbana: Univ. of Illinois Press, 1988.

Sterling, Eleonore. *Judenhass: Die Anfänge des politischen Antisemitismus in Deutschland (1815–1850)*. Frankfurt a. M.: Europäische Verlagsanstalt, 1969.

Stern, Frank. *The Whitewashing of the Yellow Badge: Antisemitism and Philosemitism in Postwar Germany*. Oxford: Pergamon Press, 1992.

Stoler, Ann Laura. *Race and the Education of Desire: Foucault's History of Sexuality and the Colonial Order of Things*. Durham, N.C.: Duke Univ. Press, 1995.

Strobel, Ferdinand. *Der Katholizismus und die liberalen Strömungen in Baden. Teildruck: Der Kampf mit dem kirchlichen Liberalismus*. Speyer: Pilger-Druckerei, 1938.

Tannen, Deborah. *You Just Don't Understand: Men and Women in Conversation*. New York: Morrow, 1990.

Taylor, Barbara. "Socialist Feminism: Utopian or Scientific?" *People's History and Socialist Theory*. Ed. Raphael Samuel. London: Routledge and Kegan Paul, 1981.

―――. *Eve and the New Jerusalem: Socialism and Feminism in the Nineteenth Century*. New York: Pantheon, 1983.

Teutsch, Friedrich. "Geschichte der jüdischen Gemeinde vom Westfälischen

Frieden bis zur Weimarer Republik im Spiegel des Quadrats F 3." *Jüdisches Gemeindezentrum Mannheim F 3: Festschrift zur Einweihung am 13. September 1987, 19. Ellul 5747.* Ed. Oberrat der Israeliten Badens et al. Mannheim: Verlagsbüro v. Brandt, 1987.

Toews, John Edward. *Hegelianism: The Path Toward Dialectical Humanism, 1805–1841.* Cambridge and New York: Cambridge Univ. Press, 1980.

Toury, Jacob. "Die Revolution von 1848 als innerjüdischer Wendepunkt." *Das Judentum in der Deutschen Umwelt 1800–1850.* Ed. Hans Liebeschütz and Arnold Paucker. Tübingen: J.C.B. Mohr, 1977.

―――. *Soziale und politische Geschichte der Juden in Deutschland 1847–1871: Zwischen Revolution, Reaktion und Emanzipation.* Düsseldorf: Droste, 1977.

Townsend, Mary Lee. *Forbidden Laughter: Popular Humor and the Limits of Repression in Nineteenth-Century Prussia.* Ann Arbor: Univ. of Michigan Press, 1992.

Treitschke, Heinrich von. *Deutsche Geschichte im Neunzehnten Jahrhundert: Fünfter Teil.* Leipzig: G. Hirzel, 1914.

Trigano, Shmuel. "The French Revolution and the Jews." *Modern Judaism* 10 (1990).

Tschirn, Gustav. *Zur 60jährigen Geschichte der freireligiösen Bewegung.* Gottesberg: Hensel, 1904/5.

Wagner, Hans. *Aus Stockachs Vergangenheit.* Singen/Hohentwiel: Verein für Geschichte des Hegaus, 1967.

Walkowitz, Judith. "The Making of an Outcast Group: Prostitutes and Working Women in Nineteenth-Century Plymouth and Southampton." *A Widening Sphere: Changing Roles of Victorian Women.* Ed. Martha Vicinus. Bloomington: Indiana Univ. Press, 1977.

―――. "Male Vice and Female Virtue: Feminism and the Politics of Prostitution in Nineteenth-Century Britain." *Powers of Desire: The Politics of Sexuality.* Ed. Ann Snitow et al. New York: Monthly Review Press, 1983.

Walter, Friedrich. *Mannheim in Vergangenheit und Gegenwart.* Vol. 2. Orig. ed. 1907. Reprinted Frankfurt a. M.: W. Weidlich, 1978.

Watt, Jeffrey R. *The Making of Modern Marriage: Matrimonial Control and the Rise of Sentiment in Neuchâtel, 1550–1800.* Ithaca: Cornell Univ. Press, 1992.

Watzinger, Karl Otto. *Geschichte der Juden in Mannheim 1650–1945.* Stuttgart: Kohlhammer, 1984.

Weech, Friedrich von, ed. *Badische Biographien.* Vols. 1 and 4. Heidelberg: F. Bassermann, 1875, and Karlsruhe: G. Braun, 1891.

Weeks, Jeffrey. *Sex, Politics and Society.* New York: Longman, 1981.

Weiland, Daniela. *Geschichte der Frauenemanzipation in Deutschland und Österreich.* Düsseldorf: ECON Taschenbuch Verlag, 1983.

Weiss, Karl. *125 Jahre Kampf um freie Religion.* Ed. and completed by Lilo Schlötermann. Mannheim: Freireligiöse Verlagsbuchhandlung, 1970.

Werner, Michael. "Heinrich Heine—Über die Interdependenz von jüdischer, deutscher und europäischer Identität in seinem Werk." *Juden im Vormärz und in der Revolution von 1848.* Ed. Walter Grab and Julius H. Schoeps. Stuttgart and Bonn: Burg, 1983.

Wirtz, Rainer. *"Widersetzlichkeiten, Excesse, Crawalle, Tumulte und Skandale": Soziale Bewegung und gewalthafter sozialer Protest in Baden 1815–1848.* Frankfurt a. M.: Ullstein, 1981.

Wittig, Gudrun. *"Nicht nur im stillen Kreis des Hauses": Frauenbewegung in Revolution und nachrevolutionärer Zeit 1848–1876.* Hamburg: Ergebnisse Verlag, 1986.

Yerushalmi, Yosef Hayim. *Assimilation and Racial Anti-Semitism: The Iberian and the German Models.* New York: Leo Baeck Institute, Inc., 1982.

Zang, Gert, ed. *Provinzialisierung einer Region: Regionale Unterentwicklung und liberale Politik in der Stadt und im Kreis Konstanz im 19. Jahrhundert. Untersuchungen zur Entstehung der bürgerlichen Gesellschaft in der Provinz.* Frankfurt a. M.: Syndikat, 1978.

Zeldin, Theodore. "The Conflict of Moralities: Confession, Sin and Pleasure in the Nineteenth Century." *Conflicts in French Society: Anticlericalism, Education and Morals in the Nineteenth Century.* Ed. Theodore Zeldin. London: Allen and Unwin, 1970.

Zimmermann, Mosche. *Hamburgischer Patriotismus und deutscher Nationalismus: Die Emanzipation der Juden in Hamburg 1830–1865.* Hamburg: Hans Christians Verlag, 1979.

Zonana, Joyce. "The Sultan and the Slave: Feminist Orientalism and the Structure of *Jane Eyre*." *Signs* 18/3 (Spring 1993).

Zucker, Stanley. *Kathinka Zitz-Halein and Female Civic Activism in Mid-Nineteenth-Century Germany.* Carbondale and Edwardsville: Southern Illinois Univ. Press, 1991.

INDEX

PRINCETON STUDIES IN CULTURE/POWER/HISTORY

The History of Everyday Life: Reconstructing Historical Experiences
and Ways of Life *edited by Alf Lüdtke*

The Savage Freud and Other Essays on Possible
and Retrievable Selves *by Ashis Nandy*

Children and the Politics of Culture *edited by Sharon Stephens*

Intimacy and Exclusion: Religious Politics in Pre-Revolutionary Baden
by Dagmar Herzog